THE GLOBAL WHITE SNAKE

CHINA UNDERSTANDINGS TODAY

Series Editors: Mary Gallagher and Xiaobing Tang

China Understandings Today is dedicated to the study of contemporary China and seeks to present the latest and most innovative scholarship in social sciences and the humanities to the academic community as well as the general public. The series is sponsored by the Lieberthal-Rogel Center for Chinese Studies at the University of Michigan.

Resisting Spirits: Drama Reform and Cultural Transformation in the People's Republic of China
Maggie Greene

Going to the Countryside: The Rural in the Modern Chinese Cultural Imagination, 1915–1965
Yu Zhang

Power over Property: The Political Economy of Communist Land Reform in China
Matthew Noellert

The Global White Snake
Liang Luo

The Global White Snake

Liang Luo 羅靚

University of Michigan Press
Ann Arbor

Published in the United States of America by
the University of Michigan Press
Manufactured in the United States of America
Printed on acid-free paper

First published August 2021

A CIP catalog record for this book is available from the British Library.

ISBN 978-0-472-13261-4 (hardcover : alk. paper)
ISBN 978-0-472-03860-2 (paper : alk. paper)
ISBN 978-0-472-12915-7 (ebook)

To My Daughter

Ingrid Xinyuan Cassel

羅欣苑

Contents

Digital materials related to this title can be found on the Fulcrum platform via the following citable URL: https://doi.org/10.3998/mpub.11901257

Acknowledgments

Do not underestimate the regenerative power of popular culture and the generations of young people creating and consuming it. For constantly inspiring and challenging me, I thank my daughter and all my undergraduate and graduate students and assistants throughout the genesis of this book. For reading the full manuscript at different incarnations, I thank Aaron Phillip Balivet, Michael M. J. Fischer, Wilt L. Idema, Peter Kalliney, Leo Ou-fan Lee, Emily Mokros, David Rolston, Linh Vu, Guimei Wang, Mary Zimmerman, and four anonymous reviewers. Their invaluable feedback and tremendous generosity have improved the manuscript in immeasurable ways.

Xiaomei Chen, Wilt Idema, Leo Ou-fan Lee, Ban Wang, and David Der-wei Wang have been sources of intellectual inspiration and moral support throughout this project. Srimati Basu, Jianjun He, Andrew Maske, Douglas Slaymaker, Shui-Yin Sharon Yam, Charlie Yi Zhang, Lisa Zunshine, and other members of the Asian Studies Research Group at the University of Kentucky, Brenna Byrd, Jeanmarie Rouhier-Willoughby, and other members of the Folklore and Mythology Working Group at the University of Kentucky, Pär Cassel, Huaiyu Chen, Jianhua Chen, Liana Chen, Xiao-Yin Chen, Cerise Lim Jacobs, Seong Un Kim, Sangjoon Lee, Jinying Li, Melody Yunzi Li, Kenny Kwok-Kwan Ng, Indrani Pal-Chaudhuri, Jun Pow, Jeffrey L. Richey, Flair Donglai Shi, Yanshuo Zhang, and Zhou Long have also read portions of the book in various stages of its development and offered expert advice from their distinctive perspectives. I am deeply grateful for their careful reading and candid feedback.

I have benefited from stimulating conversations at conferences and workshops, before and after performances, and with archivists, colleagues, creative artists, editors, family and friends, librarians, and mentors over the years, in person or through other means of communication. For their contribution to this book, and at risk of omitting many more names than I can list here, I thank Eva Aggeklint, Nadia Atia, Anna Bosch, Molly Thomasy Blasing, Liang Cai, Cao Zhihong, Ingrid Xinyuan Cassel, Dongshin Chang, Cha Taegeun, Anarchichi Chen, Claire Chen, Hsiang-Yin Sasha Chen, Chen Sihe, Chen Yongguo, Yu-yu Cheng, Lik-kwan Cheung, Moon Choi, Hyaeweol Choi, Choi Young Hee, Eileen Cheng-yin Chow, Tarryn Li-Min Chun, Joscha Chung, William Christie, Brian James DeMare, Hilde De Weerdt, Kirk A. Denton, Daisy Yan Du, Huaiqing Duan, Christopher Dreyer, Shengyu Fan, Jin Feng, Feng Xinhua, LeAnn Fields, Géraldine A. Fiss, Jiexiang Fu, Fu Jin, Mary Gallagher, Jie Guo, Li Guo, Maggie Greene, Hao Lan, Kaoru Hayashi, Michel Hockx, Hong Seok-Pyo, Jiangfeng Hu, Zhiyi Hu, Rania Huntington, Rachel Jacobe, Ji Jin, Fumiko Joo, Alexa Alice Joubin, Jung Sun-Kyung, Echo Sihui Ke, Molly Kim, Seung-kyung Kim, Kim Sooyeon, Ko Chia Cian, Eunhua Lee, Haiyan Lee, Seonju Lee, Jie Li, Li Lidan, Li Wei, Yi-Chieh Lin, Chiung-yun Liu, Liu Hongtao, Jianmei Liu, Siyuan Liu, Liu Xiangyu, Christine Luk, Christopher Lupke, Lü Hong, Sean Macdonald, Paul Magee, Roald Maliangkay, Xuefei Min, Moon Hyun Sun, Darcy Paquet, Shaw-Yu Pan, Park Jaewoo, Jayoung Park, Bo Pu, Yin Qian, Yu Qian, Anne Rebull, Karen Redrobe, Ke Ren, Andrew Rodekohr, Carlos Rojas, Joanna Rutter, Sang Hai, Sheng Zhimei, Soh Yoojin, Song Ki-Jeong, Mingwei Song, Allison Arkell Stockman, Ronald Suleski, Hongmei Sun, Akiko Takenaka, Toni Tan, Keiko Tanaka, Mimi Tang, Xiaobing Tang, Tao Qingmei, Tom Teasley, Chao Tian, Tian Qinxin, Karen Thornber, CJ Torres, Tuo Jianing, Geling Yan, Tseng Yong-Yih, Nicolai Volland, Amanda Vredenburgh, Margaret Wan, Wang An-chi, Dylan Pengfei Wang, Shuge Wei, Wen Yuhang, Emily Wilcox, Kwok Sze Wing, Hang Wu, Shengqing Wu, Wu Xueshan, I-Hsien Wu, Hui Faye Xiao, Jiwei Xiao, Catherine Xiaowen Xu, Yang Lianfen, Naiqiao Yang, Yang Chia-hsien, Yang Xiaobin, Yoon Sun Yang, Yu Dongyun, Yu Hongyan, Yu Sheng-Kuan, Paola Zamperini, Ghadir Zannoun, Chuntian Zhang, Ke Zhang, Yingjin Zhang, Jamie J. Zhao, Zhao Qun, Xifang Zhao, Zhongliang Zhang, and Zhou Zhiqiang.

At the University of Kentucky, I am fortunate to be surrounded by a supportive intellectual community at the College of Arts and Sciences headed by Dean Mark Kornbluh and Associate Dean of Inclusion and Internationalization M. Cristina Alcalde. I must also thank our excellent department chairs Jeanmarie Rouhier-Willoughby and Jeffrey N. Peters and wonderful department managers Liliana Drucker and Katie Holzhause at the Department of Modern and Classical Languages, Literatures, and Cultures. I have also benefited from our employee education program, improving my Japanese language skills with the help of superb language teachers Yoko Horikawa, Koji Tanno, and Atsushi Hasegawa. I must also thank my Korean teachers at the Lexington Korean School, Heesung Choi, Sue Kyeung Son, and Hyeon Gu Lee, for their help in keeping the language alive in the community. With the help of student leaders and many Korean native speaker volunteers, I was able to introduce informal Korean language instruction on campus and finally brought Korean language instruction to the University of Kentucky with a grant from the Korea Foundation.

I am deeply grateful to Ewha Institute for the Humanities at Ewha Womans University in Seoul, Korea for granting me a full-year research professorship funded by the National Research Foundation of Korea to help develop transdisciplinary and transcultural humanities in East Asia in 2014–2015. It was at the excellent Ewha Language Center that I also started my formal Korean language training. I brought this valuable experience to Shanghai, China, in the summer of 2016 and convened an international workshop on the White Snake legend at Fudan University, where I was supported by a three-month research fellowship at the International Center for the Studies of Chinese Civilization. In the summer of 2017, I received a two-month visiting fellowship at the Humanities Research Center of Australian National University in Canberra, Australia, where I was able to interact with a wide range of international scholars working together on the question of the stranger through interdisciplinary perspectives. Earlier treatments of some of the material in this study have appeared in the journals *Frontiers of Literary Studies in China* (vol. 11, no. 1, 2017), *Literature & Modern China* (vol. 1, no. 1, 2019), and *CHINOPERL: Journal of Chinese Oral and Performing Literature* (vol. 39, no. 2, 2020). I am grateful to the editors of these journals for their insightful comments.

In the summer of 2018, I wrote the first draft of what became this book in my mother's apartment in Chongqing, China. Throughout the writing and revision process, my family has been a constant source of joy, love, and support. This book is for them: Pär, Ingrid, my mother Guangzhen, and my late father Fuxu, as well as my parents-in-law Åsa and Jan. It is dedicated to Ingrid as she graduates high school and enters college in the eventful year of 2020. Her generation embodies the power of the White Snake. May that power be with her and enable her to brave any challenges in life.

List of Illustrations

A Note on Translation, Romanization, and the Order of Names

All translations not otherwise credited are my own. Romanizations of Chinese terms are based on pinyin, Japanese terms are based on modified Hepburn, and Korean terms are based on modified McCune-Reischauer. However historical usages and regional diversities are respected, and exceptions are made when proper names, surnames, and other terms are more widely known in their alternative Romanizations. Exceptions are also made when quoting others' work, where the transliteration system originally chosen by the author is respected. The order of surnames and given names appear according to the convention of the country where they originated from, hence Asian names appear with the surname listed first, with the exception of those who are active outside Asia and have adapted the order of first name first.

CHAPTER 1

Introduction to the White Snake Legends

When I tell my English-speaking friends that I am writing a book about the White Snake, many of them think of the nineteenth-century German fairy tale from the Grimm Brothers,[1] some bring up the English hard rock band Whitesnake,[2] and one has even referenced the humanoid Whitesnake figure from the popular Japanese anime and manga series *JoJo's Bizarre Adventure*.[3] The Chinese legend of the White Snake, with a long oral tradition, an illustrious written record within China, and a vibrant history that has traversed national boundaries in Asia and throughout the world, is, however, largely invisible in these anecdotal accounts and first impressions. More importantly, it has not hitherto attracted the scholarly attention it merits.

This book brings the Chinese White Snake legends and their extensive, multidirectional travels within Asia and across the globe to the attention of Anglophone readers. Such travels across linguistic and cultural boundaries have generated distinctive traditions, as the White Snake has been reinvented in the Chinese, Japanese, Korean, and English-speaking worlds, among other linguistic and cultural traditions.[4] However, this study is not intended as an exhaustive account of the myriad transformations of the White Snake legends and their global travels, as historical productions and new creations are constantly being rediscovered and regenerated. More importantly, it is also not a study of textual variations of the White Snake legends with a systematic analysis of their various degrees of proximity with some fixed core narratives, as the diverse and distinct retellings included in this study are fully embraced and valued in their own right. Together, these narratives contribute to stories of radical tolerance for hybrid identities and sexualities, love across traditional boundaries, subversion of authorities, and valuing the strange and the uncanny. They also demonstrate that regardless of elitist and nationalistic condemnations, the wild popularity of these narratives has persisted even—or especially—in times that demanded great social conformity. As a result, the global travels of the White Snake tell a story not of "cultural appropriation" but of "culture as appropriation." It suggests that culture itself is that which appropriates; its artifacts are always already in the process of mediation and transformation. This ability to travel and transform is what keeps a culture alive, as it sheds skin after skin and regenerates itself time and again.[5]

The vibrant Anglophone White Snake configurations from the turn of twentieth century to the twenty-first century attest to the contemporary and transnational qualities of the White Snake phenomenon, whose impact on global cultural productions appears to be gaining momentum every day.[6] Moreover, the inter-Asian voyages and global circulations of the White Snake legends have enabled them to become repositories of diverse and complex meanings for a great number of people throughout the world, serving as reservoirs for polyphonic expressions ranging from the attempts to consolidate established power to their powerful oppositions in celebration of minority rights and activism, which are key issues confronting our contemporary world today.[7]

In the Sinophone sphere, the White Snake legends enjoy tremendous popularity in the People's Republic of China (hereafter PRC) and are frequently referred to as its "national people's intellectual property" (*guomin IP* 國民IP),[8] assigning commercial and nationalist values to fantastic legends in a neoliberal fashion. Mandarin Chinese productions of the White Snake legend have toured the world in recent years, with National Theatre of China's *Green Snake* (*Qingshe* 青蛇) directed by leading avant-gardist stage director Tian Qinxin 田沁鑫 at the Kennedy Center in March 2014, and the Beijing opera (*jingju* 京劇) *Legend of the White Snake* (*Baishe zhuan* 白蛇傳) with *jingju* superstar Zhang Huoding 張火丁 in the title role at the Lincoln Center in September 2015.[9] Moreover, a dynamic range of Sinophone White Snake productions originated outside of Mainland China has led and are still leading experiments in choreography, media spectacle, and radical expressions of gender and sexual identities.[10]

GENDER AND SPECIES, AND MEDIA AND POLITICS

Although one can hardly find a single overarching interpretative perspective in the intricate webs connecting the Chinese White Snake legends, the fluidity and intersection of gender and species and of media and politics do emerge as key entryways into some of the most influential iterations of the legends. Many versions of the legend recount how a white snake spirit transforms itself into a beautiful woman and goes to West Lake in Hangzhou,[11] either to fulfill her predestined role on earth or to experience the beauty of the human world. She meets a handsome young man named Xu Xian at the famous Broken Bridge and quickly begins a sexual relationship with him. In the meantime, her destruction of innocent humans and other living creatures and her violation of the boundary between the human and the nonhuman attract the attention of Fahai 法海, a Buddhist abbot with the power to recognize and exorcise demons and spirits. White Snake is forced to drink realgar wine during the Dragon Boat Festival;[12] this leads her to show her serpentine form to Xu, scaring him to death. She risks her life to steal a magic herb to revive Xu, but Fahai tricks Xu into leaving his wife and accompanying him to the Golden Mountain Monastery. White Snake and her companion Green Snake,[13] in an attempt to reclaim Xu, mobilize water spirits under their command and fight Fahai's heavenly soldiers. However, she is defeated partly because of her pregnant body. She barely escapes to the Broken Bridge, where she reconciles with a repentant Xu. After giving birth to a boy, she is imprisoned by Fahai under the Thunder Peak Pagoda and is released decades after.[14] The story's profound uncanniness lies in the humanity of the nonhuman, manifested in the snake woman, who metamorphasizes, in many instances, from a human-devouring demoness to a human-saving goddess.[15] Such an uncanny transformation operates on both the level of narrative and the level of meta-narrative. After all, the story both contains and enacts a tale of metamorphosis—a snake becomes a woman (on the story level), and a demon becomes a goddess (on the meta-story level).

While some earlier versions of the legend feature a righteous Buddhist abbot as the vanquisher of the monstrous White Snake, many modern and contemporary versions recast the abbot as the ultimate villain, who is presented as prejudiced and heartless and uses brute force to separate the snake woman from her human lover. In the centuries following the earliest known versions, the more conservative versions of the legend have sometimes been retold and revived, with the White Snake portrayed as monstrous and dangerous and the monk painted in a positive light. However, more often than not, the White Snake, together with her companion, the sometimes transgender Green Snake, serves important antiauthoritarian functions in various fantastic narratives by fighting the Buddhist abbot, who is an agent of religious and morally reactionary authorities.

Gender and species, as well as media and politics, fluidly intersect in the legends' multidirectional travels. The relatively recently acquired "humanity" of the snake women is exemplified by their capacity for compassion, love, devotion, fertility, and maternity in these stories. But these same narratives also exhibit numerous partial inversions of this premise; that is, not only are the snake women both nonhuman and good, but many humans, such as the Buddhist abbot Fahai, are actually bad. These narratives foreground the compassionate and loving qualities of "humanity" as in fact independent of species, attributes shared by good humans and nonhumans alike. Such a subversive understanding challenges the basic narrative and philosophical premises inherent in the very term "humanity."

This subversive White Snake legend reconfigures itself again and again throughout Chinese history, and through each reincarnation, it presents transmigration and metamorphosis as essential features of reality. The various retellings of the legend suggest that boundary-crossing intensifies conflicts between order and anarchy and between content and form. The legend simultaneously demonstrates our fear of hybridity and our readiness to welcome it, the fight between conservation of form and formal creativity, and the maintenance of purity and spiritual liberation.[16] Over several centuries, various permutations of the White Snake legend exerted significant influence in the process of cultural transformation and political change across Asia and beyond.

For example, throughout the Late Imperial and modern times in China, the White Snake legends have been used by different agents to promote diverse, often avant-gardist, and frequently political, causes—such as marriage freedom, women's rights, grassroots revolutionary spirit, queer love, and transgender rights—in the Chinese-speaking worlds and beyond. The legend was used to promote women's liberation and the PRC's new marriage law in the early 1950s and became an iconic site of homosexual expression in Taiwanese experimental theater of the 1970s. In some cases, the legend has become the basis for popular tourist sites and theme parks, celebrating the traditional didactic messages and ignoring the antiauthoritarian interpretations, or commodifying traditional Chinese culture as contemporary fashion.[17] In other cases, it serves as a fountainhead for minority rights activism and carries on the spirit of antiauthoritarianism with renewed urgency, which connects a culturally specific and contextually embedded legend to a global neoliberal economy and its discontents.[18]

It is no exaggeration to say that the Asian market in general and the Chinese market in particular have long been in love with the White Snake, pushing the legend to the forefront of public discourse while capitalizing on its potential for profit, in and outside China. The first commercial success of White Snake–themed films occurred in Shanghai in 1926, followed by later Chinese, Malay, Japanese, and Korean film productions throughout the mid- to late twentieth century. In the early 1990s, the fifty-episode Taiwanese television drama *New Legend of Madame White Snake* (*Xin Bainiangzi chuanqi* 新白娘子傳奇) took Mainland China by storm.[19] Its impact on Chinese and

Figure 1: White Snake struggles to reach for Ah Xuan in an ink painting animation style. In *White Snake: The Legend Begins* (*Baishe: yuanqi*), directed by Amp Wong and Zhao Ji. Light Chaser Animation Studios and Warner Bros., 2019, 2:08. Screenshot by author. Courtesy of Light Chaser Animation.

Asian popular cultures is still keenly felt today, as seen most prominently in the waves of remakes and adaptations in Mainland China, Hong Kong, Taiwan, and Singapore, among other places. One of the most recent major adaptations from Mainland China is the 2018 sixty-episode internet drama series *The Destiny of White Snake* (*Tianji zhi Baishe chuanshuo* 天乩之白蛇傳說). The production stars some of the most popular young actors and established veterans in the Chinese-language television and film industry, has garnered major investment for its big-budget production and sensational publicity, and has even incited protests from organizations claiming to speak on behalf of two hundred million Buddhists in China and arguing that the series "tarnishes the reputation of Buddhism."[20]

On January 11, 2019, a new animation film directed by Amp Wong (Huang Jiakang) 黄家康 and Zhao Ji 趙霽, *White Snake: The Legend Begins* (*Baishe: yuanqi* 白蛇: 緣起), the very first animated coproduction by the Beijing-based Light Chaser Animation and the US-based Warner Bros., was released in Mainland China, again arousing a sensational popular following, while also garnering critical acclaim (fig. 1).[21] On April 3, 2019, yet another thirty-six-episode internet drama series *New Legend of Madame White Snake* (*Xin Bainiangzi chuanqi*), created by the Chinese video site iQiyi, one of the largest video streaming sites in the world, premiered on its own platforms in both Mainland China and Taiwan and finished its first run on May 10, 2019.

Taking the name of the 1992 Taiwanese TV series, the 2019 internet drama series pays tribute to its namesake from twenty-seven years earlier by adopting its theme songs and inviting key actors from the 1992 series for cameo performances, successfully creating a new media sensation throughout the Chinese-speaking worlds and beyond.[22] Meanwhile, a new English-language stage production based on the Tony Award–winning playwright and director Mary Zimmerman's play *The White Snake*, which I first saw in 2014 in Wuzhen, China, was unveiled at the Constellation Theatre Company in Washington, DC, from April 25 to May 26, 2019.[23]

How should we understand the seemingly endless regenerative powers of the White Snake legends? What does their pervasive and long-lasting popularity suggest? In *Retelling/Rereading: The Fate of Storytelling in Modern Times*, Karl Kroeber reminds us that "storytelling is perhaps humanity's primary tool for changing reality," and "genuine storytelling is essentially antiauthoritarian."[24] The fluidity of gender, species, media, and politics exemplified by the White Snake legends' various permutations have animated a wide range of religious, philosophical, and political transformations throughout the past centuries, across Asia and beyond. This study investigates the relationship between fantasy and reality in the global travels of the White Snake legends and the power such global retellings exert in their interrogation and shaping of reality. In this study, I pay special attention to the migration of the White Snake legends across historical demarcations and geographical boundaries and to how the retelling of these legends in different media have impacted contemporary politics and popular culture. At the center of the White Snake legends is how gender and species, and media and politics intersect to produce decentering and dissenting powers. At the same time, such antiauthoritarian and transgressive powers, as expressed in the "humanity of the nonhuman" and culminating in the "righteousness of the demoness," may lead to a new conservatism and a return to conventional ethical judgments, demonstrating a complex, dialectic relationship between authoritarianism and antiauthoritarian tendencies.

METAMORPHOSES AND REGENERATIONS

Forbidden love, sexual attraction, and spiritual salvation are recurring themes in the White Snake legends. To some extent, these widely resonant themes account for the legends' enduring popularity. But what is it in the White Snake legends that particularly lends them to the myriad transmigrations across different languages and media, endowing them with regenerative power in disparate historical and geopolitical contexts? What is it that specifically makes the White Snake legends important case studies for students of the avant-garde and the popular, the folk and the political, the experimental and the commercial, from traditional to modern and then contemporary times? The continuing allure of the White Snake legends stems from both their shifting content and their ever-changing forms. Since the legends themselves are overtly about metamorphosis and regeneration, their thematic content and their highly mutable forms are dynamically aligned. The changing forms of the White Snake legends speak to disparate philosophies, politics, and ethics; they also embody changing technologies, media, formal conventions, and practices across Asia and beyond.

The relationship, transference, and transgression among gender, species, media, and politics are of central importance here. The White Snake is a snake who, through self-cultivation over thousands of years, achieves human speech and the ability to assume human form. Animals (sometimes rocks or plants, among others) able to do this are known as *jing* 精 in Chinese. *Jing* can act in demonic ways, neutral ways, or benevolent ways.[25] In a culture that places a moral premium on the ideal of chastity and sexual segregation in particular, as well as purity and the preservation of boundaries in general, violating the reverence for classification and the integrity of established categories suggests impurity, contamination, even peril. This was especially true from the tenth century onwards because of the increasing influence of neo-Confucianism. The White Snake demoness destabilizes such fixed boundaries, representing an antithesis to such traditional worldviews. However, simply treating the nonhuman White Snake as impure and contaminating cannot fully explain the core teaching in early White Snake legends, that is, the damage to "male essence" as a result of sexual entanglement with the snake woman.[26] From this point of view, the White Snake needs to be contained not only because she is impure, but more importantly, because of the seductive sexuality she embodies, which bewitches males and damages their bodies.

However, many later versions of the legend demonstrate how such violations of boundaries result not in contamination, disease, or decay, but in regeneration and creativity. The contemporary persistence and relevance of the White Snake theme instantiates the "nonhuman turn" that has recently emerged in the studies of the humanities in Western academia,[27] by articulating the political potential and affective power of the "alien" bodies of animals, children, and women (who are often considered subhuman or even nonhuman) as ways to resist the dominance of human-, adult-, and male-centered narratives. The White Snake legends' empowerment of suppressed voices accounts in part for their wide-ranging resonance with audiences far beyond the borders of the geopolitical entities of China and the wider Chinese-speaking worlds.

A key example of the White Snake's global travels is filmmaker Miyazaki Hayao's 宮崎駿 encounter with the legend through the 1958 film *The Tale of the White Serpent* (*Hakujaden* 白蛇伝, released as *Panda and the Magic Serpent* in the US in 1961), Japan's first full-length color animation based on the Chinese legend. This encounter has been repeatedly cited as the decisive moment in the development of a leading animator of our times. Miyazaki, whose 1988 *My Neighbor Totoro* and 2001 *Spirited Away*, among many other films, inspired the imagination of generations of fans worldwide, first saw *Hakujaden* when he was a teenager. So enraptured was Miyazaki by the film, about a young boy who falls in love with a snake goddess, that he returned several times to the theater to see the film and later admitted to having "fallen in love" himself with the snake goddess. He wrote in a 1979 essay, "I was hooked when I saw *Hakujaden*, and I wound up choosing to become an animator because of it."[28]

The power of the snake goddess is itself one of animation—inspiriting and quickening the imagination, as it did that of young Cerise Lim Jacobs 林曉英, who, growing up in a traditional Chinese family in colonial Singapore, watched the Cantonese opera version of the White Snake legend religiously: "When I think of Madame White Snake, I think of sitting cross-legged on my grandparents' cold tile floor, feeling the cold tile against my skin, and the warmth radiating from three generations of women. Because we crowded around the black-and-white TV set, mesmerized, as we watched the White Snake sing her heart out."[29] Later on, Jacobs turned to the White Snake legend, a staple offering in Chinese opera, when writing a song cycle as a birthday present for her music-loving husband.[30] That song cycle evolved into the 2011 Pulitzer Prize–winning opera *Madame White Snake*, composed by Zhou Long 周龍, with libretto by Cerise Lim Jacobs herself.[31] After her husband's passing, Jacobs further developed the legend of the White Snake into the *Ouroboros Trilogy*, adding a prequel and a sequel to the White Snake opera (making it *Naga*, *Madame White Snake*, and *Gilgamesh*) and using the Greek symbol of the snake who eats its own tail to epitomize the cycle of love, death, and rebirth.

From Zhou Long and Cerise Lim Jacobs's *Madame White Snake* opera to the many stagings of Mary Zimmerman's *The White Snake*, at the Oregon Shakespeare Festival in 2012, in Wuzhen, China, in 2014, and in Washington,

DC in 2019, the White Snake has emerged as a well-known motif in global Anglophone culture in the twenty-first century.[32] Meanwhile, White Snake continues to play a significant role in cultural productions in the contemporary Sinophone world.[33] From at least the eighteenth century, the White Snake legends have also created their own tradition in modern Japanese culture, inspiring generations of experimental writers and filmmakers from Ueda Akinari 上田秋成, Tanizaki Jun'ichirō 谷崎潤一郎, and Mizoguchi Kenji 溝口健二, to the above-mentioned Miyazaki Hayao, among others. This modern Japanese tradition has, in turn, facilitated a distinctive Korean cinematic connection to the White Snake legend through the legendary Korean filmmaker Shin Sang-ok 申相玉 신상옥, as well as sustained coproduction between Hong Kong, South Korea, and Taiwan, among other locations. The 1956 Japan–Hong Kong coproduction *Madame White Snake* (*Byaku fujin no yōren* 白夫人の妖恋) and the 1978 Hong Kong, Taiwan, and possibly South Korea coproduction *Love of the White Snake* (*Zhen Baishe zhuan* 真白蛇傳) are two prominent examples of a complex web of inter-Asian connections.[34]

LEGENDS OF THE WHITE SNAKE

The legend of the White Snake is widely regarded as one of the four great folk legends of China.[35] It is often said that the White Snake's prototype can be traced back to "Li Huang" 李黃, a short tale from the *Extensive Record of the Strange* (*Boyi zhi* 博異志), a source dated to the ninth century. The "Li Huang" tale is also included in the *Extensive Record of the Taiping Era* (*Taiping guangji* 太平廣記), a massive, thematically arranged compendium of short classical tales and other writings about strange events and topics from previous centuries compiled in the final years of the tenth century.[36] The "Li Huang" story can be retold as follows.

In the year 807 in the Tang dynasty capital of Chang'an, a man named Li Huang was waiting for his appointment to a position at the capital. He wandered into the Eastern Market and spotted an extraordinarily beautiful woman dressed in white sitting in an oxcart. He was told that the woman was a widow and that her mourning period was over, so she needed money for new clothes. He inquired as to whether she might be willing to remarry and was not given a direct answer, whereupon he gave her cash to buy brocades. He was promised repayment and was asked by the woman to follow her oxcart back home. Upon arrival, he was invited to stay the night. When he entered the courtyard, he was greeted by a woman in blue, who claimed to be the aunt of the woman in white. The woman in white finally appeared, and "her white skirt was dazzling, her pure skin lustrous, while the simple elegance of her words and bearing was not different from the divine immortals."[37] She then suddenly retreated, while the woman in blue returned to propose the woman in white's services to Li in exchange for thirty thousand coins. Li happily obliged and upon receipt of the agreed amount was welcomed with a big feast.

Li stayed for three days and thoroughly enjoyed himself (a sexual relationship with the woman in white is strongly implied). On the fourth day, he was asked to leave and was promised an opportunity to return. Li desired to return home, so he took his leave. When he mounted his horse, his servants noticed that he smelled strongly of rotten fish. Upon returning home, he made up a story to excuse his absence. He felt very sick and asked for a blanket so he could lie down. Although he was still speaking, his family and friends noticed that his body was melting under the blanket. When they lifted the blanket, all they saw was a puddle of water. The whole family was terrified. They questioned the servants who had accompanied him and were told the whole story. When they went to look for the house of the woman in white, they found an empty garden. A honey locust tree was found there, with two sets of fifteen strings of cash (one string is worth one thousand copper coins) hanging from its branches.[38] When they questioned the neighbors, they were told a huge white snake was often seen at the base of the tree.

It is intriguing to see that many key elements later consolidated in the seventeenth-century vernacular short story version of the White Snake legend already appeared in "Li Huang" centuries earlier. The woman in white in this story is indeed a huge white snake, and the woman in blue a model for the sister/maid/nurse figure in later versions, while the central plot of the man's bewitchment is already the chief storyline here.[39]

In addition to the tale of "Li Huang," two other short classical tales, "The Wife of County Magistrate Sun" (*Sun zhixian qi* 孫知縣妻) and "The Student Qian Yan" (*Qian Yan shusheng* 錢炎書生) are relevant here. Both of these tales are found in the *Record of the Listener* (*Yijian zhi* 夷堅志), a large, late twelfth-century compilation of "record of anomalies" (*zhiguai* 志怪) tales by Hong Mai 洪邁.[40] The first tale recounts how county magistrate Sun married a woman of extraordinary beauty but was warned never to look at her when she took a bath. After ten years of marriage, he finally peeked and found a huge white snake coiled in the tub.[41] He ran to his study and was determined never to return to her bed, but finally returned out of fear. He fell ill and died within a year. The second tale is about a young student named Qian Yan who was living alone in a monastery when he encountered a beautiful girl. The girl visited Qian every night, and as a consequence, he neglected his studies and became increasingly emaciated. Concerned, his friend introduced him to a priest of a nearby temple, who gave him a protective amulet. Upon seeing the amulet, the girl turned into two snakes, one large and one small, and never appeared again.[42]

It is telling that, in these rather primitive tales, the snake seductresses take the form of women and have sex with men for the express purpose of robbing them of their male essence.[43] In most cases, the man is a student or an official, which suggests that the feminine principle is a threat to the life of the mind and of the bureaucracy, that is, the rational faculties of self and of society. These male victims eventually will die at the hands of the seductresses, unless they are saved by the timely intervention of an exorcist. This largely explains why the Buddhist abbot was enshrined in the seventeenth-century vernacular version of the White Snake legend as a semidivine exorcist who saves the young man from being endangered by the White Snake.

Whereas the above classical accounts are told succinctly, the vernacular short stories that emerged later are filled with enticing details and descriptive language, mimicking aspects of a professional storytelling performance. The first vernacular short story to feature a white snake demon is titled "West Lake's Three Stupas" (*Xihu santa ji* 西湖三塔記), from a collection of stories titled *Vernacular Stories from Qingping Mountain Studio* (*Qingping shantang huaben* 清平山堂話本) published in the mid-sixteenth century with some stories dating to the thirteenth or fourteenth century.[44] Any summary of such a text suffers from the omission of the poetic descriptions and entertaining details that lend the story its distinctive charm. However, for the purpose of outlining the transformations of the White Snake legends over time, a summary follows.

Sometime between 1174 and 1189, during the Song dynasty, a man named Xi Xuanzan 奚宣贊 went to West Lake during the Clear and Bright Festival (Qingming jie 清明節) for tomb sweeping and came upon a young girl who had lost her way.[45] He took the girl home for ten days and was visited by an old woman in black, who claimed to be the girl's "granny." They invited him to their home, where he met a woman in white, the girl's "mother." When Xi Xuanzan looked more closely at the woman, "she appeared as beautiful as a flower and as white as jade, so that his heart and mind were shaken and moved."[46] Xi then witnessed the woman in white killing her previous "husband" and eating his heart and liver in front of him, after which Xi became her "husband" and was kept there for over half a month. Sickened, physically and mentally, he begged to go home, but when a new man was brought to the woman in white, Xi knew he would now suffer the same fate as the man before him. However, the little girl whom he had rescued earlier saved him, and he made it home safely.

The next year, again during the Clear and Bright Festival, Xi went out to catch some birds and fell into a trap set by the woman in black. He was captured and brought back to the woman in white and was kept there as her sex slave for another half month. He was again threatened with death and once again was saved by the little girl and returned home. A Daoist immortal surnamed Xi, the uncle of Xi Xuanzan, finally intervened on his behalf, summoning a divine warrior to drive out the three demons of West Lake, whose real forms were then revealed: the woman in black turned out to be an otter, the girl a black chicken, and the woman in white a snake. Three stone stupas were constructed to capture the three demons in the lake, and Xi Xuanzan became the immortal's disciple.[47] The three West Lake monsters (including the sexually aggressive and human-eating "woman in white," who turned out to be a white snake) in this thirteenth-to fourteenth-century vernacular story are still distinctly evil, although the little girl who repeatedly saved the male protagonist does display a humanity that will be amplified in later versions of the White Snake legend.

Between the fourteenth and the seventeenth centuries, West Lake seems to have become strongly associated with the image of the White Snake, who is transformed as a beautiful woman and appears at the side of the lake. She forms a sexual relationship with the young man Xu Xian 許仙 (or Xu Xuan 許宣, likely developed from the Xi Xuanzan character in "West Lake's Three Stupas"). Eventually, her transgressive sexuality and violation of the human-nonhuman boundary attracts the attention of Fahai. Often there is a subplot in which the White Snake defeats a Daoist priest before the intervention of the Buddhist exorcist, possibly signaling the rising influence of Buddhism over Daoism.

The seventeenth-century vernacular tale "Madam White Is Kept Forever under Thunder Peak Tower" (*Bainiangzi yongzhen Leifengta* 白娘子永鎮雷峰塔) is one of the earliest, fullest versions of what is clearly the White Snake story. It is also one of the most popular versions of the legend and is often regarded as the "standard" version. It highlights the "lust, caution" parable embedded in the story and repudiates the snake woman's lustful nature and her destructive power,[48] while upholding the Buddhist abbot as a defender of social norms and natural human relations. The story is included in a 1624 vernacular story collection compiled by Feng Menglong 馮夢龍 and titled *Stories to Caution the World* (*Jingshi tongyan* 警世通言). The full collection has been translated into English by Shuhui Yang and Yunqin Yang, with the "Madam White" story comprising more than thirty translated pages,[49] as summarized here.

Between 1132 and 1162, during the Song dynasty, a man named Xu Xuan lived with his sister and worked as an assistant in an herbal medicine shop. On a visit to West Lake during the Clear and Bright Festival, Xu Xuan was caught in the rain, when he chanced upon two beautiful women, one clothed in white and one in green, apparently mistress and maid. Sharing a boat with the women on the way home, Xu was enchanted by the woman in white and lent his umbrella to her. The next day, Xu Xuan went to fetch his umbrella from the woman's home and was entertained with food and wine. The woman in white proposed marriage, but worried about his lack of money, Xu Xuan hesitated.[50]

When the woman in white presented him with fifty taels of silver, Xu happily agreed to the marriage. Upon his return home with the money to seek permission from his sister, he discovered that the silver was part of those missing from the government. Xu Xuan's brother-in-law, who worked for the government, was charged with the task of finding the thief; Xu was interrogated and told the police where the silver had come from. When the arresting officer arrived at the residence of the woman in white, they found a deserted house. The women had disappeared; only the rest of the stolen silver ingots remained. Xu was then exiled to Suzhou where the woman in white (Madam White) and the woman in green (Little Green) magically reappeared. With Little Green and their host in Suzhou serving as witnesses, Madam White then married Xu Xuan. Six months slipped by while the two lost themselves in delirious pleasure. However, Madam White repeatedly caused Xu Xuan trouble (dressing him up in stolen clothes, poisoning the well water to cause plague so as to help his pharmaceutical business), but she was always able to win his forgiveness using her seductive charm. When Xu Xuan was exiled to Zhenjiang, Madam White and Little Green followed him again. At the sight of Abbot Fahai of the Golden Mountain Monastery, the snake women dived to the bottom of Yangtze River to escape. Finally, however, Abbot Fahai trapped Madam White with his golden alms bowl and confined her under Thunder Peak Pagoda. Thereafter, Xu Xuan joined the Buddhist order and became a monk.[51]

The legend subsequently went through a major transformation during the Qing dynasty (1644–1911), especially from the eighteenth century onward. An exception, however, is the 1738 *chuanqi* 傳奇 attributed to Huang Tubi 黃圖珌, which was often considered closer to Feng Menglong's 1624 vernacular tale than to later eighteenth century performance versions of the legend.[52] A more radical shift of the White Snake legend took place in the late eighteenth century, manifested in a 1777 *chuanqi* attributed to Fang Chengpei 方成培, an 1806 thirteen-chapter vernacular story attributed to Yushan zhuren 玉山主人, and a *tanci* 彈詞 version attributed to Chen Yuqian 陳遇乾, with a preface dated 1809.[53] The narrative changes and developments that these late eighteenth and early nineteenth-century versions record likely appeared first on stage in local opera and storytelling performances. They present White Snake as an endearing character and recast Abbot Fahai as the destructive power, or at least an agent of higher authorities who create obstacles for lovers' unions and who separate families and loved ones. Most of these texts, with the exception of the medium-length rendition attributed to Yushan zhuren, lend themselves to fully fledged plays ranging from thirty to fifty-odd scenes, and often take hours, if not days, to perform in full length. They often focus on romances between the young male and female leads and conventionally demand big happy final scenes that tie up all loose ends.

These genre developments signal a key transformation in the retelling of the White Snake legend: responding to strong social, political, and cultural factors, the legend underwent an important transformation in its thematic focus. The White Snake performances' popularity, reflecting the demands of the large number of ordinary theatergoers, helped to redefine good and evil in the White Snake legend, turning the Buddhist abbot into the ultimate villain and the snake woman into an increasingly humane and righteous protagonist.[54] The happy ending—in particular, the birth of a son, and the son's deliverance of his mother from her imprisonment under the Thunder Peak Pagoda, as well as the snake woman and her human husband's ascent to heaven—further popularized the legend and its protagonists.

Later versions of the White Snake legend have since incorporated both the lustful and loving natures of the White Snake, rendering her the embodiment of the exotic and the erotic in the legend's many renditions in no less than a dozen local dialects and operatic forms throughout the eighteenth and nineteenth centuries. The continuing relevance of the White Snake in reflecting and even shaping contemporary popular culture is intimately linked to the various forms of transgression that she now embodies: gender and species, media and politics. The present work is particularly invested in the ways these legends have traveled over time and space, defying historical demarcations, as well as linguistic, geographical, national, and cultural boundaries, and in how such retellings come not only to reflect but also to shape and impact contemporary politics and popular culture.

THE POWER OF TRANSMIGRATION

The foregoing summary and analysis of the earliest extant versions of the White Snake legends from "Li Huang" onward provide the foundation for analyzing the subsequent reinterpretations that are the focus of this book. Just as the White Snake and her sister/maid Green Snake represent changing expressions of the female gender and sexuality through various incarnations of the legend, her human husband Xu Xian and the Buddhist abbot Fahai similarly serve as moral, religious, and political indicators of the patriarchal human world. Fahai's role, in particular, changes from that of a religious and moral authority to that of an authoritarian oppressor, answering ordinary theater audiences' demand for a happy ending for the human/nonhuman lovers while also signaling a collaboration between grassroots antiauthoritarian politics (as expressed in the demands of the audience) and cultural visions of the educated elite (as articulated in the literati versions of the tale).[55] Importantly, the desire for a happy ending did not simply originate from popular demand; it was very much a generic requirement of the Southern Chinese theatrical tradition (*nanqu* 南曲) because of its social and religious functions.[56]

In 2017, the Mexican director Guillermo del Toro offered an intriguing contemporary cognate for the White Snake legend in his film *The Shape of Water*. Both stories have at their heart the transformation of a monstrous other (in the eyes of mainstream powerholders) into an uncannily beautiful beloved (for their human lovers). In his Academy Awards acceptance speech, del Toro acknowledged that "fantasy . . . tell[s] about things that are real in the world today."[57] *The Shape of Water* exemplifies what del Toro refers to as the inherently political quality of both fairy tales and the horror genre, the impulse of the fantastic being "completely anarchic and antiestablishment"—something shared by the transgressive, antiauthoritarian thrust of the White Snake legend.[58] Among the striking similarities between *The Shape of Water* and the White Snake legends are forbidden romances between humans and nonhumans, the power of water as a symbol of boundary transgression, the villains and their political agendas, and the marginal identities of the supporting characters. But more importantly, both stories revolve around hybridity: on the one hand, the hybrid human/nonhuman water creatures—snake woman and fish man—are by their nature transgressive triggers of anxiety, fear, and horror; on the other hand, they are exotic, seductive, and beautiful, arouse curiosity and affection, and throw into relief the attraction of the uncanny.[59] The snake woman and the fish man combine the tantalizing allure of the horrifying and the exotic: the beauty-in-horror, that is to say, the alluring nature of something that is physically or culturally transgressive, which simultaneously repels and compels.

In this sense, the White Snake legends, like *The Shape of Water*, can be read on a psychological level as a story about the struggles between our conscious and social selves and the unconscious that stands apart from and at odds with society. That psychological drama is exteriorized in both stories as political allegory. Like the character Strickland in the movie, the Buddhist abbot Fahai in the early versions of the White Snake legend battles hybridity in the name of order and purity. Like del Toro's film, which is firmly in the camp of transgressive lovers, legends of the White Snake have, in reinterpretations and retellings over time, come to champion the species-crossing relationship at their heart. Indeed, over the course of Chinese history, White Snake legends exhibit a trend toward greater tolerance of hybridity, ambiguity, impurity, and boundary crossing—in other words, a growing cultural syncretism.[60] Whenever that tendency confronts hostility from the reigning authorities and their drive to purify, we witness not only the rise of authoritarianism and totalitarianism, but also the potential for the fantastic to challenge and reshape reality.

Importantly, there are some subtle differences in how the "nonhuman" was dealt with in the seemingly converging representations discussed above. The White Snake legends were rooted in the Chinese tradition, a tradition that enables cross-species transmigration between humans and other species.[61] This fluidity between the human and the nonhuman through the act of self-cultivation enables acts of self-transformation, for any species, by an innate power circulating within the world or cosmos.[62] This fluid concept of the boundless flow of energy is deeply ingrained in an egalitarian conception of the interconnectedness of all species between heaven and earth. This departs from the embodiment of "hybridity" as expressed in *The Shape of Water*, where the representation of the beloved as a visible hybrid between an amphibian animal and a human male is different from the beautiful female image of the White Snake in the Chinese legends. On the other hand, one could argue that the fish man is revealed, through the eyes of the mute lover, as not a hybrid "beast" but a beautiful lover; similarly, one could also emphasize that there is always the danger of the White Snake exposing her monstrous "true self" from beneath the robes of a beauty.

In this sense, it seems more fitting to describe White Snake's state of being as closer to the concept of transmigration or reincarnation, or a conceptual hybrid, rather than a hybrid of two species. On the other hand, the son of White Snake and Xu Xian, as highlighted in some versions, may better personify the idea of a hybrid. Ironically, in quite a few White Snake texts from the Qing dynasty, the son, as a hybrid, becomes the best embodiment of a central Confucian virtue, filial piety. His topping the list in the imperial examination becomes the foundation of the White Snake's salvation. In this sense, the White Snake legends truly embody the complex, and often ironic interplay between the traditional and the experimental, the human and the nonhuman, and order and anarchy, with its central power and danger rooted in the possibility of transgressing boundaries.

ASPIRATIONS IN THE REMAKING OF THE LEGENDS

Although the White Snake has long been a popular cultural trope throughout the Chinese-speaking worlds and beyond, there is, remarkably, no book-length academic or general interest work on the White Snake theme in the English language, with the exception of Pei-yi Wu's 1969 dissertation and Wilt Idema's 2009 book and two recent dissertations.[63] Existing Japanese- and Korean-language scholarship focuses mainly on the White Snake theme in premodern narratives and its fictional and dramatic adaptations, with the exception of recent works looking into cross-fertilizations between East Asian countries.[64] Chinese-language scholarship is often more concerned with the legend's gender politics and visual adaptations in recent years, with the exception of Zhang Lianhong's important research focusing on the 1950s.[65] English-language scholarship, meanwhile, tends to highlight the legend's metamorphoses in traditional music genres and opera films in the Chinese diaspora, foregrounding issues of translation and censorship.[66]

Synthesizing original source materials and scholarship in Chinese, Japanese, Korean, and English, I examine the avant-gardist, political, and popularizing aspirations in the remaking of the White Snake legends in the contemporary world. In doing so, my intent is to break up the compartmentalization of the premodern, modern, and contemporary in the study of cultural transformations and political changes. At the same time, as my study traverses Mainland China, Hong Kong, Japan, South Korea, Taiwan, and Singapore, I focus on both the distinctions and the commonalities running through inter-Asian and global theatrical, political, and popular cultural articulations of the White Snake motif and narrative.

Conceived both chronologically and thematically, this study follows three broadly defined historical moments in the coming of age of modern

Chinese culture from the Late Imperial and early Republican period, to the Cold War period, and then to the contemporary moment. More importantly, I emphasize constant thematic intersection and exchange between the three temporal parts and the remarkable resilience of the White Snake legends in serving as forces of convergence rather than divergence, continuity rather than rupture.

Specially, I highlight the connections between the Anglophone retellings of the White Snake legends by American missionaries and diplomats from the late nineteenth century to American cultural reproductions of the legends in the early twenty-first century, and take the multimedia, multilingual, and multisite reincarnations of the legends in Chinese-, Japanese-, and Korean-language productions throughout "the long twentieth century"[67] as its central case studies. The three parts are the following: Part I, "The White Snake at the Turn of the Twentieth Century"; Part II, "The Profound Humanity of the Nonhuman during the Cold War"; and Part III, "The Specter of the Past in Contemporary Popular Culture." The spheres of gender, species, media, and politics all intersect in each part.

Part I consists of two chapters. Following this introductory chapter, chapter 2, "The White Snake Problem versus the White Snake Industry," recounts how the figure of the White Snake came alive through a network of religious, modernist, and commercial discourses in the vibrant print and visual cultures throughout the late nineteenth and early twentieth centuries. Accounts by Western missionaries and diplomats in China at the time, such as Samuel I. Woodbridge's 1896 book *The Mystery of the White Snake* and Frederick D. Cloud's 1906 book *Hangchow, the "City of Heaven"* served as both tourist guides and primers on China. Their perspectives on the White Snake accentuated the conflict between animal worship and the worship of God. They framed the White Snake legend as a remnant of primitive animism but were at the same time hopelessly seduced by its magic. As a result, in spite of their missionary and diplomatic objectives, they ended up popularizing the legend and contributing to its changing iconographies in the Anglophone worlds at the turn of the twentieth century.

The second part of the chapter takes as its starting point the above Anglophone missionary and diplomatic accounts, reading them against entries featuring the legends of White Snake from the pages of one of the most influential Chinese-language newspapers, *Shanghai News* (*Shenbao* 申報, 1872–1949), among many other Chinese-language sources, probing the technological breakthroughs in theatrical representations, the shifting performative paradigm regarding gender roles, and the sociopolitical debates over what is considered normative. As an industry, the White Snake legends animated new possibilities of being human in China's many transitional paths from an imperial dynasty to a modern republic, through deep engagements with the new media scenes at the time.

Chapter 3, "The Fall of the Pagoda and the Rise of the White Snake," deals with the collapse on September 25, 1924, of the Thunder Peak Pagoda, the historical structure under which the White Snake was said to have been imprisoned, located near West Lake in Hangzhou. The pagoda's fall triggered an intellectual earthquake, which had a much more profound impact than the physical collapse of the already decaying structure. Major cultural figures of the time, including Yu Pingbo 俞平伯, Liu Dabai 劉大白, Liu Gonglu 劉公魯, Sheyu 舍予, Gao Jianfu 高劍父, Lu Yin 盧隱, Xu Zhimo 徐志摩, and Lu Xun 魯迅, among others, offered timely and spirited reflections on the event through a diverse range of genres, such as essays, poems, letters, paintings, and photographs, and demonstrated the intriguing and imposing presence of the White Snake legends and the Thunder Peak Pagoda in Chinese intellectual and cultural imaginations.

Only a couple of years after the pagoda's fall, the first commercial film adaptation of the White Snake legend was produced by a Shanghai film company; the first two parts premiered in 1926 and the third and final part (covering what happens after the White Snake's imprisonment under the pagoda) in 1927. Printed cards inserted in cigarette packs based on the 1926 film series featured naked animal, female, and child bodies, sensationalizing and animating the image of the White Snake amid a polyphonic urban milieu.[68] An experimental film featuring the White Snake as a modern femme fatale also appeared almost simultaneously. Here the avant-garde, the commercial, and the popular intersect to create a synergy of modernity.[69] This "White Snake Modern," with its commercial and popular successes, initiated a long tradition of diasporic imagination regarding the White Snake theme. Intriguingly, the rhetoric of resurrecting the pagoda, both physically and imaginatively, propelled new waves of the White Snake's rise across a wide media spectrum in an inter-Asian and global context. The travels of the legends of the White Snake continue as the talks of rebuilding the pagoda reopen, year after year.

Part II, "The Profound Humanity of the Nonhuman during the Cold War," also consists of two chapters. Chapter 4, "The White Snake Legend in Postwar Japanese Cinema," shifts the focus to three Japanese-language "White Snake" films and scrutinizes their role in connecting Chinese legends and Japanese literary traditions, linking the modernist 1920s to the geopolitics of postwar Japan. In an uncanny fashion, the three Japanese films at the center of this chapter—Mizoguchi Kenji's 1953 *Ugetsu* (*Ugetsu monogatari* 雨月物語), Toyoda Shirō's 豊田四郎 1956 *Madame White Snake* (*Byaku fujin no yōren*), and Tōei Dōga's (Tōei Animation 東映動画) 1958 animation *Hakujaden*—all from the 1950s, deeply echo the Japan-inspired Chinese artist Tian Han's 田漢 1926 call for artistic creation based on a Chinese legend. In addition, these films also bear fascinating resemblances to the purported invention of love and modern sensibility in the Anglophone renditions of the legend in the Late Qing and early Republican Era, as discussed in chapter 2, as well as the visualization and canonization of the legend in Chinese pictorial journals and commercial films throughout the Republican era, as examined in chapter 3.

The continuities are striking. However, the issue of national representation becomes complicated when texts and images travel across linguistic and cultural spheres, in particular, between geopolitical entities recently at war and positioned at different sides of the Cold War divide. It is remarkable how the idea of love—whether forbidden, a result of "witchcraft," or manifested in a greater harmony that grows out of benevolence—emerged as a central thread stitching together the three postwar Japanese "White Snake" films, at a moment when the inhumanity of the Japanese Imperial Army and its aggressions toward its Asian neighbors was becoming an object of moral and ethical self-interrogation for many Japanese. The dynamic transitions between black-and-white film (*Ugetsu*) and color film (*Byaku fujin*), between live-action films aimed mainly at adult audiences (*Ugetsu* and *Byaku fujin*) and animation packaged for families and children (*Hakujaden*), reveal the importance of a media-centered approach in examining the White Snake legends in postwar Japanese cinema.

Chapter 5, "Reconfiguring the White Snake in Korean Cinema in an Inter-Asian Context," focuses on three films with a strong Korean connection as they reinvent the White Snake legend, both inside the Korean film industry and through the industry's collaboration and distribution efforts in East and Southeast Asia from the 1960s to the 1970s. Two of the films are Korean-language productions made in Korea—*Madam White Snake* (*Paeksa buin* 白蛇夫人 백사부인) and *Snake Woman* (*Sanyŏ* 蛇女 사녀). In fact, they were directed by the same legendary Korean director, Shin Sang-ok, in 1960 and 1969, respectively.

The third film's directorship, nationality, and even language are considerably more ambiguous. Credited to different directors in scholarly and popular sources originating from South Korea, Hong Kong, Mainland China, and the United States, the film is listed in the Korean Film Archive as a Korean-language film made in Korea, in the Hong Kong Movie Database as a Mandarin-language fantasy film made in Hong Kong, in Mainland China as a Taiwan, Hong Kong, and South Korea coproduction, and in the Internet Movie Database in the United States as a coproduction between Taiwan and Hong Kong with no trace of Korean involvement. Such an extremely variegated picture presents a fascinating case study for any researcher interested in continuities and connections across historical periods and geopolitical locations in East Asian filmmaking. Indeed, in the Korean film industry, these "White Snake" films were viewed as more accessible for export because of the broader market outside Korea in Chinese-speaking Southeast Asia.

Together, Chapters 4 and 5 highlight the inter-Asian connections among Mainland China, Japan, Hong Kong, South Korea, Taiwan, and Southeast Asia in revamping the White Snake legends under Cold War conditions. They explore the broad context of postwar inter-Asian inspiration and influence, coproduction, marketing, and consumption in the "White Snake Industry." Embedded in the Japanese and Korean connections is the role of Hong Kong as a Cold War cultural powerhouse, inheriting early cinematic legacies from Shanghai, coproducing with Japan, South Korea, and Taiwan, and exporting to Southeast Asia, revamping the White Snake legends in vivid shapes and colors. The legends' various retellings, both inside and outside the film industry, worked together to transform them into a story of love and reconciliation, and helped to create a stable master narrative—but one that would then be overturned amid the changes of the global 1980s and beyond.

Part III, "The Specter of the Past in Contemporary Popular Culture," consists of three chapters. Chapter 6, "Reconfiguring the Legend in Mainland China and Hong Kong," follows the fate of the fictional White Snake impersonator in Geling Yan's 1998 novella *White Snake* (*Baishe*), who was a renowned White Snake performer on stage but was accused of being "worn shoes"[70] offstage during the Cultural Revolution (1966–1976). The fate of this White Snake dancer serves as an allegory for the life-shaping power of art, as the political trauma wrought by the Cultural Revolution on the Chinese mainland is transmuted into the personal trauma of coming to terms with one's own lesbian identity. The blurring of gender boundaries, particularly for women, echoes what Lilian Lee has described as the "running wild" milieu of Hong Kong in the 1980s, crystalized in the Green Snake image she created in her own novel *Green Snake* (*Qingshe*), at the time.[71]

I treat Yan's novella *White Snake* as a broad metaphor for the fate of the White Snake legends during the Maoist Era (late 1940s to late 1970s) in Mainland China. In it, the experimental and the popular, as prescribed by the regime's cultural policies, intersect.[72] Yan's text also gestures toward what came to be known as the postmodern, postsocialist, and postcolonial developments,[73] both in the Mainland and in Hong Kong, as expressed in the avant-garde theaters of Taiwan and Singapore, in the revisionist Green Snake–centered narratives of Lilian Lee's novel and Tsui Hark's film, in the 3D martial arts film *It's Love* (*Baishe chuanshuo* 白蛇傳說) starring Jet Li (Li Lianjie 李連傑) as the Buddhist abbot, and in the experimental staging of the legend by celebrated theater director Tian Qinxin in Mainland China and in the United States, among other places.

In the context of Yan's *White Snake* and its gender politics, the contradictions in the cultural politics of the Cultural Revolution need to be spelled out. On the one hand, the reigning ideology of the time advocated rebellion against authority, bureaucracy, and establishment and hence unwittingly unleashed and catalyzed gender and sexual experimentations, particularly among the young. On the other hand, the official discourse repressed sexual desires in the name of an asexual revolutionary comradeship and designated antiestablishment gender and sexual experimentations as aberrant.[74] In such a self-proclaimed "revolutionary" regime, the officially designated "anti-revolutionary" or "counterrevolutionary" elements may in fact serve as the most revolutionary inspirations in reshaping gender and sexual relations for years to come.

In chapter 7, "The White Snake Legend in the United States in the Twenty-First Century," we return to the Anglophone connections of the White Snake legend a century later, after witnessing the legend's transformations throughout the twentieth century in Chinese, Japanese, and Korean cultures, through changing media representations, and across historical and geopolitical divides. This return delineates how the obsessions of the American missionary and diplomat as examined in chapter 2, which solidified the Anglophone White Snake tradition, are manifested in new configurations in a cluster of Anglophone productions in the first decades of the twenty-first century. The three texts examined are Zhou Long's four-act opera *Madame White Snake*, with libretto by Cerise Lim Jacobs, which premiered in Boston in February 2010 and in Beijing in October 2010; Tony Award–winner Mary Zimmerman's one-act play *The White Snake*, first performed at the Oregon Shakespeare Festival in 2012, brought to Wuzhen Theatre Festival in China in 2014, and staged at the Constellation Theatre Company in Washington, DC, in 2019 under the direction of Allison Stockman, among other iterations; and the short fashion video *The Legend of Lady White Snake* by the Indian-born fashion-model-turned-photographer Indrani, created in 2013 to publicize a major new line of fashion and released as an award-winning film in 2015.

For the audience in Boston and other locales outside the Chinese-speaking worlds, the Chinese legend itself serves as a kind of exotic environment in Zhou Long's opera, while the Western operatic form and its characterizations reinforce such exoticism for the audience at the Beijing Music Festival, as they may very well already be familiar with the legend in Chinese. As to Zimmerman's play, it is distinguished from other White Snake adaptations by its forking narrative arcs and the possibilities for the audience to creatively interact with the performances. In Indrani's digital video, through the intertwining of poetry, photography, and fashion, we see the themes of gender and species, media and politics coming together, in the director's insistence on using digital media to foster queer subjectivity and celebrate the life and work of a queer designer, whose at once inspired and tortured existence has left lingering echoes and extensive legacies in the world of contemporary fashion. Such a digital video accentuates the plasticity, the shape-shifting, and the transformative qualities of the metamorphosis tales that are at the center of the legends of the White Snake.

The concluding chapter, chapter 8, "The Eternal Bodies of the White Snake," takes as its starting point a Korean webtoon and its afterlife in Chinese. The chapter then zooms in on the 2019 internet drama *New Legend of Madame White Snake* (*Xin Bainiangzi chuanqi*), which claimed to be the only authorized remake of the 1992 Taiwanese TV series of the same name; the 2019 animation *White Snake: The Legend Begins* (*Baishe: yuanqi*), which was touted as the first US-China coproduced animation and as a triumph of Chinese animation at the same time; and the 2016 adaption of the legend with an all-child cast, the television series *Star* [sic] *of Tomorrow: Legend of the White Snake* (*Xiaoxigu: Baishe zhuan* 小戏骨: 白蛇传).

This chapter argues for a historical and contextual reading of the body politics embedded in these contemporary multimedia retellings of the White Snake legends. The bodies of females, children, and animals, already important in the early versions and increasingly prominent in the most recent retellings, bridge the realms of human and nonhuman and of adults and children. Moreover, the bodies of females and children are alike in having been, throughout history and across cultures, controlled and used by those more powerful, often adults and men. As attested throughout our investigations, the White Snake legends have served transgressive functions through their modern retellings by blurring the boundaries between human and nonhuman. The bodies of females, children, and animals emerge as renewed manifestations of the powerfully humane "nonhuman."

Throughout this study, the White Snake serves to deconstruct the human-, adult-, and male-centered narratives of the cultural mainstream and creates transgressive, creative spaces to explore the confrontations between the past and the present, the folk and the literary, the avant-garde and the popular, and between socialist and postsocialist political and cultural ideals. The White Snake legends instantiate the ways in which, in their telling and retellings, and in their transference across generations and across media, cultural narratives can model and inspire individual identity formation and transformation. At the same time, the retellings and transferences could provide impetus for social change, with the distinctive political potential and affective power of the fantastic at the center of the reconstructed narratives.

THEORETICAL IMPLICATIONS

The inter-Asian connections emerging throughout the course of the White Snake legends' travels, in which linguistic, cultural, and political registers and literal and metaphorical translations become the mechanism of migration, situate the legends and their afterlives into a global framework beyond the narrow focus of the geopolitically Chinese nation-state. Moreover, rather than taking a Sino-centric approach and treating the English, Japanese, Korean, and other iterations of the legends as derivative and of lesser importance, this study focuses on the travels of the legends in multiple directions, and on how such travels, through translation and adaptation, came back to shape and impact modern and contemporary Chinese culture and politics. Such reverberations are crucial in teasing out the multidirectional and multinational coproduction, in real or metaphorical senses, of the White Snake legends in contemporary times, across linguistic, historical, and geopolitical boundaries.

There are strong theoretical implications of such multidirectional movements across borders. Adaptation (translation across media) and migration (translation to other cultural and political contexts) are two central theoretical threads in the travels of the White Snake legends.[75] With its dual focus on "thick descriptions" of the textual travels of specific legends and an earnest theoretical articulation of translation and adaptation based on such an empirical approach,[76] this study responds to some of the central debates in the field of world literature, in particular, between Franco Moretti's advocating "distant reading" through a world system–style macro analysis and David Damrosch's focus on close reading and insistence on micro-analysis in its specific linguistic and cultural contexts.[77] My approach can also be framed through the folklore-anthropology-structuralist traditions as inspired by

Vladimir Propp's syntagmatic approach and Claude Lévi-Strauss's paradigmatic model, which both recognize recombinatorial motifs without abandoning their specificities in their deployments across languages and cultures. Propp's approach has a syntagmatic leaning toward the empirical and the inductive and Lévi-Strauss's a paradigmatic leaning toward speculative and the deductive. This provides a middle ground to the universalizing impulses as reflected in Joseph Campbell's concept of "monomyth" or Stith Thompson's focus on classification.[78]

As a result, I take a synthesizing approach that profits from both Moretti's vision of the world system and Damrosch's attention to cultural differences. My preoccupation with the travels of the White Snake legends echoes Moretti's interest in examining the movement of a specific literary form. However, rather than aiming at revealing any laws or systematic trends through big data analyses, I am more in tune with what Damrosch would demand regarding close reading and empirical studies: illuminating linguistic and cultural differences in the locations to which the legends migrated, examining how translation and adaptation work in concrete, specific situations, and determining how, as a result, literary and cultural changes and accommodations might have taken place over time. In this study of the Chinese White Snake legends, I set out to practice such a theory of translation and adaptation, not only between languages and cultures but also across media, and situate it between the Moretti and the Damrosch models. It is my hope that the theoretical implications of approaching translation and adaptation in intercultural and intermedia contexts will invite further conversations beyond the China field and beyond a specific interest in the fantastic and the legendary.

In addition to participating in the aforementioned dialogue within the field of world literature and the study of folklore, this study also insists on exploring historical continuities and convergences in specific national and cultural contexts. Rather than reiterating the standard argument about Mainland China as an oddity in Cold War Asia, this project demonstrates that there are multidirectional exchanges, interplays, coproductions, and mutual inspirations between Communist China and its Asian neighbors and beyond. Moreover, by putting this Cold War episode into a longer historical framework, as I do in this study's three-part design, I am not only demonstrating convergences between China and the wider world during the Cold War period but also suggesting continuities between the pre–Cold War and post–Cold War moments throughout the long twentieth century.

In this sense, the convergence argument happens in two ways. The first of these hinges on historical continuity: from the late nineteenth-century

American missionary objections to the "superstitious" qualities of the Chinese White Snake legends, to the modernist and Maoist struggles against "superstition" and the intellectual remaking of the legends into a positive revolutionary "myth" during the Cold War, and then to the legends' return in postsocialist and postmodern conditions as minority discourse, a renewed antiauthoritarian, revolutionary discourse in the age of "farewell to revolution." The other convergence argument involves the cultural cross-fertilizations between the often simplistically categorized Communist Mainland China and the anti-Communist Asian countries and regions, along with their Western allies during the Cold War. Studying the travels of the Chinese White Snake legends allows a broader perspective in the study of China, the East Asian region, and their global connections, as no culture can be fully understood in isolation. Situating the legends in their Asian and global contexts also reveals sustained dialogues involving adaptations, appropriations, translations, retranslations, and multidirectional exchanges between Chinese and other Asian cultural traditions and beyond.

More importantly, by putting Chinese studies in closer dialogue with studies of other Asian traditions, I hope not only to energize Chinese studies but also to contribute to studies of Japan, Korea, Hong Kong, Taiwan, and Southeast Asia. The White Snake artifacts produced in Japanese, Korean, and other Asian languages and dialects initiated their own literary and popular traditions in their respective linguistic and cultural contexts and became treasured contributions, or forgotten treasures, in the literary and cultural history of these national and regional traditions. With more and more students and scholars acquiring more than one Asian language for their research and with the continued interest in inter-Asian and transnational networks, this approach could be useful to anyone interested in cultural adaptation, translation, migration, and transnationalism in the broadly defined field of Asian studies, in which multiple Asian languages, geographical locations, and cultural traditions interconnect and interact in a multidirectional fashion.

PART I

The White Snake at the Turn of the Twentieth Century

CHAPTER 2

The White Snake Problem versus the White Snake Industry

THE WHITE SNAKE PROBLEM

> The status of the Chinese popular mind in its abnormal cravings, may be compared with the physical condition of a fever patient. Unable, through ignorance, to extend the operations of thought further than the borders of the Inner Land, and requiring something far beyond the resources of China to satisfy the natural and normal desire, it has peopled the earth, the air, and the sea with all sorts of ghosts, hobgoblins, fairies and dragons. For this lamentable fact, the Buddhist doctrine of transmigration is largely responsible. Certain it is, that the people think that animals and reptiles were once men, and men were once animals and reptiles. Such being the case, it is no wonder that the ordinary and commonplace occurrences on this planet seem tame and insipid when put alongside the thrilling adventures of their imaginary heroes.[1]

So begins Samuel I. Woodbridge's introduction to his 1896 English rendition of the Chinese White Snake legend, titled *The Mystery of the White Snake.* Woodbridge seems to have regarded the White Snake legend as a key to deciphering what he saw as the feverish "Chinese popular mind." Regardless of whether he had been directly influenced by French psychologist Gustave Le Bon,[2] Woodbridge used scientific language, especially medical and psychological terminology, to diagnose the problems of the "Chinese popular mind" and thus find their "root causes." Curiously, Woodbridge's scientific, medical, and psychological inquiries into the "Inner Land" of the Chinese physical and mental landscapes convinced him of the primary role of "the Buddhist doctrine of transmigration" in Chinese popular beliefs. Wielding the weapons of the latest scientific thinking, Woodbridge found such a Chinese mentality abnormal and lamentable, and he earnestly sought for its salvation.

Woodbridge's introduction to his translation, dissecting the Chinese legend and the Chinese popular mind from the perspective of the modern, and in this case, the Western Other, provides an intriguing starting point for exploring the global travels of the White Snake legend in English, Chinese, Japanese, Korean, from the late nineteenth century to the present day. This chapter first examines Woodbridge's and his contemporary American diplomat Frederick D. Cloud's English renditions of the White Snake legend. It then delves into popular representations of the White Snake in contemporary Chinese press, using *Shenbao* as a prime example, supplemented by a wide range of other textual and visual materials. By combining and contrasting the Anglophone and the Sinophone representations, we find a complex picture regarding the White Snake legend's transformation at the turn of the twentieth century and beyond. This transformation is characterized by two parallel trends, at the same time secularizing and spiritualizing, forming an intricate tapestry of converging and diverging trends that extend throughout the modern metamorphoses of the White Snake legends.

An American missionary active in China in the late nineteenth century, Woodbridge created a rendition of the Chinese legend that was serialized between September 4 and October 16, 1896, in the pages of the prominent English-language newspaper *The North-China Herald*, published in Shanghai. The serialized chapters were then collected and printed at the office of *The North-China Herald* later the same year, as a slim thirty-four-page pamphlet selling at fifty cents per copy,[3] a significant but still affordable price tag at the time. In the same introduction, Woodbridge goes on to offer his detailed diagnosis of what he saw as the problem with the Chinese popular mind and its possible cure:

> The *nil admirari* attitude of the Chinese, that is apparent even to the most casual observer, may be partly accounted for by the fact that in every department of thought and action their traditions contain the deeds of demigods more exceedingly wonderful than any actual sublunary character ever produced. . . . In order to render the native intellect capable of receiving and assimilating true knowledge, the fever above mentioned must first be reduced. We believe that the plain Gospel of Jesus Christ, with its long train of beneficent effects upon the world and mankind, will clarify the mind of the Chinese, as well as accomplish the farther reaching and more enduring result of saving their souls.[4]

Looking from a modern, secular perspective, we can certainly discredit Woodbridge's proposal for "saving Chinese souls" by observing its propagandizing nature. Indeed, his propagation of Christianity had as its target what he perceived as the most influential religion in China at the time, Buddhism.

Examined from a secular viewpoint, which became increasingly influential in China after the May Fourth movement of the early twentieth century,[5] the objectivity of Woodbridge's perspective certainly becomes suspect. Indeed, he had been serving as a missionary of the Presbyterian Church of the United States in China for well over a decade by the time he published this introduction in 1896.

However, such a criticism of Woodbridge's "religious propaganda" is colored by an unjustified presentism, which I would like to avoid in this study. Instead, I would like to reconsider Woodbridge in his historical context and examine in more detail what he identified as a decisive influence on the Chinese popular mind, "the Buddhist doctrine of transmigration." As introduced in chapter 1, White Snake's power in the legend lies in the snake's ability to metamorphose into human form, and belief in that kind of transformation is as old as Chinese culture itself, as demonstrated in *The Animal and the Daemon in Early China* by Roel Sterckx, a leading scholar of animals and spirits in the Chinese tradition.[6] So it is indeed quite a stretch to attribute such beliefs to Buddhism, a later import from India during the Han dynasty (206 BCE–220 CE). In fact, even in Buddhist belief, once you are reborn in a certain form, you cannot change it as long as that incarnation lasts—a rather inflexible sort of transmigration, where the boundary between human and nonhuman still holds, at least during one lifetime. This fixed form for life, even after taking into consideration the role of mediation, is vividly expressed by contemporary Chinese writer and Nobel laureate Mo Yan in his novel *Life and Death Are Wearing Me Out* (*Shengsi pilao* 生死疲勞),[7] in which the male protagonist is reborn as a donkey, an ox, a pig, a dog, and a monkey, before finally being born again as a human.[8]

In Woodbridge's diagnosis, "the thrilling adventures of their imaginary heroes" and the "exceedingly wonderful" demigods were detrimental to the Chinese popular mind and hindered the capacity of the Chinese to receive and assimilate "true knowledge." On the front page of his pamphlet,[9] Woodbridge included the Chinese translation of Romans 1:23, 不崇永生上帝之榮反拜速朽世人禽獸昆蟲之像 (*buchong yongsheng Shangdi zhirong fanbai suxiu shiren qinshou kunchong zhixiang*), which, in the English Revised Version of the Bible popular in the 1880s, appeared as "[they] changed the glory of the incorruptible God for the likeness of an image of corruptible man, and of birds, and four-footed beasts, and creeping things."[10] Woodbridge likely took the Chinese translation of Romans 1:23 from Joseph Edkins's *Correcting the Mistakes in Buddhism* (*Shijiao zhengmiu* 釋教正謬).[11] Using the legend of White Snake as a prime example, Woodbridge framed his translation of it as an endeavor to critique Buddhism and animal worship, foregrounding what he saw as a shortcoming of the Chinese "popular mind" and thereby spreading the Gospel of Jesus Christ.

Inspirations from Kentucky

Although framed as a means to promote Christianity and critique Buddhism, Woodbridge's rendition of the White Snake legend nonetheless presents an intriguing early representation of the Chinese legend in the English language that is both accessible for popular consumption and worthy of critical engagement. My undergraduate students at the University of Kentucky provided some early inspirations for my own thinking, as quite a few of them readily identify with Woodbridge, who, like them, grew up Christian in Kentucky. One of the central questions they posed is, if the reader cannot categorize the White Snake as a beast or a human, was Woodbridge's original intent in telling this story successful? One student, a girl of mixed racial background who was born and raised in northern Kentucky, considered Woodbridge's portrayal of the White Snake extremely "ambiguous." For her, the persona that Woodbridge had wanted to build up, the enchantress who bewitches, does not provide room for human love or value. However, throughout the story, the White Snake is given surprisingly humane qualities. For instance, Woodbridge tells the reader that she "loved devotedly."[12] Such personification adds complexity to the reader's perception of the White Snake, who is both demon and human and who simultaneously possesses the power to love while being a "brute creation," as Woodbridge insisted early on in his narrative.[13]

Another seemingly trivial question raised by my Kentucky students has to do with Woodbridge's choice of names for the characters. Having read English translations of many other (often later) Chinese versions, my students questioned the radically Westernized names for some leading characters, such as Albia (for the White Snake) and Flora (for the Green Snake). One student worried whether this would undermine "the longstanding cultural value of the legend." Another responded by highlighting the "Westernized and mysterious mood" fostered by these names and observed that the name "Albia" conveyed "a magical aura" that seemed appropriate for the White Snake character, while the name "Flora" suggested a close relationship with nature and wildness and thus corresponded with the Green Snake's somewhat "beast-like" persona. The students' final question, however, has to do with Woodbridge's radical shift of purpose from earlier Chinese versions, from cautioning its audience to "beware of desire" to "spreading the Gospel." One student concluded, "This is a first-hand example of the plasticity of folklore and how interpretations can alter the storyline just a little bit to elicit new ideas. For me, this provides more evidence that the storyteller has no control over the story, and it is in fact the readers that make the story meaningful and unique."[14]

Accounts by American missionaries and diplomats, including Samuel I. Woodbridge's aforementioned *Mystery of the White Snake* (1896) and Frederick D. Cloud's *Hangchow, the "City of Heaven"* (1906), functioned as tourist guides and as cultural primers on China for contemporaneous English readers. Their perspectives on the White Snake legend accentuated the conflict between "animal worship" and the worship of God and framed the legend as a folk remnant of primitive animism, awaiting religious and modernist salvation.[15] The correlation between Christian teaching and modern enlightenment may seem odd to many today, but many among Woodbridge's and Cloud's generation of Western missionaries, diplomats, businessmen, and travelers still saw Christianity and Western culture, including science and technology, as one indivisible whole. This view persisted even when *On the Origin of Species* was published in 1859 and caused much concern about how science and faith could coexist and even after modern textual criticism of the Bible caused similar concerns and controversies.

More importantly, Woodbridge and Cloud afforded the White Snake legend its immortality in the English language through their extensive and often loving engagements with the Chinese material, strengthened by their lived experience in Zhenjiang, Hangzhou, and Suzhou—important cities along the Grand Canal (Da yunhe 大運河) that are central to the White Snake narratives.[16] Although the spread of Woodbridge's and Cloud's renditions of the White Snake legends may well have been largely limited to English-reading communities in China, the authors did publish and circulate their writings through prominent channels closely connected with both the missionary and the diplomatic circles. As a result, and sometimes unwittingly, they further popularized the White Snake legends in the English-reading world at large and contributed to their changing iconographies at the turn of the twentieth century.

The Mystery of the White Snake

To make the Chinese White Snake legend more relatable to readers of English and to suggest meaningful distinctions between the human male protagonist and the snake women, Woodbridge names his characters in evocative ways. As my students pointed out, the White Snake is given a Latinate name, "Albia," while her human husband is referred to only as "Hanwin" (Hanwen 漢

文), using his courtesy name in Chinese without even mentioning his family name Hsu (Xu 許). Hanwen's married sister and her husband, two minor human characters, are both given fully Anglicized names and first names only, "Grace" and "Leigh," respectively. Hanwen is the only character in Woodbridge's rendition whose Chinese name is preserved. Woodbridge describes Hanwen as "very handsome" at the beginning of the narrative and remarks that "he had beautiful eyes, and was graceful in body, and of a happy, cheerful disposition."[17] Moreover, Woodbridge constantly emphasizes Hanwen's "beauty" throughout the narrative in an effort to justify other characters' emotional attachment to him. In contrast, the White Snake is introduced as a "brute creation," who, having "spent eighteen hundred years in meditation, seeking to attain perfection," would never be able to reach that state.[18]

Later in the story, Woodbridge introduces a Daoist priest Manetho of Mow Mountain (Maoshan daoshi 茅山道士), as a noted exorcist who becomes overpowered by Albia. Woodbridge's naming of the Daoist priest invites association with Manetho the ancient Egyptian priest[19] and lends a mythical quality to this minor character, who is used mainly to buttress the display of Albia's supernatural powers. Woodbridge's verdict on the legend, at least as stated early in his translation, echoes the premise he lays out in the introduction. He sees the legend as demonstrating the "feverish" state of the Chinese popular mind and the need for a cure. And that cure, Woodbridge announces in the first installment of his rendition of the White Snake legend, was the plain teaching of Jesus Christ.

Judging by both content and format, we can see that Woodbridge may have based his version on the first Western-language translation of the White Snake legend, Stanislas Julien's 1834 rendition in French, *Blanche et Bleue, ou Les deux couleuvres-fées; roman chinois*, itself based on the 1806 Chinese version of the legend, *The Strange Tale of the White Snake* (*Leifengta qizhuan* 雷峰塔奇傳), attributed to Yushan zhuren,[20] as the French version had already been introduced in an English-language summary in late 1834[21] and an English rendition based on the same Chinese source text was serialized in full in 1864. Another possible influence was the Chinese American activist Wong Chin Foo 王清福's 1888 short story written in English, "Poh Yuin Ko, The Serpent-Princess," presented as "translated from the original" and published in *The Cosmopolitan*.[22] This cluster of texts in Chinese, French, and English, published between 1806 and 1888, became some of the most likely candidates to have influenced Woodbridge's 1896 English rendition, either directly or indirectly. This textual lineage supports the general impression of missionary's lack of meaningful interaction with actual Chinese performances on stage, as reflected in Pearl Buck's biography of her father, who also served as a missionary in Zhenjiang at the time and knew Woodbridge personally.[23]

The nineteenth-century *tanci* version *The Complete Illustrated Righteous Snake* (*Xiuxiang yiyao quanzhuan* 繡像義妖全傳, *The Illustrated Righteous Snake* hereafter), attributed to Chen Yuqian, may also have had some influence. It was first printed in an edition with an 1809 preface and became popular through numerous performances and reprints throughout the nineteenth century.[24] It is also likely that Woodbridge may have known another version of the legend collected in the early Qing story collection *Beautiful Tales of the West Lake* (*Xihu jiahua* 西湖佳話, 1673, chapter 15).

Regardless of his actual sources, Woodbridge's intimate touch in portraying his male protagonist Hanwen is rather different from both Feng Menglong's focus on the "lust, caution" morality tale in the vernacular story and Chen Yuqian's focus on the righteous White Snake in the *tanci* version. Woodbridge makes important choices to highlight the emotional intimacies of his protagonists, especially Hanwen. Accentuating the male perspective and likely influenced by the 1806 Chinese version attributed to Yushan zhuren and its French and English renditions, he first follows Hanwen in Hangzhou as he is apprenticed to an apothecary's shop. Woodbridge then moves on to the Pure Winds Cavern in Sichuan to introduce the White Snake. He introduces her as a creature of deception, who lied to the God of the North Star and swore, "If I am not speaking the truth, let the Thunder Peak Tower crush my body,"[25] prefiguring her future imprisonment. Woodbridge then introduces the Green Snake, who fights the White Snake at their first encounter and loses miserably. This is also how Woodbridge shows the White Snake to possess "a superhuman power over nature and man."[26]

Woodbridge continues to emphasize Hanwen's good looks, his "thoughts of love" in the springtime, and, most important, his "love at first sight" upon seeing the beautiful White Snake by the West Lake: "the young man's heart beat rapidly," and he "stood rooted to the spot . . . completely bewitched."[27] After lending his umbrella to Albia and Flora in the rain, Hanwen goes to their residence to claim it and is entertained with food and drink. Woodbridge has Hanwen declare his passion for Albia first; she promises to be his wife afterwards, a rare occurrence in any White Snake rendition that the human male takes the lead in confessing his love, with Wong Chin Foo's 1888 short story as the only precedent and a possible influence.[28] Our tour of the male psyche continues as Woodbridge includes an account of the snake woman's theft of silver, which causes the young man's exile to Suzhou, echoing plot developments in Chinese versions of the story beginning with Feng Menglong. Here Woodbridge brings the human sensibility of his snake woman protagonist

Albia to the forefront, reassuring readers that she longs for Hanwen, "whom she now loved devotedly."[29]

In one of the most climactic scenes in the legend, Woodbridge renders Albia's startling transformation in graphic language: "Oh, horror! A large snake with a head like a bushel, and eyes flushing fire discovered up in the bed. Slowly uncoiling itself, with fangs gleaming, and month dripping blood, it moved towards him, hissing as it came!"[30] As a result of having been forced to drink realgar wine, she transforms to her original snake form, scaring her husband to death. Albia then risks her life to seek a precious herb that will restore him. Fated to be the mother of the God of Literature (Wenqu xing 文曲星) and to be crushed under Thunder Peak Pagoda for lying to the God of the North Star, she is given the herb to save the father of her future son.[31] Intriguingly, Woodbridge grants full humanity to Albia right after this scene, as he has her suddenly appearing to be dead after being attacked on her homeward journey, no different from any mortal.[32] Albia has to be revived, and upon arriving home, she revives her husband and regains his "love and trust" by using a handkerchief to produce the magical illusion of a dead White Snake.[33]

In humanizing the demonic White Snake and even granting her divinity, Woodbridge goes as far as to depict Albia as impersonating the Goddess of Mercy (Guanyin 觀音) to direct the local Prefect to Hanwen, so he can cure the Prefect's wife and gain business and good reputation.[34] When Albia finds out that Hanwen has again been arrested for the goods she stole, we learn that "her heart was burdened with grief for she loved him tenderly."[35] Woodbridge then has Albia cross-dress as "a finely dressed young man," with Flora as "a servant," delivering money to Hanwen's brother-in-law in Hangchow (Hangzhou) before following him to the city of his exile, Zhenjiang.[36] Albia and Hanwen are reunited in Zhenjiang and live happily together until Fahhai (Fahai) meets Hanwen and advises him to leave his snake wife: "The White Snake wields a wonderful power, and will exert it to the utmost to bewitch you and bring you back, because she loves you devotedly, and, were she not of the brute creation, would be a model wife."[37] Here Woodbridge really seems to have had difficulty reconciling Albia's identities as both a bewitching snake spirit and a possible "model wife" full of humanity, especially on the question of her love for Hanwen. He continues to buttress her humanity through her confession of devotion to Hanwen: "I did evil only that good might come to him."[38]

Albia and Flora flood Golden Island (Golden Mountain Monastery) and rampage through the city of Zhenjiang to reclaim Hanwen, and Albia meets Hanwen again in Hangzhou. Yet despite the destruction they have wrought,

Hanwen cannot fulfill his promise to become a monk because "the love he had always cherished for his wife, the natural feeling for her distress, and the many proofs of her devotion to him" hold him back.[39] The couple settle in Hangzhou with the help of Leigh and Grace. Albia assumes full human vulnerability when the vengeful Manetho sends his pupil, the "centipede ghost," to harm her: "When she looked up, just before her, stretched along his full length, crouched the venomous insect, his fangs all showing ready to strike. Albia screamed in terror, and fell swooning to the ground."[40]

Here Woodbridge has deprived Albia of all her supernatural power and made her a fragile wife. Albia's full humanity is later confirmed when she gives birth to a perfect human boy, "Dream Dragon" (Mengjiao 夢蛟). Intriguingly, Woodbridge has Albia confess her identity to all present when she is captured by Fahai's bowl: "I must tell you now that I am the White Snake of Pure Winds Cavern. In a former life my husband rescued me from a beggar who was about to kill me, and I have tried to recompense him as well as I could. All my actions towards you, dear husband, have been prompted by love."[41] In the end, Woodbridge manages to maintain the "happy ending" already popularized in his sources, where there is no villain: Fahai fulfills Buddha's order and sets the White Snake free upon her son's attaining the highest rank in the imperial examination; as a result, Hanwen and Albia both reach perfection and ascend to heaven.

Woodbridge's evident love for the Chinese legend and his intimate portrayals of its loving, impulsive, and devoted young protagonists, be they a human male or a snake woman, seem to have been at odds with his pronounced purpose of critiquing the animal worship of the Chinese popular mind "polluted" by Buddhism. Quite remarkably, within such an imaginary world filled with ghosts and goblins, Woodbridge did manage to bestow love and devotion, as well as psychological depth, on humans and nonhumans alike, making his English-language text a new and rather successful contribution to the feverish world created by the Chinese popular mind, the world he set out to condemn and redeem. However, for Woodbridge, love was not feverish, because it was based on human emotions and modern sensibilities.

Having reimagined a "superstitious" legend into a modern love story, Woodbridge could be considered to have brought the Chinese legend into the orbit of romantic English literature.[42] Such a framework, in which indigenous traditions are found lacking and Westernization are considered to bring "true" versions of modern practices into them, has generated thoughtful debates.[43] By representing the White Snake legend as a love story, a theme already started to take hold in Late Imperial China, Woodbridge contributed to romantic English literature as well as to the modern reinvention of the White Snake legends. The link between this form of Westernization and Woodbridge's chief purpose, Christianization, needs to be spelled out. His express purpose of spreading Christianity, as we will see, was not always well served when he entered more deeply into the role of a participant-observer of the Chinese popular mind that he had set out to reform.

In 1895, one year before the publication of *The Mystery of the White Snake*, Woodbridge had already published his translation of another Chinese legend, *The Golden-Horned Dragon King, or The Emperor's Visit to the Spirit World*,[44] also at *The North-China Herald* office in Shanghai. The front page of the sixteen-page pamphlet bears the Chinese epigraph "*Jing guishen* (*er*) *yuanzhi*" 敬鬼神 (而) 遠之, attributed to Confucius in *The Analects* and translated by James Legge as "while respecting spiritual beings, to keep aloof from them."[45] Legge's translation was published in multiple volumes beginning in the early 1860s and was reprinted in the early 1890s.

However, in his translator's preface immediately following this cover page, Woodbridge alerts his readers that it would be a mistake to suppose that the classics (such as those translated by Legge) "form the mainspring of Chinese popular thought and action."[46] Arguing for the central importance of the imaginary realm in Chinese life, Woodbridge reminds his readers that "the people believe a story like this (the Dragon King) as thoroughly as we do the history of George Washington" and that "while comparatively few people study Confucius, all classes, men and women, old and young, rich and poor, eagerly devour and digest stories like the 'Golden-Horned Dragon King.'"[47] It is revealing to consider this earlier volume in the context of *The Mystery of the White Snake* and how Woodbridge left behind the teachings he quoted from the Bible and the *Analects* on the front pages of both books.

Only a few years later, in 1900, Woodbridge wrote in a prefatory note to another of his translations from Chinese, *China's Only Hope*, a rendition of Chang Chih-tung's (Zhang Zhidong 張之洞) *An Exhortation to Learning* (*Quanxue pian* 勸學篇), that his own translation was wrought "with a free hand," as he believed "that a strict adherence to mere words is slavish, and that the spirit and genius of translation consists in conveying the thought of one language into another by the shortest and quickest route."[48] This statement offers insight into Woodbridge's unique engagement with the Chinese originals. It might seem a big leap from the retelling of the Dragon King and the White Snake legends to a translation of treatises on the future of China sanctioned by its emperor at the time.[49] However, both texts served Woodbridge well in providing platforms for his attempts to cure the Chinese popular mind of the effects of Buddhism and to explore the possibility that Christianity could provide the solution for the problems China was facing. Zhang Zhidong's position of encouraging foreign learning while maintaining Confucian teachings, in particular, proved of special interest to missionaries such as Woodbridge and Griffith John, who wrote an introduction to *China's Only Hope*.[50]

Woodbridge was eventually commissioned to write *Fifty Years in China* (1918), a book of church history to be used as a textbook on the China mission (1867–1917) of the Presbyterian Church in the United States. In the section on "superstition," he wrote, "The Chinese firmly believe that there are demons in the air, demons on land, in the earth, in the water—'*in all things too superstitious*.' The clog to all progress in China consists in what the people call *fengshui*, literally *wind and water*."[51] Readers of Woodbridge's rendition of the White Snake legend knew what he was referring to when he emphasized the impact of "superstition" on the Chinese popular mind: "The outcome of all this is the deep impression on the minds of the deluded people of the terrible power possessed by revengeful demons and ghosts," and "no foreigner even now can fathom the depth of these devilish beliefs, and strange as it may seem, the revolution which has opened the way for the Gospel in such a marvelous way has done little to break the chains of superstition that have bound the common people for such a long period."[52]

Because of the projected textbook's anticipated large female readership and the need to address women's issues in mission work, Woodbridge included a whole chapter titled "Woman's Work for Women" and specifically mentioned "the marvelous transmigrations of the 'White Snake'" as an example of the "lesser literature" preferred by Chinese women.[53] Although, in the context of church history, Woodbridge was obliged to frame the legend of the White Snake as a negative example of "disastrous consequences" to the Chinese imagination,[54] one has to recognize the weight he bestowed upon the legend and the serious attention he gave to it in what became the official history of the US Presbyterian mission in China.

Hangchow, the "City of Heaven"

Frederick D. Cloud's *Hangchow, the "City of Heaven,"* written in 1906 while he was serving at the American Consulate in Hangzhou, also treats the White Snake legend in the context of serious discussions concerning both church and state. Though designed as a comprehensive guide to the city of Hangzhou and including captivating accounts of its history and geography,

Cloud's book also features extensive reports on local Christian missionary activities and another substantial rendition of the White Snake legend, apparently considered worthy of being included in a handbook ostensibly focused on the transmission of "reliable and practical knowledge."[55] Where Woodbridge quotes from the Bible on the front page of his White Snake pamphlet, Cloud prefaces his handbook with the popular saying, "Heaven is above; beneath are Soo (chow) and Hang (chow)" (*shangyou tiantang xiayou Su Hang* 上有天堂下有蘇杭), phrases used to denote the appeal of these two prosperous cities.[56]

Moreover, unlike Woodbridge, Cloud clearly identifies his sources in his foreword, with a detailed footnote at the beginning of his rendition, where he explains the popularity and high esteem of the White Snake legend in Chinese cultural life, manifestations of which included an annual performance in the imperial palace. Cloud identifies his retelling as following the version known locally in Hangzhou, and "as told" by others to him and "supplemented from an edition titled *Hsiu-hsiang-i-yao-ch'uan-chuan*" (*Xiuxiang yiyao quanzhuan, The Illustrated Righteous Snake*).[57] What Cloud cites here is precisely the 1809 *tanci* version attributed to Chen Yuqian, a version in wide circulation at the time of his writing.

Cloud introduces the legend of the "White Snake" and the "Green Fish" in his section on West Lake earlier in the book, as perhaps the most famous of all legends related to the lake.[58] He again refers to the legend in his introduction of Thunder Peak Pagoda, under which the White Snake and the Green Fish, "two goblins or witches" feared by the people "were captured and buried forever," according to "ancient folklore."[59] He even predicts the pagoda's fall, which happened almost twenty years later in 1924, reasoning that the tendency for visitors to carry away bits of brick from its ruined walls for good fortune would cause it to crumble within a few decades.[60]

After describing many of Hanzhou's historical and cultural sites of interest, Cloud moves to retelling the White Snake legend.[61] Sixteen coarsely sketched illustrations in the *tanci* version attributed to Chen Yuqian tell the White Snake legend in sixteen visual installments (fig. 2).[62] Carefully examining the sixteen illustrations side by side with Cloud's retelling provides further evidence concerning the possible connections between Cloud's and Woodbridge's renditions and the *tanci* version. The two English renditions a decade apart both resemble *The Illustrated Righteous Snake* to some extent: Woodbridge takes more liberty in structural elements than Cloud due to heavy influence from the aforementioned cluster of texts from 1806 to 1888, and Cloud's account echoes Woodbridge's version but with subtle variations and closer connection to the 1809 *tanci* version.

Figure 2: (left) "Traces of the Immortal" (*Xianzong*); (right) "Sent into Exile" (*Fanpei*). Both in *The Complete Illustrated Righteous Snake* (*Xiuxiang Yiyao quanzhuan*), based on a manuscript by Chen Yuqian, edited by Chen Shiqi and Yu Xiushan, 1809, 1–2. Full-text available at Waseda University Library: http://archive.wul.waseda.ac.jp/kosho/he19/he19_03304/.

Whereas Woodbridge focuses on the male protagonist Hanwen from the start of his narrative, both the *tanci* and Cloud's version emphasize "traces of the immortal" to highlight the White Snake's nonhuman characteristics. The two English versions converge from time to time throughout the storytelling process, with Cloud continuing to humanize the White Snake as Woodbridge did, endowing the snake woman with psychological depth and the ability to love. For example, Cloud explains away the White Snake's theft of silver as the act of a woman "desperately in love," who simply wanted to marry her lover "at once." In this context, when the White Snake discovers that Hanwen has been exiled because of the stolen silver, she is "filled with bitter remorse and deep sorrow."[63]

Since Cloud's rendition of the White Snake legend is part of a handbook on Hangzhou and Suzhou, it also focuses on its connection to the two cities, as in "So Suchen and Greenette left 'beautiful Hang' and went to dwell in 'beautiful Soo'" following Hanwen's exile to Suzhou.[64] Cloud makes sure to bring his readers' attention back to the two cities, the presumed real protagonists of his book. Where Woodbridge gives Latinate names to the snake women for the benefit of his Western readers, Cloud preserves the original Chinese names more closely. He refers to the White Snake by her given Chinese name, Suchen (Suzhen 素貞), literally, "white" (meaning "pure") and "chaste," and he translated Green Snake's name, "Little Green" (Xiaoqing 小青), faithfully as "Greenette." He even provides footnotes explaining these choices.[65] However, compared to Woodbridge's literary flair and intimate understanding of the Chinese language,[66] Cloud's rendition appears somewhat drier, with fewer juicy details.

This nuanced difference in style is indicative of Cloud's unique approach to the legend of the White Snake. He created his version as part of a diplomatic project to acquaint his Western readers with practical knowledge about China. Cloud took his Chinese sources seriously, including *The Illustrated Righteous Snake*, and even attempted to replicate its illustrations with documentary photographs. Keeping in mind his mission to write a handbook that could serve as a travel guidebook of the two cities, Cloud sprinkles his city handbook and his rendition of the White Snake legend in particular with contemporary photographs of the city, its people, and landscapes.

Cloud introduces the city of Hangzhou early in his book through a bird's-eye-view photograph (fig. 3), foregrounding a bridge with two human figures on top, reminding the viewers of the White Snake legend. This "location shot" effectively sets the stage for his translation of the legend later in the book. He continues to introduce practical information about Hangzhou, including its seat of government, the *yamen*;[67] a photograph of himself standing in front of such a provincial office was included.[68] In fact, in the legend of the White Snake, the *yamen* is an important locale, as it is there that Hanwen is interrogated and sent into exile. Similarly, Cloud's inclusion of a photograph of the Hangzhou Bore[69] could well have been meant to prepare his readers for the climactic confrontation between the snake women and the Buddhist abbot Fahai in the legend's famous "water battle" scene.

Significantly, Cloud constantly emphasizes his perspective as an American diplomat. After introducing Hangzhou, its *yamen*, and its famous tidal bore, Cloud goes on to include a beautiful scene of West Lake, "viewed from the American Consulate."[70] The consulate was apparently situated at the lake-

Figure 3: "The City—A Bird's-Eye View." In Frederick D. Cloud, *Hangchow, the "City of Heaven"* (Shanghai: Presbyterian Mission Press, 1906), after p. 10. Full-text available at https://archive.org/details/hangchowcityofhe00clourich/mode/2up.

side, with gentle hills in the background, its occupation of prime real estate in the Chinese provincial capital showcasing the privilege and importance of American diplomacy. A second photograph of the lake (fig. 4) shows a close-up view of the Broken Bridge where White Snake and Hanwen first meet and are later reunited. One of the first photographs in Cloud's book to feature the people of Hangzhou, the scene's framing suggests that the photographer was facing the boat and captured the moment when the boat was about to pass under the bridge. The image's three Chinese figures, with the two passengers covering their faces and eyes, probably to avoid both the direct sunlight and the Westerner's intrusive photographing, prepared Cloud's readers for the central role that the act of sharing a boat with strangers plays in the White Snake legend.

Finally, Cloud introduces Thunder Peak Pagoda with a striking image. With a compelling focus on a stele inscribed with calligraphy, the pavilion housing it, and a human figure with an umbrella, all of which stand in front of the pagoda, this image of Thunder Peak Pagoda (fig. 5) accentuates the close proximity between the pagoda and traces of human activity. As both the umbrella and the pagoda serve as important phallic symbols at different moments in the White Snake narrative, the contrast between the umbrella

Figure 4: "A Lake Scene." In Frederick D. Cloud, *Hangchow: the "City of Heaven"* (Shanghai: Presbyterian Mission Press, 1906), after p. 40. Full-text available at https://archive.org/details/hangchowcityofhe00clourich/mode/2up.

as a token of love and the pagoda as a symbol of oppression adds dynamism to the image when it is viewed in the context of the legend. In subsequent pages, documentary photographs continue to serve as literal illustrations for Cloud's rendition of the legend.

The first illustration of the legend, "A Chinese Grave, Hangchow,"[71] directly precedes the account of Hanwen's visit to his family's "ancestral tombs" to perform his "filial duties."[72] Quite fittingly, the second illustration, titled "On the Grand Canal" (fig. 6), features multiple single-sailed boats traveling on the busy canal, which connects Hangzhou with Zhenjiang before extending all the way north to Beijing. The surrounding text treats Hanwen's exile to Zhenjiang and the snake women's following him there by boat, presumably along the Grand Canal. Intriguingly, in addition to the Chinese boats, Cloud's documentary photo prominently foregrounds a boat with American flag, dancing in the wind and fully displaying its power.

The final illustration, positioned after the last page of the legend and

Figure 5: "Thunder Peak Pagoda." In Frederick D. Cloud, *Hangchow: the "City of Heaven"* (Shanghai: Presbyterian Mission Press, 1906), after p. 42. Full-text available at https://archive.org/details/hangchowcityofhe00clourich/mode/2up.

before the section on Suzhou and titled "A Canal Bridge near Hangchow" (fig. 7), features a long view of more than a dozen human figures atop a canal bridge with the shadow of both the bridge and the human figures captured in the water beneath. The photographer, likely Cloud himself, must have been observing the bridge and the small crowd from a distance; thus, he would have been part of the scenery that the domestic Chinese visitors to the Grand Canal were appreciating.

We know very little about Frederick D. Cloud other than that he was the author of this handbook on Hangzhou and served as the vice-consul at the American Consulate when the book was published in 1906. However, we do know that Cloud's book was published by the Presbyterian Mission Press in Shanghai. Although not all diplomats looked kindly on the activities of missionaries at the time, Cloud's case does suggest the possible, perhaps even intimate, connections between diplomats and missionaries. It is intriguing to consider how much weight the American diplomat, closely connected to the Presbyterian mission, gave to retelling the White Snake legend in a book

Figure 6: "On the Grand Canal." In Frederick D. Cloud, *Hangchow: the "City of Heaven"* (Shanghai: Presbyterian Mission Press, 1906), after p. 88. Full-text available at https://archive.org/details/hangchowcityofhe00clourich/mode/2up.

Figure 7: "A Canal Bridge near Hangchow." In Frederick D. Cloud, *Hangchow: the "City of Heaven"* (Shanghai: Presbyterian Mission Press, 1906), before p. 103. Full-text available at https://archive.org/details/hangchowcityofhe00clourich/mode/2up.

on the Chinese city Hangzhou. Two years later, Cloud was already listed as the American vice-consul-general of Shanghai, a substantial promotion.[73] For both Woodbridge and Cloud, the legend of the White Snake served an important function in their missionary and diplomatic careers, which were themselves closely intertwined. The legend formed and informed their understanding of the nature of the Chinese popular mind, especially its reliance on the Buddhist doctrine of transmigration and metamorphosis to form an intimate connection between the human and the nonhuman.

THE WHITE SNAKE INDUSTRY

The case of Woodbridge and Cloud demonstrates the centrality of the White Snake legend in missionary and diplomatic narratives of late nineteenth-century Chinese society. Did the American observers overstate the case? Did the voices and opinions that appeared in China's Anglophone press at the time truly capture the spirit of the Chinese popular mind, which they so desperately sought to understand and remold? Close readings of entries related to the White Snake legends from the pages of the influential Chinese-language newspaper *Shenbao*, as well as other relevant sources, complement the missionary and diplomatic accounts and illustrate how the White Snake came alive in the commercial practices, intellectual discourse, and everyday lives of the Chinese people at the time. Combing through advertisements, news reports, and occasional essays, we see the Chinese world of the White Snake open up in print, on the stage, and in the streets. This allows us to pursue a number of key inquiries concerning a range of contemporary developments: technological breakthroughs in theatrical representation, shifting performative paradigms regarding gender roles, and sociopolitical debate over what was considered normative, triggered by the prominence of the snake women in the retelling of the legends at the turn of the twentieth century and beyond.

New White Snake Performances, 1870s to 1920s

Upon stepping inside a major theater in Shanghai in the 1870s and 1880s, one would have seen "exquisite and colorful 'new-style' lanterns from Fujian and Guangdong" (*Min Guang linglong xiqiao xinshi dengcai* 閩廣玲瓏細巧新式燈彩) adorning the stage.[74] A variety show might have been in session, and some versions of the White Snake legend would very likely have been one of its highlights.[75] Just a decade or two later, in the 1890s, you would have

Figure 8: "Jiuxian dan performing *Reaglar Trap*" (*Jiuxian dan zhi Xionghuang zhen*). Illustration by Liu Chun, in "Best Plays of the Theater Circle in the Past Thirty Years" (*Sanshi nianlai lingjie zhi nashouxi*) series, *Illustrated Daily* (*Tuhua ribao*), no. 291 (1910): 8.

been able to see "machines imported from Britain, Western hydraulic special effects, and blooming iron lotuses" (*Yingguo jiqi xiyang shuifa tielian kaihua* 英國機器西洋水法鐵蓮開花) on the White Snake stage, according to *Shenbao* advertisements.[76]

A series of more than 180 illustrations of contemporary stage performance, titled "Best Plays of the Theater Circle in the Past Thirty Years" (*Sanshi nianlai lingjie zhi nashouxi* 三十年來伶界之拿手戲), was featured in *Illustrated Daily* (*Tuhua ribao* 圖畫日報) throughout the year 1910, spanning close to two hundred issues during the second half of the daily's lifespan.[77] These vivid illustrations of highlights of the theater stage from 1880s to the 1910s

Figure 9: "Wang Jiuzhi performing *Thunder Peak Pagoda*" (*Wang Jiuzhi zhi Leifengta*). In "Best Plays of the Theater Circle in the Past Thirty Years" (*Sanshi nianlai lingjie zhi nashouxi*) series, *Illustrated Daily* (*Tuhua ribao*), no. 333 (1910): 6.

provide a wealth of information on stage setting, costume design, and use of props, as well as identify representative popular highlights among contemporary theater repertoire. Two illustrations (figs. 8 and 9) attest to the popularity of various White Snake performances at the turn of the twentieth century: one features Jiuxian dan 九仙旦 performing the White Snake in the role type of a "martial female" (*wudan* 武旦) in "Reaglar Trap" (*Xionghuang zhen* 雄黃陣), an alternative title for an often-performed highlight from the White Snake repertoire, "Stealing the Magic Herb" (*Dao xiancao* 盜仙草); the other illustrates Wang Jiuzhi 王九芝 performing the White Snake in the role type of a "female lead" (*qingyi dan* 青衣旦) in *Thunder Peak Pagoda* (*Leifengta*), a highlight often known as "The Pagoda Crumbles" (*Daota* 倒塔) and showcasing White Snake's son returning as an accomplished scholar and rescuing his mother from under the Thunder Peak Pagoda.

At the turn of the twentieth century, "new" (*xin* 新) became the most prominent keyword in advertisements for White Snake performances, although actual stage practice seems to have largely continued with the "colorful lantern" tradition of the preceding few decades. The advertisements emphasized that the performances in the early 1900s were "new-style" festival plays (*yingjie xinxi* 應節新戲), the results of "new theater reforms."[78] The reforms mentioned here were undertaken at the turn of the twentieth century by theater practitioners and their literati patrons, who emerged as some of the leading theorists of theater reform at the time.

A recent Chinese-language study names the collaborations between opera singer Mei Lanfang 梅蘭芳 and scholar Qi Rushan 齊如山 as the foundation for the "Mei Lanfang Paradigm" of reforming traditional theater in the 1910s and 1920s.[79] In addition to technical modernity in the form of innovative set design, the reformers often envisioned theater as a site for social reform. Some even went as far as to promote idealistic political agendas at the expense of economic expedience. Many worked to increase the social status and respectability of theater itself. Historian Joshua Goldstein has examined this phenomenon using the case of the Xia Brothers and the New Stage (Xin Wutai 新舞台), their important venue for theater reform in Shanghai in the early 1900s.[80]

In 1913, both New Stage's and Mei Lanfang's performances of the White Snake attracted the attention of *Theater Illustrated* (*Tuhua jubao* 圖畫劇報), a daily newspaper specializing in reviewing and illustrating theater performance, founded by the theater reformer and later filmmaker Zheng Zhengqiu 鄭正秋 in November 1912 in Shanghai. In particular, the New Stage's "complete version" of the White Snake (*Quanben Baishe zhuan* 全本白蛇傳) attributed to Xia Yueshan 夏月珊 was advertised with a vivid illustration of White Snake's transformation into a giant serpent, which frightened her husband to death (fig. 10). The New Stage performance of White Snake, illustrated and widely circulated in the popular press, became so influential as to inspire many future cartoons using this scene to comment on political and social affairs.[81] A few months later, the same illustrated newspaper published a glowing review of Mei Lanfang's White Snake performance, praising his impersonation as "eyes exuding tenderness and love, accompanied by graceful lily steps" (*hanqing momo lianbu shanshan* 含情脈脈蓮步珊珊[sic]; fig. 11).

Technical innovations on stage became the most visible signs of a com-

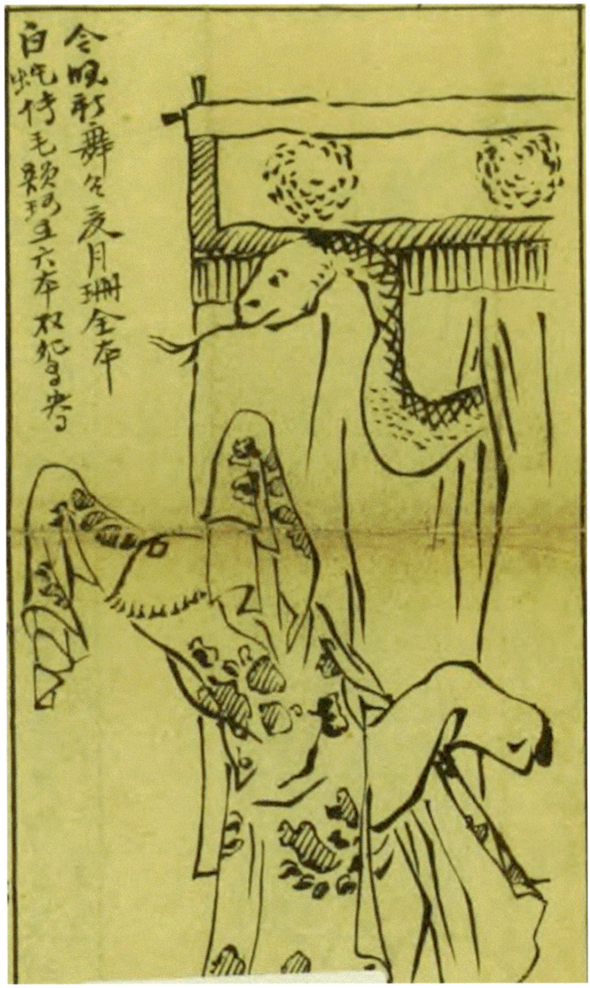

Figure 10: "Xia Yueshan's complete version of *Legend of White Snake* at New Stage tonight" (*Jinwan Xin Wutai Xia Yueshan quanben Baishe zhuan*). *Theater Illustrated* (*Tuhua jubao*), May 5, 1913, 2.

mercial modernity in the new world of White Snake performances. The performances of the early 1910s continued the trajectory from the 1870s, with "new additions of water monsters all over the stage" (*xintian mantai shuiguai* 新添滿台水怪) for a New Year's performance in 1911.[82] "Fantastic and colorful props on revolving stage" (*huanshu caijing qiaozhuan wutai* 幻術彩景巧轉舞台) and "various new-style automated spirits and monsters imported from foreign countries" (*waiyang yundao xinshi gezhong huodong jingguai* 外洋運到新式各種活動精怪) were further advertised for a January 1912 performance, which coincided with the formal establishment of the Republic of

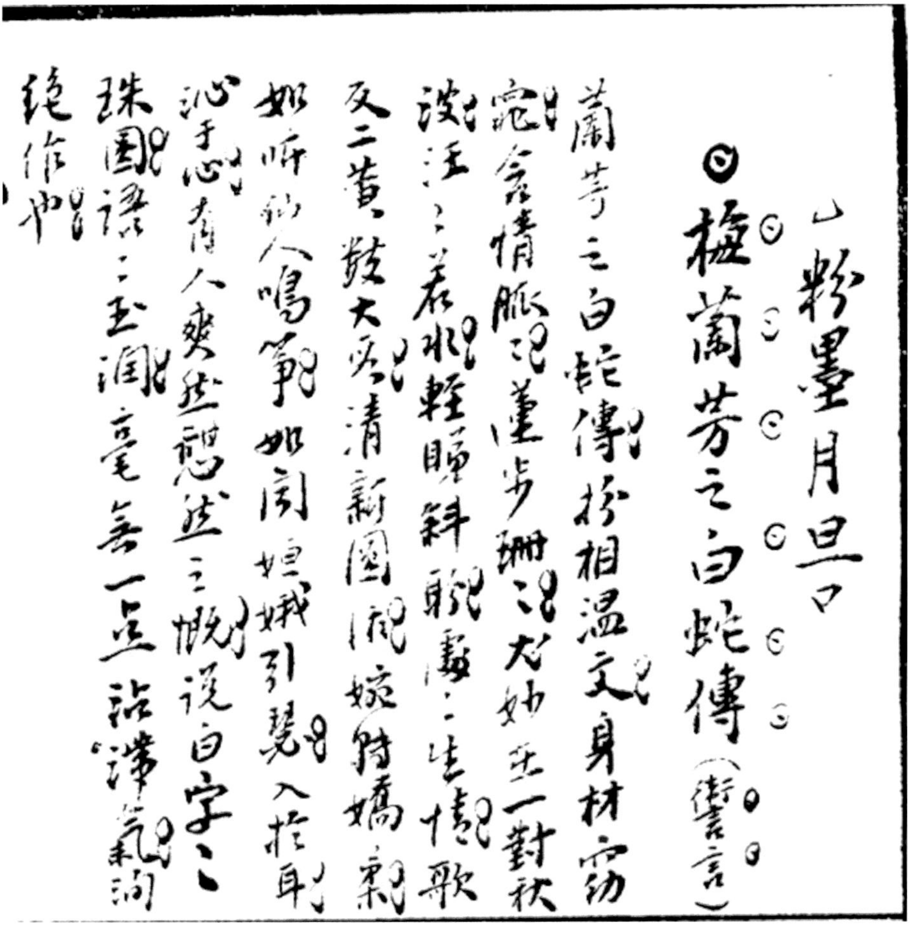
粉墨月旦

梅蘭芳之白蛇傳

Figure 11: "On Mei Lanfang's *Legend of the White Snake*" (*Mei Lanfang zhi Baishe zhuan*). Review by Shiyan, in *Theater Illustrated* (*Tuhua jubao*), November 15, 1913, 3.

China after the fall of the Qing dynasty in 1911.[83] An advertisement promoting a performance "with about eight thousand gallons of real water on stage, with fighting taking place in real water" (*mantai zhenshui you liuwan yubang zai shuizhong dazhan* 滿台真水有六萬余磅在水中大戰) for the Dragon Boat Festival in 1913 claimed such a spectacle "had never been seen in Chinese theater before" (*Zhonghua xiju congwei youguo* 中華戲劇從未有過).[84]

Technical modernity continued to be a selling point in the mid- to late 1910s, with advertisements underscoring "newly added special props and backdrops" (*xintian tebie bujing* 新添特別佈景), "various wild animals" (*yeshan gezhong qinshou* 野山各種禽獸), and automated "magic" figures on stage.[85] Reacting to the increasingly flamboyant White Snake performances featured in *Shenbao*, Woodbridge lamented in 1918 that the fall of the imperial dynasty and the founding of the Republic had done little "to break the chains of superstition" to dispel the Chinese obsession with enjoying the White Snake performances on stage.[86]

Woodbridge's lamentation notwithstanding, an advertisement for a Little Stage (Xiao wutai 小舞台) performance of the White Snake legend in 1915 highlighted more than technical modernity, promoting a performance based on "aesthetic quality" (*meishu xingzhi* 美術性質) and "completely cleansed of superstitious elements" (*jiang mixin zhidian shanchu jinjing* 將迷信之點刪除盡淨). This signaled a radical departure from the past. Audiences who had seen the older versions of the White Snake were urged to attend the new version, demonstrating that a self-conscious aspiration toward ideological modernity was starting to infiltrate commercial theater.[87] In intellectual circles, Cai Yuanpei 蔡元培 famously advocated "using aesthetic education as a substitute for religion" (*yi meiyu dai zongjiao* 以美育代宗教).[88] This attitude was ironically similar to Woodbridge's identification of the relationship between White Snake and Hanwen as love, a view inspired by his Christian beliefs and his desire to rid China of Buddhist "superstition."[89]

Performances of newly composed *tanci* fiction (*tanci xiaoshuo* 彈詞小說) featuring both men and women appeared on the White Snake stage in 1914.[90] A shift from the fantastic to the realistic, and even the farcical, was also apparent in this transition. The story's fantastic and magical elements, when stripped of "superstition," i.e., folk spirituality, appear to have become merely laughable. The exquisite scenery used in the productions included "real boats, real water, comical dialogues and farcical plots" (*zhenchuan zhenshui bingjia huaji yankou* 真船真水並加滑稽談口).[91] In 1917, an advertisement for the Laughing Stage (Xiao wutai 笑舞台) even went so far as to promote laughter as a secret path to maintaining "health" (*weisheng* 衛生, literally, "hygiene").[92] Consequently, from the late 1910s to the early 1920s, White Snake performances began to be considered as "farce" (*quju* 趣劇).[93] In 1926, the terms used to refer to particular White Snake performances changed to "festival serial plays" (*yingshi lianhuanxi* 應時連環戲) using camera "tricks" (*qulike* 屈力克) and "burlesque" (*huajixi* 滑稽戲).[94] However, many performances appear to have been excerpts rather than productions of the entire play.[95] One example was "Flooding Golden Mountain Monastery" (*Shuiman jinshan* 水漫金山), the White Snake's battle with Abbot Fahai on the seventh day of the seventh month in the lunar calendar, which was performed as a festival play.[96] Combining stage performance with film, such experimental festival plays highlighted the White Snake legends' adaptability to and influence on new media formations, as well as their longevity in serving ritualistic and spiritual functions in Chinese popular life. As a result, it is important to revisit the development of a secular, realistic aesthetic in the White Snake performances, while keeping in mind their ritualistic and spiritual elements as served by the festival productions mentioned above.

The Popularity of Jingju, Tanci, *and* Yueju

In the early decades of the twentieth century, *jingju* (often translated as "Peking opera" or "Beijing opera"), *tanci*, and *yueju* 粵劇 (often translated as "Cantonese opera") emerged as the three most influential performance genres used to render the White Snake legends in Shanghai.[97] The leading *jingju* female impersonator Mei Lanfang first received attention for his White Snake performances from the Shanghai press in 1913.[98] By 1914, his works were already reported to enjoy a "nationwide welcome" (*quanguo huanying* 全國歡迎), especially his performances of the White Snake legend.[99] In 1917, another female impersonator Shang Xiaoyun 尚小雲 advertised his "brand-new embroidered costume from Guangdong and special scenery with colorful electric lights" (*quanxin guangxiu xingtou tebie diancai beijing* 全新廣繡行頭特別電彩背景), along with a radically revised plot for his White Snake performances,[100] while yet another performer, Ouyang Yuqian 歐陽予倩, joined the ranks of White Snake impersonators in 1918.[101] The continued popularity of female impersonation in portraying the White Snake might seem to be at odds with the legend's radical reinterpretations using technical innovations and realistic settings. However, the Chinese patrons who bought tickets to the performances and prompted more advertisements in *Shenbao* evidently did not see the shift in performance paradigms as a dichotomy based on traditional versus modern approaches, or old versus new styles. By the time Woodbridge lamented the lack of change in the Chinese popular mind during the early years of the Republic, the world of the White Snake had developed into a robust industry affecting the lives and livelihoods of a large number of consumers and practitioners. By the late 1910s, female White Snake performers such as Fen Juhua (粉菊花, artistic name of Sun Qiao'er 孫巧兒; fig. 12) emerged on the male-dominated stage and started to develop avid followings.[102]

However, although the 1914 performance of the newly composed *tanci*

Figure 12: "Fen Juhua performing Reaglar Trap" (*Fen Juhua zhi Xionghuang zhen*). Illustration by Ding Na, in *Grand World* (*Da Shijie*), September 2, 1919, 2.

fiction already featured a mixed cast and female performers gained popularity in the late 1910s on *jingju* stage, female impersonators still dominated. Moreover, from the mid-1910s onwards, the still male-dominated *tanci* style of performance became one of the most important vehicles for the White Snake narratives' popularization. If, in 1916, you had entered one of Shanghai's popular Western-style restaurants such as Heaven Beyond Heaven (Tian wai tian 天外天), or one of the leading entertainment venues such as the New World and the Grand World (Da shijie 大世界), you would likely have heard the Wu brothers (Wu Yusun 吳玉蓀, Wu Xiaosong 吳小松, and Wu Xiaoshi 吳小石) retelling the White Snake legend, accompanied by the Chinese string instruments the *pipa* 琵琶 and *sanxian* 三弦.[103] Later, the twin brothers Wu Xiaosong and Wu Xiaoshi became exceedingly popular for their joint performances in some of the leading venues. *Tanci's* popularity was so enduring that it not only became one of the major genres widely featured in product endorsements following the rise of radio broadcasting but also survived the political vicissitudes of the 1930s and remained popular into the 1940s. It has endured many transformations and still enjoys a special following in contemporary Chinese popular culture.[104]

At the same time, the Cantonese opera actress Li Sut-fong (Li Xuefang 李雪芳) carved out her own space as a White Snake performer in an urban milieu dominated by *tanci* and male performers. Her 1919 charity performance boasted striking "new costumes, electric lights and colorful special effects, which complemented her singing" (*jiapei xinzhuang dianguang xiaying wucai binfen yu gesheng xiang paihe* 加配新裝電光霞影五彩繽紛與歌聲相拍合).[105] Such a spectacular performance focusing on its flashy appearance and visual stimulus would come under attack in theater reform movements from the early 1950s onwards, as both the Cantonese style and the "Shanghai School" (*Haipai* 海派) of traditional Chinese theater performance were condemned as superficial, or worse, decadent, in the changed climate of the new Communist regime.[106] In the early 1920s, however, such a flashy style was what the Shanghai audience wanted. Riding on her popularity, a "full biography" of Li was published in October 1920; it included stage photos, a full version of the White Snake performance text, and cover calligraphy by the late Qing Cantonese reformer Kang Youwei 康有為.[107] The book went into a second printing in just a month. Commentaries published in *Shenbao* in the mid-1920s, which praise her for "leading the trend of the times" (*fengmi yishi* 風靡一時), further attest to Li's extreme popularity in Shanghai.[108]

Stage Performance, Urban Gossip, Print Culture, and Intellectual Lamentations

The Shanghai stage performances of the White Snake legends are best understood as participating in dialogue with a vibrant industry of urban gossip and print culture. Some of the earliest newspaper stories to exemplify this phenomenon appeared in the 1880s. In 1882, one writer claimed that he received a letter from a friend in Suzhou describing a male white snake god (*sheshen* 蛇神) as the protector of a house.[109] A year later, another report portrayed the White Snake as a snake spirit (*shejing* 蛇精), a rapist who disappeared after being struck by lightning.[110] The popularization of these male spirits, either protective gods or evil demons, as urban legends and in print, fostered from the 1880s an urban milieu that was receptive to illustrated White Snake theater books and that witnessed the transition of the White Snake from urban legends to aesthetic products of theatrical artifice.

The physical forms and materiality of the White Snake books ranged from stereotype (*qianban* 鉛板) to lithography (*shiyin* 石印) to copperplate (*tongban* 銅板); from simple illustrations (*huitu* 繪圖) to detailed prints with brocade cases (*jingyin jintao* 精印錦套); from exquisitely drawn portraits in eight volumes (*xiuxiang bace* 繡像八冊) to Western-style bound books in two volumes (*yangzhuang erce* 洋裝二冊).[111] Such a rich and diverse print culture was again intimately connected with the performances on stage. A commentary published in 1916 lamented the reduction of the original *kunqu* performance of the White Snake legend to the two climactic scenes: "Broken Bridge" (*Duanqiao* 斷橋) and "Making Sacrifice to the Pagoda" (*Jita* 祭塔), scenes featuring the reunion of the White Snake and her human husband in the former, and her salvation by her grown son in the latter.[112] The year 1917 saw the reprinting of *A Collective Biography of Female Storytellers* (*Shuoshu nüxiansheng hezhuan* 說書女先生合傳), first published in 1872 and featuring storytellers famous for their renditions of the White Snake legends.[113] This was a testament to the urban readership's fascination with an early female storytelling tradition that was fast disappearing, but now, with new interest in female performers on stage, possibly about to make a return.

From the 1920s onwards, materials regarding the White Snake legends became ever more extensive and attuned to the changing intellectual climate. We start to hear voices of modern intellectuals commenting on the White Snake performances in the increasingly influential "Free Talk" (*Ziyou tan* 自由談) supplement in *Shenbao*, with a 1921 piece by Shu Sheyu 舒舍予 (better known as Lao She 老舍) challenging the newly introduced stage conventions such as using modern signage to indicate the passage of time.[114] But such specific critiques of a particular production choice were nothing compared to a broader series of attacks from educated urban elites, who protested the vulgarity of the story and the ludicrousness of the whole White Snake phenomenon in celebrating traditional aesthetics in increasingly modernizing China, quite different from Lao She's attempt to maintain traditional practices on the White Snake stage. There were calls for banning performances of the White Snake legends throughout the following decades. The nature of this antagonism echoed Woodbridge's diagnosis decades earlier. A 1941 piece openly called for the abolishment of the superstitions surrounding the Dragon Boat Festival and related White Snake performances.[115] Some cultural elites went even further, objecting to all forms of the White Snake legends, as they believed that these fantastic and "superstitious" aspects of traditional culture were detrimental to the cultivation of modern sensibilities.

On the other hand, some intellectuals, as was likely the case with Lao She, wanted to retain the performances' more traditional aspects and praised the performers' rigorous traditional training; what they opposed was the effect of the recent technical innovations, as they believed these new trends were "dumbing down" or vulgarizing the legends.[116] Such intellectual lamentations also unintentionally highlighted the fascinating stage innovations that appeared in White Snake performances throughout the late nineteenth and early twentieth centuries. The leading entertainment venue New World advertised from early June to mid-July 1922 that the famous "Ten Scenes of the West Lake," introduced in vivid detail in "Ten Beautiful Views" in Frederick D. Cloud's 1906 *Hangchow, the "City of Heaven,"*[117] had been meticulously recreated on stage. In addition, renowned craftsmen had ingeniously created a machine-operated White Snake, complemented by "electric lighting and real water" (*diandeng zhenshui* 電燈真水) on stage for that specific performance.[118]

Sounding the White Snake: Shaping New Media, New Practice, and New Sensibilities

Despite opposition from intellectuals, *tanci* White Snake emerged as one of the most versatile and easily adaptable to new technological and media developments.[119] At the same time, this storytelling form also informed and shaped creative ways of experimenting with new media. Pathé Records, the leading record company in Shanghai at the time, announced in 1923 that it had recorded *tanci* storyteller Wu Yusun, the oldest Wu brother, performing *Jade Dragonfly* (*Yu qingting* 玉蜻蜓), *Golden Phoenix* (*Miao jinfeng* 描金鳳), and *The White Snake* on three records, celebrating his career in advance of his imminent retirement.[120]

The three Wu brothers' popularity warranted a full article in the "Storytelling Commentary" (*Shuoshu xiaoping* 說書小評) section of *Shenbao's* local supplement.[121] The article praised the three as leaders among the young generation of members of the Guangyu Guild (*Guangyu she* 光裕社), the longest running (est. 1776, renamed 1912) and most influential professional storyteller association based in Suzhou.[122] Highlighting the younger twin brothers Wu Xiaosong and Wu Xiaoshi, the article emphasized that the two were not only famous for storytelling but also performed in plays on stage at night in the Grand World. The impressive daily earnings of the three Wu brothers at a few dozen yuan, the highest among all Guangyu Guild members, further evidenced their popularity. Moreover, the twins were presented as emerging entrepreneurs, engaging in various other business practices beyond storytelling.

On June 8, 1929, Stage of Heavenly Cicada (*Tianchan wutai* 天蟬舞台) staged *Legend of the White Snake* (*Baishe zhuan*) and *Thunder Peak Pagoda* (*Leifengta*) together in the same day to celebrate the Dragon Boat Festival. The first was a version of White Snake presented as an annual production on the Dragon Boat Festival that was restaged (*chongpai* 重排) every year, the second was a new production starring Zhou Xinfang and picked up the story where the first left off.[123] The advertisement went on to refer to the first play, *Legend of the White Snake*, as a profound and noble performance that teaches humans about dehumanization through nonhuman and animal metaphors.[124] In addition, Xiang Peiliang's 向培良 one-act "spoken drama" (*huaju* 話劇) piece "White Snake and Xu Xian" (*Baishe yu Xu Xian* 白蛇與許仙) was highly praised in *Shenbao* as an innovative experiment on the incorporation of folk legends into stage performance, an in-depth character study, as well as an attack on old opera, with the cultural and political implications that it would in turn promote new theater education, hence giving people "a desire to create" (*chuangzao de yuwang* 創造的慾望) and "the will to strive upward" (*xiangshang de yizhi* 向上的意志).[125]

Around the time that Woodbridge died in Shanghai and in distinct contrast to the concerns he had voiced, Chinese urban commercial culture in the mid-1920s was investing White Snake legends with the power to inspire change in perspective and behavior. Thus, it is no surprise that the White Snake legends became some of the most popular tools for product endorsements in the 1920s and afterwards, by means of radio broadcast performances and through other media platforms. The "hundred-year machine" (Bailing ji 百齡機) tonic, advertised as good for the human body in the same way that lubricating oil is for machines, became a prime example, a fad of the day, attracting believers such as the leading popular writer Zhou Shoujuan 周瘦鵑.[126]

A 1933 advertisement in *Shenbao* endorsing this tonic used the daily White Snake radio performances of *jingju* singers Zhou Fengwen 周鳳文 and Wu Jianqiu 吳劍秋 to promote the "hundred-year machine" tonic to fans of the White Snake opera.[127] Another advertisement later that year used Yang Renlin's 楊仁麟 daily *tanci* storytelling White Snake performance on Yong Sheng Radio Station (Yongsheng diantai 永生電台) to promote a big winter sale at Minghua Department Store.[128] Other radio advertisements featuring White Snake performances in the forms of traditional opera, *tanci* storytelling, and spoken drama, among others, endorsed even more wide-ranging products such as Five Butterfly Brand cigarettes (Wudiepai xiangyan 五蝶牌香煙, with free White Snake cards purportedly painted by the late painter

Zhou Muqiao 周慕橋, famous for calendar posters); diamond rings; enamelware; glasses; fresh American orange juice; popsicles; and Three Friends tonic tablets (Sanyou buwan 三友補丸) with a specially issued songbook.[129]

The extreme popularity of the White Snake performances at the time is also evidenced by the fact that when patriotic Chinese needed to raise money to buy airplanes for the war against Japan in the early to mid-1930s, the White Snake again came to the rescue—or was pressed into service. In particular, two fundraising events by Guangyu Guild, the Suzhou-based storytelling society, were recorded in 1933 and 1936, among other dates, at which its members—on one occasion joined by the famous Wu Brothers—performed the White Snake legend in the style of a dramatized storytelling performance (*shuxi* 書戲) for a whole day to raise funds to buy airplanes for the resistance against Japan.[130]

The popularity of the White Snake performances generated other commercial activities, such as using the exhibition of two giant snakes, one white, the other green, as a major attraction for a leading entertainment venue, the Xu Garden (Xuyuan 徐園) in Shanghai. It was first announced in *Shenbao* that two giant snakes, both more than nine meters long, were found in Quzhou, Zhejiang Province; the body of the white snake was said to be transparent and jade-like (*touming ruyu* 透明如玉), while the body of the green snake was a clear green, also resembling jade (*bijing rucui* 碧淨如翠).[131] A follow-up advertisement announced that the snakes had arrived in Shanghai and would only be available for viewing for three days from noon to midnight in the Xu Garden.[132] Two days later, another advertisement urged the Shanghai public to view the snakes, as it would be the last possible day. It also recounted an incident that had taken place the day before, when the two "divine snakes" (*shenshe* 神蛇) apparently went wild at high noon, breaking through their cages and terrifying the viewers.[133]

The use of "divine snakes" serves as a reminder of the urban legends concerning snake gods circulating in *Shenbao* in the 1880s[134] and echoes Woodbridge's observation on the remarkable continuities of the Chinese popular mind's appetite for spiritual beings in the form of snakes.[135] The Xu Garden advertisement went on to assure readers that the snakes were now safely under control by means of magical talismans and would not be able to cause any further trouble.[136] Following these advertisements, a certain writer with the pen name of Sanduo 三多 contributed an editorial, a sort of "voluntary advertisement" (*yiwu guanggao* 義務廣告).[137] The author quoted the full report recounting the Xu Garden incident and then commented that, notwithstanding the rumor that Madame White and Xiao

Qing had visited Shanghai in 1934 in the form of the giant snakes on exhibit, snakes were still just snakes and could not possibly transform into beautiful women in real life.

The Rong Stage Dominates White Snake Performances

Although educated urban intellectuals often condescendingly criticized both the form and the content of White Snake performances, and specifically their commercialization, the commercial appeal and concomitant economic success of such performances suggest that White Snake productions facilitated both technical innovations and sociocultural experiments. For example, the theaters that housed the White Snake performances in the summer heat pioneered good-quality air conditioning in the 1930s.[138] Moreover, starting in the early to mid-1930s, the Rong Brand United Stage 榮記共舞台 (Rong Stage hereafter), owned by the Shanghai Green Gang leader Huang Jinrong 黃金榮, became one of the leading White Snake performance venues. *Shenbao*'s final advertisement for a White Snake performance on the Rong Stage was dated May 27, 1949, the very day the newspaper ceased printing. Judging by other advertisements that refer to 1933 as the heyday of White Snake performances there, this span of at least more than fifteen years makes the Rong Stage one of the most innovative and successful White Snake venues.[139]

A four-day advertisement campaign, running from May 16 to 19, 1935, promoted Rong Stage's newly revised performance as "both humorous and amorous" (*huaji xiangyan* 滑稽香艷), with fantastic plots, "scientific devices" (*kexue jiguan* 科學機關) and "sceneries with sound effects" (*yousheng bujing* 有聲佈景).[140] The distinguishing feature of this production, the advertisement stressed, lay in its "secret *tanci* script" (*tanci miben* 彈詞秘本), which departed dramatically from other popular versions and was especially rich in farcical materials. The advertisement went on to identify this version of the White Snake *tanci* narratives with the deceased storyteller Wu Xigeng 吳西賡, father of the three Wu brothers. The Rong Stage's rhetoric of presenting this new performance as simultaneously innovative and representing a hidden tradition may sound contradictory at first glance. However, touting its version as a dramatic departure from other versions and identifying it with a renowned storyteller who represented the secret ingredients for popularity in a long tradition, Rong Stage achieved its dominance and sustained its longevity with White Snake performances. The advertisement campaign also highlighted details in the technological innovations of the Rong Stage, stressing its sound, movable scenery, real rain onstage with sound effects, and its spectacular grand finale, which utilized an automated landing stage to facilitate the snake women's flying movements.[141]

Demonstrating their commitment to leading technological innovation, the Rong Stage went on to announce that there would be no public performances on May 17, 1935, in order to test their cutting-edge stage devices, enabled by electric technology. The same advertisement went on to highlight the cinematic quality of their stage performance, claiming that the fantasy on stage was similar to "the performance of past events in film" (*yingxi lide biaoyan jiushi* 影戲裏的表演舊事), namely flashbacks. The production featured Zhang Yinglin 張英麟 as Xu Xian, an actress "who excels in both male and female roles"; Mei Xuefang 梅雪芳, who has "the reputation of being a female Mei Lanfang," as the White Snake; and Tong Yuejuan 童月娟 as Green Snake, an actress "who can pass as a seventeen- or eighteen-year-old" (and who would act as the Green Snake a few years later in the 1939 film *All Quiet in the Pagoda*, or *Huangta chenyuan* 荒塔沉冤).[142] These women were highlighted as the performance's major attractions. Moreover, the theater promoted itself as an advocate for "entertainment for the people" (*pingmin yule* 平民娛樂), hence their willingness to reduce prices and stage "accessible plays" (*tongsu xiju* 通俗戲劇).[143]

The following day's advertisement shifted attention to the audience and claimed that the Rong Stage had reduced the length of its performance to avoid tiring out the audience by making them sit for too long. Other reform measures included meticulous casting, abolishing opening acts, and advocating for the "pure artistry of *jingju*" (*chuncui jingju yishuhua* 純粹京劇藝術化).[144] These measures, though packaged as representing "an innovative spirit" (*gexin jingshen* 革新精神), had much to do with audience demands.[145] This marketing strategy demonstrates how commercial theaters at the time had to distinguish themselves by not only catering to popular taste but also proclaiming the uniqueness and progressiveness of their offerings.

That same advertisement further elaborated on the Rong Stage's effort to focus on the exquisite script and the emotional lyrics of the White Snake play. It claimed that ordinary versions being performed elsewhere could not possibly compare to the intricate plot and artistry of their version. The next day's advertisement, on the other hand, focused on the fight scene between the Crane God, the Deer God, and the White Snake, which it described as "similar to watching a big production foreign film featuring wild animals" (*haosi kan waiguode yeshou jupian* 好似看外國的野獸巨片), likely referring to *King Kong*, which had recently opened in Shanghai in 1933, and possibly showing the influence of *Tarzan, the Ape Man*, released in the United States in 1932.[146]

Moreover, the Rong Stage advertisement claimed that the set design of their production exceeded all previously established standards in extravagance and expense.[147]

Echoing the strategy employed by the Laughing Stage in the mid-1910s, a June 1935 advertisement for the Rong Stage promoted the health benefits of watching White Snake performances, as laughter could aid digestion and their performances could be counted upon to have the most humorous materials. Indeed, according to the advertisement, watching the Rong Stage performances "would be like consuming soda tablets after food, good for relieving symptoms of indigestion" (*haobi fanhou chi sudapian nengzhu xiaohua buliang zhizheng* 好比飯後吃蘇打片能助消化不良之癥).[148] In the months after this advertisement campaign, the Rong Stage took even more creative steps to consolidate its leading position in staging the White Snake. A further strategy to attract audiences appeared in July 1935: regardless of the ticket price (ranging from ten to sixty cents), the theater promised to provide each ticket holder with a free bottle of fresh American orange juice (worth twenty cents).[149]

The Rong Stage continued to feature White Snake performances at least until *Shenbao* ceased publication in 1949. However, there were a few extended ruptures from 1935 to 1939 and then from 1939 to 1942 owing to the outbreak of the Second Sino-Japanese War (1937–1945) and continued economic uncertainties during wartime. The first White Snake advertisement after 1935 that I was able to locate is dated to June 1939: it reiterated the great reputation of the Rong Stage in the past and emphasized the especially fine performances expected this time around (fig. 13). This advertisement highlighted the newly constructed fantastic stage settings of more than thirty movable pieces, plus giant pythons from Vietnam, and the aerial flying stunts in their new performances.[150] The next White Snake advertisement that I was able to locate dates to June 1942, another three years later. It claimed that their previous night's performance had been packed and that its success was rooted in the Rong Stage's continued popularity for the preceding nine years. The major attractions were their "brand-name animatronic snake" (*laopai dianshe* 老牌電蛇); amazing real clouds on stage, "shockingly invented by European experts" (*Ouzhou zhuanjia jingren faming* 歐洲專家驚人發明); and "movable scenery in the 'Flooding the Golden Mountain Monastery'" (*huodong "Shuiman jinshan"* 活動水漫金山) scene.[151] An advertisement two years later went even further, presenting the Rong Stage White Snake production as "a mixture of *jingju* and film, and a combination of variety show and entertainment" (*jingxi yingxi hunwei yiti zashua youxi bingzai yitai* 京戲影戲混爲一體雜耍游藝併在一台), a truly intermedia experience. The last advertisement for

永安跑冰場

端午節 粽子飯 每客二角

仙樂 夜花園今日開幕

北極歷險記

中歐飯店

遊藝界

冠生園 飲食部

黃金大戲院

大舞台

白蛇傳

卡爾登大戲院

最後一天

二本 文素臣

Figure 13: A page of *Shanghai News* (*Shenbao*) during the Dragon Boat Festival (Duanwu jie), June 21, 1939, 5. It includes an article titled "Theatre Stages Compete to Perform *Legend of White Snake*" ("Wutai jingyan Baishe zhuan") and advertisements for various theater performances of *Legend of White Snake* and *Thunder Peak Pagoda* (*Leifengta*), including at Crystal Theater (Huangjin daxiyuan).

the Rong Stage appeared on *Shenbao*'s last day in existence, on May 27, 1949, in which the "golden brand" (*jinzi zhaopai* 金字招牌) of the Rong Stage was again highlighted and a future performance date was announced.[152]

Throughout the Rong Stage's engagement with the White Snake performances, and both long before and after its lifespan, dozens of other theaters in Shanghai, some of them affiliated with leading department stores and other companies, also experimented with White Snake performances. Among the most important ones were Crystal Theater (Huangjin daxiyuan 黃金大戲院, literally Golden Grand Theater), contemporary to the Rong Stage and with the same owner, Huang Jinrong; and the Newer Stage (Gengxin wutai 更新舞台), opened in 1923 and burned down in 1932, after which the Rong Stage became dominant in performing the White Snake. A 1934 report from an *Eastern Times* (*Shibao* 時報) special issue on theater announced Shang Xiaoyun's four performances in female lead roles at Crystal Theater.[153] The first among them was his impersonating Bai Suzhen (白素貞 White Snake's human name) in *Thunder Peak Pagoda.*

Similar to the Rong Stage's dominance throughout the second half of the 1930s, the Newer Stage was the talk of the town in the late 1920s. Famous for its revolving stage and its machine-operated stage scenery beginning in the mid-1920s, it also led the way in experimenting with the White Snake performance on stage. Multiple reports on the Newer Stage's newly arranged White Snake performance populated Shanghai daily newspapers and entertainment news starting in mid-November 1928, with photos of two particular scenes in the much-anticipated new production: one appeared to be about the much-publicized "dream scene" (*mengjing* 夢景) in the new production involving the miraculous appearance of Guanyin; the other was obviously about the snake women's fight against Abbot Fahai at the Golden Mountain Monestary.[154] Although the surviving photos are of rather poor quality, one can still appreciate the potential attraction of this new production for its contemporary audience, as both scenes require cutting-edge technology and meticulous stage settings for their time, featuring Guanyin's appearance amid clouds and the snake women's riding ranging waves on stage.

In addition to the Newer Stage and Crystal Theater, Jade Treasure Theatre (Lübao juchang 綠寶劇場), affiliated with the Xin Xin Company (Xinxin gongsi 新新公司), for example, announced its "costume comedy *New White Snake*" (*Guzhuang xiju Xin Baishe zhuan* 古裝喜劇新白蛇傳) in a 1940 advertisement. It presented its version as a revisionist account that brought justice to Lady White after thousands of years of injustice. Their promotion of the "newness" of their performance highlighted a modernized plot and a "scientific arrangement" cleansed of ideologically "poisonous elements" (*dusu* 毒素), replacing superstition with flesh and blood and deeply rooting the familiar legend in humanity and rationality.[155]

CONCLUDING REMARKS

The 1924 collapse of Thunder Peak Pagoda, under which the White Snake was said to have been imprisoned, and the 1948 burning of the Golden Mountain Monastery, which according to the legend was flooded by the White Snake in her fight against Abbot Fahai to claim her husband, triggered waves of stage performances and intellectual responses. It were as if the real-life disasters echoed the power of the fictive White Snake, whose destruction of these symbols of oppression had appeared in the legend's many popular retellings and had made her an antiauthoritarian rebel figure, who was fighting for her right to love and humanity. A September 29, 1924, advertisement in *Shenbao*, just days after the fall of Thunder Peak Pagoda on September 25, 1924, promoted a unique White Snake performance that featured the panoramic reverberation throughout West Lake and the surrounding hills caused by the pagoda's collapse, the machine-operated dramatic reappearance of the White Snake, and the havoc caused in the city of Hangzhou by the freed White Snake.[156]

In the same newspaper, an entry from April 18, 1948, soon after the Golden Mountain Monastery burned to the ground in real life, connected the monastery's destruction to the pagoda's 1924 fall. It contended that the burning of the monastery should be treated as a symptom of the "conflict between heaven and human" (*tianren jiaojing* 天人交警) and a more serious omen than the fall of the pagoda more than twenty years before.[157] However, a 1948 "Free Talk" opinion piece used the burning of the Golden Mountain Monastery as a starting point to criticize the Fahai Mentality. According to the author, Abbot Fahai's intervention in the relationship between the White Snake and her human lover, analyzed from the perspective of Freudian psychoanalysis, could be explained as motivated by the Abbot's conscious or subconscious jealousy of Xu Xian, White Snake's husband. Indeed, leading modern Chinese writer Lu Xun had similarly condemned Fahai soon after the pagoda's fall in October 1924.[158] In the 1948 "Free Talk" piece, the author simply concluded that what should have burnt was not the monastery, but the Fahai Mentality![159]

In sum, White Snake performances in Shanghai from the late nineteenth to the early twentieth centuries were at the center of popular culture and everyday life, powerfully shaping and reflecting popular imagination and new media development. The folk, the popular, and the avant-garde intricately intersected in retelling the White Snake legends in the context of urban entertainment and commercial popular culture; technological, economic, and political changes; and the intellectual and popular projects of disenchantment and possible re-enchantment. Beyond the life of *Shenbao* (1872–1949), which had been pivotal in promoting the White Snake performances in Shanghai, a July 9, 1950, news article from Hong Kong's English-language *South China Morning Post* connected Shanghai with Hong Kong in recreating the White Snake. The article featured the miraculous reappearance of the Cantonese opera actress Li Sut-fong, extremely popular in Shanghai in the late 1910s and early 1920s. After some thirty years, Li returned as Mrs. Henry Wei, for two nights of White Snake performances, at a new historical moment, for the Hong Kong Society for the Protection of Children.[160] In Part II of this study, chapters 4 and 5 take off from this Shanghai–Hong Kong connection to explore how the White Snake legends gained new life outside Mainland China through transnational cinematic coproduction and international distribution in Hong Kong, Japan, South Korea, Taiwan, and Southeast Asian regions.

White Snake legends were reenvisioned, revised, re-formed, retold, and reinterpreted to suit a variety of points of view and purposes while also challenging others, both social-cultural and political. The legends' resilience and resonance can keep becoming relevant again and again, and the complicated relationship between the "old" and the "new" that runs throughout these narratives, deserve further scrutiny. From technological breakthroughs to shifting gender-related performance paradigms, from the legends' gender politics to the social debates triggered by the White Snake narratives, these *Shenbao* and other popular accounts in Chinese supply the cultural context for Woodbridge and Cloud. In particular, they contextualize the writers taking the White Snake legends so seriously and bringing them into the Anglophone world at a time contemporary to the Chinese popular obsessions with the snake women. As an industry, the White Snake legends did not stop at being problems that the American missionary and diplomat needed to solve in order to treat the "feverish Chinese popular mind" and "save Chinese souls." Rather, these White Snake legends animated new possibilities of being human in China's many transitional paths from an imperial dynasty to a modern republic, through deep engagements with the new media scenes of the time, in various print forms, via radio air waves, on performance stages, and in the daily lives of Chinese people.

CHAPTER 3

The Fall of the Pagoda and the Rise of the White Snake

THE FALL OF THE PAGODA AND THE VISUALIZATION OF A VANISHED PAST

September 25, 1924, was a sunny day in Hangzhou with some light wind. At 1:40 p.m., Yu Pingbo was playing *weiqi* 圍棋 (often translated as "go," the Japanese name for the game) with Tiyuan 體圓, a monk from Guanghua Monastery (Guanghua si 廣化寺), upstairs in the Yu family house across the West Lake from the Thunder Peak Pagoda.[1] The pagoda had been in ruins for many centuries. Suddenly Yu sensed some commotion and looked out toward the pagoda. The only movement he could see was yellow dust rising to the sky. In an instant, the pagoda had collapsed completely, and Yu had missed this once-in-a-lifetime opportunity to witness it. According to him, the wind was blowing in the direction opposite to his house, and there was not much noise.[2]

Yu rushed downstairs and attempted to reach the pagoda across the lake, which until that day had been deserted due to an ongoing conflict between warlords. However, that afternoon, many boats suddenly reappeared, all moving toward the collapsed pagoda. When Yu reached the site, it was already past four in the afternoon. He climbed up the hill and looked around, but he could see only numerous pieces of brick in a huge yellow mound. A large crowd was thronged on top of the decayed structure. Many carried bricks with them when they left the site. The bricks were rather big; the ones with characters carved on them were quite difficult to find. Yu took a brick that he considered "defective," without characters but perforated by a horizontal hole, and returned home with it.[3]

Yu's detailed account of the immediate aftermath of the Thunder Peak Pagoda's fall brings us to the historical site and precise moment of its collapse. This chapter chronicles the impact of that collapse that afternoon in September 1924. Since the White Snake was said to have been trapped under the pagoda, legend dictated that the pagoda's collapse would allow the White

Snake to emerge from her subterranean prison. The pagoda's sudden fall in real life created a visible, tangible embodiment of the White Snake legend, as if providing physical traces and material evidence of the power of the White Snake. The collapse triggered an intellectual earthquake, whose impact upon the legend's popular discourses was far more profound than the physical collapse's effect on the surrounding landscape.

Popular pictorial magazines and publishers, including *The Eastern Miscellany* (*Dongfang zazhi* 東方雜誌), *Pictorial Weekly of the Eastern Times* (*Shibao tuhua zhoukan* 時報圖畫週刊), Shanghai Martial Painting and Photography Press (Shanghai zhanshi xiezhenguan 上海戰事寫真館), *Railway Bulletin* (*Tielu gongbao* 鐵路公報), and *The Young Companion* (*Liangyou* 良友), joined in on the general fascination, along with major cultural figures such as Yu Pingbo, Liu Dabai, Liu Gonglu, Sheyu, Gao Jianfu, Lu Yin, Xu Zhimo, and, most famously, Lu Xun. These and other individuals and institutions offered reflections on the fall of the pagoda in a diverse range of genres, including photograph, painting, essay, poem, letter, and film.

These various responses recorded and discussed the Thunder Peak Pagoda's collapse in the style of cultural commentary and with the immediacy of photojournalism. Thus, they created an association between the White Snake legend and the world of current affairs, investing the legend with the cultural gravitas normally attached to historical events. For some, reifying and commemorating the final collapse of this long-decaying pagoda reaffirmed its cultural and spiritual importance in the Chinese popular religious imagination in general and in the Buddhist tradition in particular. For others, it provided a catalyst for emerging modern reinterpretations of the White Snake legend that shifted the paradigm from "his story" to "her story," transforming the male-centered narrative of admonition, which warned human males about the danger of nonhuman seductresses, into a story that featured a righteous female protagonist who fought against patriarchal and institutional oppressions. Collectively, these wide-ranging responses demonstrated the intriguing and imposing presence of the Thunder Peak Pagoda and the White Snake legend in the Chinese intellectual and popular imaginations.

Bricks, Scriptures, and Visuality: Relics from and Memories of the Thunder Peak

The Eastern Miscellany included in its September 25, 1924 issue, reputedly published on the day the pagoda fell, a high-definition full-page photograph of the now-collapsed pagoda (fig. 14),[4] crowded with visitors like Yu Pingbo. Moreover, the magazine not only published a creative collage showing the

Figure 14: "The Collapse of the Thunder Peak Pagoda, a Great View by the West Lake" (*Xihu shengji Leifengta zhi bengtui*). *The Eastern Miscellany* (*Dongfang zazhi*) 21, no. 18 (September 25, 1924): 1.

history of the pagoda, but also managed to include two brief articles directly addressing its collapse.

Likely one of the very first visual representations of the Thunder Peak Pagoda's collapse, this full-page collection of photographs is remarkable for several reasons. First, it is an important piece of photojournalism, giving the first close-up look of a site and an event that would later exert a lasting impact on the Chinese popular imagination. Second, its creativity sets the bar for later visual representations of the Thunder Peak Pagoda, innovatively insetting a high-quality photograph of the still-standing pagoda in close-up with an unusually clear portrayal of the collapsed pagoda. The bricks from which the pagoda had been built were piled up in a huge mound, from which visitors and onlookers busily retrieved the souvenirs of their choice, jostling one another in their attempts to select the most desirable pieces. The image corresponds closely to the scene described in multiple accounts by Yu Pingbo, published days and months later. Third, the camera angle suggests that the photographer set up his equipment in a particularly fortunate location, elevated above the site of the collapsed pagoda but close enough to capture the man in the white gown posing in the foreground. The man's stance in front of the brick mound seems to indicate that he may have caught sight of the camera.

Two short pieces accompanied this memorable photo. One was referenced in the photo itself and published to "fill the blanks" on page 48 of the issue, titled "A Record of the Thunder Peak Pagoda after Its Catastrophic Collapse" (*Jiehou Leifengta ji* 劫後雷峰塔記). Chunfeng 春風, author of the piece, speculated that the concurrent entrance into Hangzhou of warlord Sun Chuanfang's 孫傳芳 army might have stolen the "thunder" from the fall of the Thunder Peak Pagoda. However, like Yu Pingbo, the author focused mainly on the bricks, each of which was said to be pierced by a hole containing a piece of Buddhist scripture. The article included detailed measurements, allowing readers to imagine holding in their hands just such a hefty brick retrieved from the ruins. It also reported that a large number of beggars and other impoverished persons had set up camp on the mound of ruins, from which they collected bricks and the scriptures hidden inside. Other visitors to the site competed to buy the scriptures, causing prices to rise from twenty cents to twenty dollars apiece, in just two or three days.[5]

Marked as "excerpted from the *Eastern Times*" (*jielu Shibao* 節錄時報),[6] this piece gives rise to a range of questions concerning the authenticity of its publication date and its source of information. How could the piece have been published on the day of the collapse, if it documented the rising prices of souvenirs two or three days later? How could it be an excerpt from another newspaper reporting on the event, if it was indeed published on the same day as the event itself? These discrepancies confirm that the actual date of publication for this issue of *The Eastern Miscellany* must have been later than the printed date of September 25, 1924. But by presenting the publication date as the day the pagoda fell (which was also the originally scheduled date for the bimonthly magazine's second September issue), *The Eastern Miscellany* was able to generate significant shock value for its readers, both at the time and more than ninety years later.

The other short piece published in the same issue, titled "On Retrieving Scriptures from the Thunder Peak Pagoda" (*Leifengta dejing ji* 雷峰塔得經記) by Sun Jinglu 孫儆盧, acts as a sequel to the first piece. Sun, like Yu Pingbo, was among the first individuals to reach the site of the collapsed pagoda. He began with an introduction to the scriptures hidden in the bricks. He then recalled having previously received a portion of the Huayan Sutra (*Huayan jing* 華嚴經), which had been carved into the top of the pagoda, when the monks made copies of it because they feared its imminent disappearance. Upon the pagoda's collapse, Sun was able to retrieve three more volumes of the same scripture.[7] With these two pieces in mind, we can better appreciate

Yu Pingbo's interest in the Thunder Peak Pagoda and his disappointment at missing the exact moment of its collapse. Like the two pieces from *The Eastern Miscellany*, Yu's account also originated in a deep interest in the physical structure of the pagoda itself, including both the bricks with which it was built and the Buddhist scriptures hidden inside them.[8] Although not published on the same day as the pagoda's collapse, Yu's account was one of the first to report on the fall with vivid personal details. It took the form of a letter to his friend Gu Jiegang 顧頡剛, which was dated October 4, 1924, only a little over a week after the fall of the pagoda.[9]

The interest in Buddhism and Buddhist material culture displayed by Yu Pingbo, Chunfeng, and Sun Jinglu was far from unusual among Chinese intellectuals in the 1920s. Many notable cultural figures at the time, including Li Shutong 李叔同, Su Manshu 蘇曼殊, Lu Xun, Zhou Zuoren 周作人, Xu Dishan 許地山, Tian Han, and Feng Zikai 豐子愷 had intimate contact with Buddhism and Buddhist practices, which helped to shape and inform their literary and cultural activities. More importantly, this phenomenon was a continuation of the longstanding Buddhist influence on Chinese literature and culture from premodern times.[10] As Huaiyu Chen points out in his study of the development and transformation of portrait eulogy as an important medieval Chinese literary genre, the increasing influence of Buddhist principles in the intellectual and artistic practices of the medieval literati class gave rise to a new visual culture in which the idea of depicting a "true appearance" (*zhenrong* 真容), "true image" (*zhenxiang* 真像), and "true body" (*zhenshen* 真身) assumed a new significance.[11] This was especially applicable to the visualization practices that resulted in the development of portrait-making as a means of commemorating the body and the virtue of the dead.[12]

Similarly, Yu Pingbo's approach to commemorating and personifying the fall of the Thunder Peak Pagoda emphasized its corporality. Yu continued to publish several important pieces concerning the event in two substantial essays and two classic-style poems from 1924 to 1928.[13] When he produced a compilation of his essays in 1930, he included the following sketch among the illustrations for the collection (fig. 15). Titled "Memories of the Thunder Peak" (*Leifeng huiyi* 雷峰回憶), it was drawn by Yu's good friend, the artist Feng Zikai, another modern intellectual deeply influenced by Buddhist thought. Although not primarily invested in the White Snake legend, the photographs and articles that appeared in *The Eastern Miscellany*, as well as Yu Pingbo's writings and Feng Zikai's sketch nonetheless provide some of the most immediate and highly visualized accounts of the fall of the Thunder Peak Pagoda, which was often directly linked with the release of the White Snake.[14]

Figure 15: "Memories of Thunder Peak" (*Leifeng huiyi*). Drawing by Feng Zikai, in Yu Pingbo, *Yanzhi cao* (Beijing: Zhongguo wenlian chuban gongsi, [1930] 1998), unpaginated.

Indeed, visuality emerged as a central concern for a populace that was highly affected, in some cases even traumatized, by the pagoda's collapse. With its enigmatic physical presence and its associations with the enchanting legend of the White Snake, the pagoda had long occupied an important position in both Chinese popular imagination and Buddhist iconography. In addition to the responses mentioned above, a wide range of other works highlighting the visuality of the event emerged immediately after the collapse. The genres included photography, pencil drawing, traditional Chinese painting, oil painting, poetry, and myriad forms of popular and scholarly essays, all of which joined performance genres such as *jingju*, *tanci* storytelling, and various forms of local operas to compete in representing the Thunder Peak Pagoda in the imaginary realm after it ceased to exist in the physical one.

Legend, Art Photography, and War Drawing: Timely Journalism and the Chinese Popular Imagination

Founded in 1904 in Shanghai, the *Eastern Times* is regarded as one of the three major newspapers of the time. Its pictorial supplement, known as *Pic-*

torial Weekly (*Tuhua zhoukan* 圖畫週刊), employed professional photojournalists and was said to have ushered in a new era in pictorial journalism.[15] This influential periodical provided one of the earliest visual accounts of the pagoda's collapse, in the form of a collage that appeared on October 5 of that year.[16] The collage consists of an elaborate assemblage of historical and contemporary images, which combined to represent the relevance of the pagoda and the impact of its collapse. The top two images each present a close-up view and a long view of the Thunder Peak Pagoda as it appeared before its collapse. Conventionally, these scenes of the pagoda are considered two of the "Ten Great Views of the West Lake" (*Xihu shijing* 西湖十景), and the long view in the evening glow (*Leifeng xizhao* 雷峰夕照) has been canonized in the Chinese imagination as the ideal embodiment of the lyrical beauty that characterizes *Jiangnan* 江南, the region south of the Yangtze River.[17] Its close association with the White Snake legend imbues the physical structure with a magical aura, consolidating its iconic position in the Chinese popular imagination.[18] Prominently positioned just below the title art is an image of the fallen pagoda, titled "Thunder Peak Pagoda after Its Sudden Collapse" (*Turan qingdao zhi Leifengta* 突然傾倒之雷峰塔), taken by a certain Mr. C. Y. Tu (Tu Zheyin 屠哲隱; fig. 16).

C. Y. Tu went on to publish in 1930 a bilingual collection of art photographs (*yishu shenying* 藝術攝影), to which Chinese luminaries Cai Yuanpei, Chen Lifu 陳立夫, Ye Chucang 葉楚傖, Hu Hanmin 胡漢民, and Chen Wanli 陳萬里, and J. B. Powell, editor of *The China Weekly Review*, all lent their calligraphy and writing to certify the importance of his work. Xu Beihong 徐悲鴻, a leading painter at the time, wrote a glowing preface in beautiful calligraphy to add his artistic stamp of approval.[19] The collection of fifty extraordinary black-and-white photos is exquisitely presented, with poetic Chinese titles accompanied by rather plain English translations. According to Tu's preface, published in Chinese at the front and in English at the back of the volume, he had embarked on a career in amateur photography seven years before and considered his camera to be his "second life." He went on to ask for "the encouragement of all who are sympathetic" toward photography, as it was "an art form only recently introduced into China."[20]

Tu's eye-witness photograph of the collapsed Thunder Peak Pagoda is one of the most immediate and visually shocking representations of the event. Its effect is similar to those created by the unattributed photo in *The Eastern Miscellany* and Yu Pingbo's letter to Gu Jiegang. However, its content is quite different. Compared to other "post-collapse" photographs and written accounts, Tu's picture is remarkably devoid of human activity. With his camera tilting up toward the sky, Tu captured the piles of bricks immediately in

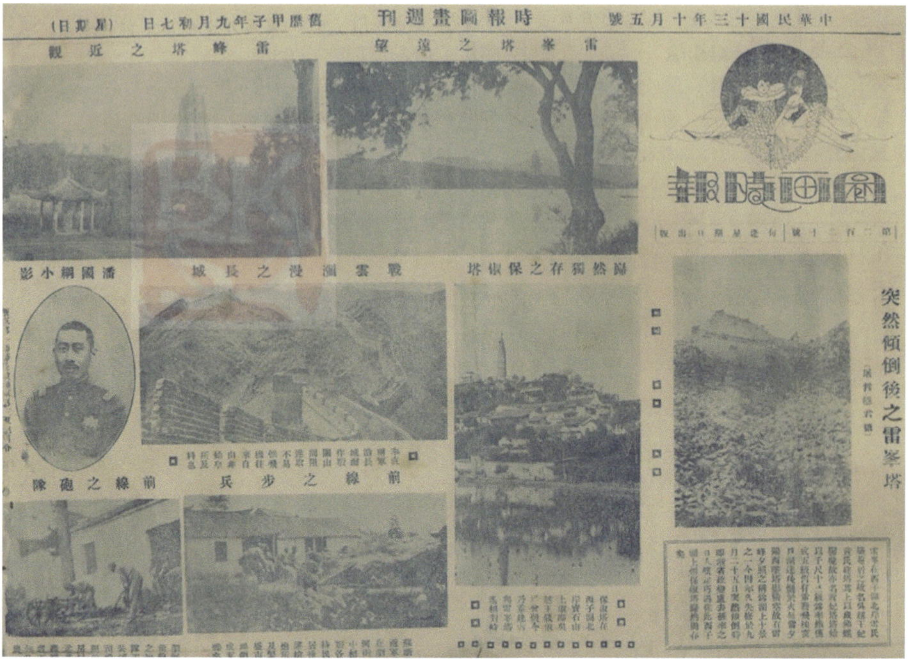

Figure 16: "Thunder Peak Pagoda after Its Sudden Collapse" (*Turan qingdao zhi Leifengta*) in context. By Mr. C. Y. T, *Pictorial Weekly of the Eastern Times* (*Shibao tuhua zhoukan*), no. 220, October 5, 1924.

front of him and the pagoda's ruins on top of the brick mound. The ruins, surrounded by piles of bricks, fill up more than two thirds of the frame; the rest is sky. Not a single trace of the crowds, onlookers, and brick-pickers mentioned in Yu Pingbo's accounts is in view. One cannot help wondering how Tu managed to capture this perfectly "uncontaminated" shot, how long he had had to wait, and what he might have done to rid the crowds of people that appear to have always been at the site.

There is an intriguing contrast between Tu's art photograph of that same pagoda, cleansed of human traces, and the emphasis on human activity associated with Thunder Peak Pagoda in other representations. Quite remarkably, in addition to the three photos representing the Thunder Peak Pagoda's past and the present, the same issue of *Pictorial Weekly of the Eastern Times* also featured Baoshu Pagoda in a scenic shot titled "Baoshu Pagoda Towering Alone" (*Weiran ducun zhi Baoshu ta* 巋然獨存之保俶塔), with captions personifying the skinny structure and its lonely existence after the collapse of the

Thunder Peak Pagoda. Even more intriguingly, these scenic and landscape photos were juxtaposed with a series of four journalistic images, bringing the viewers back to the contemporary historical context of a fragmented country suffering from armed conflict between warlords. One of the top two photos features the Great Wall amid the "war clouds" (*zhanyun* 戰雲), referring to the fighting between the Fengtian and Zhili warlord armies. The other presents a portrait of Pan Guogang 潘國綱, division commander of the First Division of the Zhejiang Army.

As detailed in Yu Pingbo's and other contemporary accounts, Pan Guogang's Zhejiang Army left for Ningbo when Sun Chuanfang's Fujianese troops entered Hangzhou on the same day that the Thunder Peak Pagoda collapsed.[21] The two bottom photos in the collage feature the city of Liuhe as the front line of the Jiangsu-Zhejiang conflict, showing foot soldiers fighting in the streets among piles of brick rubble, evidence of the damage caused by heavy artillery fire and eerily evocative of the brick mounds left by the collapse of the Thunder Peak Pagoda.

A vivid line drawing of the pagoda's collapse (fig. 17) appeared in a series of drawings featuring scenes from the contemporaneous Jiangsu-Zhejiang and Zhili-Fengtian conflicts. The caption described the pagoda's collapse as having occurred "for no reason" (*wuduan* 無端) and calls it "a terrifying incident for those who heard about it" (*wenzhe huanghe* 聞者惶駭) and "probably not a good omen" (*kongfei jiazhao* 恐非佳兆). The series in which the drawing appeared, the four-volume *Complete Collection of Paintings on Jiang-Zhe and Zhi-Feng Wars* (*Jiang Zhe Zhi Feng xuezhan huabao daquan* 江浙直奉血戰畫寶大全), was published on the Double Ninth Festival in 1924 on the ninth day of the ninth month in the lunar calendar, shortly after the fall of the pagoda. The entire series featured contemporary subject matters, pioneering the use of serialized drawings (*lianhuan hua* 連環畫) to represent contemporary events such as war and revolution.[22]

The creative mind behind this innovative approach belonged to Hu Yaguang 胡亞光 (1901–1986), a pioneer in the development of Western-style painting in China. The grandson of business tycoon Hu Xueyan 胡雪巖, he had studied Western-style painting with Zhang Yuguang 張聿光 (1885–1968). Zhang had been a student at the Jesuit-established T'ou-Sè-Wè Painting School (Tu shanwan huaguan 土山灣畫館) in Shanghai and had pioneered stage design for *jingju* at the New Stage, a leading venue for the White Snake performances discussed in chapter 2.[23] With Hu Yaguang in charge and Sun Buyue 孫步月, Hu Xiao'e 胡小萼, and Jin Shaomei 金少梅 joining the effort, this album documented, in highly economic and vivid strokes, how the ongo-

Figure 17: "Thunder Peak Pagoda at the West Lake Fell for No Reason" (*Xihu Leifengta wuduan tanhui*). In *Complete Collection of Paintings on Jiang-Zhe and Zhi-Feng Wars* (*Jiang Zhe Zhi Feng xuezhan huabao daquan*) 4 (October 7, 1924): 9.

ing wars both had historical impacts and permeated the mundane details of daily life. It is fascinating to see the collapsed pagoda in terrible ruins included in this collection and characterized as belonging to this series of "pictorial treasures" (*huabao* 畫寶) that depict the "bloody battles" (*xuezhan* 血戰) between the northern and southern warlords. That the pagoda collapsed at the precise moment that Sun Chuanfang's army entered Hangzhou seems to have reinforced the real-world implications of the legendary and the fantastic. The inclusion of visual depictions of the fallen pagoda in this documentary album of the ongoing war further cemented the link between fantasy and reality.

Shadows of the Pagoda: Coming to Terms with the Fall through Visual and Textual Representations

On October 31, 1924, just a little over a month after the fall of the Thunder Peak Pagoda, *Railway Bulletin: Shanghai-Nanjing and Shanghai-Hangzhou-Ningbo Route* (*Tielu gongbao: Hu Ning-Hu Hang Yong xian* 鐵路公報: 滬寧滬杭甬線), the official journal of these routes of the national railway system, published two striking images of the pagoda (fig. 18) as part of a series of illustrations featuring famous sites and tourist destinations along the relevant railway lines. The Thunder Peak Pagoda matched the criteria of the series perfectly, so it is no surprise that two haunting images were included immediately after the table of contents of this issue.

The images are striking for several reasons. One distinguishing feature is the representation of human activity that appears in these still frames. The image of the pagoda before its collapse includes a group of people dressed in the long gowns favored by scholars and gathered in front of the structure. Two figures dressed in shorts standing off to the side appear to be laborers or servants. In the other remarkable close-up of the pagoda after its collapse, two human figures have taken up central positions at the front of the frame. Standing at the base of the mound of the brick ruins, a young man with a dark jacket faces directly into the camera. He appears to be holding something in his hand, possibly a brick or fragment of scripture fished from the ruins. Another figure, positioned even closer to the camera, stands with his back to the viewer. He is wearing a light two-piece outfit, his arms are spread wide, and he appears to be carrying something in his right hand. Following the tilted camera angle toward the middle of the frame, one can see a few more figures on the brick mound, evidently collecting pieces from the rubble. At the top of the mound, about two dozen human figures can be observed standing, squatting, sitting, and picking through the ruins of the collapsed pagoda.

These vivid images recreate the appearance of the vanished Thunder Peak Pagoda, immortalizing it through remembrances, representations, and reflections. More specifically, the men's presence in the ruins only makes sense with awareness of the site's past and the pagoda's history. Similarly, Liu Dabai opened his 1925 essay "After the Collapse of the Thunder Peak Pagoda" with poetic recreations of the "before" and "after" views of the structure. He contrasted the hustle and bustle of visitors crowding in the shade of the weeping willows during one of the "elegant gatherings" (*yaji* 雅集), which he recalled participating in more than ten years before, with the wild grass, beggars, and

Figure 18: (left) "Thunder Peak Pagoda before Collapsing" (*Weidao zhi Leifengta*); (right) "Thunder Peak Pagoda after Collapsing" (*Yidao zhi Leifengta*). Both in *Railway Bulletin: Shanghai-Nanjing and Shanghai-Ningbo Route* (*Tielu gongbao: Hu Ning-Hu Hang Yong xian*), no. 150 (October 31, 1924): 4–5.

vagabonds now clustered around the decaying and lonely structure. He went on to lament that even the crumbling pagoda of his memory had now ceased to exist. Thus, Liu's perspective on the collapse of the Thunder Peak Pagoda reveals three layers of historical time, with the "post-collapse" present serving as a reminder of a disappearing past and an equally evanescent present, both of which are now only memories.

Liu's essay goes on to embrace a polyphonic soundscape in which competing voices express their views on the fall of the Thunder Peak Pagoda. Voice number one marvels: The pagoda collapsed precisely when warlord Sun entered the city. How strange! Voice number two worries: Madame White can now escape from the pagoda and flood the Golden Mountain Monastery for a second time. How scary! Voice number three proposes: With the hegemony of the evil monk Fahai finally overthrown, Madame White is free to find Xu Xian and live happily ever after. How wonderful! These three perspectives are only a few of the manifold reactions envisioned in Liu's essay. Liu's own position, however, remained unique. He poured his poetic energy into portraying the Thunder Peak Pagoda and the opposite Baoshu Pagoda as a romantic pair, with the Thunder Peak Pagoda as masculine and the Baoshu Pagoda as feminine. Now that its lover, the Thunder Peak Pagoda, has collapsed. How can the lonely, slim Baoshu Pagoda sustain its remaining days? How melancholy![24]

A similar strategy of remembrance and reinvention, albeit in a soberer tone, appears in the travel journal of Ding Huikang 丁惠康, a medical student at Tongji University in Shanghai. Ding had toured Hangzhou extensively with friends in April 1923, just a year and a half before the collapse:

> When we look toward the south, Thunder Peak Pagoda soars toward the clouds, as if inviting us tourists for a visit. We then rode the boat to the Evening Bell Pavilion, in front of the Monastery of Peaceful Mercy and under the Hill of Southern Screen. According to our boatman, when the monastery bell rings, the sound of the bell shakes the hills and leaves lingering echoes. That is why the monastery is named after its bell. There is an old well for transporting wood, a historical site from the times when Abbot Jiying built the monastery with transported wooden logs. The monks of the monastery lit the well with candles, and we could still see heads of the wooden logs sticking out. This is how remarkable the power of Buddhism can be. We went out of the monastery toward the Thunder Peak Pagoda. The pagoda is made of bricks and its color has turned into a reddish brown after suffering from ravages of war, very similar to the color of an old monk's patchwork vest. Just when we were about to sit down and meditate, broken bricks started to fall one after another from the pagoda. The pagoda is indeed decaying gradually.[25]

Ding likely had taken the intriguingly titled photo "Under the Crotch of the Thunder Peak Pagoda" (*Leifengta zhi kuaxia* 雷峰塔之胯下; fig. 19) during this 1923 trip described in his diary. He most likely had stood under the pagoda, inside what he named "the crotch," to take this picture featuring the silhouettes of two of his friends posing in front of what appears to be the outline of a mini pagoda created by the cave-like opening on the ground level of the Thunder Peak Pagoda. The peculiar perspective of the close-up and the innovative camera angle make Ding's photograph a most unusual portrayal of the still-standing structure, breaking with the tradition that generally represented the pagoda as one element in a larger scene, similar to the composition of a landscape painting.[26]

Ding Huikang was an active participant in the China Photographic Soci-

Figure 19: (left) "Under the Crotch of the Thunder Peak Pagoda" (*Leifengta zhi kuaxia*). Photograph by Ding Huikang, *Shanghai Pictorial* (*Shanghai ribao*), no. 6, unpaginated; (right) "Rowing to Return" (*Guizhao*). Photograph by Ding Huikang, *The Pictorial Weekly of the Eastern Times* (*Tuhua shibao*), no. 256 (April 19, 1925): 7.

ety (Zhongguo sheying xuehui 中國攝影學會) and contributed a large number of his photographs to its pictorial weekly. In addition, he also published widely in the aforementioned *Pictorial Weekly of the Eastern Times*, as well as in other leading pictorials and general interest magazines. A couple of months before the publication of the "crotch" photo, Ding published "Rowing to Return" (*Guizhao* 歸棹), a poetic portrayal of a boatman's silhouette outlined by the arch-like opening under a bridge (fig. 19). Apparently taken from the side of the bridge closest to the boatman, it is strongly reminiscent of American diplomat Frederick D. Cloud's photo "A Lake Scene" in his 1906 guidebook to Hangzhou. Both photographs evoke the White Snake legend, for which the image of a boat carrying human figures is a key symbol.[27] In the "crotch" photo taken under the Thunder Peak Pagoda, Ding Huikang seems to have further developed his interest in setting human figures against a well-lit background to produce a poetic silhouette; at any rate, he risked his life to capture the image, remaining inside the decaying structure despite the threat posed by the fall of loose bricks.

Indeed, Thunder Peak Pagoda had long maintained an enigmatic existence, exhibiting a silhouette of visual, religious, and symbolic significance in the Chinese popular imagination. The Buddhist origin of the pagoda, as a structure to preserve sacred relics, directly connected the structure to the idea of death, afterlife, and the otherworldly. The term "pagoda" as it appears in various Asian languages, including *tǎ* 塔 in Chinese, is thought to have derived from the Pali word *thūpa*, its Sanskrit pronunciation being *stūpa*.[28] The pagoda's physical structure was originally meant to evoke shadowy, spectral associations with the border between life and death, this world and the other shore. The Thunder Peak Pagoda was often represented as a silhouette against a darkened landscape and the ominous sky above, as in the "Lingering Shadows of the Thunder Peak Pagoda" (*Leifeng yiying* 雷峰遺影), a photograph collected by a certain Chen Efu 陳遏夫 and published in *The Half Moon Journal* (*Banyue* 半月) in 1925. In this rather obscure photograph, the shadow of the collapsed pagoda is again juxtaposed with a silhouette of a human figure posing under the weeping willows on the riverbank with what appears to be a farming instrument on his shoulders and a giant full moon hanging in midair. Such a focus on the pagoda's shadowy qualities became pervasive, as in another photograph titled "Undulant Shadows of the Thunder Peak Pagoda" (*Leifeng boying* 雷峰波影) by Yinsheng 吟笙, published in *Southern Pictorial* (*Nanfang huabao* 南方畫報) in 1925.[29]

In the Chinese language, the character *ying* 影 (shadow) is derived from the character *jing* 景 (view), creating a visible representation of the conceptual link between the two: a shadow can only be created when there is an image that has already formed a view. A copperplate print of a painting by Liu Gonglu, titled "An Old View of the Thunder Peak Pagoda" (*Leifeng jiujing* 雷峰舊景; fig. 20), amplifies the idea of the pagoda's "shadowy" presence as the "view" had indeed ceased to exist by the time the painting was created; here the figurative "shadow" of memory is reflected in the semiotic and lexigraphic relationship between sceneries and shadows. According to the painting's inscription, Liu visited Baoshi Hill (*Baoshi shan* 寶石山) for a tour on March 6, 1926, *after* the collapse; he painted the already vanished pagoda from memory, based on his recollections of previous visits. In this sense, the painted pagoda was literally a spectral stand-in for the physical structure that had disappeared almost two years before.[30]

Liu Gonglu was a legendary figure in the cultural scene at the time, active in *jingju*, painting, calligraphy, film, and connoisseurship of antiques and objects related to celebrities of all sorts. Famous for his professional *jingju* skills, long queue, and antique opium pipe and for frequenting the pleasure quarters and maintaining friendships with courtesans, he often appeared in the leading pictorial journals of the day, posing with actors and courtesans. His paintings, as well as items in his collection of painting and calligraphy by famous actors and personal friends, were also much sought after and widely printed by those journals. In an essay recalling Liu's eccentricities after his death, well-known cultural critic Zheng Yimei 鄭逸梅 fostered a ghostly mood at the beginning of his essay, using such descriptions as "dancing of ghostly shadows" (*guiying chongchong* 鬼影憧憧).[31] Here writing, similar to painting, became a way of not only remembering the dead but also fending off the ghosts: an imaginary pagoda was erected in place of the physical one that had collapsed.

Liu's "young survivor" (*yishao* 遺少) identity and his eccentricities in art and life are apparent in his painting of the Thunder Peak Pagoda, which is executed in the ink brush (*shuimo* 水墨, literally "water-ink") painting style, using economic brush strokes and a dynamic display of varying shades to create a lingering view of the Thunder Peak Pagoda after the collapse. Here "young survivors" is used in contrast to "old survivors" (*yilao* 遺老), the former referring to figures active in Republican China who had experienced the later years of the Qing dynasty in youth, and the latter, referring to those who were already mature adults during this same period. The nostalgia associated with the "young survivors" cultural circle echoes the idea of painting from memory to recreate a lost icon. Such an activity, in turn, helps us understand the attraction of the Thunder Peak Pagoda and its associated White Snake legend for both Liu and the reading public, who were fascinated by his creations.

Liu's outline of the pagoda, with wild grass growing out of the cracks formed by the decaying bricks, comes alive in very few strokes. The hills, trees, and a pavilion were all outlined with a masterful touch, very much in the style of traditional Chinese ink brush landscape paintings. Published in copperplate, a recent trend in pictorial printing, in *The Pacific Pictorial* (*Taipingyang huabao* 太平洋畫報), Liu's painting presents a fascinating hybrid: it is at once a timely reflection on a real, historical event, but also an event characterized by powerful, reverberating associations with the world of legend and fantasy; at once a representation of the refined tradition of ink painting and a beneficiary of the latest advances in printing technology, published in a leading modern journal. Leading oil painter Chen Baoyi's 陳抱一 contemporary contribution on the same subject seems rather old-fashioned in comparison, its title and angle undistinguished, and the entire composition poorly printed and presented in the much more obscure journal *Light of the Triangle* (*Sanjiao zhiguang* 三角之光).[32]

The same issue of *The Pacific Pictorial* that published Liu Gonglu's paint-

Figure 20: "An Old View of the Thunder Peak Pagoda" (*Leifeng jiujing*), by Liu Gonglu, in *The Pacific Pictorial* (*Taipingyang huabao*) 1, no. 1 (1926): 32, copperplate.

ing also carried a photo-essay with two photographs of the Thunder Peak Pagoda by Sheyu, likely the courtesy name of Shu Qingchun 舒慶春 (Shu Sheyu), better known by his pen name Lao She.[33] Titled "On Photographing the Thunder Peak Pagoda" (*Leifengta paizhao ji* 雷峰塔拍照記), this striking photo-essay recounts the author's many visits to the pagoda from 1915 on.[34] Although Lao She left China for London on September 14, 1924, it is possible that he had visited the Thunder Peak Pagoda in the spring of 1924, just prior to its collapse. However, it is unlikely that he was able to visit the site again in the spring of 1925, after the pagoda fell. This leaves us with the question of how Lao She was able to return to Hangzhou to make his "after-collapse" visit to the site of the ruined pagoda. Was this Sheyu in *The Pacific Pictorial* in 1926 really the Shu Sheyu who had criticized developments on *jingju* stage in *Shenbao* in 1921?

Whatever the identity of the photographer and essayist, the motif of contrasting the "before and after" images of the Thunder Peak Pagoda and the complex range of emotions that might be evoked by the pagoda's collapse were apparent in the photo-essay and were clearly echoed in Lu Yin's 1927 essay "Under the Thunder Peak Pagoda" (*Leifengta xia* 雷峰塔下).[35] Using an intimate epistolary format made all the more poignant by being addressed to a deceased lover and containing reminiscences about their romantic encounters four years before, this piece highlights themes of remembrance, forgetting, and tragic love as determined by fate, themes central to the White Snake legends and to Lu Yin's generation of May Fourth women writers. Named only by a single Chinese character, Han 涵, the lover whispers to the first-person female narrator, "We are leaving a major trace of our lives under the Thunder Peak Pagoda!" The female narrator bemoans how, only a year from that moment, the Thunder Peak Pagoda would collapse, and how her lover would follow suit only a month later. She explains in the story that she would feel thankful rather than saddened by the fall of the pagoda, for only by erasing its physical structure can she possibly hope to bury the remaining traces of their ill-fated romance. Here, rather than serving as a symbol of patriarchal oppression, the pagoda acts as a witness to the modern lovers' tragic romance; its collapse becomes a kind of catharsis for the young woman who has lost her lover. The collapse of the pagoda is successfully incorporated into a tragically romantic milieu closely linked to human emotions and experiences, a revamping of the White Snake legend from the perspective of a modern female writer.

The implied "before and after" logic reappeared as a visual and virtual specter in other representations of the collapsed Thunder Peak Pagoda. A photograph by Huang Weiqing 黄維慶 titled "Already Collapsed Thunder Peak Pagoda" (*Yidao zhi Leifengta* 已倒之雷峰塔; fig. 21) and published in 1927 presents the pagoda in all its scenic perfection as it appeared *before* collapsing, with the lake reflecting the pagoda's beautiful shadow as background and a pair of swans swimming at the center of the frame to accentuate its poetic quality. Strikingly, another photograph published in 1927, Yu Shaochang's 余少常 "Setting Sun over the Thunder Peak Pagoda" (*Leifeng xizhao* 雷峰西照; fig. 21), similarly employs the swan motif while adding trees, a boatman, and riverbanks, all of which are both long-cherished components of Chinese-style landscape paintings and key elements in the White Snake legend. Moreover, Yu inscribed the photograph in his own calligraphy, detailing the occasion of its presentation: the ten-week anniversary of the martial arts group Jingwuhui's 精武會 founding in 1920. Complete with his seal, Yu's creation represents a seamless hybrid between painting and photography, making his contribution to the Thunder Peak Pagoda visual repertoire a truly unique one. Yu's artful photograph, like many other visual creations, served

Figure 21: (left) "Already Collapsed Thunder Peak Pagoda" (*Yidao zhi Leifengta*). Photograph by Huang Weiqing, *The Young Companion* (*Liangyou*), no. 22 (December 30, 1927): 32; (right): "Setting Sun over the Thunder Peak Pagoda" (*Leifeng xizhao*). Photograph by Yu Shaochang, *Foshan Martial Arts Monthly* (*Foshan jingwu yuekan*) 2, no. 3 (1927): 11.

to fill the physical void left by the pagoda's collapse and was immortalized on the magazine page as a living visual specter. In its call for submissions in 1925, *Foshan Martial Arts Monthly* (*Foshan jingwu yuekan* 佛山精武月刊), where Yu's photo was to be published a couple of years later, had especially welcomed landscape photographs and paintings (*you fengjing tupian touzeng zhe yousuo huanying* 有風景圖片投贈者尤所歡迎).[36] Here the relationship between painting and photography, as well as the way that calligraphy was used to blend the two genres, was emphasized. In fact, when Yu's photograph was published, it was sandwiched between prints of exquisite calligraphy and paintings, blending photography with traditional visual media.[37]

This hybridization of painting and photography is also a feature in one of the most celebrated, highly visible, and widely published paintings of the Thunder Peak Pagoda, Gao Jianfu's "Evening Illuminations over Thunder Peak" (*Leifeng wanzhao* 雷峰晚照; fig. 22), which likely first appeared in *The Eastern Miscellany* in April 1926.[38] In the years that followed, the same painting by Gao was republished in a wide range of journals, most notably as the frontispiece in *The Young Companion* in December 1927, the same issue where Huang Weiqing's "Already Collapsed Thunder Peak Pagoda" photo also appeared.[39]

Figure 22: "Evening Illuminations over Thunder Peak" (*Leifeng wanzhao*). Painting by Gao Jianfu, *The Eastern Miscellany* (*Dongfang zazhi*) 23, no. 7 (April 10, 1926): unpaginated.

Gao Jianfu's painting, and his life story, became legendary even during his lifetime. In 1927, *Literature of the Masses* (*Minzhong wenxue* 民眾文學) published a piece titled "Mr. Gao Jianfu's Painting" (*Gao Jianfu xiansheng zhihua* 高劍父先生之畫), calling him "the first of our old-style painters to go abroad to study" (*woguo jiu huajia chuyang zuizao zhi yiren* 我國舊畫家出洋最早之一人). In 1935, Xu Beihong's essay "On Mr. Gao Jianfu's Painting" (*Tan Gao Jianfu xiansheng hua* 談高劍父先生畫) traced Gao's lineage to the Ming dynasty (1368–1644) painter Lin Liang 林良.[40] Xu applauds Gao's painting as a celebration of the liveliness and rich energy that had always characterized traditional Chinese painting. He then recounts his pleasant relationship with Gao Jianfu, his brother Gao Qifeng 高奇峰, and another Cantonese painter named Chen Shuren 陳樹人 when they had all been together in Shanghai about twenty years before. Xu laments the unpredictability of life now that Gao Qifeng has passed away, while thanking Premier Wang Jingwei 汪精衛 for his support for the arts,[41] which had enabled Gao Jianfu's tour of the capital with his paintings. Xu compares Gao's paintings to the "dignified and respectful sound of ritual instruments" (*huangzhong dalü zhisheng* 黃鐘大呂之聲) and claims that those who like music that is soft and sentimental, decadent, and obscene (*mimi zhiyin* 靡靡之音), might not be able to appreciate Gao's style. Xu goes on to connect Gao's revolutionary past with his painting and his kind and humorous character with his work and praises him as learned and authentic (*boda zhenren* 博大真人). Finally, revising his previous assessment of Gao's paintings as food that is too flavorful to be eaten in quantity (*qiwei taixian buyi duoshi* 其味太鮮不宜多食), he praises Gao's art as having returned to its simple and unadorned nature (*pushi* 樸實), thus reaching a higher level of cultivation.[42]

The dialectics between realism and fantasy, between present decay and the shadowy past, and between human actions and nonhuman ruins come together again in the romantic poet Xu Zhimo's long engagement with the Thunder Peak Pagoda and its association with the White Snake legend. Xu Zhimo wrote two relevant poems in September 1923 during a trip to Hangzhou. He specifically designated one as written in the "Hangzhou vernacular" (*Hangbai* 杭白) and simply titled it "Thunder Peak Pagoda" (*Leifengta*):

Over there is the ancient tomb of Madame White
 (the boatman points to the place where wild grass grows tall);
Guest, you have heard about the beautiful legend of the West Lake,
 Madame White is a loving demoness.

In pursuit of her love, she suffered instead,
As she loved a useless Xu Xian, her lover;
Believing the words of a monk, he was confused for a short while,
Taking a begging bowl, he covered his wife's original form with it.

It has been hundreds of years now,
How pitiful that she has been suppressed under the Thunder Peak
Pagoda,
A decaying ancient pagoda, desolate but still formidable,
Stands alone as the evening bell of Southern Screen sounds![43]

Xu's other poem, written earlier in the same month, is titled "The Shadow of the Moonlit Thunder Peak Pagoda" (*Yuexia Leifeng yingpian* 月下雷峰影片), and reads as follows:

Let me gift you the shadow of the Thunder Peak Pagoda,
Amidst thick dark and white clouds in the sky;
Let me gift you the tip of the Thunder Peak Pagoda,
Where the shadow of the bright moon floats in the heart of the soundly sleeping waves.
Deep dark nights, beautiful shadow of the pagoda,
round and round colors of the moon, long and slender shines of the waves.
Imagine you and I were rowing an uncovered little boat,
Imagine you and I created a flawless dreamscape![44]

Here Xu Zhimo's "dreamscape" is romantic rather than demonic. For Xu, the Thunder Peak Pagoda is merely the "ancient tomb of Madame White" (*Bai niangniang de gumu* 白娘娘的古墓), who is a "loving demoness" (*duoqing de yaomo* 多情的妖魔). Like Woodbridge's reinvention of love in his retelling of the legend, Xu and his contemporary, the female writer Lu Yin, invest the image of the White Snake and her lover Xu Xian with modern qualities of heterosexual love and romance. In this context, the decaying Thunder Peak Pagoda appears as both miserable and dignified, providing a dreamy backdrop for the lovers in the poems. In Xu's second poem, the shadow of Thunder Peak Pagoda in the water become items that the young lovers can exchange as romantic tokens. With the aid of the bright, round moon, the slender, shining waves, and the imagined little boat shared by the future lovers in the style of White Snake and Xu Xian, Xu Zhimo the modern poet was able to paint a complete dreamscape based on this fantastic legend.

Figure 23: “Thunder Peak in the Moonlight” (*Yuexia Leifeng*). Composed by Tianhe (Chen Tianhe), poem by Xu Zhimo, in *Music Education* (*Yinyue jiaoyu*) 2, no. 2 (1934): 1–4.

In the mid-1930s, a decade after the fall of the Thunder Peak Pagoda, "The Shadow of the Moonlit Thunder Peak Pagoda" was set to music by two different composers, first by Tianhe 田鶴 (Chen Tianhe 陳田鶴) in 1934 as "Thunder Peak in the Moonlight" (*Yuexia Leifeng* 月下雷峰) (fig. 23),[45] then by He Lüting 賀綠汀 in 1935.[46] He Lüting was an active leader of the left-wing music movement who was in charge of arranging the instrumental accompaniment for "March of the Volunteers" (*Yiyongjun jinxingqu* 義勇軍進行曲), one of the theme songs for the 1934 hit *Lovers in Troubled Times* (*Fengyun ernü* 風雲兒女), which later evolved into the national anthem of the PRC.[47] When Xu's poem featuring the romantic shadow of the Thunder Peak Pagoda was incorporated into popular songs in the mid-1930s, his interpretation of this dreamy landscape and its modern associations became a poetic link connecting the pre- and post-collapse Thunder Peak Pagoda with the popularization and canonization of its romantic image through the legendary figures of the White Snake and her human lover.[48]

THE RISE OF THE WHITE SNAKE AND THE CANONIZATION OF "THE WHITE SNAKE MODERN"

In December 1924, a few months after the fall of Thunder Peak Pagoda, an essay titled "On How Madame White Would Be against Rebuilding Thunder Peak Pagoda" (*Bai niangniang fandui chongjian Leifengta lun* 白娘娘反對重建雷峰塔論) graced the pages of *Red Roses* (*Hong meigui* 紅玫瑰).[49] Listed as author of the piece, Yingchuan Qiushui 穎川秋水 claims that a tourist picked up on the shore of West Lake a manifesto written by Madame White Snake that outlined, with a heavy dose of irony, four points against rebuilding the Thunder Peak Pagoda.[50]

The first reason outlined in the manifesto has to do with the aesthetics of ruins.[51] The "author" of the manifesto, White Snake herself, maintains that the ruined site where the Thunder Peak Pagoda used to stand, set against the setting sun and lush greenery, could provoke a more profound sense of loss in a visitor's heart, and thus would be more enduring, than those views that were visible in plain sight. Secondly, the author argues that building pagodas (the author uses the transliteration *futu* 浮圖 to highlight the foreign quality of the concept) is a superstitious custom imported into China by Buddhism, and that the pagodas are mere decorations and not really useful. Instead of rebuilding a pagoda at considerable expense, why not build something useful, like a library on top of the ruins? The author's third argument has to do with eliminating unnecessary structures in Chinese society, claiming that Thunder Peak Pagoda was quite superfluous at West Lake given the presence of the Liuhe 六合 Pagoda and Baoshu Pagoda. Lastly, the White Snake finally speaks directly to the readers in the first person:

> Although considered a Buddhist treasure, Thunder Peak Pagoda was a living hell for me. Hangzhou and Suzhou are called heavens on earth, so wouldn't it be outrageous to keep this living hell standing right in front of us? Not to mention we now live in a republic, and bodily freedom has been written into the laws and regulations. Now which one of you would have the heart to rebuild it with much fanfare, to violate my freedom again?[52]

Although it seems too playful to be taken seriously, this piece, published as a direct response to the pagoda's ruin, represented a widely shared sentiment empathizing with White Snake's plight. Such a position was first and most prominently articulated in Lu Xun's celebrated piece, "On the Fall of Thunder Peak Pagoda" (*Lun Leifengta de daodiao* 論雷峰塔的倒掉), published in November 1924.[53] After the PRC's founding, Lu Xun's piece was a required and often memorized school text for generations of Chinese children (including myself) and consequently had a huge impact on their understanding of the Thunder Peak Pagoda's fall as a distinctive cultural phenomenon. For Lu Xun, who initiated and popularized this position, the fall of the pagoda meant the rise of the White Snake suppressed under it.[54] He called for celebration rather than lamentation. Rebuilding the pagoda, consequently, meant returning the White Snake to subjugation, restricting her freedom and siding with the "treacherous monk" Fahai, the evil antagonist who had separated husband and wife and broken family harmony. In this influential essay, Lu Xun specifically cited the late Qing *tanci* edition of *The Righteous Snake* as a possible influence. Not only widely published and reprinted, *The Righteous Snake* also circulated through oral traditions. Lu Xun's own grandmother had retold the legend with added embellishments when the author was a young boy.[55]

Lu Xun's Verdict and The Righteous Snake *on the Silver Screen*

"A monk should simply focus on reciting his scriptures. White Snake is obsessed with Xu Xian, and Xu Xian is happy to marry a demoness, what does that have to do with anyone else?" (*Heshang ben yinggai zhiguan ziji nianjing. Baishe zimi Xu Xian, Xu Xian ziqu yaoguai, he bieren you shenme xianggan ne* 和尚本應該只管自己念經。白蛇自迷許仙，許仙自娶妖怪， 和別人有什麼

相干呢?).[56] Lu Xun's famous verdict on the triangular relationship between the White Snake, her human lover, and the Buddhist monk led him to determine that Abbot Fahai's motive must have been jealousy, thus literally pulling the abbot down from his Buddhist altar and making him an antagonist in a narrative with a new focus on freedom of choice versus social control. Lu Xun's piece was written on October 28, 1924, just a month after the fall of the pagoda, and was published only a few weeks after it is composed. In a postscript written on November 3, 1924, he corrected his confusion of Baoshu Pagoda for Leifeng (Thunder Peak) Pagoda, and further emphasized that he had known for a long time that the White Snake was not in actuality under Thunder Peak Pagoda. But why does he keep emphasizing this understanding grounded in reality, if his whole piece rests on his belief in the fantastic story he was told as a child? It is possible to read Lu Xun's immediate reaction to the fall of the Thunder Peak Pagoda here as speaking on behalf of the Chinese popular imagination of the mid-1920s, when there was a renewed understanding of the White Snake as a righteous figure, one opposed to the pagoda's association with the evil monk. This understanding, which was gaining popularity during this time, was initiated by a range of modern, secular, and romantic sensibilities that were invigorated by the May Fourth new cultural movement. The verdict was in: the pagoda should be "overthrown" to liberate the White Snake from its hegemonic control.

Only a couple of years later, the Shanghai-based Unique Film Company (Tianyi yingpian gongsi 天一影片公司; Unique Film hereafter) released the first commercial film adaptation of the White Snake legend as a two-part film series (1926) followed by a third installment (1927). Founded in June 1925, the film company was a family business operated by four brothers of the Shaw family from Ningbo, Runje Shaw 邵醉翁, Runde Shaw 邵邨人, Runme Shaw 邵山客, and Run Run Shaw 邵逸夫.[57] These films were among Unique Film's earliest productions. Although none of the three films appear to be extant, press coverage of the films gives us an idea of their major characteristics.

The July 1926 special issue of *Tianyi Magazine* on the film *The Righteous Snake* (*Yiyao Baishe zhuan* 義妖白蛇傳) includes an extensive English synopsis of the first two installments, premiered at the Dragon Boat Festival in 1926 (fig. 24).[58] This full English synopsis, a major contribution to Anglophone retellings of the White Snake legend by a Chinese film company, is unfortunately too long to be included in full here. Instead, a brief analysis follows.[59]

Although the 1926 synopsis for *The Righteous Snake* film, similar to the two Anglophone renditions discussed in detail in chapter 2, contains traces of indebtedness to the *tanci* version (including its title), it does depart from

Figure 24: Cover page of *The Righteous Snake* (*Yiyao Baishe zhuan*), *Tianyi Magazine*, special issue no. 6, July 1, 1926.

both the Chinese *tanci* storytelling and the turn-of-the-twentieth-century American adaptations. It is also hard to pinpoint any direct influence from Woodbridge and Cloud on the textual level, as the influence of their works may very well have been limited to the circle of Western residents in China at the time or, at most, within the Anglophone reading public. Published in a largely Chinese-language film magazine, the English synopsis in *Tianyi Magazine* did reflect the popular Chinese storytelling version and provided one of the first Anglophone renditions of the White Snake legend from within the sphere of the Chinese popular imagination, a sphere the American missionary and diplomat had so earnestly sought to decipher.

Likely for its melodramatic visual effect on the silver screen, the 1926 *Righteous Snake* film, according to the synopsis, added a major plot twist during Xu Xian's exile in Suzhou. A major antagonist, Xu's ex-employer at the pharmacy where he used to work, is introduced here to add drama and conflict. The ex-employer cooks up an elaborate scheme to frame Xu Xian and destroy his new drugstore business. Recommending two of his own employees to work for Xu, he instructs them to purchase decayed medical plants for Xu's newly opened Baohe Pharmacy (*Baohe tang* 保和堂), with the aim of ruining Xu's reputation and business. Although similar to the plot devices used in previous textual and stage renditions of the White Snake legend, this new plot stands out for its focus on visual magic. The antagonist was created precisely as an opportunity for the White Snake to display her powers. She discovers this treacherous trick immediately and transforms the decayed plants into magical herbs effective for curing every disease, using her magical arts. Xu Xian's reputation as a "living genius" is thus established, and his business booms.[60]

The continued need for antagonists and melodrama even produced one of the first visual incarnations of a sexually aggressive Green Snake. She is usually the loyal sister/maid figure in service of the White Snake, but in the 1926 film synopsis, she emerges as a rival to the White Snake for the human lover.[61] Such a reformulation of Green Snake's character would make a strong comeback in the postsocialist and postmodern narratives that later appeared in both the Sinophone and Anglophone worlds, as discussed in detail in Part III of this book. The Green Snake in *The Righteous Snake* films is depicted as "proud and dissolute," and as a result, she "makes love" to Xu Xian and "is found and reprimanded" by the White Snake. Angrily, she leaves home and goes to Kunshan to "seek a lover."[62] The introduction of a new city, in addition to the three cities for which the legend was famous, namely, Hangzhou, Suzhou, and Zhenjiang, was as significant as the introduction of an antagonistic Green Snake. In Kunshan, a city about thirty miles east of Suzhou, the Green Snake seduces a young man in a fashion similar to how White Snake seduced Xu Xian in many of the earlier versions of the legend.[63]

A number of additional plot twists and coincidences were added to heighten the film's melodrama and visual spectacle. The mother of the young man from Kunshan seduced by Green Snake, having heard of Xu Xian's reputation as the "living genius" of Suzhou, sends for him to expel the evil spirit. Again, the White Snake comes to the rescue. Xu follows her advice, and the young man is instantly cured. As a result, the Green Snake returns to Suzhou to serve the White Snake and her husband again. A further new coincidence occurs when the cured young man pays a visit to his savior in Suzhou and discovers the Green Snake and some of his lost property in Xu's residence. He reports this to the magistrate, and Xu is again banished from Suzhou to Zhenjiang.[64] In the end, these elaborate plot twists serve the same narrative function—getting Xu Xian exiled again—as in earlier versions. Uniquely, this first cinematic adaptation foregrounds the sensational visual details of commercial and sexual competitions that spring from envy and jealousy and transforms pleasant host and loyal servant in many previous versions, into memorable antagonists.

Moreover, unlike any previous text, the English synopsis for *The Righteous Snake* both opens and ends with the Thunder Peak Pagoda (referred to in the synopsis as "Thunder Pagoda") and endows the structure with a single purpose—imprisoning the White Snake. The synopsis opens, "Thunder Pagoda—one of the best sceneries [sic] of the West Lake, Hangchow—was built by a Buddhist priest, named Fa-Hai, the legend says. He built it to imprison his antagonist, Pe Su-cheng, a fairy."[65] It ends, "Afterwards the priest buried the bowl on the shore of the West Lake, and upon it was built a pagoda—the Thunder Pagoda."[66] Opening and closing with the Thunder Peak Pagoda, this synopsis accentuates the pagoda's importance in the visualization of the White Snake legend. Because the synopsis, which covers only the first two parts of the film, stops before the White Snake's imprisonment under the pagoda, it leaves open the fate of the White Snake and of the pagoda. A number of important scenes (such as the return of the White Snake's son and his offering to the pagoda to release his mother) are thus reserved for future release in the much-anticipated sequel. But why would the 1926 synopsis of the very first cinematic rendering of the White Snake legend give the Thunder Peak Pagoda such prominence so soon after the physical collapse of the actual structure in September 1924?

The Pagoda in the Film

The *Tianyi Magazine* special issue on *The Righteous Snake* film offers some important clues concerning the pagoda's prominence in the film. Published prominently in the front pages of the special issue were two images, "Lingering Shadows of the Thunder Peak Pagoda" (*Leifengta yiying* 雷峰塔遺影) and "Pe Su-cheng of *The Righteous Snake*" (*Baishe zhuan zhong zhi Bai Suzhen* 白蛇傳中之白素貞).[67] Pe Su-cheng (Bai Suzhen) is the name adopted by the White Snake in her human form. The photographs, placed one after the other, suggest a direct link between the image of the recently collapsed pagoda and the rise in popularity of the image of the White Snake, as portrayed by the actress Hu Die 胡蝶, known in English as Butterfly Wu (the name *die* means "butterfly" in Chinese). Indeed, with the 1926 release of the two-part film, various images of Butterfly Wu as the White Snake began to dominate popular print media outlets.

The published intertitles (*zimu* 字幕) for the silent film also reflect the importance of the pagoda in the film's conception and execution. The phrase "Lingering Shadows of the Thunder Peak Pagoda" appears as the penultimate of the film's 340 intertitles, which suggests that the pre-collapse image of the pagoda, included in the same special issue of *Tianyi Magazine*, might have served as one of the film's concluding visuals.[68]

At this time, Unique Film had produced six films, which were listed in an advertisement titled "A Full List of Film Productions from Our Company" (*Ben gongsi chupin yilan* 本公司出品一覽) in the *Tianyi Magazine* special issue devoted to *The Righteous Snake*.[69] One report from a "test screening" (*shiying hui* 試映會) specifically mentions the amazing speed with which the company was producing new films.[70] The report maintains that *The Righteous Snake* was made and test screened soon after the opening of *The Butterfly Lovers* (*Liang Zhu tongshi* 梁祝痛史), Unique Film's fifth production, itself based on another enduring legend with a fascinating afterlife in contemporary popular culture.[71]

Unique Film categorized *The Righteous Snake* as an "unofficial history" (*baishi* 稗史) and promoted the film as following *The Butterfly Lovers'* style, which connects legendary anecdotes with stories of everyday life. The physical structure of the Thunder Peak Pagoda and its recent real-life collapse were meticulously highlighted to anchor the miraculous and the fantastic in its historical and geographical context.

However, what made the story of the White Snake "unofficial," that is, the otherworldly encounters between the human and the nonhuman, fed right into what Woodbridge had summarized as the pervasive existence of "demigods" in the Chinese popular imagination. The phenomenal success of *The Righteous Snake* film and the five preceding films from Unique Film largely rested on just such a popular thirst for things extraordinary and fantastic, albeit rooted in the seemingly ordinary and realistic, from within what the Western observer considered the "feverish" Chinese popular mind. At the same time, one can also argue that the films were popular because they were based on familiar stories, linking them to oral traditions and performance genres central to the daily lives of the Chinese people.

CONCLUDING REMARKS

On April 11, 1926, *Shenbao* published an advertisement titled "Fuchang Five Butterfly Brand Cigarette in Great Demand" (*Fuchang Wudie pai xiangyan changxiao* 福昌五蝶牌香菸暢銷), which exemplified Fuchang Cigarette Company's aggressive promotional strategies for its new products. Following popular trends, the company handed out more than ten thousand packs of cigarettes every day at the famous entertainment venue Grand World, one pack with every ticket purchase. The advertisement continued to explain how the company was "flattering with public mentality" (*yinghe shehui xinli* 迎合社会心理) and how every pack of cigarettes included a card designed by the late painter Zhou Muqiao, famous for his paintings for commercial calendar posters focusing on subject matters either from *Journey to the West* (*Xiyou ji*) or from *Legend of the White Snake*.[72] A few months later—after a series of promotional advertisements and the much-anticipated release of *The Righteous Snake*—another advertisement in *Shenbao* specifically connected the Five Butterfly Brand cigarettes and the new films starring Hu Die. With Butterfly Wu as lead actress, the new films from Unique Film and the Five Butterfly Brand cigarettes from Fuchang Cigarette Company were quite a match for mutual promotions.

A July 13, 1926, advertisement provided the details of the promotion: each pack of cigarettes included various cards (fig. 25), and the card with "Top-of-the-List Bai" (Bai Zhuangyuan 白狀元), the son of the White Snake and Xu Xian, who won first place in the imperial examination, could be exchanged for a new pack of Five Butterfly Brand cigarettes. The advertisement highlighted the cards depicting various spirits loosely related to the White Snake's water troops during her fight with Abbot Fahai—the clam spirit (card 10 of the 14 below), the butterfly spirit, the frog spirit, and the carp spirit—and

Figure 25: *The Righteous Snake* (*Yiyao Baishe zhuan*) cards based on the two-part film by Unique Film and produced for Five Butterfly Brand (*Wudie pai*) cigarettes, 1926, https://tieba.baidu.com/p/4338420505, accessed November 1, 2018.

called them "especially beautiful and lovely" (*youwei meiguan ke'ai* 尤為美觀可愛). It stated cards would be issued continuously and that the total number of cards in the series would reach a few dozen. Collectors of the painted cards should not miss such great opportunities, the advertisement urged.[73]

The company that produced this series of painted cards, Fuchang Cigarette Company, was founded by business tycoon Huang Chujiu 黃楚九, known for his advertising acumen. In the 1910s, Huang had established the

Grand World, a leading entertainment venue in Shanghai, hence the mutual promotion of the Grand World and Five Butterfly Brand cigarettes. He was also famous for promoting Bailing ji, the tonic advertised as a "hundred-year machine" to prolong human life, in the 1920s, as discussed in chapter 2.[74] Headed by Huang Chujiu, the Fuchang Cigarette Company was able to target the Shanghai public's hunger for things "novel and exotic" (*xinqi* 新奇), and the White Snake cards were very different from the usual ones with beauties from classic novels.[75] These *Righteous Snake* cards based on the two-part film featured the naked bodies of animals, women, and children, among other things, and sensationalized and animated the image of the White Snake amid a polyphonic urban milieu from the mid-1920s onwards.[76] The very fact that this series of cigarette cards has been posted on a Baidu.com discussion forum devoted to "Movie Queen Hu Die" (Dianying huanghou Hu Die 電影皇后胡蝶) speaks volumes about the popularity of the 1926 film and its leading actress. Fans of popular culture have become both active researchers of its historical and cultural contexts and fervent collectors of relevant artifacts.[77]

One of the most active discussion forums on Baidu.com related to the White snake theme, however, is on the 1992 Taiwanese TV series *New Legend of Madame White Snake* (*Xin Bainiangzi chuanqi*). Intriguingly, the White Snake iconography popularized by the 1992 series points to the aesthetic beauty of traditional Chinese costumes and the Huangmei opera–style singing popularized by opera films from the mid-twentieth century, in both Mainland China and Hong Kong. Among these, the 1962 film *Madam White Snake* (*Baishe zhuan*) produced by Shaw Brothers Studio in Hong Kong is a prominent example. The aesthetic and institutional continuities are striking. The same Shaw brothers behind *The Righteous Snake* films from Shanghai in the late 1920s established the Shaw Brothers Studio in Hong Kong in the late 1950s and ushered in the return of the White Snake during the Cold War. What distinguished the 1926 Shanghai experiments from the Shaw Brothers Studio's recreations in 1960s' Hong Kong, however, was the deliberate adoption of modern costumes for a fantastic story set in a bygone time, with few scenes switching back to traditional costumes. Unique Film's 1926 cinematic experiment belonged to a filmmaking style known as "ancient story dressed in contemporary costumes" (*shizhuang guxi* 時裝古戲), employed in the first wave of Chinese commercial filmmaking in the mid-1920s, including Unique Film's *The Butterfly Lovers*.[78]

Quite remarkably, even after critical voices argued for the incompatibility between ancient stories and modern costumes in *The Butterfly Lovers*, *The Righteous Snake* still adopted largely modern everyday costumes, with only three scenes featuring the White Snake's descending from Heaven in traditional costumes.[79] Other companies followed suit. *Dream of the Red Chamber* (*Honglou meng* 紅樓夢), a "modern costume film" (*shizhuang yingpian* 時裝影片) from Fudan Film Company in Shanghai, was said to have focused on "young people's lives in modern society." Lin Daiyu and Jia Baoyu, the names of the two young protagonists in the eighteenth-century novel upon which the film was based, are synonyms for lovers in the Chinese cultural imagination today.

Although dressing traditional story in modern clothing may have raised eyebrows among intellectuals and some everyday filmgoers at the time, such anachronist experiments produced surprising commercial returns, as the cinemas were flooded with crowds even in the summer heat.[80] Situated in the long view of history, this hybrid genre of a modern costume film that focuses on fantastic themes quickly lost popularity, as seen in the change from modern to traditional costumes in the third episode of *The Righteous Snake* film (1927). It did, however, through its unconventional mismatch between content and form, usher in a new era of commercial filmmaking that aimed at attracting the attention of its audience and fostering sensational media phenomena in a truly modern fashion. The evolution from the first two episodes of *The Righteous Snake*, with actors clad predominantly in modern everyday costumes, to the third episode with actors dressed in traditional costumes, vividly illustrates the nonlinear pathway toward traditional aesthetics in later White Snake films, as illustrated by reiterations of the legend on the big and small screens during the Cold War and in contemporary times.

Echoing the trend of giving a modern face to the fantastic legend, the experimental film *Lakeshore Spring Dream* (*Hubian chunmeng* 湖邊春夢), featuring the White Snake as a modern femme fatale, appeared simultaneously with the commercial success of the 1926–1927 White Snake films.[81] Here the avant-garde, the commercial, and the popular intersected to create a highly modern synergy. The modern attire worn by the film's young protagonists, a young playwright who has gone to West Lake to recover from a failed love affair and a charming modern woman he encounters by the lakeshore, accentuated the contemporary spirit of this modern revamping of the White Snake legend. Conceived by Tian Han and directed by Bu Wancang at the Mingxing (Star) Film Company in Shanghai in 1927, the film incorporated sadomasochistic elements and emphasized both the lustful and dangerous nature of the powerful female figure and the possessive power of the "vampire." A surviving still from the now lost film shows the femme fatale in Westernized and masculine attire—shirt, tie, and pants—standing beside the playwright's naked, tied, and effeminate body. The image suggests an aesthetic of feminine transgression and a reversal of the male gaze, placing the male body under the intense gaze of the modern incarnation of the fantastic White Snake.[82]

Alongside commercial and avant-gardist experimentations in reimagining the White Snake legend, and with the establishment of folk literature (*minjian wenxue* 民間文學) as an academic discipline, scholarly publications about the legend began to appear. *Collection of Myths about Madame White Snake* (*Leifengta; Bai niangniang* 雷峰塔 • 白娘娘) was first published in the folklore and folk literature series of National Peking University & Chinese Association for Folklore in the late 1920s in Beijing and was reprinted in Taiwan in the 1970s. Quite remarkably, in this scholarly, contemporary rendition of the White Snake legend soon after the fall of the Thunder Peak Pagoda, the narrator completely negates the White Snake's snake identity, calling the story a result of the prevailing trend of superstition in China and a sign of how the people are poisoned by the likes of monks and petty officials. The fall of the pagoda, the storyteller continues, "symbolically shows that all oppressed women will be freed someday."[83] Such a "White Snake Modern," with the aid of commercial and popular successes, initiated a long tradition of diasporic imagination regarding the White Snake theme throughout the mid-twentieth century across Asia, an early expression of which can be found in the form of two no longer-existent Malay-language films produced by The Teng Chun 鄭丁春 (Tahyar Idris, Tahjar Ederis, or Zheng Dingchun) in the mid- to late 1930s.[84]

The rise of the "White Snake Modern" eventually invited its suppression. At a time of national crisis in the mid-twentieth century, Thunder Peak Pagoda again became a symbol of stability and prosperity, and calls for its reconstruction regained popularity. In 1948, editorials and reports such as "The Prosperity of the Nation Depends on the Thunder Peak Pagoda" (*Guoyun xinglong zai Leifengta* 國運興隆在雷峰塔) and "Thunder Peak Pagoda is Responsible for the Fate of the Nation" (*Tianxia xingwang Leifengta youze* 天下興亡雷峰塔有責) appeared in popular newspapers and journals. The first piece claims that the first Chinese disciple of the Ninth Panchen Lama, the hundred-year-old Chen Jianqi 陳鑑岐, had organized a committee for rebuilding the pagoda. The plan was to raise one hundred thousand gold coins, and to rebuild the pagoda according to its previous appearance, so as to protect ancient sites. For that purpose, Chiang Kai-shek, president of the Republic of China in the midst of the civil war between the Communists and his Nationalist Party, issued a plaque with the four-character phrase *hushan zengsheng* 湖山增勝, celebrating the rebuilding effort as "adding charms to the lakes and hills." The article further cites Chen Jianqi's claim that the pagoda was not only a "famous site" at West Lake but was also connected to the fate of the nation. The author concluded that rebuilding Thunder Peak Pagoda would secure the future prosperity of the Chinese nation.[85] Similarly, in a satirical tone, the second article alleged that all of China's problems had to do with the fall of the pagoda in 1924. Now that the rebuilding effort was ongoing, the author claimed, things would get better and China would be prosperous again once the pagoda was rebuilt.[86] Such claims further canonized the Thunder Peak Pagoda in the Chinese popular and nationalistic imagination. Intriguingly, the rhetoric of reinstating the pagoda, both physically and imaginatively, propelled new waves of the rise of the White Snake across a wide media spectrum in an inter-Asian and global context. The global travels of the White Snake legends continued as discussions of rebuilding the pagoda were reopened, year after year.[87]

PART II

The Profound Humanity of the Nonhuman during the Cold War

CHAPTER 4

The White Snake Legend in Postwar Japanese Cinema

In 1926, only two years after the Thunder Peak Pagoda collapsed, the White Snake legend came up as the subject of casual conversation between the Chinese artist and filmmaker Tian Han and the Japanese painter Migishi Kōtarō 三岸好太郎. Their conversation took place at the very setting of the White Snake legend, West Lake, where Tian Han was shooting outdoor scenes for his film *V Narod*, or *Going to the People* (*Dao minjian qu* 到民間去). In an ironic twist, the Chinese filmmaker introduced a Japanese collection of legendary stories *Tales of Moonlight and Rain* (*Ugetsu monogatari*) to the Japanese painter,[1] assuring him that Ueda Akinari's work had Japanized the Chinese legend and that its *charm* (Tian's original English word) had intoxicated their contemporary and mutual friend, Japanese writer Tanizaki Jun'ichirō.

Tian continued to explain that *The Lust of the Serpent* (*Jasei no in*),[2] one of Tanizaki's earliest efforts at writing a film scenario while working at the Taishō Moving Picture Company (*Taikatsu* 大活) in the early 1920s, was a result of this sense of affinity. Tian Han went on to quote Kuriyagawa Hakuson's 厨川白村 discussion of John Keats's *Lamia*, a long narrative poem about a snake woman who drinks human blood, thus an archetype of the vampire/snake/femme fatale. He speculated that snake-woman stories might have originated in India and spread west to Greece and thence to England, as well as migrating eastwards to China and Japan. However, he was troubled that while England had the work of John Keats and Japan had that of Ueda Akinari, China only had the "unpolished" folk legend without the added refinement that would elevate the legend into a truly "artistic creation."[3]

The situation seems to suggest that Tian Han at this time either would not have been aware of the seventeenth-century artful tale produced by Feng Menglong or that he had disregarded Feng's version completely, which would explain why he considered Ueda Akinari's version of the legend as representing the artistic recreation of the White Snake in East Asia. Regardless, in this purposefully clear-cut distinction between high and low culture, the underlying nationalist message was clear: Tian Han himself would strive to be the Keats and Ueda of China and to create a real work of art based on the White Snake legend. This promise, however, would not be realized for another thirty years.[4]

In past work, I have attempted to tell the complicated story of how the White Snake legend and the femme fatale at the center of its modern metamorphoses survived and even triumphed over the requirements for the experimental and the popular in Communist China, emerging as a new canonical source for socialist theater, dance, and other performance genres throughout the 1950s.[5] This chapter is about a different and equally intriguing transformation that took place at the same time, but outside the Sinophone world. In an uncanny fashion, the three Japanese films at the center of this chapter, all from the 1950s, responded to the Japan-inspired Tian Han's call in 1926 for renewed artistic creation based on the Chinese legend. In addition, these films draw upon the invention of love and of modern sensibility in the legend's Anglophone renditions in the late nineteenth and early twentieth centuries (examined in chapter 2), as well as to the visualization and canonization of the legend in Chinese pictorial journals and commercial films throughout the first half of the twentieth century (examined in chapter 3).

The continuities are striking. However, the issue of national representation, which was at the center of Tian Han's chat with Migishi, became complicated when texts and images travelled across linguistic and cultural spheres. This was particularly true when the migration in question took place in the postwar period between Japan and China—geopolitical entities recently at war and positioned on opposite sides of the Cold War. This phenomenon raises a number of questions about the relationships that develop between language, culture, media, and national representation. In what ways did the three Japanese-language White Snake–themed films capture the spirit of the Japanese 1950s, a decade burdened by the need to "embrac[e] defeat,"[6] to emerge from the shadow of American Occupation, and to strive for national regeneration? How might the mid-twentieth-century Japanese films in turn continue to challenge and enrich White Snake narratives in the Chinese traditions?

EXQUISITE PARADISE AND FORBIDDEN LOVE

Reinterpreting Mizoguchi Kenji's *Ugetsu*, one of the most widely celebrated Japanese films from the early 1950s, as one of the first Japanese adaptations of the White Snake legend in the postwar moment, may provoke a range of emotional and intellectual reactions. Writing shortly after the dawning of a new reign era in Japan, named Reiwa 令和 after a poem in the oldest-existing Japanese poetry anthology *Collection of Ten Thousand Leaves* (*Man'yōshū* 万葉集) and used as a gesture to disassociate Japan from Chinese influences, I am aware that any effort to connect Japanese and Chinese cultural traditions may seem suspect and unwelcome by political and cultural conservatives in Japan. In spite of such political fissure, or because of it, it seems to me that such an inquiry becomes ever more important.

A representative director of what the West calls Japanese cinema's Golden Age of the 1950s, Mizoguchi has been described as possessing two contrasting sides: on the one hand, he is a master of showcasing the ultimate refinement and exquisite qualities of what is now known in the West as the Japanese aesthetics; on the other hand, he is also considered a great poet of social engagement.[7] One of Mizoguchi's most celebrated films, *Ugetsu* combines "The House in the Thicket" (*Asaji ga yado* 浅茅が宿) and "The Lust of the Serpent" (*Jasei no in*), two fantastic stories from Ueda Akinari's eighteenth-century compilation *Tales of Moonlight and Rain*.[8] Born in 1898 and coming of age in the period after World War I, Mizoguchi was an exact contemporary with Tian Han and part of his generation of the interwar international avant-garde.[9] Mizoguchi and his oeuvre must be understood in the context of a constant dialogue between the aesthetic and the political, and between the post–World War I 1920s and the post–World War II 1950s. Inspired by similar cultural resources in post–World War I Tokyo, including German expressionism and the works of Eugene O'Neill and Leo Tolstoy, Mizoguchi Kenji's and Tian Han's generation of East Asian avant-garde artists share remarkable career trajectories in using the fantastic to attack the real and in employing in their art strong female figures to critique social injustice.

"The Lust of the Serpent" is widely regarded as the longest and most complex story in Ueda Akinari's collection. It is also the one closest to its Chinese source material, the vernacular story "Madam White Is Kept Forever under Thunder Peak Tower," from Feng Menglong's seventeenth-century *Stories to Caution the World*.[10] Intriguingly, the Ueda story is also recognized as incorporating multiple allusions from Japanese sources, especially *Tale of Genji* (*Genji monogatari* 源氏物語) and *Dojoji Temple* (*Dōjōji* 道成寺).[11] Poised at the intersection of Chinese and Japanese literary traditions, "The Lust of the Serpent" embodies the interplay between the languages of connected lands and cultural traditions. Through the image of an enchantress (the serpent woman Manago 真女児, who appears during rainy weather, at hot springs, or near rivers) and the magic powers of water, the Japanese retelling of the Chinese legend offers a compelling vision of the convergence between cultural and religious practices of multiple provenances in both China and Japan.[12]

Using "The House in the Thicket" as a frame story, in which a man returns home after a long period only to be greeted by his wife's ghost, the main body of Mizoguchi's *Ugetsu* focuses on "The Lust of the Serpent," recounting the same man's sexual encounter with an enchanting ghost (replacing the original snake spirit) while away from home. This otherworldly rendition of the White Snake legend has initiated its own tradition in Japanese literary and cultural history, a tradition that emphasizes "lust" rather than "love," accentuating the image of a "femme fatale" at the expense of the image of the "loving wife" of some Chinese versions.[13]

In 1953, with Miyagawa Kazuo 宮川一夫, of *Rashomon* (*Rashōmon* 羅生門) fame, as cinematographer[14] and Hayasaka Fumio 早坂文雄 as composer of the musical score, Mizoguchi Kenji was well positioned to create another "refashioning" of *Tales of Moonlight and Rain*, which "continue[d] to enchant modern readers with its mysterious fantasies."[15] The following section attempts to better explore the 1953 Japanese film *Ugetsu* in the genealogy of the White Snake repertoire, in dialogue with other contemporary cinematic adaptations of the Chinese legend in Japan and beyond, and with reference to its place in Mizoguchi's oeuvre within the context of postwar Japanese filmmaking. More importantly, through a close reading of the cinematic language of *Ugetsu* and other contemporary Japanese "White Snake" films throughout the 1950s, I aim to contribute to our understanding of the humanity of the nonhuman as expressed in the complex, intertwined relationship between gender, species, media, and politics in the translingual and transnational retelling of the White Snake legends across the Cold War divide.

Between Light and Shadow: Infinite Shades of Gray

Ugetsu's famous opening and closing sequences have long been widely regarded as exemplifying Mizoguchi's masterful use of panning long shots (executed by Miyagawa's poetic camera work), employed to present the landscape of the Japanese countryside with a sense of transiency and transmigration. This cinematographic style has been described, by cinematographer Miyagawa himself and others, as recreating the sensation of slowly unrolling a handscroll (*emakimono* 絵巻物) and incrementally viewing a horizontal landscape painting. In an interview conducted for a documentary on Mizoguchi's life as a film director, Miyagawa the cameraman specifically referred to the influence on Mizoguchi of the Southern school of Chinese painting, typically executed in monochrome ink and often taking landscapes as its subject.[16] Even more fittingly, Miyagawa also recounted how he learned traditional monochrome ink paintings (*sumi-e* 墨絵) himself and how his teacher never permitted his students to use colors in their painting, as the world of *sumi-e* is a world of black and white, and infinite levels of gray. He continued to explain that what the teacher wanted was for them to make viewers feel colors by gradations in the shades of gray. He concluded that his cinematographic tone was born out of training in *sumi-e*.[17]

It is significant that Miyagawa highlighted the influence of the Southern school of Chinese painting on Mizoguchi's monochrome film aesthetics. Art historian Aida Yuen Wong has pointed out the dynamic role played by Japan in the rise of "national-style painting" (*guohua* 國畫) in early twentieth-century China.[18] In her recent study on Gao Jianfu, famous for his painting of Thunder Peak Pagoda after its collapse (as discussed in chapter 3), Wong further uses Gao's aesthetic of dilapidation (*canpo mei* 殘破美) in painting and calligraphy as a case study to illustrate the role played by Southern Chinese painting in the movement to resurrect national-style painting in China.[19]

There are a number of reversals at work. What was considered traditional Chinese aesthetics, in this case monochrome ink painting, was reinvented and institutionalized in China as national and modern with the discovery of a Westernized Japan in the early twentieth century. In contrast, in the mid-twentieth century, postwar Japan's search for a distinctive national identity, propelled by its emergence out of the shadow of US Occupation, prompted a renewed search for a shared East Asian cultural tradition, again manifested in the art of ink painting, as a way both to assert its aesthetic difference from the United States and to reconnect with its East Asian neighbors, who had been alienated by its wartime aggression. Japan's reconciliation efforts, coupled with the relative expansion of cultural and intellectual freedom immediately after the war, gave rise to the flowering of a popular culture that was, as Andrew Gordon has put it, "far less packaged or processed than it would be in later years."[20] It was in this relatively progressive intellectual milieu that *Ugetsu* was born.

It is hard to imagine how *Ugetsu* might look in color. Miyagawa called *Ugetsu* a film with "infinite gray as the basic tone," which could give "a sense of calmness to human eyes."[21] If Miyagawa's work with Kurosawa Akira 黒澤明, particularly in *Rashomon*, focused on a cinematography that heightened the contrast between black and white, his collaboration with Mizoguchi indeed accentuated the realization of innumerable shades of gray.[22] It took Mizoguchi the director and Miyagawa the cinematographer quite some time to work with American Eastman Color, which led the industry standard in the early 1950s. In fact, although the first color film in Japan was made in 1951,[23] Mizoguchi's first color film, *Tales of the Taira Clan* (*Shin Heike monogatari* 新平家物語), was not made until 1955. It is also one of only two color films in his long career.[24] Apart from the aforementioned cultural politics, which favored asserting difference from the United States by returning to an East Asia identity, what held Mizoguchi and Miyagawa back from transitioning to color?

It is important to point out here that the Chinese artist Tian Han, who largely shaped our contemporary understanding of the White Snake legend through his writing during the early 1950s in the PRC, was deeply influenced by the modernist cinematic renditions of the Chinese legend that had appeared in early twentieth-century Japan and by the legend's eighteenth-century literary precedents in the Japanese tradition. Chief among these was the work of Tanizaki Jun'ichirō, the modernist writer who adapted "The Lust of the Serpent" into a film scenario for Taishō Moving Picture Company in the early 1920s.[25] In 1933, Tanizaki wrote an essay on Japanese aesthetics titled "In Praise of Shadows" (*In'ei raisan* 隠翳礼讃), which many commentators interpreted as signaling his symbolic return to a traditional Japan. In this now canonical text, Tanizaki discussed the darkness of household pottery and its reflection of "Japanese national character," compared the aesthetic use of different shades of darkness in Japanese-style dwellings to ink painting, and praised the beauty of the shadowy Noh stage.[26]

Tanizaki attributed the genius of Japanese aesthetics to the magic of shadows, claiming that shadows lend mystery and depth to Japanese art and culture.[27] His arguments echoed the prominence of shadows in the artistic reconfigurations of the Thunder Peak Pagoda after its fall, as well as practices of traditional shadow theater in both China and Japan. However, such a gesture of signaling toward past practices should not be read as a simple return to things traditional; rather, it indicated a deeply modernist, even avant-gardist reinterpretation of Chinese and Japanese traditions, likely inspired at least partly by German expressionism,[28] with an enchanting, modernist femme fatale at the center of the layers of gray.

It is thus quite understandable that when Miyagawa the cinematographer talked about the dark tones that he preferred in cinema, many Japanese and international commentators attributed it to the traditional aesthetics of his hometown, Kyoto. Miyagawa himself, however, tended to cite German filmmakers such as F. W. Murnau as influences rather than looking back to Japanese tradition.[29] The commentators' evocation of a traditional Japan had much to do with the cultural location of Japanese film under an international gaze at the early postwar moment. It was also intimately connected with the ways in which film interpretations were propelled by a self-exoticizing strategy and thrust into an emergent rhetoric that represented Japan as a nation under national and cultural reconstruction after the devastation of World War II.

In the context of renewed international relations, the aesthetics of shadow in cinema played a significant role in formulating a particular cultural image of Japan, fittingly black and white,[30] while at the same time disregarding the modernist, avant-gardist gestures embedded in this seeming return to tradition. By contrast, the Chinese color film *The Butterfly Lovers* (*Liang Shanbo yu Zhu Yingtai*) of the same year,[31] had a very different aim and was accordingly interpreted quite differently. In 1953, the new Communist nation was eager to prove its technical advancement and to present a strong yet nonthreatening image to those members of the global community who were suspicious of the new regime.[32] In service to this goal, flamboyant colors and an emphasis on the nonthreatening feminine theatrical tradition emerged as a dominant aesthetic.

The Sound and Look of a Lady Wakasa Film: Pottery, Water, and Mutual Enchantment

The opening intertitles of *Ugetsu* specify the setting of the story as "early spring, sixteenth century," much like how *The Butterfly Lovers* presents a bygone era characterized by enchanting feminine aesthetics. Different from its Chinese counterpart's technically advanced use of color, however, *Ugetsu*'s opening scene features long panning shots of the landscape, which unfolds as in a *sumi-e*. This scene immediately fosters a sense of "innocence lost" and foreshadows the tragic fate of its human protagonists. Set on the north bank of Lake Biwa (*Biwa-ko* 琵琶湖) in *Ōmi* 近江 province (likely a reference to the West Lake setting of the Chinese White Snake legend), the unfolding story includes a series of scenes that evokes the importance of water and the feminine power of seduction, both central to Ueda's design in "The Lust of the Serpent."

Lady Wakasa 若狭, a female ghost based on the character of the White Serpent, occupies the center of this enchanting world of ethereal shadows, although she does not appear on screen until some thirty minutes into the film. Though less overly political than his series of "tendency films" from the 1930s,[33] Mizoguchi's *Ugetsu* is still endowed with a strong undercurrent of social criticism, which has invited feminist and pacifist interpretations. Though the film's frame story features the worldly pursuits of two men, Mizoguchi takes an unapologetically female-centered approach in the film itself, giving top billing to the actresses playing the three female protagonists, Kyō Machiko 京マチ子, Tanaka Kinuyo 田中絹代, and Mito Mitsuko 水戸光子. The enchantress Lady Wakasa's epitomization of the femme fatale figure in this film is considered by some to be evidence of the Americanization of the Japanese film industry in the late 1940s and early 1950s.[34] However, this putatively causal relationship between Americanization and the femme fatale warrants considerable scrutiny, as Lady Wakasa's Chinese connections raise interesting questions concerning the validity of her ostensibly American origin.

Ugetsu's frame story features the potter Genjūrō 源十郎, who is obliged to go into town to sell his wares, leaving behind his wife Miyagi 宮木 and son Gen'ichi 源市. Tōbei 藤兵衛, a farmer who dreams of becoming a samurai, follows along, leaving behind his wife Ohajma 阿浜.[35] Although the film starts off with its male protagonists' search for fame and fortune, it gradually moves away from realistic, stark portrayals of wartime hardship (which include Miyagi's death and final return as a ghost, and Ohama's rape and subsequent descent into prostitution). It shifts instead to Lady Wakasa's enchanted world, where Genjūrō joins her in a sexual rendezvous, while in a parallel story, Tōbei lives out his martial fantasy, becoming a samurai at the ultimate expense of his wife.

Genjurō's pottery serves as an instrument of initiation and enchantment in *Ugetsu*. Here, Mizoguchi diverges from phallic symbols afforded to Xu Xian in Feng's "Madam White Is Kept Forever under Thunder Peak Tower" and to Toyō 豊雄 in Ueda's "The Lust of the Serpent": in both stories, the male character's umbrella builds the connection between the world of the human males and the world of the otherworldly beauties (White Snake/Manago). By contrast, pottery, made by adding water to clay and used in everyday life to contain, is often associated with feminine qualities rather than masculine ones.

In the pottery-making scene, which introduces the artistry at the center of the mutual attraction between Genjūrō and Lady Wakasa, directing, camerawork, and music, join together to create a magical ambience. Rhythmic music aided by emotional drum beats opens the scene; from the darkened background emerges the figure of Genjūrō, making pottery in the workshop with his wife Miyagi, who turns the wheel. Genjūrō is featured at the front of the frame in profile, facing his wife, while Miyagi is in the background, facing the camera. The spiral movement of the vessel developing in Genjūrō's hands echoes the wheel spinning in Miyagi's hand, and together they perfectly match the rhythmic beats in the accompanying music, which sounds almost like the beating hearts of the couple working together (10:50). Although the ensuing dialogue between the husband and wife presents Genjūrō as an irritable man eager for quick profits, it is clear nonetheless that he has invested his life and soul into his pottery, as Miyagi relates to Ohama when the two women are keeping the fire burning in the kiln for the final tempering of the wares. This intimate exploration of Genjūrō's craft anticipates his encounter with Lady Wakasa, who treats him as an artist of exquisite skill, and his creations as objects of love and affection.

Pottery-making here serves as a metaphor for the transformation of the mundane into the miraculous. The spiral movements of the water-dripping clay as Genjūrō creates his pottery vessels has an enchanting quality. Water becomes the magical ingredient that transforms earthly clay into heavenly pottery. The pervasiveness of such water metaphors extends from the seventeenth-century Chinese legend (the White Snake as the embodiment of the feminine *yin* 陰 has the power to control water)[36] to its eighteenth-century Japanese adaptation (water is a prevalent trope in "The Lust of the Serpent"), and manifests its significance in a series of defining moments in *Ugetsu*.

The first of such moments takes place in Lake Biwa, shrouded in a heavy mist: as the two families attempt to cross the lake in order to sell Genjūrō's pottery in a prosperous city on the other side, they encounter a ghostly lone boat on the water. A meticulously arranged soundtrack again serves as the harbinger for this intense encounter. The voice of a woman singing emerges from the darkened screen, amid the muffled sounds of water and faintly discernible drum beats, which almost seem to have lingered on from the previous pottery-making scene. The singer is Ohama, a boatman's daughter and Tōbei's wife, who sings while rowing a boat across the lake. A long shot exquisitely blends the boat with the mist that hovers around it, and a nearly one-minute long take focuses on the lake water carrying the boat, with its infinite shades of gray and patches of glimmer (23:12–24:10). The boat, carrying the pottery and hence the two families' hopes, initially approaches the rather static camera from the upper far right of the frame, with the boatwoman silhouetted against the mist, and gradually emerges from the darkness to become more and more visible. The *mise-en-scène* accentuates the seamless transition between the mysterious water and the ominously darkened sky. According to cinematographer Miyagawa, the overall effect was designed to resemble the *sumi-e* style. The lyrics to Ohama's song ("In the waters of Azuchi, a little boat floats alone"), Miyagi's words to her young son Gen'ichi ("This is the lake water. Isn't it pretty?"), and her husband Genjūrō's cheerful comment ("We are finally out of danger") all direct the viewer's attention to the enchanting power of water.

Such a lyrical and peaceful atmosphere, however, must be interrupted by a ghostly encounter in order to foreshadow the real ghosts who appear later on: the rather harmless ghosts of Lady Wakasa and her old female attendant, the ghost of Miyagi after her death, and the demonic rampaging pirates and fugitive soldiers, who are the real "ghosts" and who will inflict real pain and suffering on the two women in the boat. Again, Ohama's singing, "This world is a temporary abode," foreshadows what is to come. This sense of the transience of life is resurrected in the Sino-US coproduced 2019 animation *White Snake: The Legend Begins*, discussed in chapter 8. Here in *Ugetsu*, the camera returns to a medium shot of Ohama rowing the boat. It lingers on her gaze and facial expressions, as she gradually turns to the left and then suddenly abandons the oars in her hands in shock, while gazing intensely to the left. Her astonished gaze reaches far outside the camera frame, and her singing stops abruptly.

With increasingly intensified drum beats, the scene smoothly transitions to a lone boat at the center of the *sumi-e*-like frame. Tōbei pulls the boat close, revealing a ghostly figure crouching in the boat, which prompts Miyagi to exclaim, "The ghost of the lake!" A reverse shot displays a shadowy figure with tousled hair, his body covered by tattered clothes and grasses. He answers, "I am not a ghost," while slowly revealing his forehead, widened eyes, upright nose, and muttering mouth. Shot from a relatively high angle, with full lighting and a close-up view of the facial expressions of the ghost-like man, this scene may very well be the film's most chilling. It alone could qualify *Ugetsu* as a horror film.

Significantly, the haunting figure has a message to deliver before he dies: "Watch out for pirates! Watch out for your women!" The message is clear: these are the real ghosts that should be feared in the chaos of war. The encounter prompts the two families to turn their boat back to shore, letting Miyagi and Gen'ichi off in the relative safety of their home, while the two men and Ohama continue their boat journey.[37]

This lake scene has become one of the most famous examples of Mizoguchi's visual mastery. Later, when a lady in white and her old companion emerge from the crowded marketplace to buy pottery from Genjūrō, the audience has been psychologically prepared. The veiled sedge hat with muslin side veils worn by the lady in white when she first appears in the marketplace has been dubbed a Mizoguchi "signature look,"[38] creating an exquisite, shadowy presence that evokes a bygone age and makes for a truly outlandish sight among the crowds. Thus, the persona that some commentators have interpreted as an Americanized femme fatale also exhibits traces of traditional influence, emphasized by her heavily made-up, Noh mask–like face. The camera first lingers on Genjūrō's shocked facial expression as he hands the pottery over to the lady in white, then in a quick reverse shot reveals her peculiar facial features. When the women reappear to lead Genjūrō to their manor for delivery of their purchase, a close-up shot reveals the lady in white's mysterious smile, her hat now removed. As the travelers pass through a deserted field of tall weeds, their shadows project onto a wall, accentuating the ghostly ambience. The old woman finally introduces the enigmatic young woman as Lady Wakasa, daughter of the late Lord Katsuki (40:00). As they enter the manor, Miyagawa's lyrical tracking shots display the beauty of the courtyard, the pine trees, the wooden corridors and window frames, and the paper doors; they are laden with elements representing what was perceived as quintessentially Japanese in the postwar and post-Occupation period.

The aesthetics of light and shadow appear on full display with a long shot, taken from the direction of the courtyard, that peeks through open doors. In a long take, this enchanting scene shows two maids lighting candles inside the rooms, which change from dark to lit, one after another, as if by magic (fig. 26). This sets the perfect stage for Lady Wakasa's reappearance (fig. 27). Her shadow emerges first, followed by her breathtaking, mysterious smiles, which are highlighted by her Noh-style theatrical makeup with its smudge-like "pulled eyebrows" (*hikimayu* 引眉). She approaches Genjūrō and takes his hand, completely naturally and without any hesitation, leading him to a seat while patting his back. She starts to converse with him by expressing admiration for his ceramic creations: "The blue glaze gleams like crystal," a shocking reminder to the audience that the film is indeed a monochrome representation of a world in color (43:53–43:59). Strikingly, at least for Genjūrō, the pottery he had made to earn a living takes on a new life as beloved objects in the enchanted house of Lady Wakasa. As if speaking about himself and completely humanizing the nonhuman objects, Genjūrō laments, "My wares must be at a loss to find themselves in such a noble manor" (46:37–46:41).

Faithfully following the plot as it appears in many previous versions of the White Snake legend, the old woman (who proves to be Wakasa's nurse and corresponds to the sister/maid figure in earlier versions of the legend) proposes marriage on behalf of Lady Wakasa. Suddenly, as if having received a cue, Wakasa pushes Genjūrō down in an apparent burst of desire, and the

Figure 26: The changing light and shadow in a scene from *Ugetsu* (*Ugetsu monogatari*), directed by Mizoguchi Kenji. Tokyo: Daiei, 1953. Digitally restored by the Film Foundation and Kadokawa Corporation. New York: Janus Films, 2017, 42:28. Screenshot by author.

two fall to the floor in a tight embrace. She then abruptly retreats, leaving him completely spellbound, in an almost paralyzed state, enchanted by her charm. The music rises, accompanying a location shot from the courtyard, peeking into the well-lit room through the opened window, foreshadowing Wakasa's at once famously reserved and wildly enchanting dance (48:27). Again, everything that epitomizes Japan's refined aesthetic traditions appears in full force during this sequence: costume, music, gesture, and song, all unfold in the style of a highly cultivated Noh performance.[39]

The water symbolism and the centrality of the femme fatale motif return in vivid shades the morning after Lady Wakasa and Genjūrō's wedding night. Wakasa leads Genjūrō to bathe in the hot spring; gazing at his naked body, she asks, "You think I am an enchantress, don't you?" After declaring that Genjūrō is hers and that he must devote his whole life to her, Wakasa undresses herself and joins him in the spring. Only her laughter can be heard

Figure 27: Lady Wakasa emerges from the shadows upon Genjūrō's entering her mansion in *Ugetsu*. Janus Films, 2017, 43:02. Screenshot by author.

as the camera pans away from the couple to linger on the pebbles under the running water, leaving the audience to imagine the flow of sexual energy off-screen. A beautiful panning shot smoothly transitions from the spring water and the bathing scene to a romantic spring field, where Genjūrō and Lady Wakasa are picnicking at the base of a tree in the manner of a modern romantic couple (fig. 28). Here we encounter Mizoguchi's signature "one scene, one take" treatment, where he uses long takes to first foster the full ambience of a scene, then seamlessly transitions to a new scene, creating the sensation that the camera is floating fluidly from one scene to another, stitching together the spatial realities both recently left behind and soon to come.[40] A female voice-over sings, "Love has driven me mad," as if speaking on behalf of Genjūrō.

A long take gently presents the couple's love game of chasing each other, fostering an erotic and blissful ambience.[41] Such an intensely felt ecstasy

Figure 28: Lady Wakasa entertaining Genjūrō with music and singing in *Ugetsu*. Image: http://www.janusfilms.com/films/1064, accessed June 12, 2020.

prompts Genjūrō to confess, "Even if you are a ghost or enchantress, I'll never let you go. I never imagined such pleasure existed. This is exquisite. It's paradise!" (56:30). In the meantime, in one of the most celebrated scenes of Mizoguchi's oeuvre, Genjūrō's wife Miyagi is forced to witness a rape and is herself speared by rampaging soldiers.[42] Here, Mizoguchi's "one scene, one take" functions differently. Rather than providing a seamless transition, it intensifies the contrast between the husband, who is now fully intoxicated with sexual pleasure, and the wife he has left behind, who suffers the atrocities of war.

A spellbound Genjūrō goes to town to buy kimonos and jewels for Wakasa and is noticed by a Buddhist priest, modeled on the Fahai figure. After declaring, "This love of yours is forbidden" (1:12:30), the priest inscribes Sanskrit characters as prayers to Buddha on his body, which function as talismans to exorcise ghosts (1:16:40). After finally managing to get away from Lady Wakasa and her nurse, Genjūrō wakes up in the wild field where the manor used to stand, and the sword given to him by Wakasa turns out to be a stolen treasure from the nearby temple (1:20:20). When he eventually returns home, Miyagi greets him and offers him warm sake and food, while their son sleeps soundly nearby. The next morning, Genjūrō discovers that Miyagi had been, in fact, killed by soldiers; it was her ghost that welcomed him the night before.

Ugetsu both consolidated the existing Japanese tradition concerning the

White Snake legend and engendered a new tradition that flourished throughout the mid-1950s and onwards. Mizoguchi's ingenious blending of the fantastic and the real and his paradoxical representation of sexual encounters as both ultimate pleasure and ultimate suffering were brought into full play in *Ugetsu*. As the seventy-eighth film by a veteran of Japanese film industry active since the 1920s and one of the last before his death in 1956, *Ugetsu* also registered Mizoguchi's reinvention of the modernist femme fatale from the early twentieth century to the postwar moment, as well as his consistent concern with the sacrifices of women amid war and revolution. His sympathetic identification with his female protagonists, be they human or ghost, shines through the light and shadows and lingers on.

Around the same time, Daiei Film (Daiei eiga 大映映画), the production company behind Kurosawa's *Rashomon* and Mizoguchi's *Ugetsu,* among other representative films of the Golden Age of Japanese cinema, took the lead in building an infrastructure for inter-Asian joint productions. The Federation of Motion Picture Producer's Association of Asia (FPA) was established in November 1953 by Nagata Masaichi 永田雅一, president of Daiei at the time, who toured Southeast Asia and met with film executives in the region.[43] Mizoguchi's 1955 film *Princess Yang Kwei-fei* (*Yōkihi* 楊貴妃, aka *The Consort Yang Guifei*) was coproduced by Daiei Film and Hong Kong's Shaw & Sons, with the latter contributing 30 percent of the production cost and taking charge of the film's Asian distribution. Evolved from the Unique Film Company in Shanghai, Shaw & Sons was the predecessor of Shaw Brothers Studio, an important player in coproducing and distributing White Snake films from the mid-1950s onwards.[44]

WHITE PEARL, RED SCARF, AND "THE WITCHCRAFT OF LOVE"

Madame White Snake (*Byaku fujin no yōren* 白夫人の妖恋) is a 1956 Japanese color film directed by Toyoda Shirō and produced by Tanaka Tomoyuki 田中友幸 of Tōhō Co. (Tōhō kabushiki kaisha 東宝株式会社).[45] At the time, Tōhō was known for such box office hits as *Seven Samurai* and the first of the *Godzilla* films, both produced in 1954. Crediting its screenplay to the Chinese White Snake legend and Hayashi Fusao's 林房雄 1948 novel *The Witchcraft of Madame White Snake* (*Byaku fujin no yōjutsu* 白夫人の妖術),[46] Toyoda's 1956 film starred Yamaguchi Yoshiko 山口淑子, also known as Ri Kōran (Li Xianglan 李香蘭) and Shirley Yamaguchi, as the White Snake, Ikebe Ryō 池部良 as her human husband, and Yachigusa Kaoru 八千草薫, who was active in the all-female musical theater troupe Takarazuka Revue from 1947 to 1957,[47] as White Snake's companion, Green Snake. With Miura Mitsuo 三浦光雄 as cinematographer and original music by Dan Ikuma 團伊玖磨, and Tsuburaya Eiji 円谷英二 (who had won fame by his work on *Godzilla*) as director of special effects, the film was conceived with an international market in mind and eventually won an honorable mention at the Sixth Berlin International Film Festival for its use of color.

Japanese scholarship has traced Hayashi Fusao's novel, on which the film is based, to Karashima Takeshi's 辛島驍 wartime translation of Feng Menglong's "Bai niangzi yongzhen Leifengta,"[48] as attested in a 1956 book combining Hayashi's novel, Karashima's translation of the Chinese legend, and Yasumi Toshio's 八住利雄 screenplay. Including a preface by Karashima, this book served as a sort of tie-in, riding on the popularity of the new film.[49] In a previous study, I highlighted Karashima Takeshi's association with the Chinese artist Tian Han. In *New Theater of China* (*Chūgoku no shingeki* 中国の新劇), a book on contemporary Chinese theater published in Tokyo in 1948, Karashima featured Tian Han's autograph from 1928 and praised him as "monitoring the mainstream of the Chinese new theater movement today."[50] In this context, it is useful to understand Hayashi's novel, which focused on the "craft" (*jutsu* 術) of seduction, and its 1956 film adaptation, which highlighted the witchcraft of "love" (*ren* 恋), as the result of decades of Sino-Japanese cross-influences in the reinvention of the White Snake legend. Kinnia Shuk-ting Yau, in her well-researched book *Japanese and Hong Kong Film Industries*, points out the intimate connection between filmmaking in the two locations, starting in the 1930s in Shanghai, and similarly emphasizes the underlying continuities in their prewar, wartime, and postwar developments.[51]

In the early 1920s, Hayashi Fusao, the future writer of *The Witchcraft of Madame White Snake*, and Tian Han were both active in the first Japanese student radical group, the New Man Society (Shinjinkai 新人会),[52] and both were associated with the Japanese Marxist literary magazine *Literary Battlefront* (*Bungei sensen* 文芸戦線).[53] Because of his leftist activities, Hayashi was jailed twice in the early to mid-1930s. He famously shifted his political position far to the right during his incarcerations and publicly renounced his leftist political views in 1936.[54] Hayashi then reported on the "China Incident" from Shanghai in August 1937.[55] He eventually became a proponent of the Japanese imperial system, as manifest in "The Heart of Imperial Loyalty" (*Kinnō no kokoro* 勤皇の心), his contribution to the 1942 "Overcoming Modernity" symposium in Tokyo, and most notoriously in his 1963 essay, "The Great East Asian War Was a Just War" (*Dai Toa senso kotei ron* 大東亜戦争肯定論).[56] He remained an outspoken advocate of Japanese nationalism until his death in 1975.[57]

It is significant that the 1956 color film *Madame White Snake* involved not only the (in)famous "tenkō" (転向, literally, "changing direction") writer Hayashi Fusao and special effects director Tsuburaya Eiji who, like many others, had created propaganda films for the imperial government during the war, but also the legendary former Manchurian film actress Yamaguchi Yoshiko, who had starred in a number of propaganda films in support of Japanese militarism. In fact, according to an interview, Yamaguchi may very well be the person who suggested the film project in the first place.[58] Given the notoriety of Yamaguchi's films, which eulogized the Japanese presence in Manchuria, and Hayashi's reputation as an ultranationalist, how might we thoughtfully approach this postwar film in view of its prewar genealogy and possible historical impact, as well as in the context of Yamaguchi's comeback as a leading actress in a postwar Japanese–Hong Kong film coproduction?

Inspired by Daiei's recent collaboration with Shaw & Sons in Mizoguchi's 1955 *Empress Yang Kwei-fei*, Tōhō Company was also aiming at the wider Asian market and intended to use their own coproduction with Shaw Brothers Studio as an entry point. This new Japanese film intended to "rehabilitate" the White Snake from previous versions and restore her "original" charm. The producers even hoped to export the film to the PRC, according to the published transcript of a discussion involving director Toyoda Shirō after a screening of the film in July 1956.[59]

Red Scarf, Manifested Desire, and the Significance of Color

The first color film by director Toyoda Shirō, *Madame White Snake* opens with prominent shots of the three stupas on West Lake, alluding to the important Chinese retelling of the White Snake legend, "West Lake's Three Stupas." Rather than setting the story in sixteenth-century Japan, as Mizoguchi did in *Ugetsu*, this film returns the legend to its Chinese setting, identifying the period as "the Song Dynasty" and the location "West Lake." Miura Mitsuo's lyrical camera pans across the lake: the stupas and their surroundings resemble painted landscape images used in a photographer's studio, with heavy color hues. A boat enters the scene with a girl in Chinese costume entertaining guests by playing an *erhu* 二胡, a two-stringed Chinese instrument. The camera pans to introduce a lonely young man, similarly in Chinese costume, riding in a boat rowed by a boatman. The young man touches the pink water

Figure 29: Madame White Snake emerges from darkness with red scarf in hand, wiping off raindrops and gazing at Xu Xian outside the frame. In *Madame White Snake* (*Byaku fujin no yōren*), directed by Toyoda Shirō. Tokyo and Hong Kong: Tōhō and Shaw Brothers, 1956. Hong Kong: Mei Ah Laser Disc, 05:31. Screenshot by author.

lilies floating on the lake's surface, with his right hand stretching into the water. The towering stupa is still in view in the background (3:36–3:45).

Smoke-like black clouds suddenly appear in the sky, and the camera cuts to raindrops hitting the lake, with the massive stupa still in the background. Off-screen, a voice calls, "Boatman, boatman!" The interruption leads the camera and the viewers to a young girl in blue under a willow tree by the lakeshore. The camera pans again to her left to reveal the figure of a young lady, dressed in pinkish white, her face hidden behind willow branches. After the two young women come on board, the viewer witnesses the first appearance of a red silk scarf, serving as a functional prop when the lady in white starts to use it to wipe away raindrops (fig. 29). She sits in the middle of the narrow boat, with her back toward the young man and facing the girl in blue,[60] who appears to be her maid. The lighting in the boat suddenly turns dark, suggesting the sensation of movement: the boat must have gone under a bridge.

Prompted by the young man's words in response to the girl in blue, the lady in white turns to face the young man and the camera. Right at this moment, lighting returns to highlight her exquisite beauty for the young man's and the viewer's gaze. The red scarf in her hands, as if on cue and by magic, suddenly flies toward the young man, covering his face with its sumptuous color (5:35). This opening scene ends with a colorful rainbow above the lake (6:36), as if to celebrate the two lovers' meeting and likely to echo the creator deities Izanagi and Izanami from Japanese folklore, who famously cross a rainbow bridge together.[61]

This opening scene metaphorically presents an extravagantly colorful horizontal "scroll" and sets the stage for the protagonists' initial dramatic encounter. Unlike *Ugetsu*'s dual focus on wartime realities and Lady Wakasa's world of romantic enchantment, *Madame White Snake* immediately introduces its protagonists through a chance encounter, resulting in their "love at first sight," or mutual enchantment. *Madame White Snake* is the only Japanese "White Snake" film to incorporate this initial encounter, endowed with a romantic sensibility. It mimics the style of the modernist Tian Han's adaptations in the 1920s and 1950s in mainland China, and both aim to rid the legend of the "superstitious" concepts of fate and reincarnation.[62] In fact, for this 1956 rendition, director Toyoda claimed that Madame White Snake "harbors the heart of a modern woman who would continue loving the young man she chose till the end of her life."[63] This strong woman versus weak man structure not only continues throughout Toyoda's film record but also echoes postwar democratizing rhetoric on women's liberation, which manifested as images of proactive women in postwar Japanese filmmaking and were intriguingly similar to Communist China's rhetoric of state feminism, epitomized in the slogan "Women can hold up half the sky."[64]

However, according to latter-day Hong Kong commentators, the image of the strong snake woman in Toyoda's film, as compared to Mainland Chinese and Hong Kong versions, remains unique: it is characteristically more daring, and by eliminating the son as a character, it concentrates fully on Madame White Snake's relentless pursuit of love and her sexual relationship with her human lover. Moreover, Yamaguchi's Madame White Snake, compared to other performances by Chinese actresses, contains distinctively sinister elements. The Hong Kong commentators reasoned that because Chinese audiences hardly appreciate such disturbing qualities, the image of the White Snake was gradually beautified and moralized in the Chinese versions.[65] All of this makes Yamaguchi's White Snake a more complexly tragic figure than Chinese representations.

When Xu Xian goes to fetch his umbrella the day after his chance encounter with the snake women, he is greeted at the gate by Little Green, here serving as the White Snake's maid. Together with Little Green, he enters the White Snake's exquisite, colorful residence, its interior design full of visual elements, including the red furnishings and intricately carved wooden window frames, that suggest its Chinese qualities. Madame White gives him a tour of the peony garden and confesses her love to him by the lotus pond, holding a pearl in her hand. Dropping the pearl into the pond as she speaks, she declares, "I would like to keep it [the pearl] at the bottom of the pond until you accept it [my love]" (14:00). The same white pearl returns at the end of the film when Xu affectionately holds it in his hand, symbolizing the fulfillment of their circle of love.[66] Knowing his financial difficulties, Madame White gives Xu silver so he can prepare for their wedding. At the moment the issue of money is resolved, the red scarf reappears, luring Xu into intimate contact with White in her chamber. Xu takes the money back home and presents it to his sister and brother-in-law for their approval. The red scarf duly reappears: Xu covers his face with it while lying on his bed, imagining blissful future encounters with White, as if triggered by a desire embedded in the red scarf (21:30). The scarf, indeed, becomes a token of Madame White's witchcraft of love.

When Xiaoqing (Little Green) rushes in to report Xu's arrest and suggests they desert him and run away,[67] Madame White slaps her in the face, thereby affirming her distinct qualities as a nonhuman enchantress who is nonetheless infatuated with and devoted to her object of desire (22:15). A location shot introduces Suzhou, where Xu has been exiled (26:40), and shows the two beauties in their full Chinese costumes following him to the inn where he is staying. Very much in the style of the flirtatious question Lady Wakasa directs at the naked Genjūrō in the hot spring in *Ugetsu*, here Xiaoqing serves the function of self-interrogation and self-defense: "Do you think we are monsters? She's human just like you. Look! She casts a shadow. If she's a monster, why did she follow you to Suzhou?" (30:50). Echoing Genjūrō's confession scene, here the red scarf hidden in Xu's clothes magically reappears (thanks to Tsuburaya Eiji and his special effects team) to reveal his desire, as pointed out by Xiaoqing: "The scarf in your hand betrays your true feelings" (31:15). Soon after, in an erotic bedroom scene that is one of the most explicitly sensual portrayals of sexual encounters in the whole White Snake visual repertoire,[68] the red scarf reappears to heighten the intense desire that permeates the scene's erotic ambience (36:35–37:20). The reciprocal kissing, caressing, embracing, and suggested intercourse all recall Lady Wakasa and Genjūrō's "love game" in the meadow and in the hot spring in *Ugetsu*.

Special Effects and Technologies of the "Witchcraft of Love"

The official biography of Tsuburaya Eiji, "master of the monsters" and director of special effects for *Madame White Snake*, describes the film as "filled with ambitious processes and optical effects, fanciful miniature sets, and a mighty deluge, conjured up in the film's dramatic finale."[69] Indeed, the film's all-out fantasy provided fertile ground for Tsuburaya's experiments. Trained as a cameraman, Tsuburaya had been the assistant cameraman for Kinugasa Teinosuke's 衣笠貞之助 groundbreaking 1925 film, *A Page of Madness* (*Kurutta ippēji* 狂った一頁). He joined Shōchiku 松竹 Kyoto Studios in 1926 and began to develop innovative filming techniques, including the first use of a camera crane in Japanese filmmaking. He openly acknowledged the role played by the 1933 film *King Kong* in inspiring his later work as a creator of "monster movies."[70] In fact, when *King Kong* opened in Shanghai, it inspired journalists and advertisers to compare the film's use of special effects with stage performances of the White Snake legend, especially the scenes in which White Snake fights the Deer God and the Crane God to steal the magic herb to cure her human husband, as discussed in chapter 2.[71]

Tsuburaya became head of the Special Arts Department (later known as the Visual Effects Department) at Tōhō Tokyo Studio in the late 1930s and returned to Tōhō in the early 1950s after a wartime interval of working on a series of propaganda films created at the order of the imperial government.[72] When Tsuburaya served as director of special effects for *Madame White Snake*, he had recently done the special effects for the first two *Godzilla* films (1954 and 1955) and had just finished working on the heavily reedited *Godzilla, King of the Monsters!* (1956) for its United States release. Several scenes central to the 1956 White Snake film demonstrate Tsuburaya's ambitious creation of miniatures sets and optical effects. Most notably, his work on the film was credited as the first use of the "blue-back" ブルーバック, or blue-screen system in the history of Japanese filmmaking. This practice, which has also came to be known as the green-screen system, uses a blue or green screen to separate the object being shot from its background so as to enable the postproduction recomposition of the scene and insertion of special effects.[73] Such uses of the "blue-screen" are visible in an elaborate fight sequence that pits Madame White against a Daoist who intervenes in her relationship with her lover (1:01:53–1:03:05; fig. 30).

This "blue-screen" technology, a leading feature of Japanese filmmaking at the time, enabled the display of Madame White's "witchcraft" in her fight with the Daoist who intends to overpower and exorcise her. In the blink of

Figure 30: The Daoist's fight with Madame White in *Madame White Snake* (dir. Toyoda, 1956). Through the use of special effects, the Daoist is at first visible (left, 1:02:14), then disappears (middle, 1:02:15), and then reappears as a tiny figure about to be hung from the Thunder Peak Pagoda (right, 1:02:16 min).
Screenshots available here: https://movie.douban.com/subject/1302094/photos?type=S, accessed June 22, 2020.

an eye (1:02:14–1:02:15), her opponent is blown away and disappears from the frame, attesting to her superb power over the Daoist. Such a visual effect in the live action sequences between Madame White and the Daoist could be achieved only with the use of the blue-screen with meticulously created miniature sets that create the optical illusion of the Daoist's disappearance. Similarly, both Little Green's and Madame White's on-screen transformations from their human form to their original snake form were made possible by other special effects techniques, including the use of superimposition, first used in Japanese filmmaking by Tsuburaya in 1930, in addition to the manipulation of the blue-screen and the miniature sets.

When Madame White risks her own life in search of the magic herb to revive her husband after he has been frightened to death by her appearance in snake form, she is questioned by the Dragon King: "You stole a young man's heart, took human form, and performed witchcraft" (1:16:00). This is the moment of truth for Madame White Snake—and the ingenuity of the 1956 Japanese film. She responds: "I am just a woman who loves a man. The witchcraft I used was just to show my love for him. Even a foolish girl knows this witchcraft. It's the witchcraft of love" (1:18:00). Had the film been shot in black and white and without special effects, the red scarf would have lost much of its symbolic power of representing such a "witchcraft of love."

In the film's final sequence, the magic power of the red scarf, which appears here in its longest form and its most prominent manifestation, is on full display (1:40:55–1:42:40). This is the moment of reincarnation, when Xu Xian follows Madame White to the afterlife, where both are resurrected as spirits. With the aid of special effects, they appear as translucent figures ascending to Heaven, leaving behind their physical existence on Earth (fig. 31). A melodic female singing voice envelop every gesture of their flying, and the red scarf marvelously reemerges from Madame White's body, stretching out long in the wind, connecting her body with Xu Xian's, and aiding their mutual ascendance, as if by magic.

Madame White Snake was Japan's response to a booming late-1950s Hong Kong film industry, which in turn can be read as a response to the popularity of Mainland "opera films" from the mid-1950s.[74] In pursuit of both investors and markets, Japanese filmmakers and producers looked to Hong Kong as a financial partner and distribution center for the revival of Japanese cultural influence in general and its film industry in particular at the crucial moment when Japanese culture was being remade in the immediate years after the Occupation.

Figure 31: Madame White Snake and Xu Xian ascending to Heaven in the final sequence of *Madame White Snake* (dir. Toyoda, 1956). A long red scarf prominently binds them together and possibly aids their flight (left, 1:41:49; middle, 1:42:13; right, 1:42:17). Screenshots available here: https://movie.douban.com/subject/1302094/photos?type=S, accessed June 22, 2020.

From Hong Kong to Southeast Asia

Hong Kong's English-language newspaper *South China Morning Post*, which had written about the Cantonese opera actress Li Sut-fong's White Snake performances in 1950, reported multiple times in June and July 1956 on *Madame White Snake* in connection with the Japanese film's honorable mention award at the Sixth Berlin International Film Festival. One report praised the enchanting atmosphere of gardens and landscapes (though they were mostly studio shots), the high-caliber acting, and the film's advanced use of color—the reason for its honorable mention at the festival. The articles further highlighted the film's magnificent scenes of "magical happenings" (special effects).[75]

Shaw Brothers Studio's investment in the film was a good incentive for its multilingual promotional and distribution efforts in Hong Kong and throughout Southeast Asia. One Chinese-language poster for Shaw Brothers' Lido Theatre opening of the film (fig. 32) in Ipoh, Perak, Malaysia, on March 21, 1957, labels the dubbed version of the film "a legendary love story in a matchlessly grand Mandarin-language production, rich in luxurious colors, majestic splendor, amorous contents, and gods and spirits" (*haohua qicai fuli tanghuang xiangyan shenguai lian'ai chuanqi guoyu kuangshi weizhi* 豪華七彩富麗堂皇香艷神怪戀愛傳奇國語曠世偉制),"[76] intriguingly echoing languages used in early twentieth-century *Shenbao* advertisements for White Snake stage performances. At the center of the poster is the title, *Baishe zhuan*, in three beautifully calligraphed Chinese characters, and to the right is Yamaguchi Yoshiko's disembodied head, showcasing her beautifully made-up face and the Chinese-style arrangement of her hair. Her meticulously outlined eyes, eyebrows, and lips, in particular, are designed to attract the attention of even a casual observer. Framing the upper edge of the poster are the White Snake and the Green Snake as two beautiful women, using magic to control the flood that appears in their final battle with Abbot Fahai. The Chinese descriptions in the middle of the poster boast of the film's technical achievements. Meanwhile, the scenes of grandeur are described as piled up with gold and jade, an intentional reference to the high production cost of the film.

Another Chinese-language poster published by S. P. W. Ltd. Singapore (fig. 32),[77] likely created as a set with the previous poster, listed Shaw Brothers as owning the film's screening rights. Intricate designs resembling snake shapes frame the poster itself; and an exaggeratedly large image of the Green Snake appears in the upper right, the White Snake and her human lover embrace each other in the lower left, and the Shaw Brothers Studio logo is prominently displayed in the lower right. The Chinese and English titles frame the

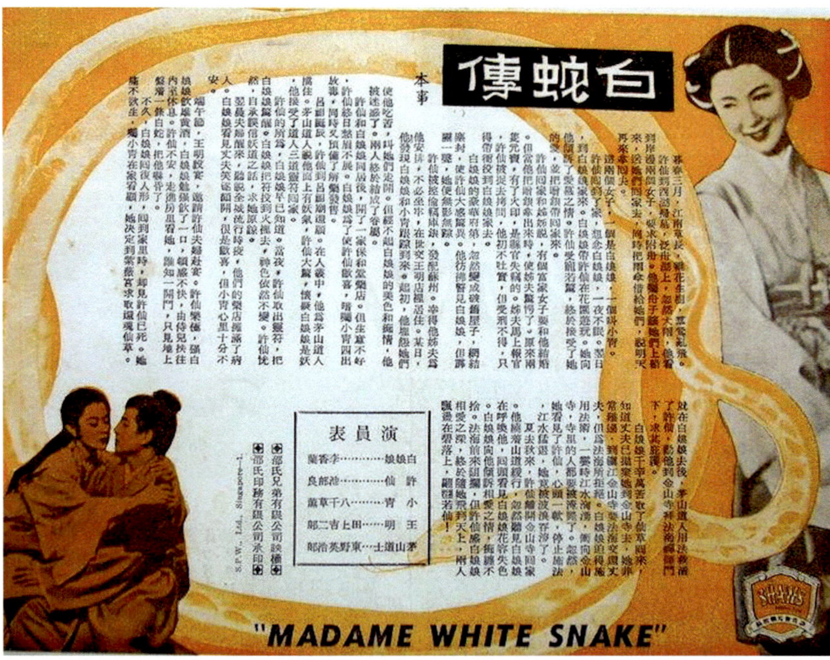

Figure 32: (top) Chinese-language poster used for the premiere of *Madame White Snake* (dir. Toyoda, 1956) at the Lido Theatre, Ipoh, Perak, Malaysia, on March 21, 1957; (bottom) Chinese-language poster published by S. P. W. Ltd. Singapore, listing Shaw Brothers as having the screening rights of the 1956 *Madame White Snake*. The posters are likely a set and are available at https://movie.douban.com/subject/1302094/photos?type=R, accessed June 13, 2020.

upper and lower middle of the poster, and a framed list of the Japanese cast is printed above the English title. A detailed synopsis is also given.

An existent full-color Thai-language poster also attests to the 1956 film's reach beyond the Sinophone Southeast Asia. This poster features colorful drawings of the White Snake and Xu Xian at its center and the flooded Golden Mountain Monastery in the background,[78] as well as the two protagonists flying together to Heaven with the White Snake's red silk scarf disproportionally highlighted. Except for the three Chinese characters for *Baishe zhuan* in red, all descriptions are in Thai. In addition, more than ten years after the 1956 film's initial run in Hong Kong, the *South China Morning Post* again reported in March 1970 an opening of "The Legend of the White Snake, A Tōhō Production," in the Oriental, a landmark local theater. The profound impact of the 1956 Japanese White Snake film lingers on much longer in Hong Kong and throughout Southeast Asia, as shown in its multilocational and multilingual commercial posters and advertisements.

This episode of a postwar Japan–Hong Kong coproduction complicates our understanding of the Japanese and Hong Kong film industries in the postwar period in a number of important ways. Hong Kong's unique geopolitical position in Cold War Asia, as part of the British colonial empire yet closely connected to Mainland China, created its privileged status as a commercial and cultural powerhouse. Hong Kong was an important commercial partner and a key cultural consultant to Japan as it reinvented its film industry after the war; it also reaffirmed Japan's nation-building process at the crucial postwar moment vis-à-vis China, the United States, and its former colonies in Asia. At the same time, Japanese special effects technologies and use of color enriched its Hong Kong partner's technical expertise and provided important inspirations for the development of postwar Hong Kong cinema and its future collaborations with Taiwan, South Korea, and other regional cinema centers.

FLOWERS, ANIMALS, AND HUMANS

Lady White (Bai-Niang, or Pai Niang 白娘; fig. 33) is the title character of the 1958 film *The Tale of the White Serpent* (*Hakujaden*), often touted as Asia's first full-length color animation,[79] whose appearance is intriguingly reminiscent of the image of Yamaguchi Yoshiko's White Snake in *Madame White Snake* (fig. 33). The flowers decorating their characteristically Chinese hairstyles, their dark eyebrows and eyelashes, the profile, smile, earrings, and even clothing style, all suggest an intriguing resemblance between these two versions of the

Figure 33: (left) Madame White Snake in *Madame White Snake* (dir. Toyoda, 1956). Hong Kong: Mei Ah Laser Disc, 1:08:06. Screenshot by author. (right) Lady White (Bai-Niang) in *Hakujaden* (*The tale of the White Serpent*), directed by Yabushita Taiji. Tokyo: Tōei Animation, 1958, 07:15. Screenshot by author.

Chinese White Snake—one filmed in live action, the other animated, both created in postwar Japan and only two years apart.

One of the first mature examples of Japanese animation, *Hakujaden* received an award at the 1959 Venice Children's Film Festival, a year after its release. It was distributed in the United States in 1961 as *Panda and the Magic Serpent*, with the Chinese American actress Lisa Lu (Lu Yan) as the English voice actor for Bai-Niang (White Snake), and the Japanese American actress Miiko Taka as Xiaoqing (Green Fish). Regarded by some commentators as a "bootleg" copy of the Japanese original, the United States release was subjected to "shoddy redubbing," with only the Japanese songs left intact and with one animal character, a duck, sounding exactly like Disney's Donald Duck. "Panda" in the title of the US release refers to one of the two sidekicks of Hsu Hsien (Xu Xian), the White Snake's lover (fig. 34). The other is Mimi, a red panda mistaken for a cat in the US release.[80]

With an eye on the global market, the Japanese film industry continued to explore new media venues for representing both the White Snake and the postwar Japanese desire for reconciliation with the wider world and for cultural rejuvenation. Made through the newly founded Tōei Animation (*Tōei animēshon* 東映アニメーション) company in Tokyo, *Hakujaden* aimed to represent the White Snake as a beautiful enchantress, in a full-color, feature-length animation. The film was expected to be distributed widely in the United States and Europe, popularizing its delicate balancing act initiated by

Figure 34: Panda and Mimi, Hsu Hsien's (Xu Xian) loyal friends in *Hakujaden* (dir. Yabushita, 1958), 9:22. Screenshot by author. This animated film was imported from Japan to the United States and released as *Panda and the Magic Serpent* with English dubbing in 1961.

the Japanese with neighboring Asian countries and regions, and the U.S. and Europe, at the height of the Cold War.

The high-tech color-animation features went hand in hand with the film's political relevance and its market viability. Packaged as a film for children and family, *Hakujaden* combined avant-gardism with comic appeal. The pedagogical and the commercial came together to usher in a new era of Japanese animation, represented by such figures as the leading contemporary animator Miyazaki Hayao, who is famed for being inspired by the White Snake animation, as discussed in chapter 1.[81] Susan Napier underscores Miyazaki's uses of enchantment, seen especially in "his richly realized fantasy worlds and his memorable female characters."[82] Ian Condry lists Nausicaä, Satsuki and Mei, Kiki, San of Princess Mononoke, Sen/Chihiro, and others as examples for such memorable characters, to which I would also add Ponyo the fish girl, among others. Each of them bearing traces of the 1958 White Snake animation's substantial impact.

In any history involving the Cold War context, the United States is always a significant presence between Japan and China, and this is especially the case in animation history. Tōei Animation was deeply influenced by Disney. The film's technical innovations, including the use of multiplane cameras, rotoscoping, squash-and-stretch, the use of color, and even the genre of the musical, were largely borrowed from Disney. These techniques had been used in the 1937 Disney feature film *Snow White and the Seven Dwarfs*, which Tōei Animation studied extensively and used as a model. The Fordist assembly-line structure of cell animation production in Tōei Animation also resembled Disney to a large extent. Most historical documents indicate that Tōei Animation chose to recreate a Chinese legend and to collaborate with Shaw Brothers in Hong Kong because of market concerns. They hoped that this popular Chinese legend would help the film reach wider audiences in the Chinese-speaking worlds and beyond. This market-driven approach also became a key reason that Japanese film companies, whether live-action or animation-based, joined coproduction efforts with Taiwan and South Korea, in addition to Hong Kong, for many more postwar films. This wider context of postwar inter-Asian coproduction is likely the most important factor in understanding the 1958 White Snake animation in the context of the mutual attraction between Tōei Animation and things Chinese.[83]

From Live Action to Animation

Tsuburaya Eiji's use of superimposition, "blue-screen," miniature sets, and other ambitious processes to produce special effects in the 1956 live-action *Madame White Snake* had reinvigorated the White Snake film repertoire. Only two years later, Tōei Animation's *Hakujaden* was touted as the first full-length color animation in Japan. Ōkawa Hiroshi 大川博 had founded the animation company in 1956 with the express purpose of creating animated films to rival those of Disney and with an eye to exporting Japanese culture to the world. As there were few experienced animators among the many staff members hired for the newly created animation studio, the production team resorted to rotoscoping, common in Disney's animation, in which sequences were filmed with actors and then a selection of stills from the developed film served as the basis for the drawings. Tōei Animation relied extensively on this technique, linking live action with early animation.[84] Although the 1956 live-action film *Madame White Snake* was never mentioned explicitly as a direct influence, the creators of the 1958 animation must have been keenly aware of such a recent precedent, particularly since Shaw Brothers had collaborated on both (although collaboration for the second ultimately fell through).

Given this connection with Shaw Brothers, *Madame White Snake* may have served as an alternative live-action version on which the animators could base their drawings. With this in mind, it is fascinating to consider the distinctive and differing qualities between the animation of the humans and that of the animals in *Hakujaden*, especially the cute little panda, which was highlighted in the title for its American release. According to Thomas Lamarre, because the 1958 film was produced before the craze that brought so many of the animals from China into zoos around the world, the panda was quite a rarity in Japan at the time. It took over a year for the filmmakers to get their hands on even a photograph of a panda to serve as a model for the animator. There was no way to attempt anything close to rotoscoping a panda. As a result, the panda's energy, and that of many other prominently featured animals (all of which were extras created for the 1958 animation and absent in earlier versions) is notably different from that of the human characters with their live action–inspired movements. Whereas the human characters merge effortlessly into the landscape, with their beautifully detailed clothes, idealized expressions, and gestures reminiscent of live-action cinema, the animals bounce, roll, stretch, and bend. The animals also feel closer in style and movement to the kind of animated expression globalized through Disney—the so-called squash-and-stretch technique.[85]

Hakujaden's opening scenes consistently echo the "special effects" found in the live-action film from two years before. Under Xu Xian's gaze, Bai-Niang's disappearance through the use of magic (9:36–9:37; fig. 35) reminds the viewer of her live-action counterpart's magical defeat of the Daoist in the 1956 film, in which the White Snake blows her adversary right out of the frame. Remarkably, in the 1958 animation, Bai-Niang's spirit travels through a seemingly infinite space, presented realistically and in the style of science fiction, as she flies through the air to reach the red star where the Dragon King lives (59:06–59:39; fig. 36). This is a notable departure from the "superstitious" Chinese versions, which feature a journey heavenwards to see the Jade Emperor or down into the underworld to see the King of Hell.

Bai-Niang's flight through space instantly brings to mind the typical flight gestures adopted by the nuclear-powered and peace-loving hero of the TV animation *Tetsuwan Atomu* 鉄腕アトム, known as *Astro Boy* in the United States, which was created with "limited animation" in 1963 (fig. 36). Daisy Yan Du points out the influence of the Monkey King from the 1941 Chinese animation *Princess Iron Fan* (*Tieshan gongzhu* 鐵扇公主) on Astro Boy, in addition to its connections to Pinocchio, Mickey Mouse, Mighty Mouse, and Superman.[86] Astro Boy first appeared in 1951, when Tezuka Osamu 手塚治虫 published a short manga series featuring the character; but the animated version with Astro Boy's iconic flying pose was not created until

Figure 35: Bai-Niang appears and disappears in *Hakujaden* (dir. Yabushita, 1958). Left: Bai-Niang found, 9:36. Right: Bai-Niang disappears, 9:37. Both screenshots by author.

Figure 36: (top) Bai-Niang flies through outer space, 59:17; (bottom) Bai-Niang's flying gesture, which was a likely predecessor for Astro Boy, 59:38. Screenshots by author. Both in *Hakujaden* (dir. Yabushita, 1958).

1963. Consequently, the image of Bai-Niang flying in space can be added to the long list of influences on the flying Astro Boy. Although Bai-Niang's flight through space in the 1958 animation may well have served as timely inspiration for Astro Boy's iconic pose, the latter emerged as such a masterpiece of postwar Japanese anime that it largely overshadowed the Bai-Niang character in the history of animation. Most importantly, the central theme of the humanity of the nonhuman connects Monkey King, Bai-Niang, and Astro Boy in their shared desire to become human and to experience human emotions.[87]

Often considered a model for "full animation" in contrast to the later "limited animation" represented by *Astro Boy*, the animated *Hakujaden* nonetheless exhibits many of the distinguishing features of "limited animation," including an enhanced focus on story and feeling, rather than on movement. Paul Roquet discusses what he calls the "cosmic subjectivity" of Japanese anime of the 1980s, regarding it as representing a new "religion boom" focused on a search for new forms of "authentic" sensation beyond social or historical frameworks.[88] He connects such cosmic subjectivity to the popular "new academicism" bestsellers of the mid-1980s in Japan, which sought to rethink human existence through emergent perspectives drawn from various disciplines, including poststructuralism, postmodernism, ecology, and cybernetics.[89] Foreshadowing such a cosmic subjectivity more than two decades earlier, Bai-Niang's spirit must fly through the realistically depicted infinite cosmos to reach her destination, where she will give up her identity as a "spirit" and her magic powers in order to be able to love like a real human (1:00:42–1:02:00).[90] Here, the enchanted white flower, replacing the red scarf, serves as a purer, more child-friendly symbol of love (rather than lust) as well as "the flower of life," that is, a magic cure to bring back her dead lover.

The abundant use of animal sidekicks recalls the numerous animal drawings on the cigarette cards based on the 1926 silent film series *The Righteous Snake* and serves as a prominent reminder that the White Snake films consistently used the nonhuman to represent a deeper level of humanity. Rather than depicting specific humans acting against an impersonal backdrop, the use of animal characters points to the "cosmic interpenetration of subject and environment in their very design."[91] Aimed at children and families, the 1958 Japanese White Snake animation, with the addition of its animal sidekicks and with its plot twists and prominent Japanese elements, departs further from the Chinese legend than any previous version, which is likely part of the reason why collaboration with Hong Kong finally fell through. For example, the giant catfish, which has long symbolized earthquakes in Japanese folk belief and evoked the fear of both earthquakes and often-consequent flood, is enlisted here to create a huge storm. The image of a rainbow, already seen in the opening of the 1956 live-action film, appears in the ending scene of the 1958 animation, creating a magical aura again because of the association with the rainbow bridge in Japan's creation myth. However, the most remarkable, or from the perspective of most of the Chinese-speaking audience, the most shocking change lies in the ending, when the Buddhist abbot becomes a benevolent figure who sends Bai-Niang and her human lover off on a boat to live happily ever after. The "Disney of the East" indeed delivered a magical happy ending for all.

"Disney of the East" and Connections between China and Japan

According to its published history, Tōei Animation's founding announcement looked forward to the possibility of overcoming the "international inaccessibility" of Japanese-language entertainment by using drawings and movements that could be readily grasped internationally.[92] The issue at stake here was international representation and marketing in the postwar period for Japanese cultural industry. In hiring animator Ōtsuka Yasuo 大塚康生, Tōei Animation aimed to create feature films that could potentially be exported throughout the world, not only to the United States. The animated film *Hakujaden,* as the company's first release in 1958, is thus based on a Chinese legend and coproduced with Hong Kong. It was intended for export to other Asian regions, and via Hong Kong, it was sold to and screened in Taiwan, Singapore, Malaysia, Thailand, and the United States and Brazil, among other locations.[93]

In this postwar moment, Tōei Animation was but one company in an animation industry that was reaching far beyond Japan's national borders to aim at regional and transnational coproduction and marketing. In this context, it is illuminating to excavate the history of mutual influence between the Chinese and Japanese animation industries both before World War II and after. Daisy Yan Du's meticulous study has revealed the far-reaching influence of *Princess Iron Fan* in Japanese animation. As Du explains, when the Chinese Wan Brothers' *Princess Iron Fan* was swiftly exported to wartime Japan in 1942, it inspired the sixteen-year-old Tezuka Osamu, creator of *Astro Boy,* to become a comics artist and prompted the Japanese navy to commission Japan's own first feature-length animated film, the 1945 *Momotaro's Divine Sea Warriors* (*Momotarō: umi no shinpei* 桃太郎: 海の神兵).[94] Given these long-obscure historical circumstances and keeping in mind the predominant impact of Disney and Hollywood on postwar Japanese culture, a more nuanced picture focusing on the multidirectional relationship among the animation industries in Japan, Hong Kong, Mainland China, and the United States can be painted.

Indeed, the White Snake legend, the influence from early Chinese animation, and coproduction with Shaw Brothers in Hong Kong were hardly the most important elements in the postwar Japanese animation industry's development. Given Disney's tremendous impact, it is probably very difficult to position the 1958 White Snake animation as the pivotal element in the history of Japanese animation. As mentioned above, most scholars would credit *Astro Boy*, instead of *Hakujaden*, as the origin of Japanese anime, because the postwar Japanese animation industry was dominated by the so-called "limited animation" on TV (i.e., the Tezuka model), rather than what was perceived as "full animation," which was found in feature films (i.e., the Tōei Animation model). However, such a sharp divide itself should also be questioned. In this chapter, we have seen the muddiness of such categories as "full" and "limited" animation and the intricate connections between monochrome and color, and live-action and animation productions. It is indeed difficult to ascertain what elements truly "animated" postwar Japanese animation industry. A range of factors, from *kamishibai* 紙芝居 ("paper play"), manga, puppet animation,[95] shōjo 少女 magazines, Disney cartoons, and geopolitical and market considerations, all joined together to breathe life into the White Snake legend and postwar Japanese animation, resulting in such an exquisite production as the 1958 *Hakujaden*, a white pearl and a magic flower that should not be left unexcavated.

CONCLUDING REMARKS

The humanity of the nonhuman continued to emerge as the central trope in White Snake adaptations throughout the Cold War, and its lineage in postwar Japan provides a particularly intriguing case, culminating in the prominence of a range of additional animal characters in *Hakujaden* and brings to mind the use of "animal sidekicks" in the 1926 *The Righteous Snake* by the Shanghai Unique Film Company discussed in chapter 3. The themes of gender, species, media, and politics continue to intertwine in the history of Japanese adaptations of the White Snake legend, as the snake woman femme fatale continued to enchant on and off screen, through the shades of gray between light and shadows, in flamboyant colors, and through special effects and animation, from Lady Wakasa in Mizoguchi Kenji's 1953 *Ugetsu*, to Madame White Snake as impersonated by the legendary Yamaguchi Yoshiko in Tōhō's 1956 *Madame White Snake*, and finally to the exquisitely animated Bai-Niang in Tōei Animation's 1958 *Hakujaden.*

It is remarkable how the idea of love—whether forbidden, a result of witchcraft, or manifested in a greater harmony that grows out of benevolence—emerged as a central thread stitching together the three postwar Japanese "White Snake" films, at a moment when the inhumanity of the Japanese Imperial Army and its aggressions toward its Asian neighbors were becoming objects of moral and ethical self-interrogation for many Japanese. With its dual storyline, Mizoguchi's *Ugetsu* masterfully combines the fantastically enchanting world of Lady Wakasa (literally a ghost from a bygone age) and the wartime reality of sixteenth-century Japan, a thinly veiled device to examine the atrocities of any war, especially the sexual exploitation of women and in this particular case "comfort women" as one of many Japanese war crimes. For Genjūrō the potter, Lady Wakasa's manor became an exquisite paradise with its overflowing sexual pleasure; but such a fantasy world must be framed by the reality out there, most prominently embodied by the rape of one woman and the killing of the other, both at the hands of rampaging soldiers.

The forbidden love between Genjūrō the human and Lady Wakasa the ghost in *Ugetsu* evolves into "the witchcraft of love" in the 1956 *Madame White Snake*, where Madame White Snake relinquishes her magic power in order to save her human lover, ending with the now human couple's death and their spirits' ascent into the sky. This ending in particular resembles the ending of *The Butterfly Lovers*, a 1953 Mainland Chinese *Yue* opera (越劇, Shaoxin opera) color film based on the same legend as the 1926 silent film *The Butterfly Lovers.*[96] This humane love story was further elevated to the realm of universal love in the 1958 animation *Hakujaden*, in which Fahai, a symbol of "feudal oppression" in Lu Xun's 1924 essay and in many Mainland Chinese adaptations throughout the twentieth century, becomes a benevolent figure representing the merciful teachings of Buddhism, under the instructions of the Buddhist Goddess of Mercy, Guanyin. Indeed, the animation movie turned the legend into a fairy tale, the Asian counterpart of *The Little Mermaid*, in which the mermaid gives up her nonhuman attributes out of love for a human being.[97]

As masculinity continued to be threatened and besieged, the symbol of the fated love between the White Snake and her human lover shifted from the umbrella to pottery, and then to a white pearl and a red scarf, and finally to the musical instrument *erhu* and the flower of life.[98] The dynamic transitions between black-and-white film (*Ugetsu*) and color film (*Madame White*), between live-action films aimed mainly at adult audiences (*Ugetsu* and *Madame White*) and animation (*Hakujaden*) packaged for families and children, reveal the importance of a media-centered approach in examining the White Snake legend in postwar Japanese cinema. Such thematic and formal metamorphoses were largely intertwined with changes that took place in the postwar Japanese film industry as part of the national rejuvenation efforts that immediately followed the US Occupation, when Japan increasingly emerged as a central player in regional and global film industrial networks, in spite of, or precisely because of, the cultural Cold War in Asia.

CHAPTER 5

Reconfiguring the White Snake in Korean Cinema in an Inter-Asian Context

SINO-KOREAN CINEMATIC CONNECTIONS

The 1929 Shanghai performance of Oscar Wilde's play *Salome*, translated into Chinese by Tian Han when he was a student in Tokyo in 1920, featured an artistically exceptional cast, among them a young man of nineteen named Jin Yan 金焰. With his melancholic expression, Jin was cast as the Young Syrian who was desperately but secretly in love with the title character.[1] Under Tian's tutelage and facilitated by his extensive stage experience with Tian's Southern Land Institute (Nanguo she 南國社),[2] Jin Yan went on to be known as the "movie emperor" (Dianying huangdi 電影皇帝) of 1930s China, starring opposite such famous leading actresses as Ruan Lingyu, Wang Renmei, Chen Yanyan, and Li Lili. With the translation of a Japanese-language biography of Jin Yan into Korean in 1996, and a Korean-language biography into Chinese in 2006,[3] scholars working in these languages began to appreciate the significance of Jin Yan's (Kim Yŏm 김염 hereafter) Korean identity and decades-long Chinese career. Though English-language scholarship developed later, Anglophone scholars did finally start to take Kim Yŏm's contributions to Sino-Korean cinematic connections seriously, viewing them as an inspiration for the development of a new approach to transnational cinema that could combat nationalism without being complicit with globalization.[4] More importantly, for our purpose of understanding the Korean connection in the White Snake legend's reinvention in the postwar and postcolonial period, the complex relationship during the Cold War between Japan and the anti-Japanese sentiments pervasive in both a divided Korea and a fragmented China must be taken into careful consideration.

Born in current-day Seoul in 1910, the year Korea became a Japanese colony, to a family later known as Korean independence fighters, Kim Yŏm's life trajectory connects early Korean and Chinese anti-Japanese activists and sentiments. Because his family fled Japanese colonial control and settled in northeastern China, Kim grew up in China and became fluent in Chinese.

He ventured to Shanghai in 1927, when its film industry was overtaken by the immensely popular first commercial adaptation of the White Snake legend, the 1926 two-part *Righteous Snake* and its 1927 sequel. However, this commercial performance milieu would be increasingly politicized. In her article "The Korean Valentino," Hye Seung Chung argues that Kim, by playing anti-imperial heroes in Shanghai for Chinese and (diasporic) Korean audiences, became a powerful symbol of Sino-Korean unity at a time when anti-Japanese sentiments could not be openly expressed in Korea.[5]

Kim Yŏm is only one example of the intricate, if intermittent, Sino-Korean cultural and cinematic connections that took place throughout the long twentieth century, situated amid complex relationships with Japan, the United States, Hong Kong, Taiwan, and other geopolitical and cultural entities across Asia. In fact, Tian Han, who introduced "The Lust of the Serpent" to his Japanese friend at West Lake in 1926, had closely associated with Korean activists of the generation of Kim's father in the late 1910s and early 1920s in Tokyo. As discussed in chapter 4, as a young Chinese student in Tokyo, Tian was active in the New Man Society, a radical student association with members from Japan, China, Taiwan, and Korea (the latter two being Japanese colonies at the time), and the Cosmo Club, a cosmopolitan organization in Tokyo with five official languages—Esperanto, English, Japanese, Chinese, and Korean.[6] Although secret police records show that these young international activists were often closely monitored,[7] interwar Tokyo and Shanghai still provided a relatively sheltered venue for the meeting of like-minded, openly left-leaning and anti-imperialist activists of various origins. Since the film industries in Shanghai and Hong Kong were intimately connected through the flow of talent and capital between the two cities, starting from the interwar period and continuing into the postwar era,[8] the kind of early Korean film connections in Shanghai exemplified by Kim serve as important threads to connect now obscure regional associations in an inter-Asian context. Cinematic recreations of the White Snake legend produced during the postwar transformations of East Asian societies provide some of the key examples of such regional associations, which feature frequent coproductions among companies in Japan, Hong Kong, South Korea, and Taiwan.

The three "White Snake" films examined in this chapter exemplify just such a series of transnational connections, which appear both in the reinvention of the White Snake legend by the Korean film industry and through its collaboration and distribution efforts in East and Southeast Asia from the 1960s to the 1970s. Two of the films are Korean-language productions made in Korea—*Madam White Snake* (*Paeksa buin*) and *Snake Woman* (*Sanyŏ*)—both of which were directed by the same legendary director, Shin Sang-ok, in 1960 and 1969, respectively.[9] However, the directorship, nationality, even language of the third film, the 1978 *Story of White Snake* (*Paeksajŏn*), also known as *Love of the White Snake* (*Zhen Baishe zhuan*, or *Xin Baishe zhuan*), is considerably more ambiguous. The film is credited to a range of different directors in both scholarly and popular sources originating from Korea, Hong Kong, Mainland China, and the United States.

The first two Korean "White Snake" films, with a relatively less complex production history than the third, still present any serious researcher with a couple of challenging issues. Shin Sang-ok's first attempt at adapting the White Snake legend for cinematic treatment, *Madam White Snake*, sold some seventy thousand tickets when it opened in theaters in 1960, a better than average record for its time but still no box office triumph.[10] His second attempt, the 1969 *Snake Woman* (often considered a remake of *Madam White Snake* and mistakenly catalogued in the Korean Movie Database (KMDB) as *Dead Woman*), sold 150,000 tickets.[11] Indeed, compared to Shin's sensational *Eunuch* (*Naeshi* 內侍 내시) from the previous year, which featured female same-sex desire on-screen and had a box office record of 320,400 according to the same database,[12] *Snake Woman* also fell short of being a triumph. However, its ticket sales, at a little less than half of *Eunuch*'s, were still much better than many other films of the same year. For example, *Women of the Yi Dynasty* (*Ijo yŏin chanhoksa* 이조 여인 잔혹사), another film by Shin Sang-ok from 1969, sold only 105,608 tickets.[13]

The box office sales for the 1978 *Love of the White Snake (Story of White Snake*) is more difficult to gauge, as the only available figure is the one listed in the Korean Movie Database, which could very well represent the limited sale of the film as dubbed for the Korean market. However, since the film is better known as a Hong Kong–Taiwan coproduction and a Mandarin-language film in the much larger Chinese-speaking markets, the Korean box-office record has limited value as gauge of sales.[14] This might have to do with a phenomenon that Sangjoon Lee has described as a "counterfeit coproduction," whereby a Korean film studio would bypass the limitations imposed by government import quotas by classifying an imported film as a Korean coproduction. Shin Films was already practicing this strategy at this time.[15] Similarly, from the Korean point of view, Shin Sang-ok's Korean "White Snake" films were conceived as more suitable for export because of their potentially broader market appeal in East and Southeast Asia. As a result, considering only Korean box-office numbers for the three "White Snake" films fails to account for these potential overseas markets.

Although the Korean box-office numbers from decades ago may not be reliable measures of the contemporary popularity and historical impact of these now largely forgotten "White Snake" films, they do provide a glimpse into these films' relative popularity in Korea when they appeared. There is a stark contrast between their past popularity and their current obscurity, both in Korea and elsewhere. This circumstance invites further scrutiny. These films' significance in the larger framework of White Snake legend recreations across linguistic and cultural borders under the conditions established by the Cold War should not be relegated to the dustbin of history.

SHIN SANG-OK'S FIRST WHITE SNAKE FILM

Shin Sang-ok made *Madam White Snake* in 1960, one year before his widely popular *Chunhyang* (*Sŏng Ch'unhyang* 成春香 성춘향). Both films starred actress Ch'oe Ŭn-hŭi (崔銀姬 최은희), but it was the latter that catapulted Shin and Ch'oe into what is considered the golden age of their collaboration. As a result, *Madam White Snake* has been largely forgotten both in the historiography of Korean cinema and as part of Shin's and Ch'oe's careers. Most Shin Sang-ok filmographies fail to include the film. In the otherwise excellent essay on Shin from the Korean Film Archive,[16] there is no mention of this 1960 White Snake film. The article moves directly from the box office hits *A Romantic Papa* (*Romaensŭ ppappa* 로맨스빠빠) and *To the Last Day* (*I saengmyŏng tahadorok* 이 생명 다하도록), both made in 1960, to the 1961 sensation *Chunhyang*. In the most recent and most comprehensive research on Shin in English, Steven Chung gives only passing mention to Shin's 1969 film as *Dead Woman*, possibly following the mistranslated title listed in the Korean Film Archive and KMDB, as *Sanyŏ* can mean both "dead woman" and "snake woman," depending on which Chinese character is implied by the title's first word *sa* 사, 死 ("dead") or 蛇 ("snake").[17] Thus, we are left with two questions. First, how might a close examination of Shin Sang-ok's contribution, in Korean, to the White Snake cinematic repertoire allow us to rediscover Shin himself? And, second, what can the 1960 and 1969 Korean White Snake films tell us about the legend's translingual metamorphosis and about transnational cinema in practice?

In his research on the trans-Asian studio system, Sangjoon Lee delineates postwar coproduction efforts between Japan, Hong Kong, South Korea, and Taiwan, along with other entities. However, *Madam White Snake,* made in 1960, came before many of the key developments facilitating such efforts.

These developments included the Park Chung Hee government's first five-year plan for economic development in 1961 and Run Run Shaw's relocation of the family's motion picture business from Malaya/Singapore to Hong Kong, which was completed in the same year.[18] But while institutional connections lagged behind, personal and incidental connections were at work. According to Sangjoon Lee's interview with Pak Haeng-ch'ŏl 박행철, director of physical production for the 1960 *Madam White Snake* and planner for the 1969 *Snake Woman*, Shin Sang-ok handed him a script of the 1956 live-action film *Madame White Snake* (*Byaku fujin no yōren*), in Japanese. This attests to the strong Japanese influence found in the Korean "White Snake" films.[19] Shin's production company, Shin Films, was founded in 1960, the same year he made *Madam White Snake*. The subsequent development of cultural infrastructure allowed Shin Films to thrive. The record-breaking ticket sales for *Chunhyang* in 1961 convinced Shin of the possibility of treating film as a serious enterprise, increasing his confidence. With commercial success came international recognition. At the Ninth Asia-Pacific Film Festival in Seoul in 1962, when his 1961 *A Guest and Mother* (*Sarangbang sonnimgwa ŏmŏni* 사랑방 손님과 어머니, aka *The Houseguest and My Mother*) won the award for best film, Shin first met Run Run Shaw. The encounter led to joint production efforts between Korea and Hong Kong in the years that followed.[20]

The postcolonial Korean film industry was built upon a foundation created by Japan-educated artists. Shin Sang-ok is a typical case, and Shin's *Madam White Snake* was the culmination of his activities before the dramatic takeoff of his career in 1961. He was trained in fine arts in Tokyo from 1944 to 1945 and returned to Korea shortly after the country established its independence after thirty-five years of Japanese colonial rule. Shin began his film career as an assistant production designer for the first postwar Korean film, *Hurrah! For Freedom* (*Jayu manse* 自由萬歲 자유만세, aka *Viva Freedom!*), directed by Ch'oe In-kyu (崔寅奎 최인규) and released in 1946. The film portrayed an anti-Japanese resistance fighter, even though the director, like most of his peers, had been very active in making pro-Japanese propaganda films until right before Japan's surrender. Shin learned the fundamentals of filmmaking from Ch'oe, and his background in painting has been credited as making him a master of *mise-en-scène*.[21] At the start of his film career, Shin's big breakthrough was the 1958 *Confessions of a Female College Student* (*Ŏnŭ yŏdaesaengŭi kobaek* 어느 여대생의 고백), which earned enough capital to fund the establishment of Shin Films in 1960. According to the oral history project on Shin Films conducted by the Korean Film Archive, Shin's highly effective filmmaking process in the 1960s was borrowed from the Japanese-style hierarchical system of production that he brought back to Korea in the mid- to late 1950s.[22]

Shin is touted by the Korean Film Archive as the only Korean director to have worked in the film industries of South Korea, Hong Kong, North Korea, and Hollywood.[23] I would add to this already very impressive list that he also had a deep understanding of the Japanese and Taiwanese film industries because of his early training in Japan and his later distribution efforts in Taiwan. Much like Kim Yŏm who portrayed anti-Japanese fighters on-screen in 1930s Shanghai, Shin Sang-ok made anti-Japanese films in North Korea after he and Ch'oe Ŭn-hŭi ended up there in 1978. This activity could be interpreted as fulfilling an unrealizable promise in an increasingly precarious South Korea under the control of the Park Chung Hee government.[24] Such a sentiment was evident in Kim Jong-il's October 1983 discussion on film with Ch'oe Ŭn-hŭi and Shin Sang-ok, secretly taped by Ch'oe and quoted in Suk-Young Kim's monograph on North Korean propaganda, *Illusive Utopia*.[25] In order to better understand the complex background of Shin's North Korean film activities, it is important to consider the fate of Shin Films from 1975 to 1978, when Shin's filmmaking license was revoked by the South Korean Park regime. Shin and Ch'oe subsequently made some twenty films for the North Korean film industry while in the Democratic People's Republic of Korea during the early 1980s. After their miraculous escape in 1986, Shin went on to make a series of films in Hollywood in the 1990s. Where do Shin's 1960 *Madam White Snake* and related films fit in relation to all these other enterprises? The following section attempts to resituate this largely forgotten film in its historical, geopolitical, and cultural context.

The Shadow of **Ugetsu** *and Holding Hands at First Sight*

The 1960 *Madam White Snake* was a low-budget project that took only ten days to film and had 90 percent of its scenes shot on a sound stage. In light of this, it is understandable that such a film would be overshadowed by the big-budget commercial hits produced both before and afterwards and would remain obscure amid the many dazzling works in Shin's long and illustrious career. And yet, when considered in the larger context of the entire White Snake repertoire (from instantiations in the oral tradition, textual and visual print publication, and film and animation, including silent and sound, monochrome and color), this much-overlooked film reveals layers of cultural influence and multidirectional cinematic enchantment between Mainland China, Japan, South Korea, Hong Kong, Taiwan, the United States, and regions of Southeast Asia.

There are, first of all, a number of significant plot changes in the White Snake story, even when compared to the 1956 Japanese film *Madame White Snake*, whose script is said to have been the basis for the 1960 Korean adaptation. In Shin's 1960 film, Madam White Snake is a thousand-year-old snake that has transformed herself into a human without permission. Thus, although she falls in love with and marries a young pharmacist named Hŏ Sŏn (許仙 허선, performed by Sin Sŏng-il 申星一 신성일),[26] she is ordered by the Buddhist Goddess of Mercy (Kwanŭm bosal 觀音菩薩 관음보살) and Abbot Fahai (Pŏp'ae sŏnsa 法海禪師 법해선사) to return to the world of the gods before the seventh day of the seventh month. Grieving, she prepares to say goodbye to her beloved husband. But before she can return to the world of the gods, she is entrapped by a man who attempts to rape her, fails to return by the promised deadline, and risks her life to save her husband. Touched by this display of true love, the Goddess of Mercy instructs the abbot to permit the pair to live happily together.[27]

This Korean version of the White Snake legend includes elements borrowed from other legends. For example, the seventh day of the seventh month in the lunar calendar, written in both Chinese and Japanese as 七夕 (*qixi* or *tanabata*), is indeed a date long associated with the romantic reunion of star-crossed human and nonhuman lovers, but it is normally found in the popular legend of the Cowherd and the Weaving Girl (*Niulang zhinü* 牛郎織女).[28] Moreover, the idea that the White Snake must return to heaven by a set date may also be borrowed from the immensely popular film *Heavenly Match* (*Tianxian pei* 天仙配), in which the Seventh Sister of the fairies (Qi xiannü 七仙女) must also leave her human lover and return to heaven. The legend of the Cowherd and the Weaving Girl is also widely known in Korea as *Kyŏnu chingnyŏ* 牽牛織女 견우직녀.[29] The use of seventh day of the seventh month in the lunar calendar as a key marker of the White Snake's return in the film, then, could be considered a Korean invention. Shin and his team likely picked this date with wide cultural resonance in East Asia, possibly with a broader Asian market in mind.

The 1960 *Madam White Snake* opens with intertitles superimposed on tracking shots of Hŏ Sŏn (Xu Xian) playing flute on a boat, with a solo melodic female voice singing in voiceover. This latter feature bears traces of the 1956 Japanese live-action film's opening shots, while Hŏ Sŏn's music-making calls to mind the 1958 Japanese animation's focus on the flute as the young man's instrument of enchantment. A reverse shot reveals the character Chŏng A (青兒 정아), depicted as a young girl, and places Hŏ Sŏn under her gaze. The camera pans to reveal the other young lady, standing next to Chŏng A and wearing a muslin veil over her face, in the manner of Lady Wakasa of the 1953 Japanese black-and-white film *Ugetsu*. Indeed, *Ugetsu* stands out as a major stylistic influence on the Korean film. This connection is partly reinforced by *Ugetsu*'s and *Madam White Snake*'s shared use of monochrome, which stands in contrast to the color used in the other two Japanese White Snake films discussed in chapter 4, the 1956 *Madame White Snake* and the 1958 *Hakujaden*. In addition, the moment when Lady Wakasa reveals her face in *Ugetsu* is reprised at the opening of the 1960 *Madam White Snake*, when the mysterious woman pulls her veil aside to reveal her face for the camera and the audience, with a reverse shot disclosing Hŏ, the object of her gaze, outside the frame (fig. 37).

Although the style of the 1960 Korean film seems most closely related to Mizoguchi Kenji's aesthetically sophisticated *Ugetsu*, its plot elements largely resemble those found in the 1956 *Madame White Snake*. As in the Japanese live-action film, dark, smoke-like clouds and rain appear at the opening of the 1960 Korean film, facilitating the protagonists' encounter by means of a shared boat. Raindrops again hit the lake water, very much resembling the opening scene of the 1956 *Madame White Snake*, with a nod to *Ugetsu*'s monochrome aesthetics. However, Shin's ingenious use of bodily contact, especially hand-holding, is a striking feature of this otherwise conventionalized component of the White Snake cinematic repertoire, distinguishing his film from previous ones.[30] Little more than three minutes into the film and before any introductions have taken place, the male protagonist is already shown holding the hands of the mysterious woman under the pretext of helping her to board the boat (3:15; fig. 37). A few minutes later, he again holds her hand, ostensibly to help her disembark, while he holds the umbrella over her (5:31). The woman then goes on to propose sharing the young man's umbrella—an example of Shin's creativity, at once demonstrating the snake woman's otherworldly ignorance of the constraints that pertain in the human realm, while at the same time throwing into relief the anomalous quality of the young man's voluntary hand-holding, which seems completely at odds with his conventional characterization as passive and weak. In fact, this characterization of the human lover may have been inherited more from the 1958 Japanese animation *Hakujaden* than the 1956 Japanese live-action film, as the Disney prince–like character in the animation may well have been the most positive portrayal of the human male to date in the White Snake repertoire.

Still, the shadow of *Ugetsu* lingers. When Hŏ goes to search for Madam White's residence to fetch his umbrella, the camera portrays him walking through an alleyway, with his shadow accentuated on the wall, creating an

Figure 37: (top) Pulling aside the veil, 2:16; (bottom) Holding hands at first sight, 3:15. Screenshots by author. Both in *Madam White Snake* (*Paeksa buin*), dir. Shin Sang-ok. Seoul: Shin Sang-ok Production, 1960. Full film with English subtitles available from Korean Film Archive's YouTube channel: https://youtu.be/69DhzDrHVeI.

ambience reminiscent of the scene in which Lady Wakasa leads Genjūrō through a deserted field to reach her manor. Hŏ's hesitation at the door, as he struggles to decline Chŏng A's invitation to enter, eerily resembles Genjūrō's fight against temptation, as both characters know what lies beyond that threshold. Spiritual echoes of *Ugetsu* aside, the Chinese-style interior design in Shin's Korean recreation shows considerable visual similarity to the 1956 Japanese version, although the Korean sets were shabbier, a natural consequence of the film's quick production schedule, and its black-and-white props were dull in comparison to the Japanese film's flamboyantly colored ones. Here, the leading actress Ch'oe Ŭn-hŭi comes to the rescue. Not a single previous White Snake film demonstrates the White Snake's power of seduction in such an elaborately choreographed fashion. In fact, the "dance to seduce" sequence is entirely absent from the Japanese live-action *Madame White Snake* and the animated *Hakujaden*, and even Lady Wakasa's highly choreographed dance sequence in *Ugetsu*, with its infinite shades of gray, literally pales beside Ch'oe Ŭn-hŭi's performance.

Dance to Seduce and Lovers' Chat in a Moonlit Garden

A lyrical sequence lasting more than two minutes brilliantly displays the seductive beauty of Madam White (and of the enchanting actress Ch'oe Ŭn-hŭi, who plays her; fig. 38). Flaunting a flower decoration inherited from White Snake's hairstyle in the 1956 and 1958 Japanese versions, a fluffy feather fan, and earrings, Shin Sang-ok's White Snake approaches the object of her desire with alluring steps, complemented by her charmingly tender hand gestures and enchanting smiles and glances (fig. 38). The camera affectionately lingers on her shapely body, accentuating her beauty from head to toe. Her elaborately tailored Chinese-style costume overshadows all previous attempts at portraying White Snake's dress: a suggestively open bodice, pendulous sleeves, and a lotus-like short skirt on top of a mermaid-like long dress all combine to highlight her feathery fan, which serves as the ultimate instrument of enchantment, as did the red silk scarf in the 1956 *Madame White Snake*.

At the end of this elaborate ritual to greet and seduce, Madam White presses Hŏ's hand for about ten seconds (12:54–13:03) while proposing to give him a tour of the garden. This is highly reminiscent of the moment in *Ugetsu* when Lady Wakasa holds Genjūrō's hands while leading him to his first meal in her manor. Lady Wakasa seems to treat the moment as an opportunity to demonstrate her love for both Genjūrō's pottery and the man. Indeed,

Figure 38: (top) Dance to seduce, 09:48; (bottom) Close-up of Madam White (Ch'oe Ŭn-hŭi) at the end of her seductive dance, 10:56. Screenshots by author. Both in *Madam White Snake* (dir. Shin Sang-ok, 1960).

hand-holding leads to a confession of love in both films. Similarly, bodily contact also connects the 1956 *Madame White Snake* with the 1960 Korean film. When Madam White confesses her feelings while holding Hŏ's hand, she admits to feeling "*as if* they have known each other from a previous life," in effect accentuating the feeling of the secular present in the style of a romantic chance encounter. She continues with a daring proposal involving the key word "love": "If you love me . . . , let me feel your warm blood" (*Saranghashin damyŏnt't, tangshinŭi ttŭgŏun p'irŭl chŏegedo hŭrŭge haejuseyo* 사랑하신다면. . . , 당신의 뜨거운 피를 저에게도 흐르게 해주세요). The lovers consummate their liaison right then and there (16:01–17:20).

Here, the White Snake legend emerges as an intriguing outlet for the self-expression, both personal and political, of generations of experimental artists throughout East Asia. Shin's film is but another manifestation of such romantic impulses, with some twists on the gender politics in a heterosexual relationship. A crane shot shows the couple having a lovers' chat on a bench in the flower garden under the moonlight, with the human lover's head on Madam White's lap, immediately reminding viewers of the meadow scene in *Ugetsu*, but with the effeminate Hŏ and the assertive White subverting many of our stereotypes about the positioning of the two genders.

The camera zooms in to a medium shot of the couple. Hŏ's confession, "Darling, I'll never doubt you again no matter what people say," resembles Genjūrō's confession in the hot spring. Touched by her lover's genuine emotion, Madam White holds Hŏ's hand tenderly, smiling at him from above (39:30). Another crane shot takes on the subject position of Madam White gazing at her lover, again from above, and Hŏ continues, "I'll never leave you no matter what happens" (40:05). Although the male lover does most of the talking, Madam White dominates the screen with her striking presence. The camera lingers amorously on her tender, almost motherly smiles. When Hŏ stretches his hand to serve as a pillow for Madam White, she leans on his hand while still gazing affectionately at him (40:12), yet all the time subverting the gendered positioning, as the one on top and in the spotlight.

Mutual Love and Devotion, and the Humanity of the Nonhuman

The kind of affectionate, mutually loving gaze exchanged by the lovers in *Madam White Snake* cements Shin Sang-ok's focus on mutual devotion between the snake woman and her human lover. Shin has created a radically different human lover in Hŏ Sŏn, drawing more from the 1958 Japanese animated "Prince Charming" than from any other versions, although the human lover remains in a supporting role throughout the narrative. Still, Hŏ Sŏn is the first male lead to hold Madam White's hand just three minutes into the film, and that is only the beginning. He is caring and considerate of others; he is loyal and resilient. He buys brocades for his sister, demonstrating his appreciation for others' care and love. When tortured and forced to disclose the origin of the stolen silver, he says to his torturer, "To be honest, I did it," a shocking change for viewers more familiar with the passive, almost hopelessly lame characterization of the human lover in most previous representations. In a demonstration of his devotion to his fellow human beings, during his journey into exile, he carries another dying convict on his back, even while he suffers from heat and thirst himself and finally collapses on the road.

With such a worthy object of her love and desire, White Snake emerges as a most devoted wife, a wise spirit who chooses well in love. The question of whether Xu Xian deserves the White Snake was a thorny issue for Tian Han when he was revising the story for his *jingju* version of *The White Snake* in Mainland China between the early 1940s and the mid-1950s. Like Shin in his cinematic attempt in South Korea, Tian attempted to beautify the image of Xu Xian to make him worthy of White Snake's love.[31] In Shin's 1960 film, White Snake continues to save Hŏ (Xu) from troubles both when she herself unintentionally causes them and when she has been wrongly accused. Like other ordinary human beings with means at the time, she bribes a prison official to secure Hŏ's release from jail. She then risks her life to seek an herb to cure the townspeople, when a "quack shaman" blames her for a plague outbreak. When Hŏ is arrested again because the official who attempted to rape White Snake was frightened to death upon seeing her original form, the White Snake turns herself in to save her lover. She earns Hŏ's final confession of love, in a sense, through her own complete devotion to him.

Hŏ's final declaration of love is an elevated version of the one he delivered at the moonlit garden: "I don't care if you are a brute or a white snake. There are so many wicked people among human beings. Compared to them, you are an angel. You should have God's blessing" (1:24:09–1:24:27). Hŏ's words prove to be prophetic; when the White Snake misses the deadline for returning to the gods and is about to be taken away by the Buddhist abbot, the tragic lovers rush toward each other and meet in the water, leaving the abbot alone on the boat. Although they might have drowned, the lovers are washed ashore with their hands tightly clasped. Seeing their mutual love and devotion, the Goddess of Mercy chants "Mercy is the heart of Buddhism" and pardons their transgressions; she orders the abbot to revive them and let them go anywhere they wish. The film ends with Hŏ carrying Madam White to the boat; the moment is reminiscent of the film's opening scenes, in which Hŏ held Madam White's hand as he helped her on and off the boat. The two lovers ride away together in the boat and live happily ever after, showing the influence of the 1958 Japanese animation that ends with the same scene.

Humanity Aided by Special Effects

In the plot of *Madam White Snake*, Shin portrays White Snake's nature as more humane than that of most human beings. In the film's special effects, the humanity of the nonhuman is expressed in vivid fashion. The female protagonist is a magical snake woman, after all, and she can fly through clouds, search for life-saving herbs, shift between her snake and human forms, and sneak out of a prison cell through window openings so narrow that "only a snake could have possibly done it." Given the circumstances under which the film was made, the achievement of such "magical happenings" is impressive. The reviewer of the 1956 *Madame White Snake* in Hong Kong uses precisely that term to refer to the special effects in the White Snake film. Special effects then became a selling point for the White Snake films in the years that followed, including the 2011 Mainland Chinese 3D film *It's Love (Baishe chuanshuo)* that featured the martial arts star Jet Li as Abbot Fahai.[32]

An investigation into who was in charge of special effects for the 1960 Shin Sang-ok film may help explain how it could have achieved such special effects on such a tight schedule. The opening credits of *Madam White Snake* list Kang Sŏng-pŏm 姜聖範 강성범 as art director, Yi Sang-man 李相萬 이상만 as in charge of "effects," and Chŏn Tae-chun 田大俊 전대준 as in charge of props, or miniature sets. A veteran of the Korean theater movement from the 1930s and an experienced film artist, Kang Sŏng-pŏm started his career in film toolmaking and lighting, and moved on to the stage art department as a device manager for live performances in the postwar era. He continued to work in both theater and film, creating ingenious devices such as realistic artificial rainfall on stage.[33] *Madam White Snake* was made only a year before Kang Sŏng-pŏm's death, the end of a long and distinguished career of special effects achievements.[34] In the case of Yi Sang-man, although he was credited as responsible simply for "effects," his contribution must have focused on sound, as his career had been mainly in radio broadcasting and film sound.[35] As for Chŏn Tae-chun, we know only that he was in charge of props for both *Madam White Snake* and *Chunhyang*, and was active as a prop designer from the late 1950s to the mid-1960s.[36] Although special effects were in use and continuously developing from the 1930s to the 1950s, in Japan and later throughout Asian film industries, the application of the specific terminology "special effects" or "visual effects" took much longer to codify. In many cases, special effects were all classified under the rubric of "film arts," and a director of special effects appears in the records simply as "art director" in the various relevant languages. This was the case for Kang Sŏng-pŏm's work on *Madam White Snake*: his role is identified in Chinese characters in the film credits simply as 美術 (*misul* 미술, or "art design"). Around this time, the field of special effects emerged as an important contact zone connecting cinematographers, designers, and technicians from Japan, Korea, Mainland China, Hong Kong, and Taiwan, among other Asian countries and regions throughout the journey of the White Snake legend's inter-Asian and global travels.

SHIN'S FORGOTTEN SECOND ATTEMPT

The 1960s were a golden age for Shin Films, reflected in the frequent coproduction and distribution efforts, led by Shin Sang-ok, that took place between the Korean, Hong Kong, and Taiwanese film industries. As a result, Shin Films productions began to be exported to Taiwan, Southeast Asia, and the United States in the early 1960s.[37] Shin Films' 1964 collaboration with Yueh Feng 岳楓, director of what is likely the most popular "White Snake" film of the period, the 1962 *Huangmei diao* film *Madam White Snake* (*Baishe zhuan*) by Hong Kong's Shaw Brothers and starring the "Queen of Asian Cinema" Lin Dai 林黛, resulted in *Princess Talgi* 妲己 (*Piryŏnŭi yŏwang talgi* 비련의 여왕 달기, or *The Last Woman of Shang*), another portrayal of a legendary femme fatale from the Chinese past.[38] This collaboration may have resulted from the meeting of Shin Sang-ok and Run Run Shaw at the Ninth Asia-Pacific Film Festival in Seoul in 1962. Its focus on reconfiguring the enchantress would also manifest in Shin's 1969 *Snake Woman*, a remake of his 1960 *Madam White Snake*. Another collaboration between Shin Films and Shaw Brothers' featured yet another film on the femme fatale, *Thousand-Year Fox* (*Ch'ŏnnyŏnho* 千年狐 천년호), also from 1969.[39]

In Shin's second attempt to reconfigure the snake woman, a young craftsman witnesses a thousand-year-old snake woman killing his teacher in a cave and promises not to mention the killing to anyone. After this, the thousand-year-old tree where the snake lives is cut down to make a perfect Buddhist statue, which the young craftsman is responsible for carving. The snake woman transforms into a beautiful woman and tempts the young craftsman. The two marry, and she gives birth to a son. Under orders from the Demon

King (Mawang 魔王 마왕), the snake woman tries to kill her husband, but the love she has developed for him prevents her from following through with the murder. The Demon King then turns the snake woman into a rock, but the Buddhist Goddess of Mercy transforms her back into a woman.[40] She lives happily ever after with the craftsman, whose statue eerily resembles both the snake woman and the Buddhist Goddess of Mercy.[41]

Shin's engagement with the philosophy of artistic creation and the pursuit of creative perfection in the film *Snake Woman* suggests a number of cross-cultural comparisons.[42] As with most earlier versions, the 1969 Korean film continues with the themes of love and devotion, in both life and art, and between the unconventionally human and nonhuman couple (who is nonetheless conventionally heterosexual). However, there is a special focus here on the role of the child. Although various Chinese versions of the White Snake legend and the American missionary Woodbridge's 1896 English-language retelling include the birth of a perfect human boy,[43] most later versions from the 1950s and early 1960s did not allow the snake woman to experience motherhood. In this sense, Shin's second attempt at retelling the White Snake story returns to early Chinese (especially Buddhist) versions of the legend, as the snake woman is again granted the ability to bear a perfect human boy. Her childbearing is the ultimate proof of her humanity, as it allows her to perform the roles of devoted wife *and* loving mother, a continuation of the logic long employed by Chinese literati and American missionaries, which treats the ability to love and reproduce as grounds for being human. This elevation to motherhood and the White Snake's expression of the unconditional love with which motherhood is commonly associated are central to the representation of the snake woman's humanity in the 1969 film. However, this is only part of the story. Like the transgressive protagonist, *Snake Woman* itself is a fascinating hybrid, simultaneously inviting classification as a romantic fantasy, a horror film, and a martial arts film, with the latter two categories gaining increasing influence in a trans-border Asian market from the late 1960s onward.

The film's 1969 audience would probably not have hesitated to consider it a horror film, nor would today's audiences, who are more experienced with the genre. The opening has the feeling of a horror movie, with two craftsmen deep in the mountains, searching for thousand-year-old trees to make a perfect Buddhist statue. Thunder strikes and rain falls only a few minutes into the film, right after they find the perfect ancient tree. The men are forced to take shelter for the night in a cave, and there they see something they should never have witnessed. The camera follows the old craftsman's gaze, under a mysterious blue light, and reveals a phosphorescent snake slithering on a platform-like stalagmite. We see the snake gradually transform (enabled by superimposition technology; fig. 39). First, pieces of phosphorescent clothing become visible, then the feet appear, and finally the head of a woman rises from under the gradually emerging clothes.

With her snake form slowly fading away but still visible, the snake woman twists and turns, while an eerie soundtrack punctuates her every move (7:05–7:20). A shot/reverse shot brings the viewer back to the terrified old man (under natural lighting), pupils diluted and mouth wide open. What ensues is the ultimate proof of the snake woman's inhumanity: she exhales a dark, smoke-like poison, killing the terrified old man right in front of his young partner and the film audience. However, when the panicked young craftsman turns back to look at the snake woman, her expression softens, almost to a discreet smile (fig. 39). The mysterious blue light still shines on her profile, in an above-shoulder close-up, and her phosphorescent clothes are still visible (8:57).

The snake woman speaks: "You are so handsome! I won't kill you, but don't tell anyone what you saw today, no matter how close you are to them, otherwise I'll kill you!" The camera lingers on the young man's face as he looks back, showing him affixed by her intense yet almost endearing gaze as she issues her threat (9–9:40). The film thus opens with the deadly snake woman killing one man and falling in love with another. This establishes a complex and ambivalent ambience for the hybrid expression of horror and romantic fantasy.[44] The snake woman's first appearance as a human, and a beautiful young girl at that, accentuates the storyline's focus on a romantic chance encounter, as in Tian Han's experiments in the 1920s and early 1950s, in the 1956 Japanese live-action film, and in Korean retellings of the legend. In accordance with White Snake legend convention, the snake woman first appears in the rain; unconventionally, however, she appears alone. The sister/maid/nurse figure, which appears in all previous versions, is eliminated here to leave room for the development of a new kind of intimacy later in the story—the close relationship between mother and child, a result of the heterosexual romance at the center of the film.

At the snake woman's first appearance as a beautiful human girl, the mysterious blue light seems to still linger on her, the color echoed in the sleeveless blue outer piece she wears on top of a lighter long-sleeved dress and in the light blue bundle she carries. Her hairstyle, the white hair ornament, the style of her clothes, and her facial features all resemble the snake woman as portrayed by Yamaguchi Yoshiko and Ch'oe Ŭn-hŭi in the Japanese and Korean

Figure 39: (top) The emerging snake woman, 7:13; (bottom) A descreet smile after seeing the handsome young man, 8:57. Screenshots by author. Both from *Snake Woman* (*Sanyŏ*), dir. Shin Sang-ok. Seoul: Shin Films, 1969.

live-action films, respectively.[45] The enchantment between the lovers is mutual, very much like the lovers in *Ugetsu*. The young craftsman's artistry as a maker of lifelike Buddhist statues, like Genjūrō's mastery of pottery-making, increases his sexual appeal in the snake woman's eyes. In the process of struggling to create the perfect statue, the young man uses the snake woman as a model; she thus becomes the object of his worship. As he becomes the object of her intensifying desire, their mutual worship and desire intermingle.

As he did in his 1960 *Madam White Snake*, Shin Sang-ok continues in this 1969 version his philosophical focus on hands in the mutual enchantment between the lovers, using hand-holding as a catalyst for sexual initiation. He first introduces the young man's artistry through a scene featuring the crafting of the hand for a Buddhist statue (18:06). After the artist's failed attempt to use the mysterious young girl as a model for the Buddhist statue, the film lingers on a lyrical moment, with a long shot showing a pair of boats floating on water in a golden sunset, reminding viewers of *Ugetsu*'s water scenes and foreshadowing the scenes of intimacy that follow. The struggling artist awakens to witness the exquisite beauty displaying her humanity, caring for the bedridden widow of the old man she killed at the beginning of the film. The widow's dying wish then prompts the young man to marry the mysterious beauty. Baek Niang 白娘, as she is introduced in this film (a name that echoes the female protagonist's name in the 1958 Japanese animation) promises to take good care of Seong Dong (Xu Xian); Seong in turn promises to make the most perfect Buddhist statue and thus to fulfill his life's mission and the dying wishes of his teacher (the old man) and his teacher's widow. In an exquisitely composed bedroom scene, the dangerous blue light is replaced by a romantic rosy pink glow (fig. 40). As he gently undresses Baek Niang, the artist-craftsman's hands are highlighted in a close-up that accentuates the sensuality of their intimate contact.

What most distinguishes this 1969 version, however, is the fact that the film immediately cuts to a scene five years later, after the birth of the couple's son, when this three-member nuclear family pays a visit to the old couple's grave and offers sacrifice to the dead (fig. 40). Seong lovingly declares, "I am so happy to have a good wife like you" (29:40). Indeed, the snake woman has not only become a good wife but also acquired full humanity through motherhood. Speaking as a loving mother to her young child, the snake woman makes the most touching confession to date in the White Snake cinematic repertoire: "Mom is a bad and scary white snake, and dad is not aware that he is making a Buddhist statue out of the tree I used to live in. I want to live with both of you for a long time, but I am so scared of the Demon King's order, what should mom do?" (41:38–42:10).

Figure 40: (top) A bedroom scene lit in rosy pink, 28:37; (bottom) A happy family five years later, 29:41. Screenshots by author. Both from *Snake Woman* (dir. Shin Sang-ok, 1969).

Figure 41: (top) Snake woman's use of magic to fight the Buddhist, 32:09. Screenshot by author; (bottom) The Buddhist's alms bowl as a weapon to counter the snake woman's magic, 1:08:58. Screenshot by author. Both from *Snake Woman* (dir. Shin Sang-ok, 1969).

Although intending to be a good wife and loving mother, the snake woman is chased by a Buddhist priest (Fahai), whom she had earlier defeated but whose golden bowl eventually becomes resistant to her powerful magic. In the meantime, Seong's rivals in making the statue deemed the craftsman's hands the most dangerous threat to their own success. They torture him, almost destroying his hands. Thus, the craftsman, who relies on his hands to create, is deprived of the basic means by which his life is sustained. "I am going to make the Buddha using my heart," he declares (54:11), and soldiers on with wounded hands, carving the hardwood and the details for the face of the statue. The facial features that emerge from the wood have two appearances: half resembles the features of the snake woman, while the other half remains those of the Buddha. Unwittingly, he has projected into the Buddhist savior's facial features those of his beautiful wife, the loving mother of his child, whose snake identity is still unknown to him. In the end, the statue he carves is the Buddhist Goddess of Mercy. He truly is making the statue with his heart. For the viewers, who are aware of his wife's real identity, the sensation of witnessing the hybrid figure, the snake woman and the Goddess of Mercy, must be nothing less than shocking and, indeed, terrifying.

Controlled by the Demon King, the snake woman loses her newly acquired humanity in a flash. She is on the verge of sucking blood from her human husband's neck, as if having resumed her vampire-like character from the opening of the film. The horror genre lingers throughout this Korean film and returns to haunt the otherwise romantic fantasy: the pitch of the music rises to accentuate the urgency of the scene, and the characteristic blue lighting returns to signal the reappearance of the snake woman's terrifying, bloodthirsty persona (1:07:36). This is the moment of truth for the snake woman: can she resist evil and remain good?

The cry of her human son saves the snake woman from utterly losing her newly acquired humanity and the father from danger. It is through motherhood that she redeems herself, and it is through her sacrifice for and support of her husband that the perfect statue is finally created. Seong the husband/father can eventually declare, as did Genjūrō and other male protagonists of the "White Snake" films throughout the 1950s and 1960s in both Japan and Korea, "I love you regardless of who you are!" (1:31:05). Seong's reasoning is similar to the reasoning of those other husbands: "There are so many bad humans. Although she is a brute, she cared for so many people and she still loves me. She is better than a human" (1:32:22–1:32:35). The ultimate savior for this unlikely couple is, again, the Buddhist Goddess of Mercy, who remains a key figure in the latter twentieth-century renditions, from the 1956 Japanese live-action film to the 1969 Korean revamping. In the 1969 version, in particular, the Buddhist abbot himself turns out to be Goddess of Mercy in disguise.[46] She resurrects the snake woman from her snake skin-like dress, allowing her to rejoin her husband and young boy and to live happily ever after.

A KOREA, HONG KONG, AND TAIWAN COPRODUCTION?

In 1974, Shin Sang-ok ventured to Hong Kong to make *The Ghost Lovers* (*Yannü huanhun* 艷女還魂, or *Panhonnyŏ* 반혼녀) for the Shaw Brothers. The film again featured a ghostly femme fatale and was one of the last films he made before his arrival in North Korea in 1978. Shin's Hong Kong career is one of the many examples of cinematic connections between the Korean, Hong Kong, and Taiwanese film industries. The genesis of the 1978 film *Love of the White Snake* is yet another example.

In the Korean Movie Database, *Love of the White Snake* is listed as a Korean-language film made in Korea, under the title *Paeksajŏn* 白蛇傳 백사전, with directorial credit given to Choi Dong-joon (Ch'oe Tong-chun) 崔東俊 최동준. It takes multiple cross-searches in the same database to discover the name Lee Han-sang 이한상, listed only in Korean and cited as a codirector from Hong Kong for the same film.[47] It has one official English title, *Love of the White Snake*; but its Chinese title is *Zhen Baishe zhuan* (True legend of the White Snake) or *Xin Baishe zhuan* (New legend of the White Snake), depending on the source. The Hong Kong Movie Database lists the film as a Mandarin-language fantasy film made in Hong Kong and credits the film to the same Korean director, Choe Dong-joon (as spelled in Hong Kong), but with Si-ma Ke 司馬克 as his codirector.[48] In the comprehensive film review section of the popular Chinese website Douban, the film appears as *Zhen Baishe zhuan* (True legend of the White Snake), with Li Hanxiang 李翰祥 as its sole director; Taiwan, Hong Kong, and South Korea are listed as production countries and regions, and reviewers speculate whether Si-ma Ke is in fact Li Hanxiang.[49]

According to most Chinese-language sources, *Love of the White Snake* was made in 1978 by First Films (which was based in Hong Kong but shot films in Taiwan). The film copy I have access to lists its producer as Wong Cheuk Hon (Huang Zhuohan 黃卓漢), who founded First Films in 1967, and states the film was made to commemorate First Films' tenth anniversary. Importantly, it also lists Nishimoto Tadashi 西本正 as one of the special effects directors,[50] effectively linking Shaw Brothers' 1962 *Madam White Snake*, for which Nishimoto served as cinematographer under his Sinicized name He Lanshan 賀蘭山, with the 1978 *Love of the White Snake*, advertised as "a masterpiece created by dozens of special effect experts from Japan" (*shushi Riben teji zhuanjia jiezuo* 數十日本特技專家傑作).[51]

The young Taiwanese director Chen Chi-hwa (Chen Zhihua 陳誌華) who is listed as the film's executive director (*zhixing daoyan* 執行導演) worked closely under Li Han-hsiang, listed as director under the name Sima Ke. Chen was a member the Grand Motion Picture (GMP 國聯) Film Company established by Li in Taiwan in the 1960s. He worked in both Hong Kong and Taiwan throughout the 1970s and onward, collaborating with King Hu and Jackie Chan, among other important industry players. Li Han-hsiang was a legendary director from Mainland China who started his film career in Hong Kong in the late 1940s and early 1950s (working particularly with the Shaw Brothers). He moved to Taiwan in the 1960s to establish GMP, returned to Hong Kong in the 1970s, and then to Mainland China in the 1980s to continue making films, especially costume dramas.[52]

Finally, in the US Internet Movie Database, the film is listed as *Love of the White Snake* and is credited to codirectors Ke Szema (Sima Ke) and Chi-Hwa Chen (Chen Zhihua). It is described as a coproduction between Taiwan and Hong Kong, but there is no mention of a Korean director or Korean involvement in the production.[53] This extraordinary nexus of contradictions presents a fascinating case study for any researcher interested in continuities and connections across historical times and geopolitical locations in postwar East Asian filmmaking, film coproduction, and film distribution.

Apart from the challenges in determining *Love of the White Snake*'s production history, however, the film is notable for the pervasive presence of the Green Snake. The Green Snake is often seen on-screen adding comedic relief and displaying her magic powers, along with Xu Xian, who appears to be a more likable character compared to earlier versions. In this 1978 film, the Green Snake's magic powers include making rain and changing objects into people, specifically, two rocks and four leaves into two male servants and four maids. The gender implication of the humanity of the nonhuman, with rocks transformed into males and leaves into females, is significant here, especially in the context of the snake women's newly acquired humanity, linking animals and humans. In addition, the two rock-turned-male servants are named "White the Rich" (Bai Fu 白富) and "White the Noble" (Bai Gui 白貴), further engraving human values onto nonhuman objects.[54]

When Green Snake uses magic to make rain, it is comically interpreted to Xu Xian as "even Heaven is trying to make the guest stay" (*tian liuke* 天留客).

When White Snake needs Green Snake to be her matchmaker, she promises to share 10 percent of her future husband with her, while Green Snake insists on at least 30 percent. After seven days of waiting, Green Snake is excited to have Xu Xian to herself for three days, but White Snake uses her honeymoon as an excuse to delay Green Snake's enjoyment of her "share" of Xu Xian. This leads to a series of humorous incidents resembling a slapstick comedy. Here, Green Snake's pursuit of White Snake's human lover recalls the sexually aggressive Green Snake portrayed in the English synopsis of *The Righteous Snake*, the very first White Snake film made in Shanghai in 1926.

In contrast to White Snake's "repayment of life-saving debts [to Xu Xian]" (*bao'en* 報恩) as in earlier renditions, which emphasizes the Buddhist doctrine of transmigration and reincarnation, Green Snake hopes to be "holding [Xu Xian's] legs" (*bao datui* 抱大腿), implying her sexual interest in him, as the two phrases *bao'en* and *bao datui* share a first character with the same pronunciation *bao*. White Snake explains her delay and ultimately her rejection of Green Snake's advances toward Xu by referring to Green Snake's "demon spirit." Since her "demon spirit is not yet cleansed" (*yaoqi weichu* 妖氣未除), Green Snake will poison Xu Xian (*guanren zhongdu* 官人中毒) if she has intimate contact with him. What a horrifying thought for the loyal wife of a human male! No wonder she must protect her sexual monopoly over her husband.

Apart from these comical elements and the "magical happenings," both largely embodied by the demon spirit of the Green Snake, the most impressive character in the 1978 film is the previously mediocre human husband, Xu Xian. In this version, he not only refuses to be persuaded by Abbot Fahai's attempts to separate husband and wife, he is also always squarely on White Snake's side, quite unlike the cowardly, wavering characters of earlier Chinese renditions. He appears to have inherited good qualities not only from Tian Han's early 1950s efforts to make the human lover more likeable but also from Shin Sang-ok's further development of the character. Given our knowledge of the involvement of the Korean director Ch'oe Tong-chun and the existence of Korean-language versions of the film in the Korean Movie Database, the 1978 film *Love of the White Snake* could be better understood in the genealogy of the Korean connection to White Snake cinematic adaptations and as a coproduction between South Korea, Hong Kong, and Taiwan.

By making Xu Xian even more likable, the film further humanizes the White Snake and seems to have diluted the elements of horror in the characters themselves. Still, there are other ingenious ways of rendering horror elements in the 1978 film, which can be read as a continuation of the 1969 horror/romantic fantasy. One example is the employment of Sichuan opera theatrics, likely a result of the Hong Kong–based production crew's involvement in the film. Instead of zooming in on Xu Xian's shocked facial expression after he witnesses White Snake transform into her snake form, the film shows Xu imagining Green Snake's and White Snake's face changing (through the use of slip-screen technology) into frightening masks, like the transformations often seen in Sichuan opera performances (60:00). After Xu recovers from the shock of the transformation, White Snake has to create a fake snake in order to dispel Xu's suspicion. She claims that this snake is the auspicious "dragon of the storage" (*canglong* 倉龍), which appears when a household's storage room is full and will protect its good fortune generation after generation. This story echoes popular folk belief throughout East Asia, and Xu's willing acceptance of the deceit adds a sense of comedy to the previous scene of horror.

Love of the White Snake was a truly international, big-budget coproduction (fig. 42). It was shot on location in both South Korea and Taiwan, unlike earlier versions, which contained relatively few outdoor scenes, and was produced by a Hong Kong film company.[55] For Hong Kong's First Films, which is listed in most Chinese-language sources as the production company, having South Korean and Taiwanese coproducers may have been a matter of necessity. With its Korean and Taiwanese partners, the Hong Kong film company could secure smooth operation for on-location shooting, which is difficult in Hong Kong because of geographical limitations. The theft of the magic herb and the water battle, among many other scenes, were shot entirely on location with realistic outdoor surroundings for the first time in the history of White Snake film adaptions. Further, First Films built up distribution arms in both South Korea and Taiwan.

The film's use of special effects also reached a new level, utilizing many state-of-the-art devices and props. At the same time, the effects prominently resemble those in the 1956 Japanese live-action film starring Yamaguchi Yoshiko, featuring Tsuburaya Eiji's special effects direction. It is possible that Korean director Ch'oe Tong-chun brought to the 1978 film his familiarity with Shin Sang-ok's Korean renditions, which in turn were influenced by Tsuburaya's special effects design. One scene that shows this continuity is after White Snake gives birth to her child. In the 1978 version, as similarly seen in the 1956 Japanese version, White Snake is shown as having shrunk into a miniature version of herself, which will allow her to enter Abbot Fahai's golden bowl, as previously agreed. The Korean connection, with Ch'oe Tong-chun credited as codirector and other Korean personnel in the cast and crew, in effect linked this new film to Japanese adaptations, from the 1956 live-action

Figure 42: A Chinese-Korean bilingual color poster for the 1978 *Love of the White Snake* (*Zhen Baishe zhuan*). The title is given simply as *Baishe zhuan*, with Korean director Choi Dong-joon and Chinese director Li Han-hsiang listed together as directors. The film is described as a coproduction between Hong Kong's First Films (*Diyi yingye*) and Korea's Woo Sung Enterprises (*Jusikoesa Useongsa*). The Korean Movie Database features this poster as the image for the film, which is designated a Korean production; see https://www.kmdb.or.kr/eng/db/kor/detail/movie/K/03251/credit; also see https://tieba.baidu.com/p/3624404079?red_tag=0440089292.

version, onward through the Japanese and Korean reinventions in the 1950s and 1960s.

The Taiwan Connection in the Context of a Hong Kong–Singapore Cinematic Matrix

If the Hong Kong–Korean coproduction of the 1978 film entailed a Hong Kong production company plus a Korean codirector and Korean influence, where does Taiwan fit into the picture? The film was shot on location in Taiwan, but this was not the limit of Taiwan's involvement. It is important to revisit the long history of Taiwan's engagement with performing the White Snake on stage. Shanghai theater troupes toured Taiwan in the early 1920s at the height of White Snake's popularity in Mainland China, as discussed in chapter 2. One particular report on July 29, 1921, detailed the all-female Shanghai Ruyi Theater Troupe's (Shanghai ruyi nüban 上海如意女班) sensational return visit at the New Stage at the invitation of Xin Pingle Teahouse (Xin Pingle chayuan 新平樂茶園) in Taiwan,[56] suggesting the success of an earlier tour. The report claimed that the theater was full every night and detailed innovative promotional measures handing out lottery prizes ranging from supreme rice to a clock. The one and only attraction every night was a "complete rendition" of *The Legend of the White Snake* (*Quanben Baishe zhuan*).

For an average viewer in the late 1970s, however, the 1978 White Snake film's most visible Taiwanese connection lay in its stars, particularly Brigitte Lin Ching-hsia (Lin Qingxia 林青霞), the striking actress who plays White Snake, and her famed screen partner, Charlie Chin Chiang-lin (Chin Xianglin 秦祥林). Lin emerged as the goddess of Taiwanese romance films and TV soap operas in the early 1970s. Her crowd-pleasing screen persona had a lasting impact on bringing the romantic image of the White Snake into mainstream popular culture in the Chinese-speaking worlds (fig. 43).

If the power of its film stars put Taiwan's stamp on the 1978 film, the multilocational career of Sima Ke, the mysterious author who was credited as a codirector with Choe Dong-joon (Ch'oe Tong-chun) in the Hong Kong Movie Database, contains important clues concerning the links between the film industries of Mainland China, Hong Kong, Japan, South Korea, and Taiwan. Sima Ke, better known as Li Han-hsiang (Li Hanxiang), is known for celebrated films such as the 1963 Shaw Brothers' *The Love Eterne* (*Liang Shanbo yu Zhu Yingtai*), based on the legend of the Butterfly Lovers, which also features enchantresses and themes of metamorphosis.

Born in 1926 in Liaoning, China, Li Han-hsiang went on to study Western

Figure 43: Brigitte Lin Ching-hsia (Lin Qingxia) as White Snake in *Love of the White Snake* (*Zhen Baishe zhuan*), featured on the cover of *Jinri dianying* (Today movie [sic]), no. 49 (1978).

painting in Beijing in 1946, just as Shin Sang-ok had studied Western painting in Tokyo only a couple of years before. Expelled from school because of his political activism, he moved to Shanghai in 1948 to enter a theater school. He left for Hong Kong later the same year to find work in its nascent film industry. Li worked as an actor, set designer, and voice actor in various early postwar film ventures in Hong Kong during the late 1940s and early 1950s. While working on dubbing, he closely studied *Escape at Dawn* (*Akatsuki no dassō*

暁の脱走), a 1950 Japanese film produced by Tanaka Tomoyuki and starring Yamaguchi Yoshiko and Ikebe Ryō (the same team that later made the 1956 live-action *Madame White Snake*), with Kurosawa Akira as co–script writer and Mimura Akira as cinematographer. As Li scripted the Chinese dialogue for the dubbing of this Japanese film, he learned from its cinematography frame by frame.

Li joined the Shaw Brothers in the mid-1950s. Inspired by the success of the Mainland Huangmei opera film *Heavenly Match* (*Tianxian pei*), based on the story of Dong Yong, he created the Shaw Brothers' first color film, the *Huangmei diao* costume drama *Diau Charn* (*Diao Chan* 貂蟬), in 1958. With Lin Dai as Diao Chan and Zhao Lei as Lü Bu, the 1958 film shares the same stars with director Yueh Feng's *Madam White Snake*, released four years later. *Diau Charn* won Li the award for best director and garnered another four awards at the Fifth Asia-Pacific Film Festival in the Philippines the same year. The year after, in 1959, another of Li's films, *The Kingdom and the Beauty* (*Jiangshan meiren* 江山美人), starring the same pair of actors, broke box office records in both Hong Kong and Taiwan and won the award for best picture at the Sixth Asia-Pacific Film Festival in Kuala Lumpur. Intriguingly, it was also submitted, under Singaporean aegis, for best foreign language film at the Thirty-Second Academy Awards, which attests to its Singaporean connection and the Hollywood reach of Hong Kong–based Shaw Brothers films.[57]

In the early 1960s, Li Han-hsiang and Shaw Brothers gained international renown at the Cannes Film Festival and market dominance in Taiwan and Hong Kong for a series of Mainland-inspired costume drama featuring famous beauties from Chinese history and legend. These included the 1960 *Enchanting Shadow* (*Qiannü youhun* 倩女幽魂), the 1962 *Magnificent Concubine* (*Yang Guifei*), and the 1963 *The Love Eterne*. Riding on this popularity, Li established his film company GMP in Taiwan in 1963 and brought with him a group of talented film practitioners from Hong Kong. That same year, Li followed the sensational Taiwan box office success of *The Love Eterne* with *Seven Fairies* (*Qi xiannü*), GMP's first production made in Taiwan and largely based on the Mainland Chinese film *Heavenly Match*. As a result, Li facilitated the rise of Mandarin-language filmmaking in Taiwan, a market previously dominated by American and Japanese films.

With the opening of the Eleventh Asia-Pacific Film Festival in Taipei in 1964, Taiwan came of age as a key player in inter-Asian cinematic exchanges. Leading figures in Asian film industries at the time attended the festival. Nagata Masaichi, producer of Mizoguchi's *Ugetsu*, represented Japan; and Shin Sang-ok, director of the 1960 *Madam White Snake* (who would make a second attempt in 1969 in *Snake Woman* as discussed above), represented Korea. Loke Wan Tho 陸運濤, a Malaysian/Singaporean business magnate and founder of Motion Picture and General Investment (MP & GI 國際電影懋業有限公司, or 電懋) in Hong Kong,[58] and Run Run Shaw, in charge of Shaw Brothers, both represented Hong Kong. And Henry Kung 龔弘, chair of the festival's executive committee, Lung Fang 龍芳, Yeung Chiu 楊樵, and Hsia Wei-Tang 夏維堂, all important managers and producers, represented Taiwan.[59] Unfortunately, this forward momentum slowed after June 20, 1964, when a plane crash in Taichung resulted in the death of Loke Wan Tho and Lung Fang, together with some fifty other important film industry personnel, many of whom were in talks with Li Han-hsiang regarding coproduction. If not for this accident, the future of Li's GMP and of Chinese-language filmmaking in Taiwan, Hong Kong, and Southeast Asia might have been much brighter.

After the untimely death of Loke Wan Tho, who was a major supporter of Li's efforts with GMP and had played a key role in connecting Hong Kong and Taiwan cinema with Singapore and Southeast Asia in general,[60] political and economic pressures led Li Han-hsiang to leave Taiwan for Hong Kong. When Li wrote the screenplay for *Love of the White Snake* under the name of Si-ma Ke, he was in fact working with Shaw Brothers back in Hong Kong, on the major production *Dream of the Red Chamber* (*Honglou meng*), starring a cross-dressing Brigitte Lin, the White Snake actress in *Love of the White Snake*, as Jia Baoyu 賈寶玉 the male lead. It was also in 1978 that Li Han-hsiang made a secret trip back to Mainland China and initiated the process of returning to work in the film and television industries there, three decades after he had left for Hong Kong as a young man looking to make a name in its nascent film industry.

CONCLUDING REMARKS

In addition to the three Japanese films analyzed in chapter 4 and the three films forming the Korean connection discussed in this chapter, another three films—the Shaw Brothers' 1962 *Huangmei diao* film *Madam White Snake* (Hong Kong, starring Lin Dai), the 1975 Kung Fu film/slapstick comedy *Snake Woman's Marriage* (*Baishe da'nao tiangong* 白蛇大鬧天宮, Taiwan, starring Chia Ling 嘉凌), and the 1980 *jingju* film *Legend of the White Snake* (*Baishe zhuan*, Mainland China, starring Li Bingshu 李炳淑)—reinforce what I call the inter-Asian context of the White Snake films. These films link Hong Kong,

Taiwan, and Mainland China, in addition to Japan and Korea, and involve producers, performers, and patrons throughout East and Southeast Asia.

The 1962 Hong Kong version and the 1975 Taiwan version of the White Snake films can be understood in the context of commercial melodrama, with a strong tendency to demystify, humanize, and eroticize the image of the White Snake. In the late 1950s and early 1960s, the Shaw Brothers, who collaborated with Tōhō in Japan to produce the 1956 film, attempted to use the *Huangmei diao* film with Lin Dai in the title role to launch a new commercial venture. Like many other film practitioners at the time, both the director Yueh Feng and the leading actress Lin Dai had moved from Mainland China to Hong Kong in 1949. Where Yueh Fang contributed his experience in commercial filmmaking in 1930s Shanghai, Lin Dai brought the ability to perform and sing in Mandarin Chinese.

With the phenomenal success of Mainland Huangmei opera films such as *Heavenly Match*, *Female Imperial Son-in-Law* (*Nü fuma* 女駙馬), and *The Cowherd and the Weaving Girl* in Hong Kong and Southeast Asia from 1955 on, the Shaw Brothers launched its own Mandarin-language *Huangmei diao* film enterprise in Hong Kong (reflected in Li Han-hsiang's inter-Asian career discussed above). These included *Heavenly Maiden Spreading Flowers* (*Tiannü sanhua* 天女散花) in 1959 and *Madam White Snake* in 1962, both starring Lin Dai in the title role. The eighteen songs in *Madam White Snake*, sung by Jing Ting and Jiang Hong for the roles of White Snake and Xu Xian, respectively, were heavily influenced by *Heavenly Match* and other Mainland Huangmei opera films.[61] The popularization of *Huangmei diao* films in Hong Kong worked well with the celebration of the folk legend and the pursuit of sensual enjoyment in modern life, as embodied in three ways: by the tagline "to pursue happiness you need to go to the human realm" (*yao kuaile dao renjian* 要快樂到人間), by the image of the enigmatic White Snake in the film, and by the enchanting actress Lin Dai in real life.

The 1975 Taiwanese film *Snake Woman's Marriage* starring Chia Ling, a martial arts film resembling a slapstick comedy, saw the coming together of the comical and the erotic and the transformation of the literary into the martial, and magical into melodrama. Female singing voices functioned as narrative voiceover, developing plot and releasing emotion. The total humanization of the White Snake brought the comical and the erotic closer together, as the scholar turned martial hero saves the beauty, and, in turn, the beauty rejuvenates the spirit of the hero (*yingxiong jiumei/meijiu yingxiong* 英雄救美/美救英雄). Without prior knowledge of the abundant Japanese and Korean renditions before this version, I had always thought of the

1975 film, labeled as made in Taiwan, as the most outlandish version among the Chinese-language adaptations and have wondered where on earth the producers got their ideas. Combing through the inter-Asian connections and reflecting on how these films were responding to Mainland Chinese filmmaking from the 1950s, we discover how they provoked or facilitated the rise of Mandarin-language cinema in Taiwan in the 1970s. The eccentricities of White Snake and Xu Xian in the 1975 Taiwan film emerge as results of a gradual evolution with many precedents, including White Snake's giving up of her magic power to save her husband and Xu Xian's turning into a Disney-style "Prince Charming," both already reflected in the 1958 Japanese animation and continued to evolve in the Korean White Snake films of the 1960s.

Not completely surprisingly, a Hong Kong producer and a Hong Kong special effects director were in fact behind *Snake Woman's Marriage*. The film was likely categorized as a Taiwan production because it was shot on location in Taiwan and because its leading actress was Chia Ling, a star in both martial arts and Chinese opera in Taiwan before she entered the film industry in the early 1970s. Born into a leading opera singer's family in Taiwan, Chia was known as a multitalented performer of female roles (*dan* 旦) who excelled in both "civil" (*wenxi* 文戲) and "martial" (*wuxi* 武戲) plays in canonic operas such as *The White Snake* before making her name as a leading film actress. Chia Ling's White Snake consequently combined the literary with the martial. Produced by the Huaxing Film Company from Hong Kong, the big-budget production achieved some of the best special effects to date in Taiwanese filmmaking, including the two lifelike giant snakes and the water battle scene between White Snake's water troop and Abbot Fahai's heavenly soldiers.[62]

Such a vibrant inter-Asian cinematic mapping of the White Snake story in Japan, Hong Kong, South Korea and Taiwan, from the late 1950s to the late 1970s, presented a challenge to the Mainland Chinese film industry. As I have shown, this challenge is a result of the popularity of Mainland Chinese films from the mid-1950s onward, which supplied both cultural resources and cinematic inspirations for such an inter-Asian development. During the first few years of the cultural rebirth following the Cultural Revolution, Shanghai Film Studio produced the *jingju* film *Legend of the White Snake* as a possible response to the earlier attempts at recreating White Snake during the Cold War. This 1980 Shanghai version of the White Snake film can be best understood in the context of multiple dialogues between the film world of 1930s Shanghai, when Kim Yŏm was its "movie emperor," the tradition of opera films in the Chinese mainland during the 1950s and 1960s, and the Japanese,

Hong Kong, Korean, and Taiwanese connections from the 1950s to the 1970s, as explored in chapter 4 and throughout this chapter.

Through the enduring White Snake theme, this *jingju* film made possible a historical dialogue between the 1920s, 1950s, and 1980s, as it was based on Tian Han's *jingju* version from the 1950s, which took inspiration from the experimental quality of his silent film of the 1920s, was filmed in the late 1970s, and then was released in 1980 in Shanghai. The Shanghai femme fatale, inspired by the Japanese renditions of the Chinese folk legend, returned to Beijing in the garb of traditional Chinese theater, but her transgressive female sexuality and revolutionary energy could not be tamed. Such transgressive sexuality and revolutionary energy joined hands with the international socialism and state feminism that prevailed in Beijing during the 1950s. This hybrid image of the "new woman" combined feminism with socialism, and traditional aesthetics with modern political aspirations.[63]

The many talented actresses who made their name performing the White Snake on the Chinese opera stage beginning in the 1950s attest to the continuing relevance of the story in the cultural life and social practice of the PRC. One of these White Snake actresses would later emerge as the female protagonist in Geling Yan's 1998 novella *White Snake*, which is at the center of the next chapter. Conditioned by the immediate post–Cultural Revolution moment, the 1980 Shanghai film quite faithfully followed Tian Han's mid-1950s *jingju* version of the story. However, as one of the first feature films from the PRC in the early 1980s, its high-caliber *jingju* performance and high-tech special effects, together with its emphasis on gender and class politics from the bottom up, created a new White Snake canon in the post–Cultural Revolution context through *jingju*, a genre highly relevant but much-maligned during the Cultural Revolution.

The current chapter, together with chapter 4, has highlighted the inter-Asian connections among Mainland China, Japan, Hong Kong, South Korea, Taiwan, and Southeast Asia as the White Snake legend was reworked under Cold War conditions. The Korean connections to the White Snake films, as explored in this chapter, offer important clues for deciphering three films at the center of an inter-Asian context of on-screen White Snake recreations in the 1960s and 1970s. In excavating Hong Kong's much-overlooked Japanese and Korean connections, we see a place often dismissed as a "cultural desert"[64] emerge instead as a Cold War cultural powerhouse, coproducing with Japan, South Korea, and Taiwan, exporting to Southeast Asia, and revamping the White Snake in vivid shapes and colors and with enchanting actresses at the center. Such feminine re-enchantment could be read as an extension of the PRC's soft power in which the political propaganda of state feminism enables radical gender transgressions. However, a rebellious White Snake, among other strong female protagonists, human or nonhuman, could also serve propagandistic purposes well, as it did throughout the early 1950s in the Chinese mainland during the campaign to propagate the new marriage law.[65]

The metamorphoses of the White Snake indeed reached a new height during the Cold War. Tian Han's *jingju* version *The White Snake,* finalized in the early 1950s in Beijing, was only the beginning of a cross-genre and multimedia flowering of the theme in Japan, Hong Kong, Taiwan, and Mainland China from the 1950s to the 1980s.[66] Throughout the Cold War, supernatural materials such as the White Snake legend were creatively manipulated to popularize and celebrate modern ideas such as heterosexual love, women's rights, and the triumph of humanity. The paradoxical nature of the legend's continuing popularity throughout the Cold War in East and Southeast Asia urges us to rethink the intricate connection between myth and mythmaking in contemporary politics and popular culture. The various retellings of the legend, both inside and outside the film industry, worked together to transform it into a story of love and reconciliation and helped to create a stable master narrative—but one that would then be overturned amid the changes of the global 1980s and beyond, as Part III of this book demonstrates.

PART III

The Specter of the Past in Contemporary Popular Culture

CHAPTER 6

Reconfiguring the Legend in Mainland China and Hong Kong

Many careers have been made by impersonating the White Snake on stage and screen. The real-life actresses and actors who have performed the role of the enchanting snake woman in her various manifestations have sometimes gained fame and fortune, but they have also suffered humiliation and persecution. Their embodiment of such a dangerously seductive creature, a woman-snake hybrid, has been prone to conflation with the image of the often audacious and daring "new woman" in their own time. Chapters 4 and 5 of Part II featured such fantastic seductresses and modern femmes fatales on-screen in Japan, South Korea, Hong Kong, and Taiwan, in spaces outside Mainland China, and beyond the Chinese-speaking worlds at the height of the Cold War, with influence across Asia and beyond. This "peripheral" approach is indeed a self-conscious, revisionist interpretation of my earlier work on recreating the White Snake legend in the Mainland, with the Chinese artist and activist Tian Han's various activities at the center of a Beijing-based and Mandarin Chinese–centered approach.[1]

The many talented actresses who made their name playing the snake woman on the Chinese opera stage, in Mandarin Chinese and no less than a dozen local dialects beginning in the 1950s, attest to the White Snake story's continuing relevance in the cultural life and social practice in the PRC. The cinematic heroines that appeared largely outside its borders only lend weight to the story's cultural importance. One of these White Snake actresses, who performed in a highly experimental hybrid genre that combined Sichuan opera with Western ballet, would emerge as the female protagonist in Geling Yan's 1998 novella *White Snake* (*Baishe*). The novella is set in Mainland China between the late 1950s and the early 1980s, a period this chapter revisits from the perspective of the post–Cultural Revolution 1980s and beyond. In the same novella, the White Snake's companion, the Green Snake, inherits expressive revolutionary qualities recreated by the Hong Kong writer Lilian Lee's novel *Green Snake* (*Qingshe*), which was written and revised in Hong Kong between the mid- to late 1980s and the early 1990s and was adapted for the silver screen in Cantonese by Tsui Hark in 1993 and for the stage in Mandarin Chinese by Tian Qinxin twenty years later.

WRITING AND DANCING, THE TEXT AND THE BODY

In this chapter, I explore the ways in which retellings of the White Snake legends became means of resisting patriarchy, heterosexuality, and authoritarianism from the 1980s onwards and how these new versions of the tale provided ways for creative artists to come to terms with the socialist past of Mainland China, the colonial past of Hong Kong, and now the postsocialist, postcolonial present through projections for the future. With an emphasis on crossing boundaries between diverse artistic genres and fields, I underscore how the distinctive political potential and affective power of the fantastic can be expressed in retellings of the White Snake legends by both verbal and nonverbal means. The dialectics of writing and dancing—or, put differently, the text and the body—as embodied by Geling Yan's dancing White Snake and Lilian Lee's writing Green Snake—have long occupied philosophers, writers, dance critics, cultural historians, and religious scholars, among others, and emerges as a central concern for this chapter.

I first offer a sequence of Western theories that hierarchize writing over dancing and, with few exceptions, subsume dance into a writing-based framework. I then explore contrasting conceptualizations that Chinese theory may be able to offer, situating writing and dancing in terms of a continuum of expressive activity and, most importantly, as a multidirectional, interlocking relationship, in which each medium informs and shapes the other. For example, in *Between Dancing and Writing*, Kimerer L. LaMothe traces how the field of religious studies tends to "favor verbal media and verbal practices over other forms of religious communication." She also identifies how, within that conceptual framework, "rhythmic bodily action can appear only as what Michel Foucault calls a 'subjugated knowledge.'" She points out that even those who recognize the problem often unwittingly reinforce the hierarchy that privileges writing over dancing and text over body. This overreliance on the practice of writing as "a model, metaphor, and disciplinary method" is ubiquitous in the Western academic world and, to some degree, also in traditional Chinese music and literary theory, where dance is conceived as the outward "appearance" (*rong* 容) of music, while language (in the form of lyrical expression) is its "heart" (*xin* 心).[2]

LaMothe continues to cite a range of examples that use the language of writing to describe dancing and other movements: Catherine Bell discusses ritual action in terms of its "vocabulary," Susan Foster calls dance a form of "bodily writing," and Richard Schechner interprets the movements of Kathakali as "being written in the bodies of dancers" and "read" by them "from the inside."[3] Although one might read this tendency as an attempt to raise the status of dancing and movement to the level of writing and "articulated" knowledge, simply by using such terminology, these scholars in effect unwittingly marginalize and subordinate dancing in relation to writing within the terrains of their respective fields. However, since those fields are academic and are therefore comprised largely of written language, it seems natural that writing should be privileged over physical movement in this way; language is of course the gold standard for any evaluation that takes place in any realm dominated by written communication.

Since the early 1980s, a "transmedia" approach to "writing" and "dancing" has been favored by Kenneth King, a leading American postmodern dancer. King emphasizes the reciprocity between dancing and writing and recognizes "a double motion" that "involves a synergy, even symbiosis, that animates not only the body but also words."[4] In his pioneering 1981 essay "Transmedia," King highlights two keywords, "transmedia" and "kinetrics": the former as a "movement that connects and extends whatever we see or know, in our heads, on the page or stage, across a room, or on a screen: even across disciplines"; the latter "as the movement of bodies, ideas, images, lines, words, letters, concepts, tracks, designs, structures, *systems*, etc., through and across one another."[5] Such a synthesizing approach is relevant for our consideration of the dialectics between writing and dancing and between the verbal and nonverbal retellings of the White Snake legends.

Along the lines of Martha Graham's famous declaration that "dance is the hidden language of the soul,"[6] Danielle Knafo discusses another important aspect of the writing/dancing dialectic that was at play in the founding of psychoanalysis when Sigmund Freud and Josef Breuer filled *Studies on Hysteria* with stories of paralyzed or dystonic women's bodies.[7] Here, the bodily movements of women were used to access their psychological state, and psychosis was studied through material embodiments and physical expressions. This treatment of psychosis as a physical state is relevant to the experiences of the White Snake and Green Snake figures in the contemporary novel and novella that I analyze in this chapter.[8] In counterpoint, the field of expressive arts therapy has emerged to explore how dance may "benefit people in ways which might be healing to the soul, to their relations with others, and to their psychological well-being."[9] According to Daria Halprin, "our bodies contain our life stories just as they contain bones, muscles, organs, nerves, and blood," and "the entire repertoire of our life experience can be accessed and activated through the body in movement."[10]

In accordance with King's pioneering transmedia, synthesizing writings on postmodern dance practices and LaMothe's call for dance to be treated seriously in religious and philosophical discourses, I examine Geling Yan's creative retelling of the White Snake legend in her novella *White Snake* in relation to Lilian Lee's novel *Green Snake*, written in the diaspora and in Hong Kong, respectively, with a focus on how the relationships between dancing and writing, and fantasy and reality, function both literally and metaphorically in these narratives. In both my textual and contextual analyses, I borrow Daria Halprin's therapeutic model for accessing life experiences through the body in movement. I argue that, through a creative use of writing and dancing as key metaphors for identity formation and transformation, Yan's text offers innovative counter-narratives of gender, writing, and the body in the context of the Cultural Revolution in particular and of contemporary China in general, demonstrating the potential power of the fantastic to resist and reshape reality.

The relationship between writing and dancing, and language and the body, can be traced back to early literary and artistic traditions in China. In contemporary Chinese-language discussions of arts and aesthetics, "poetry, singing, dancing, and music" (*shi ge wu yue* 詩歌舞樂) often appear as a single expression, as if this itemization of four expressive media stands for a larger whole.[11] This reflects the intricate interrelations between the four arts as articulated in early Chinese texts such as *Ritual of the Zhou (Zhouli* 周禮). The relationship has also been further articulated by Zhu Guangqian 朱光潛, often considered the founder of the study of aesthetics (*meixue* 美學) in twentieth-century China.[12] What Kenneth King calls a postmodern "transmedia" approach was in fact elaborated in the preface of *The Classic of Poetry* (*Shijing* 詩經), likely composed during or not long before the Han dynasties (202 BC–220 AD), which states in part: "When feelings are moved within, they are manifested in words; when words are not enough, they make people sigh with emotion; when sighing becomes inadequate, they compel people to sing songs; when singing still cannot fully express, people cannot help dancing with their arms and legs."[13]

According to the great Tang Dynasty poet Du Fu's preface to one of his poems, the famous Tang Dynasty calligrapher Zhang Xu (active late seventh to mid-eighth century) greatly improved his calligraphy skills after watching female dancer Gongsun's extraordinary sword dance.[14] Zhang Xu is also said to have improved his calligraphy after watching a crane and a snake fight and carefully analyzing their movements, although no written source is available and the story borders on the legendary. The fight between the Crane God and the White Snake in the legend of the White Snake forms one of the central conflicts in the storyline, as the White Snake must seek the magic herb from the magic mountain guarded by the Crane and Deer Gods to revive her human husband.[15] The fight between a crane and a snake is also central to the founding myth of the Wing Chun school of martial arts, whose founder is said to have been inspired by the fight to create a new style of Southern martial arts that would accentuate the movements of crane and snake.[16]

In this sense, both martial arts and dancing are writing with the body in space. Writing, in turn, can be regarded as a transformation, containment, or perpetuation of energetic but ephemeral dancing movements. Indeed, calligraphy is a form of choreography—an attempt to infuse that which is written and the act of writing with rhythm and movement, to turn verbal communication into something more corporeal. The fact that calligraphy has such a prominent place in Chinese art suggests a distinctive dynamic between movement and inscription in the Chinese context, that dancing and calligraphy are not necessarily reducible to writing and reading[17] and that the choreography of movements and structures of writing emerge as an integral process in the intermedia origins of Chinese art and aesthetics. As the idea of text representing corporeality became deeply embedded, the relationship between text and the body became much closer in the Chinese and East Asian context, as Chinese characters served important functions in the development of Japanese, Korean, and Vietnamese languages from premodern times and throughout the twentieth century and beyond.[18]

Such a formulation of the dialectics between writing and dancing, text and body, signals an alternative to the hierarchizing metaphors in the Western context discussed at the opening of this chapter. In this broad Chinese context, I examine Geling Yan's *White Snake*, in connection with Lilian Lee's *Green Snake*, in its form finalized in the early 1990s. My discussion is aligned with three specific contexts: first, the expressiveness of the female body relevant to the White Snake legend and its literary canon; second, the tradition and significance of women writers in imperial, modern, and contemporary China; and third, the experience of a real-life "snake dancer" from the early 1950s to the early 1980s in China, as it corresponds to the experience of the female protagonists in the stories. These three different contexts, woven together, create an intricate tapestry that reveals the dialectics of writing and dancing, and of language and the body, throughout the latter half of the twentieth century in Mainland China and Hong Kong. Furthermore, Yan's text foregrounds the Cultural Revolution as an important chronotope for experimenting with a range of complex gender identities and female subjectivities in relation to the expressive and symbolic powers of dancing and writing in the retelling of the White Snake legends.

The Expressiveness of the Hybrid Body and the Iconoclasm of the Green Snake

On the Chinese mainland in the early 1950s, Tian Han's *jingju* version of *The White Snake* summons White Snake's maid/sister figure Green Snake back to "liberate" (*jiefang* 解放) her from under the Thunder Peak Pagoda.[19] This can be understood as the model for the young fangirl "liberating" the incarcerated White Snake dancer in Geling Yan's novella, attesting to the feminist and grassroots revolutionary spirit celebrated by the new Communist government,[20] and its possible queer implications. The key themes of dancing, writing, and the formation and transformation of gender and sexual identities are front and center in Yan's *White Snake*, a story about a cross-dressing female fan's homosexual infatuation with an actress famous for playing the White Snake before, during, and after the Cultural Revolution. The female, hybrid, dancing body is celebrated as expressive in performance, but that same body can be seen as politically suspicious in real life; the White Snake can be revered onstage and at the same time can be considered scandalous offstage. In Yan's *White Snake*, the fate of the fictional White Snake performer, who during the Cultural Revolution is accused of being "worn shoes" (*poxie* 破鞋, i.e., a loose woman) in her offstage life, serves as an allegory for the life-shaping power of performance.

The female fan of Yan's novella radically identifies with Green Snake, who in some versions of the legend is a male who wishes to marry White Snake but is transformed into her female servant after losing a bet.[21] The 2011 Pulitzer Prize–winning opera *Madame White Snake* represents Green Snake with a nod to her previous male identity, and its Opera Boston premiere in 2010 and later iterations employed a male soprano for the role, as I elaborate in chapter 7. In Yan's novella, the female fan who identifies with the Green Snake disguises herself as a man and visits the White Snake dancer every day, while the latter is incarcerated during the Cultural Revolution. These daily visits become something of a month-long therapy session for both of them. In fact, the androgynous Green Snake emerges as a key to deciphering Yan's *White Snake*.

In Lilian Lee's novel, written and revised between the late 1980s and the early 1990s in Hong Kong, Green Snake and White Snake peer down from their hiding place and witness female dancers dancing in the human realm. Initially, the snakes see the female dancers as a swirl of charm and exoticism: wild glances, bare feet, seductive music, swaying necks, flamboyant and unrefined costumes. For the reader, the dancers' bare feet might suggest an Indian origin, their twisting necks a Uyghur connection, and their seductive eyes and spirits, Salome's Dance of the Seven Veils. However, from the snake women's perspective, the female dancers' greatest charm lies in their "snake-like" waists. Naturally, that charm also pales before "the real thing," Green Snake and White Snake themselves.[22]

Lilian Lee's *Green Snake* revolutionizes the power structure governing the four main characters of the canonical White Snake story—the White Snake, the Green Snake, the human lover Xu Xian, and the Buddhist abbot Fahai and changes the rules of their power game. The fight between Green Snake and White Snake for Xu Xian challenges the stable, heterosexual relationship between White Snake and Xu Xian, also mocked in the 1978 film. Traditional conceptualizations of the White Snake/Xu Xian relationship are also challenged by emerging homosexual relationships between the Green Snake and the White Snake, and between Fahai and Xu Xian. Although the male homosexual relationship is beyond the scope of this chapter, it gained full expression in the Taiwanese experimental theater movement of the 1990s, when Tien Chi-yuan's (Tian Qiyuan 田啟元) adaptation of the White Snake tale *White Water* 白水 used male actors to perform all four roles (White Snake, Green Snake, Fahai, and Xu Xian), accentuating male homosexual expression.[23]

Similarly, Lilian Lee's *Green Snake* further challenges the singular, stable, heterosexual relationship between the White Snake and Xu Xian. In the scene below, Green Snake, a minor character in the canonic narrative but "a real snake woman" herself, turns to dance as the most effective means to express her frustrated sexual desires:

> I dance wildly. As I turn, my dress lightly brushes flowers and grasses. I face the sunshine—I have not thought about it . . .
>
> Tears streaming down, out of control.
>
> Not sure how long it's been, not knowing how many rounds I have danced so wildly. I turn around and see a man . . .
>
> "You dance really well," he tries to explain away something, "I didn't know you could dance."
>
> "What dance? It's just chaotic movements." "True, dance has its own rules."

> I abruptly sit down under the willow tree, raising my face: "I hate rules. They're so annoying: one should do this, and one shouldn't do that."[24]

Green Snake's dance expresses not only desire but also an anarchic impulse, and brings to mind Mexican director Guillermo del Toro's interpretation of the horror and fairy tale genres as "completely anarchic and antiestablishment," as discussed in chapter 1.[25] "Chaos" (*luan* 亂) is the key to Green Snake's dance. She is determined to break all rules and longs for revolutionary, earth-shattering changes. Lilian Lee's Green Snake's self-portrayal, "I dance wildly," also anticipates Geling Yan's White Snake and her self-perception of the profound chaos expressed by her dancer's body and her "blank brain." With Yan's character, the question "Who am I?" becomes the ultimate expression of such bodily and psychological struggles.[26]

However, Lilian Lee's *Green Snake*, often considered a postmodern breakthrough in rewriting the White Snake legend in late twentieth-century Hong Kong, in fact carried on an important alternative interpretive tradition in the canon in which the character of the Green Snake is accorded more power and importance, especially in the relatively "nonmainstream" branch of the tradition represented by *A Complete Account of the White Snake* (*Baishe quanzhuan* 白蛇全傳), a vernacular novel attributed to a certain Master of the House of Dreaming Flowers (Menghua guanzhu 夢花館主) at the turn of the twentieth century. In this version, Green Snake desires Xu Xian—even if it means having to share him with White Snake—and tries to seduce him.[27] This competition for Xu Xian not only introduced melodrama into the 1926 *Righteous Snake* film series but also provided the 1978 film *Love of the White Snake* with its main source of comedy. The foregrounding of Green Snake went even further on stage, as represented by Sichuan opera, as well as early *jingju* and Kunqu opera traditions, in which Green Snake's identity shifts from male to female in order for him to become a maid servant to the White Snake.

Many paintings on the White Snake theatrical performances in mid-twentieth-century China connect the multiple important trends central to the revamping of the White Snake image that I examine in this study. One of these is Guan Liang's 1956 ink painting of the "Broken Bridge" (fig. 44) scene, whose year of creation is contemporaneous with the period in which the beginning of Yan's novella is set. It highlights the spirit of the Green Snake as performed on the *jingju* stage and deeply echoes my previous study on Tian Han's avant-gardist spirit as reflected in his *jingju* version of *The White Snake*, created just a few years before Guan's painting. A leading Cantonese painter of the twentieth century, Guan reminds us the importance of Southern Chi-

Figure 44: "A Scene from *The White Snake*" (*Baishe zhuan yiduan*). Ink painting by Guan Liang, 1956. It portrays Green Snake accusing Xu Xian of betraying White Snake, who protects Xu Xian against Green Snake. The depicted scene is from "Broken Bridge" (*Duanqiao*), one of the most performed excerpts of *jingju White Snake*. Held at the National Art Museum of China.

nese painting in the development of the Japanese monochrome film *Ugetsu* in the early 1950s. Importantly, Guan Liang, like Tian Han, was a lover of stylized Chinese stage performances as a child and went to Japan to receive Western-style education in his late teens. He was influenced by both ritualized Chinese theatrical performances, which inspired Bertolt Brecht and other modernists in their artistic experimentations,[28] and by fauvism, especially Henri Matisse's "neo-impressionist" painting style. Such encounters were mediated, ironically, by Guan's experience learning realistic Western-style painting in Japan.[29] Guan Liang's 1956 ink painting "Broken Bridge" synthesizes his rich exposure to oil painting and Chinese painting, realism and impressionism and yet may appear childish at first glance, precisely because of its lack of interest in photographic realism. However, its powerfully economic brushstrokes bring out the characters' life force, highlighting the androgynous and audacious spirit of Green Snake, who is at the center of both the painting and the dramatic conflict that it depicts.

This dynamic tension that characterizes Green Snake, vividly brought to life in Guan Liang's painting, is also exemplified in the practice in some Sichuan opera performances of using two actors, one male and one female, to play Green Snake. The "tender care" and "earnest service" offered by Green Snake to White Snake in Yan's novella (using characterizations of Green Snake directly borrowed from Sichuan opera), requires a specific "secondary female" (*tiedan* 貼旦) role, while fighting White Snake in the "Subduing Green" (*Shouqing* 收青) scene, supporting White Snake in the "Water Battle" (*Shuidou* 水鬥) scene, accusing Xu Xian in the "Broken Bridge" scene and demonstrating mask-changing skills unique to Sichuan opera, require male roles ranging from "clown" (*chou* 丑), "mighty male" (*jing* 淨), to "martial male" (*wusheng* 武生).[30] The range of changing gender roles partly gives rise to the reinterpretations of Green Snake; in other words, splitting the role between a male and a female actor gives substance to the problem of restrictive definitions of the feminine. Of course, the very fact that the same role was played by two actors also suggests the Green Snake's androgynous character, manifesting both feminine and masculine attributes and archetypes.

Thus, rather than inverting or overturning the White Snake/Green Snake tradition, Lilian Lee's novel foregrounds and literalizes the expressive and transgressive desire of the androgynous Green Snake, which had long simmered beneath the surface in popular versions of the legend and on local opera stages. This "anti-traditional" tradition has continued to find expression on the modern stage. This trend was highly visible in the mid-1970s with the Taiwanese Cloud Gate Dance Theatre's (*Yunmen wuji* 雲門舞集) rendition of the story, in which stunning choreography heightened the expression of the triangular love and lust between Green Snake, White Snake, and Xu Xian,[31] and continued in the early 1990s with Tien Chi-yuan's experiments in the aforementioned *White Water*.[32] In all of these incarnations, Green Snake dances to express her repressed desires and her rebellious spirit. But, significantly, in Lilian Lee's novel, she also writes. In fact, the novel is constructed as Green Snake's autobiography. The writing and dancing aspects of Green Snake become the key to deciphering Geling Yan's novella *White Snake*, written by another female writer in the late 1990s in the diaspora, and provide a fresh perspective for our investigation of the rewriting of the White Snake legend in contemporary times.

THE WRITING WOMEN OF CHINA

The category of "writing women" has emerged as an important academic field in the study of Chinese cultural and gender history. Critical anthologies such as *The Red Brush: Writing Women of Imperial China*, *Writing Women in Late Imperial China*, *Writing Women in Modern China*, and a special issue of the journal *Frontiers of Literary Studies in China*, on "Women, Writing and Visuality in Contemporary China,"[33] have traced a long tradition of educated women who have used writing as a means of self-expression, political agitation, and critique, among myriad other uses. These timely collections reveal the voices and visions of women who have prevailed against patriarchy and political authorities to express themselves through writing for some two thousand years. The subversive, anti-patriarchal retellings of the White Snake legend should thus be contextualized within the enduring Chinese tradition of feminine/feminist writing, especially during imperial and highly politicized times.

In light of this "writing women" tradition and in recognition of the symbolic and historical significance of women's writing, I consider the emergence of a "writing Green Snake" as the most revolutionary contribution of Lilian Lee's novel to the White Snake repertoire. Even the excerpt quoted above concerning the expressiveness of the female body in dance had to be written by Green Snake herself inside the narrative. In fact, Green Snake's fictional writing under the Broken Bridge in West Lake takes place at the same time as Lilian Lee's composition of her novel in Hong Kong in the late 1980s to early 1990s. This is evident from the inclusion of time markers drawn from popular culture, such as the 1980s Cantonese pop music stars Andy Lau Tak-wah (Liu Dehua 劉德華) and Leon Lai Ming (Li Ming 黎明), at the end of Lee's *Green Snake* story. In an interview conducted in 1993, after the premiere of Tian Qinxin's *Green Snake*, Lilian Lee paid tribute to "the free creative environment at the time" in Hong Kong when she wrote the first version of the novel in 1986.[34] She recounted how she herself had rebelled against rules and conventions and had overthrown traditional characterizations, including that of the moral defender, Fahai. The parallels thus are inescapable: the writing Green Snake is the writing Lilian Lee; the rebellious Green Snake is the daring female writer herself, reinventing a legend within the vibrant cultural milieu that was late 1980s Hong Kong.

A DANCING WHITE SNAKE

When Geling Yan began writing her novella *White Snake* in the late 1990s, a decade after Lee, she brought to the work her personal experiences with the Cultural Revolution's antiestablishment politics. For eight years, Yan had been a dancer in an entertainment troupe that served propaganda functions in the People's Liberation Army in the city of Chengdu, capital of Sichuan province. Yan's story about the writing Green Snake and the dancing White Snake stitches together a representation of political and cultural history of modern China from the late 1950s to the early 1980s. Again, the story centers on a dancer famous for her role as the White Snake and on her complicated relationship with a loyal female fan. It traces the complex emotional and bodily entanglements between the young female fan and the White Snake dancer. The story is told through three explicitly divided perspectives and three corresponding accounts, official (*guanfang* 官方), popular (*minjian* 民間), and untold (*buwei renzhi* 不為人知), each perspective interposing into the other two narratives throughout the story. The third kind of account, the untold stories, is further divided into three types: the female dancer's third-person internal monologues, the fangirl's first-person diaries, and accounts of the secret meetings between the two.

The novella opens with the following résumé-like introduction of the female protagonist, the White Snake dancer Sun Likun 孫麗坤, in the first of the "official" accounts:

> Sun Likun, female, presently 34 years of age, was formerly a major performer in the Sichuan Province Performing Arts Troupe. In 1958 and 1959, she traveled to the Soviet Union's International Song and Dance Festival, where she won the Stalin Prize for the Arts. In 1962, she received First Prize in the Solo Ballet Performance category in the All-China National Dance Competition. In 1963, Beijing Film Studios made a film based on *The Legend of White Snake*, a ballet she both choreographed and performed in. At the same time, the stage version of the ballet played in seventeen cities, causing quite a sensation. In order to study and imitate the behavior of snakes, Sun had apprenticed herself to an Indian snake charmer and had helped him raise snakes. The "snake step," which she developed on her own, became her signature movement, and its performance received tremendous acclaim among ballet critics. The step even became a fad among members of the audience.[35]

The rest of the account, however, exposes Sun's "crimes" and "misdemeanors." Taken from a letter addressed to Premier Zhou Enlai and written in the highly recognizable "Mao style" (*Mao wenti* 毛文體), this account succinctly outlines the vicissitudes of Sun Likun's career, which were fully exposed to the Chinese public because of her special identity as a celebrated White Snake dancer. Interestingly, Sun's artistic achievements—the Stalin Prize in the Soviet Union in the late 1950s, her national awards, and the making of her White Snake ballet into a film, as well as her "sensational" seventeen-city nationwide tour in the early 1960s—counter the usual image of the so-called Seventeen Years (1949–1966) of the Chinese socialist era as monolithic and uninspired[36] and instead portray a lively cultural scene that crosses the boundaries of stage, screen, and popular culture.

Quite remarkably, although there is no record of any ballet-based *White Snake* film made in Mainland China in 1963, the most famous "Snake Dance" (*Shewu* 蛇舞) in the history of the PRC was created in the late 1950s and won an international prize in 1959, not in the Soviet Union, but in Finland. In her autobiography, the real-life dancer famous for her snake dance, Chen Ailian 陳愛蓮, mentions an abortive attempt on the part of Beijing Film Studios to film a dance drama version of *White Snake* in 1963,[37] with Chen performing the lead role, a coincidence that further confirms my interpretation of Yan's text as inspired by Chen's life story. "Snake Dance" was a highlight in the dance drama *Maid of the Sea* (*Yü meiren* 魚美人) as performed by the first generation of dancers educated in the PRC. With the twenty-year-old Chen Ailian as the "viperous beauty," the dance piece not only won international acclaim but also brought its leading dancer fame at home.[38] Chen toured the country and built up a huge fan base, paralleling the achievement of the White Snake dancer Sun Likun in the above "official account" in Yan's novella.

The following description of Sun Likun, taken from the first installment of the "untold story," told from an omniscient third-person perspective, sharply contrasts with the above "official account":

> Men loved her beauty, loved the seductive but spiteful look in her eyes, loved her dancer's breasts, loved her long neck, sharp chin and shoulders that sloped like flowing waters. Loved her picture with Zhou Enlai. They loved everything about her, except herself. And what was herself? Apart from her dancing, would she exist? She had never thought about this question before.[39] She had made a living from her dancing, and while making a living, she didn't analyze what "living" really was. Her fingertips, the tips of her toes, the silk of her eyebrows and the ends of her hair all poured forth feeling. Yet her brain was a blank, lagging far behind her emotions.[40]

This "untold story" concentrates on the same quality of seductiveness in the White Snake dancer that mesmerized the snake women in Lilian Lee's *Green Snake* as they watched the human dancers. The narrative highlights the double temptations of sex and power. But the deeper level of the narrative lies in Sun's self-interrogation. Despite the author's use of the third-person female singular pronoun to refer to her protagonist, the impression of peering directly into Sun's soul is unmistakable. The effect of such a question, "Apart from her dancing, would she exist?" is equivalent to the first-person self-interrogatory "Who am I?" with a sense of psychological horror accompanying this self-confrontation. With the observation/admission, "She had never thought about this question before," we see that Sun Likun does not deem herself capable of raising, let alone answering, such existential questions: "She had made a living from her dancing, and while making a living, she didn't analyze what 'living' really was."[41]

In this case, Yan intentionally lures the reader into Sun's interior world, while at the same time identifying the White Snake dancer with what Rey Chow terms "primitive passions": with her body, she "poured forth feeling," while "her brain was a blank." Indeed, Chow's key terms, visuality and sexuality, define the White Snake dancer Sun Likun.[42] Similarly, the ethnic focus and ethnographical logic prominent in Chow's work are also highlighted in the other "untold stories" in *White Snake*, with the third-person male observer serving as an important foil to Sun's self-discovery:

> She did not realize she had choreographed her entire reality, her whole material existence. She had allowed her feelings and her hopes to dance. Dance has only intuition and inference; it is a language beyond language. Early mankind had dance before language; although unfathomable, at the same time dance contains the most fundamental precision. In Sun Likun's body, brimming with dance, he had unearthed that completely forgotten precision. This discovery excited and moved him. In the face of that precision beyond language, all knowledge, all defined emotions appeared too obtuse, too concrete.[43]

According to the "he" in this instance, ultimate meaning rests in the White Snake dancer Sun Likun's body, "brimming with dance." No intellectual abstraction equals its value. Neither language nor any "defined emotion" (which we may interpret as emotion translated into and limited by language) is necessary. From Sun Likun's dancing body, full of primitive passions and beyond any linguistic expressions, the "he" in this "untold story" excavates a long-forgotten "precision" that goes beyond any language. This double-edged understanding of the primitive power of the dancing body, simultaneously demeaned in the language/body hierarchy and elevated as a more precise and higher truth, closely echoes those critics with whom we began: LaMothe's critique of the marginalization of dancing, King's transmedia synthesis between language and the body, and Halprin's reading dance as life experience and political force.

However, as readers, we do not yet completely inhabit the perspective of the "he" in the above text. But if we continue to dig into the second type of sources for the "untold stories," that is, the diaries of the female fan who becomes obsessed with Sun as early as age eleven or twelve, we may be able to better appreciate the meaning of the "precision" referenced by the "he" in the previous "untold story":

> She was wearing a pair of wide black harem pants and an India red woolen blouse. The collar almost trailed down to her shoulders. She was so beautiful. How is it possible for a person to be so beautiful?! (While writing that line, I blushed—my face is so hot!) Her long, long neck went all the way down, exposing her cleavage. She reminded me of a statue! Her bosom is really beautiful, like you'd see on a heroine in distress. It stands straight up. I'd really like to touch her, to see if it is sculpted or real. I frighten myself when I have thoughts like that.[44]

The girl in the diary, who was about to enter puberty in 1963, has seen Sun's *White Snake* five times during its seventeen-city national tour. As she prepares to watch it yet again with her friends, she discovers that tickets have long been sold out. Using the diary form, Yan is able to delineate the raging emotions inside the preteen girl when she first encounters Sun in close proximity and realizes that her strongest attraction is not to the dancer but to the dancer's body: "I've always liked dance, but since I saw her dancing, I feel I don't like dance so much as I like the body that produces the dance."[45] Was such raw emotion raging inside the female fan related to what Sun Likun self-identified as her emptiness—"her brain was a blank"?

As discussed above, in the first "untold story," author Geling Yan, who enters the female protagonist through the third person "she," has already discussed such a self-identification in Sun Likun as rooted in the idea of "dance as self." Perhaps the distinctions made between dance and body would be quite meaningless in the eyes of the dancer herself. Following the logic of "dance as self," and "self as body," perhaps the female fan's evolution from loving the White Snake dance to loving the body that creates the dance is utterly natural. When she continues to interrogate herself, asking whether "I" am "strange," whether "I" am "normal," she is at once terrified by her own imagined caressing of the White Snake dancer's full bosom while at the same time secretly enjoying the pleasures of repetitively writing down her shamefully "strange" thoughts. The idea that writing about the body of the other is a source of physical pleasure reinforces the symbiosis of writing and dancing, and text and the body.

In this context, the writing of the Green Snake in Lilian Lee's *Green Snake* mimics the writing of the author herself: it defies established rules and runs wild, reworking the complicated relationships between snake and snake, snake and human, Buddhist and snake, and Buddhist and human that appear in the established legend and literary canon. Lee's revolutionary text endows the supporting Green Snake with the ultimate power of discourse and the ability to articulate a minority perspective. The writing of the fangirl in Yan's *White Snake* is similarly endowed with a richly revolutionary implication. As an extremely important original source for the "untold stories" in the fictional narrative, the writings of the sexually ambiguous girl who falls in love with the White Snake dancer emphasize the fangirl's deep identification with the male Green Snake (of the Sichuan opera version of the story), who ultimately transforms into female form in order to better serve White Snake:

> Onstage they had just performed up to the part where White Snake and Green Snake start their battle. Green Snake tries to woo White Snake, and they are determined to test each other in battle. If Green Snake wins, White Snake will marry him, and if White Snake wins, Green Snake will become a female and serve White Snake all her life. Green Snake is defeated, and as soon as the stage lights go dark, then light up again, he has already become a female. After becoming a female, Green Snake is so loyal and brave, so attentive toward White Snake even in the smallest matters. What if he had not become a female? Wouldn't White Snake then have avoided having anything to do with that idiot Xu Xian? I really can't stand Xu Xian![46]

The fangirl's love for White Snake is transformative: it reshapes her into Green Snake. The girl's diary thus signals the emergence of the writing Green Snake in Yan's *White Snake*. Living in a time and society where the only "normal" sexual orientation is heterosexual, the fangirl turned Green Snake even secretly hopes that she/Green Snake can be male so as to love White Snake "normally." In the preteen girl's diary and through her eyes, Sun Likun's solo ballet *White Snake*, most likely based on the Sichuan opera version, transforms into a story dominated by Green Snake. Both Lilian Lee's *Green Snake* and Geling Yan's *White Snake* reveal a world seen through the perspective of the writing Green Snake. Yan's narrative, however, distinguishes itself with its dual focus on writing and dancing, and the philosophical interplay between the two, against the historical background of the late 1950s to the early 1980s before, during, and after the Cultural Revolution. The following section examines the Cultural Revolution's role in shaping and reshaping gender and sexual identities. Here, sexuality and politics have interwoven and formed an intricate dance, telling the story of two women's self-discoveries during the Cultural Revolution.

WRITING, DANCING, AND THE CULTURAL REVOLUTION AS MEMORY AND IMAGINATION

Geling Yan urges her readers to confront the psychological truth residing in the "untold stories"—that is, not in the public story performed on stage in Sun Likun's ballet, but in the private daily lives of the two characters involved. When the dancing White Snake (female dancer) meets the writing Green Snake (fangirl) again during the Cultural Revolution, the fangirl has transformed into a young man, the "he" who already appeared in previous discussions. However, this "he" is not the androgynous Green Snake returned to its original male form, as in the Sichuan opera. Rather, "he" is the now nineteen-year-old girl who, with the aid of a high-quality woolen military uniform (most likely green), has metamorphosed into Green Snake, who is both "loyal and brave" and "attentive even in the smallest matters." As a man, "he" is able to visit the incarcerated female dancer by pretending to be a special investigator sent from the Central Party Committee. In the third kind of "untold story," the fangirl secretly meets the White Snake dancer in the scenery warehouse, which transforms, for the White Snake, from her hell to her heaven, from a place of suffering to a place for healing:

> He began to speak about her dancing. "When I was very young, I once saw you dance" . . . "Is there something to investigate?" she asked. She shifted her entire weight to one leg and stretched out the other leg, her toes pointed tightly. Before his eyes, the leg rose up, and after a moment it no longer resembled a leg. It seemed as if it could be extended infinitely, so pliant and tough it was. An incredible life reawakened and unfolded in that leg. With its own soul and body, it made those shapeless pants suddenly appear to have vanished.[47]

Here, the "investigation" conducted by the "special investigator," which should be based on verbal communication, becomes instead a wordless encounter where the dancing White Snake uses her body, especially her legs, to speak. Of course, the investigation is but a convenient excuse. The real purpose of the young man/Green Snake's visit is precisely to indulge in the transporting dances emerging from the White Snake dancer's legs, each "with its own soul and body," an experience that awakens her/him to intense life forces. Throughout their daily secret meetings and, in fact, mutually therapeutic dancing sessions, the apparent naiveté and silence of the thirty-four-year-old White Snake dancer reconfirms her self-identification as a "primitive" whose salvation and revival can be achieved only through the "primitive" act of dancing. At the same time, through their encounters, the reader starts to grasp why the "he" in the above quoted accounts comes to consider corporeality the highest truth and the body's language the most accurate expression of one's psyche—in this case, a tortured one.

Unlike the carnival-like representation of the Cultural Revolution in Lilian Lee's work from the late 1980s and early 1990s—where Red Guards topple the Thunder Peak Pagoda in "a revolutionary game" ("Some of them dig out the bricks, others add firewood, and still others smash with tools"[48])—Geling Yan's *White Snake* is saturated and stamped with the writer's own life experience during the Cultural Revolution. At twelve, the same age at which the young girl in the story becomes obsessed with the dancing body of the White Snake, Yan was selected to dance in the propaganda troupe of the People's Liberation Army in Chengdu. In the novella, Sun Likun dances the White Snake on the streets and on Sichuan opera stages as a member of the Sichuan Province Performing Arts Troupe (*Sichuansheng gewu juyuan* 四川省歌舞劇院), based in Chengdu, where the Sichuan dialect dictates every aspect of everyday life. The use of Sichuan dialect in Yan's work is both a marker for the Sichuan opera version of the White Snake story, with its androgynous Green Snake at the center, and an indicator of the story's potentially autobiographical qualities.[49] In the recent Chinese box office hit *Youth* (*Fanghua* 芳華), a 2017 film based on Yan's novel and adapted to the big screen by Yan herself, four young girls in a provincial dance troupe struggle to overcome their coming-of-age pains during the Cultural Revolution. Yan calls the stories in the film her own "youthful experiences," and the characters "reflective of the comrades in arms" she encountered throughout her coming-of-age years.[50]

In *White Snake*, Yan's experience in and memory of the Cultural Revolution, combined with the experience of those she observed or came to know during that time and after (including, perhaps, the famous snake dancer

Chen Ailian), help to create a rich tapestry of lively characterizations: "A dancer who left home and entered dancing school at age ten . . . Without any education, how could I have any counter-revolutionary thought? I, who while writing the self-criticism and the confession, pored over the whole dog-eared dictionary. If I hadn't written them, I never would have learned so many characters."[51] It is tempting to imagine that, just as Yan danced at a young age like the White Snake dancer, she must also have retained her loyalty to her inner "self" despite the requisite political "shell," just like the writing Green Snake who confides to her diary:

> When I put the cover of *Red Flag* on top of one of my old movie magazines, then what I was reading became *Red Flag*. When I put the cover of *Quotations of Chairman Mao* over my copy of *Les Misérables*, then it became *Quotations of Chairman Mao*. A woolen military uniform immediately transforms me into a first-class, high-level person, receiving everyone's admiration as a wool-clad special soldier . . . Just like *Red Flag* or *Quotations of Chairman Mao*, it's what's on the outside that counts; the seeds don't betray the fruit. I'm nineteen, and this is the first time I have felt that my body is inherently androgynous . . . That's just fine with me. A purely feminine girl is both silly and insipid. . . . Will I be able to find my way through these possibilities? Is there a destiny that transcends the dichotomy of male and female? Despite having a body with a uterus and ovaries, is it possible that I am not without a choice?
>
> I despise the superficiality of girls.
> I scorn the vulgarity of boys.
> How tedious I am. How bizarre I am.[52]

Just as film magazines and forbidden "bourgeois novels" such as *Les Misérables* could be read only secretly, "abnormal" desire and extraordinary infatuation could be smuggled in only after being decorated and disguised by a high-quality military uniform. The narrator's comment, "It's what's on the outside that counts," is said with heavy irony. It is clear that she does not believe that relabeling, or redressing, changes anything. Politics and gender seem to intersect here, in a meditation on "truth." Inside the first-person narrator "I"—that is, the writing Green Snake's stream-of-consciousness narrative—such cloaked desire and sanctioned obsession become the most precise expression of a longing for beauty and transcendence. When the self-conscious nineteen-year-old "I" starts to ask, "Is there a destiny that transcends the dichotomy of male and female?" Pandora's Box is about to be opened. Behind the seemingly detached self-parody and ostensibly cold-hearted self-criticism, there lies a nineteen-year-old sneering at all normality and all social conventions. In the process of accusing "myself" of being "tedious" and "bizarre," "I" turns into "he."

In Yan's bold exploration of gender transgressions, it is possible to read her, the contemporary diasporic female writer, as quietly replacing class with gender, and foregrounding gender politics at the expense of realpolitik. However, in her crucial insistence on using the much-neglected period of High Socialism and the still-taboo Cultural Revolution as the background to the narrative, she can also be read as joining the postmodernists who are very much engaged with realpolitik and as reaffirming the interrelatedness of class politics and gender transgression.[53] The fangirl's act of dressing up as a young man of high social status to save the older woman with a dubious sexual and class background both reaffirms the blatant gender and class politics during the Cultural Revolution and challenges conventional views emphasizing their separation. Yan's novella demonstrates how class politics and gender transgression are interrelated and how transgressing one leads to the implosion and explosion of the other.

In Yan's narrative, the fangirl/Green Snake's rescue of the White Snake dancer becomes a metaphor for how "he" and "she" reencounter each other during the Cultural Revolution. If White Snake dancer's incarceration is a metaphoric winter for her life and her art, as well as a "hibernation" period, when sexual desire is dormant inside the female dancer's body, then the reemergence of "he" is warm sunshine in the cold winter. In the heat of the sun, "a spring snake was reviving after a long hibernation, limbering up to freshness and new life":[54]

> She felt as if he had come to rescue her, taking measures that were completely unfathomable to her. Yet she couldn't penetrate this young man's aloofness and politeness to discover his true mission. Sometimes she felt as if this storeroom stuffed with scenery had organized itself into a play and the wiry young man had become a character in it. She never considered whether he might be toying with her or whether he might be infatuated with her; she only felt that he was very different. She could no longer be without him, no matter who he was, even if the purpose of his existence was to torment her, to destroy her bit by bit with his cultivated manner.[55]

The White Snake dancer thus falls in love with the young man, and it is unclear if he is being deceitful or is infatuated with her, or both. Following the young man's daily visits to the dusty scenery storehouse where she has been incarcerated for the crime of being a "counterrevolutionary viperous beauty" (*fangeming meinüshe* 反革命美女蛇), the White Snake dancer begins to metamorphose into someone with a new body. She starts to dance again, only for him, fully displaying her shapely curves. Perhaps she thinks "the wiry young man" is her Xu Xian, emerging from the White Snake legend? Or perhaps her sensitive nerves already intuited the truth behind his courtesy? Regardless, the White Snake dancer has taken a path of no return: the cross-dressed fan's obsession with her has triggered her complete infatuation with "him" in return. She starts to live for "him," for "his" one or two hours of visiting time every day. When "he" tells her that the following day will be their last meeting, her whole world virtually collapses. When "he" uses his privilege to take her to a hotel room so as to be able to spend time with her alone, the unfathomable truth must finally be unveiled:

> He said he had found a tape with a selection from *The Legend of White Snake*. He turned the player on, and it emitted a seductive *erhu* solo that slowly warbled to the point of weeping. The sound quality was not good, and the music came out muffled, like real weeping.
>
> She jutted out her chin and turned her ear toward the sound. But, just as when looking into the mirror, she didn't quite dare to listen to it. It was the solo dance in which White Snake weeps. After Xu Xian has seen Lady White turn into a snake and has died of fright, White Snake dances around and around his corpse, trying to use her body heat to warm him back to life. . . .
>
> Later, when she would reflect on all this, she would recall clearly that she herself undid the first button. She took off the long since passé cardigan blouse of India red, letting out the sculpted flesh of her dancer's body. . . .
>
> In her entire life, already half a lifespan, nothing had ever presented itself in its true state. Dance *was* her life, and the vividness of her dance lay in the absence of any other reality.
>
> Still, there was no way she could evade it. Too late: a gaffe made in plain view onstage, with no opportunity to retrieve it.[56]

The figure before her, however, is Xu Qunshan, not Xu Xian. Even if the White Snake dancer wants to tangle her naked body up with "his," "he" will not be able to transform into Xu Xian. "He" is *merely* a cross-dressing female fan performing the role of the "loyal and brave" and "extremely attentive" Green Snake. "He" is Xu Qunshan 徐群山, a hill-like man (hence the Chinese word for hills 山 in his given name), and "she" is also Xu Qunshan 徐群珊, the coral-like girl (hence the Chinese word for coral 珊 in her given name) who will eventually be married off.

When the White Snake dancer's statue-like naked body has to meet the icy cold fingers of the cross-dressing girl, "the conventional love between the sexes Sun Likun had once understood was now sapped of all meaning, had become emptiness itself."[57] As readers, we will be informed of what this "emptiness" means: when Sun realizes that "he" is a female, she goes insane. In that sense, "emptiness" seems to refer to how she loses control of her own rationality and goes into the initial stage of denial. However, she has already been described, or has described herself, as "empty," early in the story. In that sense, one could read the "emptiness" here as a return to her earlier state, empty of meaning, once her infatuation is revealed for what it is, from her point of view. Rather than reading the above statement as a revolutionary negation of "conventional love between the sexes" from the perspective of a contemporary diasporic writer's postmodern take on the Cultural Revolution, we may fare better by treating it as an initial concession to the heteronormative mindset on the character's part, based on the author's own memory of the Cultural Revolution: for Sun, the White Snake dancer, sinking into madness might be the only way to liberate her body and clear her mind from social norms and political pressures.

When the White Snake dancer and the female fan meet again, it is in the psychiatric hospital where the dancer is being treated. Having assumed again a female appearance, the fangirl is able to accompany the dancer during her treatment. But the dancer falls in love with the fan all over again: this time not with the Xu Qunshan the hill-like man, but with Xu Qunshan the coral-like girl. Also called Shan-shan, the girl has an eccentric short hair style to complete her persona: "She [Sun Likun] loved her as the illusory Xu Qunshan, and she also loved her as the real person Shan-shan. She feared Shan-shan would disappear as Xu Qunshan did, yet she also feared that Shan-shan would forever exist in her life in this manner. Nevertheless, if she didn't love Shan-shan, whom could she love? Shan-shan was the only ray of sunshine in her life, a ray full of dust, but also full of true warmth."[58]

After the Cultural Revolution, Sun Likun, "the former famous dancer," is able to clear her name, just as a whole generation of intellectuals and artists did in real life. In the novella, it even seems likely that she will be able to welcome the second spring of her art and life. Her solo dance performance opens in the golden autumn of October 1980 in Chengdu. Not so coincidentally, the celebrated real-life snake dancer, Chen Ailian, who enjoyed international acclaim and nationwide fame beginning in the late 1950s but then suffered during the Cultural Revolution, also had her first solo dance concert in Beijing in 1980. But unlike Chen Ailian, whose solo concert prominently featured her "Snake Dance" as one of her most celebrated pieces, the dancer in Yan's novella intentionally omits her signature White Snake dance from the program. Moreover, Shan-shan is married off to a man the weekend after the dancer's return to the stage. Such omission and normalization safely domesticate the formerly transgressive Green Snake and quietly defuses the seductiveness of the White Snake for the post–Cultural Revolution new order.

In Yan's seemingly cold-hearted description throughout the novella, Sun Likun gains both fame and infamy because of her White Snake dance. She is accused of being an "anti-revolutionary" because of her embodiment of the viperous beauty, which counters the revolutionary narratives that require women to be "iron girls" and "good daughters of the party."[59] At her time of great suffering, she is saved by the cross-dressing Green Snake and finds her true self because of him/her; at the same time, she goes insane when she discovers that her lover is a girl. And finally, it is again the young fan who, returning to her female identity, nurses the snake dancer back from the emptiness caused by her "traumatic" encounter with the truth about her own love.

There are some crucial replacements and nifty substitutions at work in Yan's novella. The political trauma of the Cultural Revolution, for one, has largely been transmuted into the personal trauma of coming to terms with one's own sexual identity. One could argue that Yan is evading the political by focusing on the personal; however, I would rather read one as a metaphor for the other, as a synthesis in what Kenneth King calls a "double motion." The dancing White Snake fatefully falls in love with the Green Snake/fangirl, who dresses both as a man and as a woman. Some readers may consider the text ambiguous regarding whether Sun is sexually attracted to Shan-shan as a female. However, when the ending of the story details Shans-han's marriage, Sun's emotional reaction to it affirms her profound sense of loss in losing Shan-shan as a potential object of sexual love and affection.

The White Snake goes insane for "him" and is saved by "her." This blurring of gender and sexual boundaries, particularly for women, echoes what Lilian Lee has referred to as the "rebellious" and "running wild" milieu of Hong Kong in the mid- to late 1980s and is crystalized in the Green Snake image she created at the time. Yan, however, depicts the flowering of such gender anarchy during the Cultural Revolution—and intriguingly, its "correction" in the years immediately afterwards. The novella's ending suggests that the revolutionary experimentation brought about by the Cultural Revolution in the most intimate spheres of ordinary Chinese people's lives had to be cleansed, reversed, and repudiated in order for society to regain homeostasis when that period ended. In the end, the antiestablishment, unconventional gender and sexual disruptions of the narrative must be disavowed as disguises and lies in order to harmonize post–Cultural Revolution society and to effect normalization.

CONCLUDING REMARKS

Writing and dancing, in Yan's textual universe, coexist and cross-fertilize in what Kenneth King would refer to as a "transmedia" synthesis. It is largely through the Green Snake/fangirl's diary, the White Snake dancer's written self-criticism, and the fangirl's accounts of her meetings with the dancer that we come to appreciate the expressive, symbolic, and life-changing power of dance. Their relationship is thus one of symbiosis rather than of hierarchy. And yet, notwithstanding the critical role of textuality within the text itself, it is the body of the dancing White Snake that ultimately possesses the power to transcend—language, custom, conventions, and sanctions—to become the highest truth, wordless and embodied, between these two women.

Throughout Yan's novella, both the White Snake dancer and the Green Snake fangirl function as metaphorical human/nonhuman hybrids. In particular, the transgressive energies embodied by the androgynous Green Snake in the local opera version of the legend merges with the powerful persona of the antiestablishment fangirl in the story. The metamorphoses of the images of the White Snake dancer and the Green Snake fangirl throughout the novella, consequently, mirrors the regenerative power of the White Snake legends as examined throughout this study as a whole.

Although this chapter, unlike most others in this study, has focused primarily on the conventional medium of written texts and used a rather conventional approach of close reading, the transmedia qualities of the texts themselves, especially the vigorous interpenetrations between writing and dancing, text and the body, are indicative of the media-centered approach of this study as a whole. Moreover, gender and political transgressions are at the center of these retellings of the White Snake legend from the last few decades of the twentieth century to the beginning of the twenty-first century, from female writers active in what were often considered "peripheries" of Chinese culture, both in Hong Kong and outside the PRC.

Importantly, especially in the context of Yan's *White Snake* and its gender politics, the contradictions in the cultural politics of the Cultural Revolution need to be made explicit. On the one hand, the reigning ideology of the time advocated rebellion against authority, bureaucracy, and establishment and hence unwittingly unleashed and catalyzed gender and sexual experimentations, particularly among the young. On the other hand, the official discourse repressed sexual desires in the name of asexual revolutionary comradeship and deemed antiestablishment gender and sexual experimentations as aberrant. In such a self-proclaimed "revolutionary" regime, the officially designated "anti-revolutionary" or "counterrevolutionary" elements might have in fact served as the most revolutionary inspirations in reshaping gender and sexual relations for years afterwards.

In that sense, the foregrounding of the White Snake legend's gender politics in Yan's novella *White Snake* also gestures toward what came to be known, both in the Mainland and in Hong Kong, as the postsocialist and postcolonial developments in reconfiguring the legend. Such reconfigurations are expressed in multiple media: in the 2007 novel *The Human Realm: Legend of the White Snake Retold* (*Renjian: chongshu Baishe zhuan* 人間: 重述白蛇傳) by Li Rui and Jiang Yun; in the avant-garde theaters of Taiwan and Singapore; in the revisionist Green Snake–centered narratives of Lilian Lee's novel and Tsui Hark's film; in the 2011 3D martial arts film *It's Love* (*Baishe chuanshuo*); and in the experimental staging of Lilian Lee's *Green Snake* by celebrated theater director Tian Qinxin.

The Human Realm was published by Chongqing Publishing House in 2007. It was part of an international project aimed at retelling myth in contemporary times. The official website of the Myths Series describes this ongoing endeavor as "the most ambitious simultaneous worldwide publication ever undertaken." The website further explains, "Myths are universal and timeless stories that reflect and shape our lives—they explore our desires, our fears, our longings, and provide narratives that remind us what it means to be human."[60] This universalizing impulse, of course, should be seriously questioned, and a central aim of this book is to tease out the changing historical, material, media technological, and social and psychological references that make the legend's retellings far more interesting than universal human myths.[61]

The Human Realm posed the following enduring questions: What does it mean to be human? What does it mean to be in the human realm? Like Lilian Lee's *Green Snake,* this novel again transformed the formerly supporting role of Green Snake into the leading female character and pondered from her perspective a question similar to the one posed by Lee: "to be demon or human, for her, that is not the question; she likes to be neither human nor demon; why be a human if you cannot be free?"[62] Authors Li Rui and Jiang Yun's attempt to retell the White Snake story hence participates in a global chorus of myth-remaking that includes authors as diverse as Margaret Atwood, Karen Armstrong, A. S. Byatt, David Grossman, Milton Hatoum, Kirino Natsuo, Alexander McCall Smith, Tomás Eloy Martínez, Victor Pelevin, Ali Smith, Su Tong, Dubravka Ugrešić, Salley Vickers, and Jeanette Winterson. *The Human Realm*'s universal message and its transnational production seem to signal a new direction for the reinvention of the White Snake tale in the contemporary world. Again, such a universalizing message should be seriously questioned, however, as myth retelling is as old as storytelling itself. What is interesting instead about retellings is how they are shaped by and shaping their contemporary conditions.

From the early 1990s onwards, the extreme popularity of the 1992 Taiwanese fifty-episode television series *New Legend of Madame White Snake* (*Xin Bainiangzi chuanqi*) in Mainland China and throughout East and Southeast Asia paved the ways for twenty-first-century cinematic and theatrical revivals of the White Snake theme, as to be examined in chapter 8. The 2009 high-tech symphony-style *jingju* performance *Madame White Snake: Seasons of Love* (*Bainiangzi: aiqing siji* 白娘子: 愛情四季),[63] produced in Shanghai and exemplifying the "Shanghai school" of experimental *jingju* performances, may in fact have served as an inspiration for, or would at least find powerful spiritual resonances in, the 2011 Pulitzer Prize–winning English-language opera *Madame White Snake*, which also employs the trope of the four seasons to symbolize the cycle of love's awakening and decaying, as to be analyzed in chapter 7.

The 2011 special effects-heavy 3D film *It's Love*, starring Jet Li as Abbot Fahai, continues to accentuate the gray zone between the human and the nonhuman, and good and evil. It does so with a newly created character, Nengren 能忍, a young disciple of Abbot Fahai who not only falls in love with Green Snake but also turns out himself to have a hybrid identity of human and demon.[64] The film, as a high-tech martial arts romantic fantasy film, creatively reflects the genre-blending trends in the legend's Japanese and Korean cinematic adaptations throughout the Cold War (examined in chapters 4 and 5), in which fantasy, romance, comedy, martial arts and horror long intersected through the meticulous use of cutting-edge special effects.

On stage, influential Taiwanese productions such as *Resurrection from the Fire: Legend of the White Snake* (*Yuhuo chongsheng: Baishe zhuan* 浴火重生: 白蛇傳) by Lin Hwai-min (Lin Huaimin 林懷民) of the Cloud Gate Dance Theatre and the Taiwanese opera *White Snake Spectacular* (*Chaoxuan Baishe zhuan* 超炫白蛇傳) by Ming Hwa Yuan 明華園 are energizing new attempts at recreating White Snake in Taiwan and, through their international performances, have spread such energies throughout the world.[65] Ming Hwa Yuan's multimedia Taiwanese opera, for example, often takes place in huge arenas and resembles a thronged pop music concert; and the audience must wear raincoats to avoid being completely soaked by water when high-pressure water hoses are employed during the water battle scene and the whole arena turns into a battlefield between White Snake's water troop and Abbot Fahai's heavenly soldiers.[66] This focus on spectacular stage magic brings us back to chapter 2, to the *Shenbao* accounts regarding the abundance of real animals, real machines, real rains, and real floods on the early twentieth-century White Snake stage. At the same time, the focus on stage magic prepares us for chapter 7's exploration of the renewed interest in the White Snake legend in various media in the twenty-first-century United States.

It is important to further reflect on how the actual lived past and the mythical past generated by the White Snake legend join together in contemporary times and how their generative powers are used to project into the future. Geling Yan's novella *White Snake*, read together with Lilian Lee's novel *Green Snake*, reaffirms the interrelatedness of class politics and gender transgression. At the same time, their celebration of gender and sexual experimentations countered the officially sanctioned and asexual relationship of revolutionary comradeship. Such experiments emphasized queer identity as transgression, rather than as lesbian longing per se. In particular, with the Cultural Revolution as historical background, these fictional accounts actively participated in the antiestablishment politics of the time and in the formation of a post-Cultural Revolution memory ecology.[67] The question of species queerness and class queerness, together with queerness as homosexual desire, forms an important entryway into twenty-first-century retellings of the White Snake legend.

CHAPTER 7

The White Snake Legend in the United States in the Twenty-First Century

The White Snake legend, as discussed in chapter 2, was introduced to the Anglophone world in the late nineteenth and early twentieth centuries through Samuel I. Woodbridge's and Frederick D. Cloud's versions. Now, after witnessing the legend's twentieth-century transformations in Chinese, Japanese, and Korean versions, through changing media representations, and across historical and geopolitical divides, we return to the legend's Anglophone connection a century later. This chapter attempts to delineate how the obsessions of the American missionary and diplomat, which initiated the Anglophone White Snake traditions, are being manifested in new configurations in a cluster of English-language productions in the United States in the first decades of the current century, and how some of these are being reimported to the Chinese-speaking worlds with fascinating reverberations.

The chapter first examines the Pulitzer Prize–winning *Madame White Snake*, with libretto by Cerise Lim Jacobs and music by Zhou Long. It probes its Singaporean and Chinese origins and contemporary relevance, in the context of the inter-Asian connection in the White Snake legend's reconfigurations throughout the Cold War. A similarly influential text is Tony Award–winner Mary Zimmerman's play *The White Snake*, first performed at the Oregon Shakespeare Festival in 2012. The play's significance is examined in the context of its dialogue with the Chinese novel *The Legend of White Snake* (*Baishe zhuan*) written by the female writer Zhao Qingge 趙清閣 (1914-1999) and published in Beijing in 1956, and the play's China premiere at the Wuzhen Theatre Festival in 2014. A third Anglophone text, much edgier and less academic, is the short digital video *The Legend of Lady White Snake* by the Indian-Canadian-British fashion-model-turned-photographer Indrani Pal-Chaudhuri, created in 2013 to publicize a major new line of fashion and in memory of the legendary fashion designer Alexander McQueen. As a whole, this chapter considers contemporary Anglophone recreations of the White Snake legend across three media—opera, theater, and digital video—and probes the significance of the Chinese legend's enigmatic return as multilocational and multilingual popular cultural phenomena and media events in today's United States, China, and beyond.

FROM CHINESE LEGEND TO PULITZER PRIZE–WINNING WESTERN OPERA

Zhou Long's 2011 *Madame White Snake* (an opera in four acts, with libretto by Cerise Lim Jacobs) was cocommissioned by Opera Boston and the Beijing Music Festival Arts Foundation and published by Oxford University Press. It had its world premiere by Opera Boston on February 26, 2010, at Cutler Majestic Theater in Boston, with Maestro Gil Rose as music director and conductor and Robert Woodruff as stage director. It toured to Beijing for its Asia premiere in October 2010, was remounted in a new production by director Michael Counts as part of *Ouroboros Trilogy* in September 2016 in Boston, and was presented by the Hong Kong Arts Festival in March 2019, among other iterations. The project was conceived by Charles M. Jacobs and Cerise Lim Jacobs and was dedicated by Cerise to Charles, her husband. In his composer's note, Zhou Long emphasizes the "universal themes" of the Chinese legend that he grew up with, observing that it can "speak to all people." Most intriguingly, when expanding an earlier shorter piece into a full-length opera, he approached president of the Beijing Music Festival Arts Foundation Maestro Yu Long, and Maestro Yu decided to "reimport" the opera back to China, making it "a valuable cross-cultural learning and artistic experience both here in the United States and in China."[1]

The published study score of the opera lists a number of character descriptions.[2] Madame White Snake (Bai Suzhen, *soprano*) is "a powerful snake demon who assumes the form of a beautiful woman and falls in love with a mortal man." Xiao Qing (Green Snake, *male soprano*) is "a green grass snake who was in love with Madame White in a prior life and is now her servant." Xu Xian (*tenor*) is "an herbalist and scholar who falls in love with Madame White." Abbot Fahai (*bass*) of the Golden Mountain Monastery is "a devout monk who has meditated for a thousand years and believes he is one step from nirvana (*chengfo* 成佛)." The four-part chorus (soprano, alto, tenor, and bass) is composed of "the villagers and parents of drowned children," while the children's choir is comprised of "the spirits of drowned children."[3]

These succinct character descriptions outlined at the beginning of the published study score represent a collaboration between the Singaporean-American librettist Cerise Lim Jacobs and the Mainland China- and US-educated composer Zhou Long, and reflect their shared understanding of the Chinese legend and their collective conceptualization of its artistic and philosophical qualities. To start with, their identification of White Snake as a "snake demon" who "falls in love with a mortal man" aligns with revisions that, gaining prominence in the nineteenth century, transformed the White Snake character into a "righteous demoness" rather than with earlier renditions in the Chinese tradition, in which White Snake was a dangerous villainess. Such an emphasis on love, in its association with romanticism and various "other emotions, attachments, loyalties, values, and ideals" that are perceived as modern,[4] connects their interpretation of the White Snake character with a range of developments in Chinese and Asian contexts beginning in the nineteenth century that were in complex dialogue with challenges and influences perceived to come from the West. However, Jacobs does not simply romanticize the White Snake and instead imbues her with fierce vengefulness, in addition to moments of tenderness when love touches her heart.

Intriguingly, in this *Madame White Snake* opera, Green Snake is specifically designated as a man in love with White Snake in a previous life, a characterization that follows conventions in the Sichuan opera versions and echoes the desires of the cross-dressing fangirl in Geling Yan's 1998 novella, discussed in chapter 6. The casting of Michael Maniaci, a male soprano who has been praised for his rare, thrilling voice and sensational stage presence, is ingeniously fitting in bringing out the androgynous, ambiguous, and hybrid qualities of the Green Snake figure in the context of precedents in local operatic and literary forms in the Chinese tradition.[5] Acclaimed as "one of the greatest singers of his generation" who "possesses a remarkable voice, one that marries trumpeting high notes with a warm and supple middle voice and secure bottom," Maniaci proved to be a thoughtful choice given the long history of using male actors or multiple actors to bring out Green Snake's complex character on stage in the Chinese tradition.[6] With White Snake and Green Snake listed as the opera's two leading roles, Jacobs and Zhou clearly emphasize the characters and perspectives of the snake women, and in this way are similar to Japanese filmmaker Mizoguchi Kenji, who foregrounded the perspectives of his human and nonhuman female protagonists in the 1953 *Ugetsu*.

However, one distinguishing characteristic of Jacobs and Zhou's Xu Xian lies in his double identity as "an herbalist and scholar"; previous versions of the White Snake legend have long deprived Xu Xian of any "scholarly" attributes. Indeed, he is often characterized as an herbalist or a craftsman, of relatively low social status, although his skills or artistry may seem superior in the eyes of his nonhuman lover. In these versions, Xu Xian operates outside the conventional "scholar and beauty" (*caizi jiaren* 才子佳人) narrative,[7] yet the nonhuman White Snake nonetheless perceives the true value of his work. In other words, in some earlier versions of the story, Xu Xian is a worthy object of love, but it is only the magical, nonhuman snake woman that possesses the special perspective to identify his value. In the Jacobs/Zhou opera, however, that value is clear to everyone in the audience. The twenty-first-century English adaptation thus seems to bring its audience into the snake woman's magical perspective, into the changed world of our current reality, creating a more obviously sympathetic love interest for the snake woman and for our contemporary audience. By first granting Xu a scholarly background and creating a storyline in which he voluntarily gives up a potentially distinguished career as a scholar-official, Jacobs's libretto accentuates Xu's devotion to the art of healing and makes him a worthy object of White Snake's desire.

The opera's most significant revision in terms of characterization lies in its portrayal of Abbot Fahai. "A devout monk who has meditated for a thousand years and believes he is one step from nirvana," Fahai nonetheless emerges as more of a believer in human love than a believer in abstract Buddhist doctrine. Zhou Long, in composing for the opera based on Jacobs's libretto, creatively positioned the adult chorus and the children's choir in the body of the opera. In addition, the children's choir also sings four seasonal interludes to stitch the opera's four acts into a seamless artistic whole.

The instrumentation listed for the opera is as follows: Chinese flutes, *xun* 塤, *bangdi* 梆笛, *qudi* 曲笛, flute, oboe, 2 clarinets, 2 bassoons, 2 French horns, 2 trumpets, bass trombone, 3 timpani, percussion 1 [including bamboo brushes, bow, 4 yarn, metal stick, bass drum, vibraphone, glockenspiel, crotales 鐵砧琴, water cymbals 水鈸, suspended cymbal (high) 吊鈸, 2 opera gongs 京鑼, claves 梆子, 5 blocks 木魚, bass drum (on side) 低音大鼓], percussion 2 [including chimes (tubular) 管鐘, bowl chime 碗磬, mark-tree 音樹, suspended cymbal (low), sleigh bells 雪橇鈴, 3 opera gongs, wind gong 風鑼, tam tam (low) 低音大鑼], harp, *erhu*, violin I, violin II, viola, violoncello, and contrabass.[8] The fascinating blend of musical instruments, including objects from everyday life, from within the Chinese musical tradition and beyond, gestures toward "a deeply expressive opera that draws on a Chinese folk tale to blend the musical traditions of the East and the West," as described in the official Pulitzer Prize committee statement regarding Zhou Long's composition.[9]

The opera comprises a prologue and an epilogue, four interludes, and four acts. The prologue, titled "The Story," features singing by Xiao Qing, the children's choir, and the chorus. The set pieces "Spring: Awakening at the Broken Bridge," "Summer: Passion," "Fall: Decay," and "Winter: Betrayal" form the four main acts, each featuring singers drawn from the four main characters and completed with vocalists from the children's choir and the chorus. Each of the four acts is preceded by an interlude, featuring spring, summer, autumn, and winter songs, respectively, each sung by the unaccompanied children's choir. The epilogue, "Battle," features Madame White Snake, Xiao Qing, and Abbot Fahai and is again completed with contributions from the children's choir and the chorus.

The rhythm of the opera, with the songs of the four seasons serving as interludes to the four main acts,[10] and the repetition and transmigration of themes and characters from awakening, passion, decay, and betrayal, vividly symbolize the themes developed later by Cerise Lim Jacobs in what eventually became the 2016 *Ouroboros Trilogy*. The three operas—*Naga*, *Madame White Snake*, and *Gilgamesh*—depict the three-part exploration of love, death and rebirth, symbolized by the ancient Greek icon of a serpent eating its own tail. The trilogy, produced by Beth Morrison Projects and The Friends of Madame White Snake, was presented in Boston in the fall of 2016, both as individual operas and as seven-hour full-day events. It brought together an acclaimed artistic team of conductors Carolyn Kuan, Julian Wachner, and Lan Shui and composers Zhou Long, Paola Prestini, and Scott Wheeler. Many renowned Boston music institutions such as The New England Conservatory of Music, The Boston Children's Chorus, and Arts Emerson were involved in this elaborately collaborative project.[11]

Green Snake the Storyteller

Xiao Qing is the only featured singer in the prologue of the *Madame White Snake* opera, as mentioned above. She is introduced by the stage instruction, "Xiao Qing is on a darkened stage. The area is littered with debris of the aftermath of a mighty flood. Xiao Qing picks her way through the debris." The song she sings provides the narrative anchor for the whole opera:

> I am Xiao Qing, a green grass snake, the servant of Madame White Snake
> Listen, as I tell you a great love story
> Between a white snake demon and a mortal man
> You ask what can a green snake know of love?
> I remember once loving my mistress passionately

But then I was a man, and she a woman
Untouched by love's vulnerability
Desperate for her love, I tried to snatch it by force
But she drove me faraway
I lived in despair until death when we were both reincarnated as snakes
And they made me a female snake
So that I can forever be by her side
Now, I am half snake half woman
The worst of all possible worlds
All for the love of Madame White Snake[12]

Quite remarkably, Cerise Lim Jacobs and Zhou Long largely echo Lilian Lee and Geling Yan (discussed in chapter 6) in endowing Green Snake with a fascinating hybrid identity and a key role in carrying the narrative. The story begins to be enacted from here onwards, and Michael Maniaci, the male soprano in the role of Xiao Qing, continues his singing-storytelling (fig. 45). Although there is no lack of singing-storytelling styles in the Chinese White Snake traditions, as has been explored throughout this study,[13] Jacobs and Zhou's *Madame White Snake* is the legend's first enactment through Western operatic apparatuses, largely outside the constraints of Chinese theatrical conventions.

Xiao Qing as enacted by Michael Maniaci, vocally and visually, embodies what Zhou Long describes as freedom and flexibility, rather than limitation and difficulty, and the double "exoticism" resulted in the composition of a Western opera to an English libretto based on a Chinese legend.[14] While the character is indeed still dressed in green, clad in David Zinn and Zane Pihlstrom's memorable costumes, Xiao Qing in this production is not recognizable as Green Snake for an audience familiar with any previous versions of her appearance, Chinese or otherwise. Nothing of his hairstyle, makeup (including the pinkish-red highlights under his eyes and mouth), or exaggerated necklace evokes the image of Green Snake we know from earlier renditions. Only the green shades in his facial and body color and the snake-scale decorations on his forehead and right chest give some hint of the role Maniaci is embodying. Furthermore, inspired by elements from traditional Chinese opera, both musically and stylistically, Zhou Long endows Xiao Qing's song with an "exoticism" that "should be contained through an intersection between exotic environments and individual characters."[15] For the audience in Boston and other locales outside the Chinese-speaking worlds, the Chinese legend itself serves as a kind of exotic environment, while the Western

Figure 45: Michael Maniaci as Xiao Qing in the 2010 Opera Boston performance of *Madame White Snake*. Copyright Clive Grainger.

operatic form and its characterizations reinforce such exoticism for the audience at the Beijing Music Festival and the Hong Kong Arts Festival, as they are already familiar with the legend in Chinese.

Righteousness against Love, Truth against Freedom

For Western audiences, the *Madame White Snake* opera may show readily identifiable parallels from such cultural resources as the Bible: it opens with a half-woman, half-snake figure in the debris of a great flood and ends with another great flood initiated by another snake woman that destroys human lives. As the conflict between Madame White Snake and Abbot Fahai over the mortal Xu Xian intensifies, the opera again invokes universal dilemmas, asking the audience to choose between siding with righteousness (Fahai) or love (White Snake), truth (Fahai) or freedom (White Snake). The war between the good values leads to evil, as the flood overtakes both the innocent onlookers and the children, who are often the real-life casualties of war.

Figure 46: Ying Huang as Madame White Snake and Peter Tantsits as Xu Xian in the 2010 Opera Boston performance of *Madame White Snake*. Copyright Clive Grainger.

Before tragedy strikes, however, the opera convincingly fosters the ambience of love, a key motif in missionary Samuel I. Woodbridge's 1896 rendition and throughout the twentieth-century multilocational and multilingual retellings in an inter-Asian context. Most importantly, the libretto compares the snake women's immortality with the mortal man's "thirty long years of human experience," observing that the snake women are "only just exploring what it is to be human." In fact, Madame White Snake insists forcefully on her own righteousness: "I am a woman, and I love this man. How can this be wrong?"[16] Learning to love, to be loved, and to die is precisely her destiny, her desire, and what gives meaning to her existence, as is clear when Madame White Snake exclaims, "Love transforms the lowliest of us all. I am lifted by its potent power. I surrender to its thrall."[17]

The opera returns to Xiao Qing the storyteller in act 2, scene 2. This love scene between Madame White Snake and Xu Xian is portrayed solely by Xiao Qing's singing and through her perspective, accompanied only by the chorus and the orchestra (fig. 46). Xiao Qing watches her beloved mistress make love to Xu Xian with bitterness and yearning, wondering what this thing called love is.

Following the libretto's previous exploration of righteousness, act 3 probes the meaning of truth: "What is the truth but what makes the heart rejoice? . . . Trust me for the sake of our love, for the sake of our child," Madame White Snake begs Xu Xian.[18] The mortal husband is tormented by a question posed to him by Fahai, whether he knew who his wife is. His doubt about his wife had been planted the day he married her, when she insisted that he agree to let her go off, one night a month, with Xiao Qing, no questions asked. He often wondered where she went and what she did in secret. He asks Fahai to reveal the truth about his wife, while wrestling with himself internally: "Can I live with her without the truth? Can I live without her with the truth? Isn't the truth the love we feel? Isn't that the only truth that matters?"[19] Unfortunately, he concludes that this is not the case. Equipped with the potion given to him by Fahai and without realizing its deadly effects, Xu Xian opts for the truth. However, in an ensuing philosophical duet, the idea of "true selves" again comes under question from Madame White's perspective:

Our true selves?
Xiao Qing, what are our true selves?
You see my true self
Standing here, head bowed, hands open
Eyes wet, heartbroken
Waiting for you
You ask who I am
Who am I?
I am transformed
I am reborn
Each month at dawn I burst from old skin a new woman
Each month I reaffirm my humanness[20]

Xu Xian the mortal husband watches in horror and disbelief after Madame White Snake takes the potion, witnessing her human form dissolving before his eyes. He echoes her wail: "I am betrayed. It is finished."[21] The epic battle between Madame White and Abbot Fahai ensues, and the world is consumed by a raging storm and deluge. Xiao Qing the storyteller must return at this moment, illuminated by a spotlight, singing, "Love, Truth, Freedom, Righteousness, to each his own nirvana. In our fierce pursuit of our heart's desire, we corrupt the heart of Nirvana [stage goes dark, final curtain falls]."[22]

Singaporean and Mainland Chinese Origins

Opera critic David Shengold, in a 2010 review of the opera, recognized the potential for a cogent theatrical expression of the White Snake legend. Many operas, including *Armide* and *Rusalka,* share the theme of an immortal attempting love with a mortal. The element of failed marital trust, from his point of view, pertains to questions of identity and origin, evoking *Lohengrin,* only with the gender roles reversed. Nonetheless, Shengold considered Jacobs's libretto "problematic," too expository and telling the audience what to think rather than showing them through performance on stage, to the extent that he wondered, "Maybe it would play better in Chinese, or retranslated?"[23] Such a question alerts us to the fact that both the Singapore-born librettist and the Mainland China–born composer occupy hybrid linguistic and cultural positions vis-à-vis their multilocational and multilingual audiences and critics active in the English-speaking world. This multilingual and multicultural factor, in combination with Jacobs's lack of prior experience in the theater, might have been the primary reason for the critical assessments from reviewers like Shengold.[24]

As mentioned in chapter 1, seeing Cantonese and other local opera versions of the White Snake legend was an important experience for the young Cerise Lim Jacobs, reflective of her childhood growing up in a traditional Chinese family in colonial Singapore: "The immortal snake's quest for love represented for us all—grandmother, great-aunt, mother, nanny, and children—the yearning for the ineffable, the courage to follow your heart. We sat for many Saturdays, millions (perhaps billions) of us, to have our hearts broken again and again by love's death."[25] Examining Jacobs's libretto grants us a renewed understanding of what she refers to as "love's death," as materialized in the tragic ending of the *Madame White Snake* opera. In a recent interview, Jacobs also mentioned Shaw Brothers' 1962 Mandarin-language *huangmei diao* film *Madam White Snake* and its leading actress Lin Dai as major influences. Although she loved the film as a child, when recreating the White Snake legend for the opera, she was determined to remold the "fragile" and "hopeless" characterizations of the snake women as fighting against authoritarianism (*yu baquan shili duikang* 與霸權勢力對抗).[26]

The Singapore into which Jacobs was born had experienced the destruction of war and Japanese occupation and been returned to British colonial control. However, Britain's failure to defend Singapore against the Japanese had destroyed its credibility in the eyes of the people, and the postwar decades saw political awakening and rising nationalist sentiments among the local populace. Growing up in a traditional Chinese family during this period of rapid change, Jacobs absorbed the disparate influences of Chinese, Malay, Indian, and Western culture and the world religions of Christianity (she was educated by American Methodist missionaries), Islam, Buddhism, and Hinduism. During the turbulence following Singapore's independence from Great Britain and its secession from Malaysia throughout the late 1950s and 1960s, when fear of Communism was rampant in Southeast Asia, her family managed to emigrate to Australia. Jacobs dropped out of school at the age of nineteen to begin a journey that took her from Melbourne to Oxford, England; East Lansing, Michigan; Vancouver; and Pittsburgh, until she finally settled in Boston, Massachusetts.[27]

Jacobs and her collaborator Zhou were both born in 1953, the year of the snake in the Chinese twelve-animal zodiac. The year 1953 also signaled the coming of age of Japanese cinema on the world stage in the post-Occupation period, with titles such as *Ugetsu* and *Tokyo Story* attracting much international attention.[28] Most importantly, 1953 saw Tian Han's first publication in Beijing of his *jingju* libretto *Legend of the White Snake*, often considered the culminating text of years of revisions and the text that opened up the legend to contemporary popular cultural reinventions.

Born into an artistic family in Mainland China, Zhou Long, the composer of the *Madame White Snake* opera, grew up in Beijing during the late 1950s and during the years of the Cultural Revolution. Zhou was forced to give up piano and drive a tractor for five years on a rural state farm. He resumed his musical training in 1973, in the final years of the Cultural Revolution, and studied composition, music theory, and conducting, as well as Chinese traditional music. Zhou enrolled in the first composition class at the reopened Central Conservatory of Music in Beijing, right after the end of the Cultural Revolution. This entering class of 1978 is famous as the first generation of composers to receive formal education after the end of the Cultural Revolution, and Zhou's classmates include many other Chinese composers active on the world stage today, including Chen Yi (Zhou's wife), Chen Qigang, Tan Dun, and Guo Wenjing, among others. After graduating in 1983, Zhou was appointed composer-in-residence with the National Broadcasting Symphony Orchestra of China. In 1985, Zhou traveled to the United States under a fellowship to attend Columbia University, where he studied with Chou Wen-Chung, Mario Davidovsky, and George Edwards, receiving a Doctor of Musical Arts degree in 1993. He became a US citizen in 1999.[29]

In the Japanese context, Mizoguchi's *Ugetsu* was released in 1953, reviving the interwar Japanese fascination with the White Snake legend and initiating a new tradition throughout the postwar 1950s, as explored in chapter 4. Such a Japanese connection in turn opened up coproduction with Hong Kong, South Korea, and Taiwan, facilitating a distinctive Korean connection in an inter-Asian context, as examined in chapter 5. Another important text, Chinese female writer Zhao Qingge's novel *The Legend of White Snake*, published in 1956 in Beijing, serves as an important connection between the PRC of the 1950s and the United States of the twenty-first century, as we will see below.

It is important to consider the multicultural and multilingual background of the creators of the *Madame White Snake* opera in a broad inter-Asian context historically, as well as through their shared minority perspectives in their American context in the present day. Jacobs, in particular, clearly articulated that she wholeheartedly identifies with the White Snake, as "a complete outsider" (*cheche didi de wailaizhe* 徹徹底底的外來者) who, uprooted from her cultural background, had to struggle in order to survive and succeed in a new environment and as "a woman, a 'yellow-skinned' minority, an immigrant from outside" (*yiming nüxing, yige huangpifu de shaoshu minzu, yige wailai yimin* 一名女性、一個黃皮膚的少數民族、一個外來移民). Jacobs named her activist opera company White Snake Projects and established an IDEA (Inclusion, Diversity, Equity, and Access) opera foundation in order to support minority composers and librettists and help them break into mainstream American venues.[30]

THE POWERS AND POSSIBILITIES OF PERFORMANCE

In her foreword to Mary Zimmerman's play *The White Snake*, Mo Zhou 周沫, assistant director for the play's Oregon Shakespeare Festival premiere in 2012, remarks that their rendition of this "epic love story" was based on the beautiful prose text written and published in Beijing in 1956 by "arguably the most underrated female writer" Zhao Qingge, "who infuses the story with immense elegance."[31] In addition, Zhou lists Wilt Idema's *The White Snake and Her Son*, which includes a translation of a Buddhist "precious scroll" (*baojuan* 寶卷) published in 1908 as a powerful influence. She goes on to quote the Buddhist monk's comments concerning the White Snake in his preface to the Buddhist *baojuan* version, written more than a century before: "Do not regard Madame White as a demon. She does not act like one. Should she not put to shame human beings who do not act like human beings but follow the ways of demons?"[32] For Zhou and Zimmerman, this new insight on the "humanity of the nonhuman" from a religious figure leads to deeper understanding of the story. Similar wisdom and inspiration could be found in American missionary Woodbridge's and diplomat Cloud's renditions discussed in chapter 2, which were roughly contemporary with the Buddhist *baojuan* version and have also left traces in the Cold War cinematic adaptations of the legend in the Japanese and Korean contexts, discussed in chapters 4 and 5, where the humanity of the fantastic White Snake demoness was often used to reveal the demonic nature of humans in real life.

Imprinted with such early- to-mid-twentieth-century inspirations, Zimmerman's one-act White Snake play contributes to the already canonized twentieth-century practice of treating the legend as an "epic love story," with an emphasis on the humanity of the nonhuman. In Zimmerman's own words, deep down, the play is about how "you can be loved for who you truly are," regardless of which species you belong to.[33] Although Fahai was already an unsympathetic character in the early twentieth-century Buddhist *baojuan*, Zimmerman's play seems to show even heavier influence from the Zhao Qingge version created in 1950s Beijing, as we see "a surprisingly evil Buddhist monk" and "a truly unconventional marriage," all for the sake of telling a great story that would appeal to five- and ninety-five-year-olds alike.[34]

It becomes clear that the Zimmerman play is drawing directly upon the politicized interpretations of Zhao Qingge's 1956 prose text. The atheist rhetoric in the PRC of the 1950s and the use of the White Snake legend to propagate the nascent regime's new marriage law provided an impetus for reinterpretation—of the Buddhist abbot as the representative of an evil "feudal" regime and of the relationship between the White Snake and her human lover as a case of free love against arranged marriage. In this context, Abbot Fahai is referred to as "a fundamentalist monk who disapproves strongly of anyone marrying a different species." The legend becomes "a very adventurous, very romantic story," while at the same time integrating fantasy with reality.[35] Similar to the way in which the 1953 Japanese film *Ugetsu* combined wartime reality with the outlandish world of Lady Wakasa, Zimmerman's play highlights the prosperous cities and scenic sites of southeastern China, showing the human/nonhuman couple as they run a pharmacy together and focusing on their desire to lead a normal life.

The Wuzhen Experience

However, the truly remarkable features of Zimmerman's *The White Snake* reside in the writing and directing; all of her published plays must be understood in the context of their performance histories. For *The White Snake* in particular, it is important to trace its performance from its premiere at the Oregon Shakespeare Festival in February 2012 to its appearance as the concluding play for the Wuzhen Theatre Festival in China in November 2014, on which occasion I was in the audience, experiencing the thrill of live theater, Zimmerman style.[36] Zimmerman wrote the script for *The White Snake* while rehearsing the play at the Oregon Shakespeare Festival, where the production premiered. All seven iterations of that original production remained the same in terms of music, scenery, lighting, and costume. The casting also remained the same, with two Asian American actresses playing White Snake and Green Snake (Greenie), Amy Kim Waschke and Tanya Thai McBride, respectively. In Wuzhen, however, McBride, who was an excellent Greenie in all prior productions, injured herself during dress rehearsal and had to be replaced by an Anglo-American actress, resulting in a cast that was less Asian American than in other venues.[37]

Zimmerman is keenly interested in figuring out the structure of pleasure and the configuration of narrative; because of that, her play is distinguished from other White Snake adaptations by its forking narrative arcs and the possibilities for the audience to creatively interact with the narratives.[38] Through the use of multiple narrators, she brings her own take on the legend's characterizations and ending. She leaves room for alternative interpretations, while keeping her focus on how this "Romeo and Juliet–style" love story is able to transcend the barrier between the human and the nonhuman.

When I watched *The White Snake* performance in Wuzhen in November 2014, I knew nothing of the production losing its original Greenie because of an injury, and I was fully immersed in the performance. I became fascinated by the audience response to Zimmerman's English-language adaptation, which was far more enthusiastic than to the opening play of the same theater festival, celebrated Chinese director Tian Qinxin's Chinese-language play *Green Snake*.[39] Compared to Tian's postmodern rendition of the White Snake legend, from the perspective of the Buddhist abbot Fahai and featuring the sister/maid figure Green Snake as first female protagonist, Zimmerman's version seemed to me, and apparently to many other audience members, as somehow more accessible, more effective, hence more moving. Even before the opening of the performance, the audience members in the Wuzhen Grand Theatre were already presented with an inviting atmosphere imbued with strong Chinese aesthetic elements: an elegant white silk curtain featuring ink painting of bamboo leaves and branches on the left side of the curtain, and two prominent Chinese characters for "White Snake" in stylish ink calligraphy on the right (fig. 47).

Figure 47: Silk curtain featuring ink paintings of bamboo and the two characters for "White Snake" in Chinese calligraphy. Stage decoration for Mary Zimmerman's *The White Snake*, as performed in English with Chinese subtitles at Wuzhen Grand Theatre, Wuzhen, China, November 7, 2014. Photo by author.

Thematically, it is likely because that the Zimmerman play has inherited the 1950s' rhetoric of focusing on the "girl power" of the two female protagonists, in a now familiar trope, and treating them as feminist heroines of antiauthoritarian struggles. Their struggle against the Buddhist abbot, the embodiment of all evil oppressors, was conditioned by an activist "structure of feeling" pervasive in socialist China,[40] which is now making a comeback in our postsocialist nostalgia for such positive female characterizations. It is not likely that Zimmerman was knowingly mobilizing that nostalgia in her creative process. Rather, it is more likely her engagement with the White Snake source text, while drawing on a wide range of cultural discourses, came to intersect with contemporary Chinese audiences' concerns and their interest in strong heroines. It is also likely that this interest was shared by audiences who saw the performances of the Oregon Shakespeare Festival production, which played at six other venues in addition to Wuzhen, as well as at Center Stage in Baltimore, and by the audiences of the more than thirty high school and college productions around the world, including in Korea and the Philippines.[41]

Most importantly, Zimmerman's artistry in bringing out the thrill of live theater must be emphasized. "I would never be the artist I was as a child," she has remarked, quoting fellow Nebraskan Willa Cather to articulate the notion,[42] planted in her own Nebraskan roots, of live theater as a playground,

Figure 48: Amy Kim Waschke as White Snake encounters Christopher Livingston as Xu Xian in the rain. In Mary Zimmerman's *The White Snake*, performed at Goodman Theatre in Chicago, May 2014. Photo by Liz Lauren.

with an emphasis on accessibility and playfulness for any performance. With the set design as "an open field of play," Zimmerman always starts rehearsing without a single word written, and she writes her scripts in between rehearsals, taking inspiration from her company: the cast members, the costume designers, the musical accompanists, the lighting and stage technicians, and any others present. With the set design and the whole company influencing her script, Zimmerman calls them her cocreators. She values nonverbal means of communication as much as verbal ones, as expressed in the dynamic relationship she sees between dancing and writing, a theme discussed in chapter 6, and combines all the tools of the theater with meticulous storytelling, so as to blend hyper-narrativity with nonverbal communication in celebrating the act of narrative.[43]

For Zimmerman, a play must be efficient, imaginative, and original, but should also be visually spectacular and theatrical. What keeps her going in theater, according to an interview with KPBS news,[44] is finding ways of doing the impossible on stage. How do you do a rainstorm without actually importing rain for it (fig. 48)? We may be reminded, by contrast, of the emphasis

Figure 49: Tanya Thai McBride (left) as Green Snake and Amy Kim Waschke (right) as White Snake, both controlling a puppet snake riding waves of water, represented by long rippling sheet of blue silk. In Mary Zimmerman's *The White Snake*, performed at Goodman Theatre in Chicago, May 2014. Photo by Liz Lauren.

on special effects in early twentieth-century Shanghai White Snake performances and in Cold War–era White Snake films across Asia, as examined throughout this study. For Zimmerman, however, imagination is the only special effect you need. She aims to engage her audience in an intimate and interactive fashion, allowing them to draw on their own resources for images in their cultural repertoire to comprehend and experience a particular scene in the performance.

One particularly good example of representing the impossible is Zimmerman and her team's creative ways of rendering the snake women on stage. The Wuzhen performance showcased a wide range: snakes in their female forms as two actresses; snakes as two puppets (made from dryer hoses covered in silk, with painted heads) operated by each actress manipulating each snake with two sticks (fig. 49); snakes as tails protruding from under the costumes of the two actresses; as parasols lined up in the shape of big snakes; and as small toy snakes, among other presentations. Moreover, when the snake women became agitated or stressed, they tended to speak with a drawn-out hissing voice, with each "s" sounding like "sssss"; their bodies also started to twist and twirl out of control, demonstrating their more dominant snake nature bursting forth from a dormant state, especially in the case of the less-cultivated Green Snake, known as Greenie in this version. Interestingly, this type of verbalization and visualization of the snake women happens both in the opera *Madame White Snake*, which premiered in 2010 in Boston, and in Tian Qinxin's *Green Snake*, which premiered at the Hong Kong Arts Festival in 2013. In this illuminating detail, we see spiritual echoes and possible mutual influences, shared across genres and locations in the Sinophone and Anglophone adaptations of the White Snake legend in the twenty-first century.

It is reported that when Mary Zimmerman was invited to present her work at the Wuzhen festival, the organizers wanted her to bring her most celebrated play, the 2002 Tony Award–winning *Metamorphoses*, as the theme of the festival was precisely "Metamorphoses."[45] But this is not what Zimmerman herself recalls. She remembers having been invited by festival organizer Stan Lai (Lai Sheng-chuan 賴聲川), an award-winning US-born, Taiwan- and Shanghai-based playwright and theater director, to specifically bring *The White Snake* play to Wuzhen. In light of this, she was not responding with her production to Tian Qinxin's *Green Snake*, the opening performance of the festival, as the report stated. Regardless of whether Zimmerman's staging of *The White Snake* in Wuzhen was by the organizer's design, it had a similar function to Zhou Long's bringing the *Madame White Snake* opera back to the Beijing Music Festival after its Boston premiere in 2010. The travel of Zimmerman's play from Oregon to Wuzhen signals an intriguing intercultural and translingual crossing, through which a deeper understanding of what it means to be human, as presented in a legend about inter-species love, could be achieved across disparate traditions and contemporary realities in both China and the United States.

The Constellation Theater Company Production in Washington, DC

After experiencing the Wuzhen production of *The White Snake*, directed by Zimmerman herself, I saw a production on May 11, 2019, at the Constellation Theatre Company (CTC) in Washington, DC, directed by Allison Arkell Stockman.[46] This production similarly delivered on the play's distinct features of visuality, musicality, and dynamic movement and acting. It generated such a profound emotional reaction in me, a researcher who has experienced dozens of White Snake productions over the years, that I asked myself: How did it do it? Why am I so moved by a performance so familiar to me?

Beyond my own experience, the CTC production generated a strong affective reaction in its audience overall, even for those extremely familiar with the White Snake legend.[47] Aided by scenic designer and Towson University professor Daniel Ettinger's sensitive designs, which incorporated Chinese-inspired visual elements, such as wooden frames and wave patterns in the background, ink painting bamboo leaves on the floor of the intimate stage, and colorful umbrellas framing the two sides of the stage, the CTC production fosters a poetic, genuine atmosphere for the introduction of the two female protagonists.

The White Snake and Green Snake puppets designed by Matthew Pauli, an actor, clown, puppeteer, and teaching artist in the DC Metro/Baltimore area, seemed to me to be updated versions of those in the Zimmerman production, with more prominent features and more flexibility in their movements. Compared to the costume designs in the Wuzhen Zimmerman production, the CTC costumes, by DC-based costume designer Frank Labovitz, are less flamboyant but equally elegant, and I appreciated how White Snake's and Green Snake's dresses are appropriately minimalistic, with an effortless charm. I also appreciated the decision to not include a Peking opera–style head piece for White Snake, as the Zimmerman production did. The Stockman production, however, did pay tribute to the Zimmerman production in the theatrical makeup of the snake women and the theatricality of Chinese-style performances. Specifically, it judiciously followed the Zimmerman play to cite Cecilia Zung's *Secrets of the Chinese Drama*[48] and highlighted ritualistic action and its potential comical effect as an integral part of a twenty-first century Anglophone production based on a Chinese legend.

Stockman also followed Zimmerman in casting the CTC production, with prominent Asian American actors in the leading roles and actors of diverse experiences and backgrounds for the whole ensemble. Momo Nakamura, an established Japanese American stage and screen actress, brought a daring, funny, and spirited Green Snake to life through her bold and uninhibited acting. Eunice Bae, a Korean American actress, who recently portrayed the role of Cornelia in Korean American playwright Julia Cho's *Aubergine*,[49] delivered the role of the White Snake with grace, charm, and elegance. Jacob Yeh, a Chinese American actor with a long list of stage credits, excelled in embodying White Snake's human husband Xu Xian, especially in his formidable delivery of what I consider the most emotional and the most powerful line of the whole Zimmerman play, "I have no doubt that no man has been loved as I have been loved."[50]

One of the most ingenious inventions in the Zimmerman play is the creation of the character Doubt. The Stockman production fleshed out the embodiment of Doubt (played by Linda Bard) by dressing her in a full-body black cloak and having her aggressively tangled up with Xu Xian, tormenting him and causing him to waver when making important decisions. With Frank Labovitz's enigmatic costume design, lighting effects designed by Max Doolittle, and choreography by Jennifer J. Hopkins, the CTC production creates tension, intrigue, and genuinely felt emotion and enchantment within the whole ensemble of actors, whether in situations featuring extensive action and fighting or in more subdued scenes, including those with subtle chorographical elements. For example, Doubt's sustained pursuit of Xu Xian is expressed with an increasing intensity through what seems to be meticulously choreographed dance movements; this is brought into full play throughout the first half of the CTC production through Linda Bard's excellent delivery. In addition to embodying the psychological depth and the moral dilemma deeply felt by the characters, Doubt and her challenge to Xu Xian also brings moments of comical relief, as when Xu Xian is seen physically bothered and psychologically tormented by Doubt, which brought bursts of laughter from the audience.

Ryan Sellers was excellent as Fahai, the Monk "far advanced in enlightenment" but with "a villainous heart."[51] Sellers, active on the stage since 2002 as author, director, fight choreographer, and actor, was one of the most experienced and most versatile in the whole ensemble[52] and was especially strong in movement and fighting scenes. In fact, excellent acting from the whole ensemble made the CTC performance an especially memorable one. All of the ensemble members are talented performers in their own right, and each excelled in multiple roles. Indian American actress Shubhangi Kuchibhotla left a strong impression as Xu Xian's sister, as one of the customers at Xu Xian's pharmacy, as one of the Cloud Spirits, and as one of the narrators, among other roles. Dylan Arredondo, a DC-based Latino-Japanese actor, who also has a background in directing, producing, and stage and company management, excelled as Xu Xian's brother-in-law, one of the Cloud Spirits, and other roles.

Similarly, Andrew Quilpa masterfully delivered ritualistic acting instructions from *Secrets of the Chinese Drama* in the middle of Green Snake's imminent attack on Xu Xian, perceived by her as betraying White Snake's love and siding with Fahai. The humor generated by such interruptions is profound, as it breaks the action, puts it on hold, and adds dynamic energy throughout the play. The singing narrators, Jennifer Knight and Jordan D. Moral, punctuated the performance's emotional highlights with enchanting singing. In addi-

Figure 50: White Snake (Eunice Bae) and Xu Xian (Jacob Yeh) at the Lantern Festival in *The White Snake*, with the ensemble members, left to right: Momo Nakamura, Jennifer Knight, Dylan Arredondo, Andrew Quilpa, Eunice Bae, Jacob Yeh, Shubhangi Kuchibhotla, Jordan D. Moral, and Linda Bard. Written and originally directed by Mary Zimmerman. Directed by Allison Arkell Stockman. Scenic design by Daniel Ettinger, costume design by Frank Labovitz, lighting design by Max Doolittle, and properties design by Alexander Rothschild. Constellation Theatre Company, Washington, DC, April 25-May 26, 2019. Copyright DJ Corey Photography.

tion, Moral delivered a memorable performance as the boatman, serving as a magic matchmaker for White Snake and Xu Xian, while Knight gave an audacious performance as the Bodhisattva Guanyin, although her bold red costume likely raised eyebrows for any audience member familiar with the white robes typically associated with the figure. This unusual choice was made to distinguish her from the White Snake, whose signature white robes needed to be highlighted throughout, according to Stockman. However, recognizing "the boldness" of the color choice after the effect, she has noted that this detail may be reconsidered if the CTC production is restaged in the future.[53]

The ensemble's collective power and the magic it produced can be further attested in a scene close to the ending of the play, when nine of the ten ensemble members celebrate the Lantern Festival and express joy together with White Snake and Xu Xian, one month after the birth of their son, Dream

Dragon (fig. 50). Prominently featuring colorfully lit umbrellas and lanterns, this scene showcases the production's elegant scenic and lighting designs and its masterful use of props. Prop designer Alexander Rothschild, in particular, has the Midas Touch in creating miniature props that evoked the aura of physical structures too large to be represented in CTC's intimate stage: a dilapidated house which could be magically transformed into a grand villa by White Snake's divine intervention, or the notorious Thunder Peak Pagoda where Fahai would eventually suppress White Snake under. Such props, including the colorfully lit umbrellas, the miniature pagoda, and the Chinese-style red wooden stand, together fostered a sense of closure at the ending of the play, when ensemble members as collective narrators delivered some of the most powerful and most poetic lines of the whole narrative, including the final line of the Zimmerman play, "Don't be afraid. It is impossible to die alone."[54]

The production's music was provided by world percussionist Tom Teasley and Chinese dulcimer (*yangqin*) virtuoso Chao Tian. Dynamic and enchanting improvised live music corresponded to the storyline, choreography, and other theatrical elements in the play. Consequently, every performance had a slightly different feel, accentuated by the experimental musical renderings of Teasley and Tian, who are strategically located onstage, largely visible, but within the wooden frame and spatially separated from the actors upstage. Teasley has won multiple awards for his previous work with CTC, including providing improvised live music for the performance of another Mary Zimmerman play based on Chinese source material, *Journey to the West*, which I attended in April 2016.[55] Collaborating with Tian to form the music duo, Dong Xi (東西, literally East and West) and debuting their new album *Out of the Blue,* featuring music for *The White Snake* performance, brought an exciting new development in Teasley's illustrious career.[56] After the CTC production ended, Dong Xi was in residence in China for a month to continue musical explorations to break boundaries and connect people through music across linguistic and national divisions,[57] which in effect brought the White Snake legend back to China. Such multidirectional travels and mutual enrichments are at the heart of the White Snake's global travels.

More Inspirations from Kentucky Students

Translingual and intercultural crossings happen daily in the college classroom, specifically related to the metamorphoses of the White Snake legend as taught in one of my classes, offered as part of the folklore and mythology minor at the University of Kentucky, as mentioned in chapter 2. It is through the fresh eyes and minds of my students that I have come to better appreciate the body of the White Snake texts written or translated into English, as no Chinese language ability is presumed for this course. Equipped with knowledge of a wide range of White Snake sources in different media, the students are well positioned to conduct historical, contextual, and trans-media comparisons of the texts in question. As a consequence, it is not surprising that they immediately identified the "love story" fallacy of the Zimmerman play, as they knew it resulted from a relatively recent conceptual remaking of the legend over the last couple of centuries. They went even further to point out the contradictory portrayal of Fahai in Zimmerman's play, which drew on the 1950s PRC rhetoric of condemning the evil oppressor and yet continued to refer to him as "far advanced in enlightenment."[58] One student argued that it seems impossible for an individual to have certain calculated intentions or attachments to the surrounding world while truly following the Way to enlightenment; for that reason, she was not convinced by the image of Fahai as both enlightened and possessing a villainous heart, as the issue here is not the incompatibility of enlightenment and villainy per se, but enlightenment and attachment.[59]

With respect to the influence of 1950s Beijing on the play, students also noticed that the Zimmerman version highlights the human/nonhuman couple's practice of traditional Chinese medicine. One student asked, "Do medicine, magic, and philosophy intersect or overlap in this play?" Through an online discussion forum and in-class debates, we, as a class, came to a better understanding of the central importance of the Bao He Pharmacy in Zimmerman's conceptualization of the play. Indeed, in this play, the pharmacy had become a key background and plot device.[60] It came to represent Xu Xian and Madame White's trust in each other, as Xu Xian's faith and love for White Snake seemed to parallel her work at the pharmacy, which involves healing people, after all. For example, when confronting Fahai's suspicion, Xu Xian shows faith in his wife, using the service she gives to the poor and the sick as a rebuttal to Fahai's insistence that her apparent loving kindness is "a trick."[61] Throughout the play, the success of the Bao He Pharmacy and the strength of the couple's marriage/relationship go hand in hand.

A Female Writer of Socialist China: Zhao Qingge and Her 1956 Novel

It is through Mary Zimmerman's one-act play *The White Snake* that my students were reintroduced to the largely forgotten Chinese writer Zhao Qingge's 1956 novel, published in Beijing in the first decade of Communist China.

In her foreword to the 1956 Chinese version, Zhao calls the White Snake story a beautiful folktale about a "fairy maiden's pursuit of freedom and happiness" and classifies the role of the "rascally monk" as a "representative of the reactionary feudal forces." Zhao mentions her six revisions of the text, based on her watching different performances of the White Snake legend in *jingju* and in local operas. Most of these operas were based on Tian Han's *jingju* text, which had been finalized just a few years earlier. As was customary at the time, Zhao positioned her novel as a reflection of the "sharp conflict between the common people and feudal ruling classes," endowing the world of fantastic legends with class politics.[62]

In her 1997 preface to the new English-Chinese bilingual edition of the novel, Zhao reflected on how she wrote for a living in the 1950s, publishing versions of *The Butterfly Lovers*, *The Legend of White Snake*, and *Peony Pavilion* (*Du Liniang* 杜麗娘) for popular consumption, with each reprinted about eight to nine times, and with some five hundred thousand copies currently in print altogether. She speculates on the ingredients for the popularity of her novelettes: their realism, freshness, and reflections on human nature. That is to say, the protagonists' pursuit of humanity, liberty, happiness, truth, goodness and beauty, and the triumph of the victimized and the downtrodden are all qualities that appeal to a public educated in the socialist "structure of feeling" that was pervasive in Maoist China.[63] In addition to realism, Zhao also emphasizes the novelettes' unabashed romanticism and mythical qualities and states that she wrote her preface for the new edition with "readers at home and abroad" in mind.[64]

A close reading of the twelve chapters of the new English-Chinese bilingual version of Zhao Qingge's *The Legend of White Snake*, cited as the version used by Zimmerman as the source text for her 2012 play, provides important clues for a careful examination of different strategies of retelling the Chinese legend in a translingual and cross-cultural context. Zhao begins her novel by setting the White Snake up as a devoted believer in search of the Way who, "did no harm to any living being" for a thousand years."[65] Zhao portrays Xu Xian, the human lover, as so often hesitant and in doubt that Zimmerman introduced a new character, simply named "Doubt," in her play. Although both versions emphasize the White Snake's heroic qualities, Zhao's version places particular weight on her almost altruistic devotion to not only her lover Xu Xian but also "the people in distress," to the extent that Xu says to her, "I do believe that you are more caring than Guanyin, the Goddess of Mercy, herself."[66] This is a shocking comparison in the genealogy of the White Snake adaptations, in which Guanyin has often enjoyed the status of the ultimate savior for White Snake and her lover.[67] In addition, White Snake's flooding the monastery and killing innocent onlookers, which results in the ultimate tragic ending in Zhou Long and Cerise Lim Jacobs's opera, is easily avoided. Zhao, for instance, has White Snake order the water spirits to guard both banks of the Yangtze River, so that the flood she will cause will only inundate Golden Mountain Monastery and not harm the city or drown innocent people.[68] In the same vein, Zhao's Greenie is depicted as utterly devoted to her mistress, and the friendship between the two snake women is said to have transcended that between ordinary mortal sisters.

Similarly, the demonization of the Buddhist abbot Fahai reaches extremes in Zhao's version of the story. This circumstance led my Kentucky students to suspect that Fahai's negative portrayal in Zimmerman's play was directly adapted from Zhao's version, which in turn reflects the values of Maoist China. In Zhao's version, Fahai not only has "a villainous heart," he also "always used his magic to cheat good people out of their incense money, never doing anything beneficial to mankind."[69] This stereotypical image, seen in both Republican and Communist discourses throughout twentieth-century China, represents "superstition" rather than "religion" and thus merits ridicule in Zhao's text.[70] With the villainization of Fahai, an authority figure who represents a higher level of humanity in earlier versions, Zhao Qingge's text grants the human husband a broader perspective; he thus does not judge his wife and her companion as human or nonhuman. Rather, Xu Xian confesses, "Even if you really are demons, you have shown me so much affection and loyalty that I can never doubt your intentions again"; he further insists that "even if my wife is a snake demon her love is true."[71] This statement is similar to the confessions made by the human husbands in cinematic adaptations of the White Snake legend contemporary to Zhao's text, throughout the 1950s across East Asia, as discussed in chapters 4 and 5.

Having first read Zimmerman's play, my students at the University of Kentucky had to confront the sensation of reading Zhao's novel with prior knowledge of the play and the gradual realization of how much the novel influenced the play. They were also able to appreciate the ways in which, compared to previous versions of the legend, the images of the White Snake in both Zhao's and Zimmerman's texts are so much more humanized through her relationship with Xu Xian, in her playful jokes and marital arguments, and in her living as a "normal" human couple with her husband. It is through such a humanistic revamping that Zhao Qingge is able to foreground Xu Xian's doubt throughout the text and Zimmerman is able to conceive the new character Doubt. Doubt is crucial to the plot's progression and in Zhao's novel comes to represent the weakness of the human heart, a point at which love falters. Zhao's mastery of language, which Mo Zhou observes in her foreword to Zimmerman's play, is on full display in scenes of slander, flattery, rumor, blasphemy, and manipulation, such as before Xu Xian's final realization of the "truth" inherent in his wife's and her companion's actions, even when their human identities are revealed as "false."

It was also through the fresh perspective offered by my students that I came to understand that although Zhao's 1956 novel has proven very popular and far more accessible than many other White Snake renditions from her time, including Tian Han's most famous *jingju* rendition a few years earlier, it is indeed indicative of its era; its ending (in which Greenie returns to defeat Fahai and liberate White Snake from under the Thunder Peak Pagoda) was likely the only one possible during that period. To my students, such an ending feels lacking, since there is no final reunion of husband and wife or mother and son. In particular, this ending pales in comparison to the one found in the introduction to the Ma Rufei *tanci* version, translated in Wilt Idema's *The White Snake and Her Son*, which features the harmonious coexistence of Confucian, Buddhist, and Daoist teachings: the son returns to save his mother (Confucian), Xu Xian becomes a monk (Buddhist), and the human/nonhuman couple eventually reach enlightenment and ascend to Heaven (Daoist and Buddhist).[72] Such a harmonious religious convergence, of course, had become impossible in the time of Zhao's writing. However, that was not the case for Zimmerman at the turn of the twenty-first century in the United States. Her text allows room for audience intervention and experimentation, and the ending makes available a range of spiritualities and possibilities. The play's multiple narrators discuss how the story forks at the concluding point, allowing the audience to decide for themselves how they want the story to end.

POETRY, PHOTOGRAPHY, AND FASHION: DIGITAL CHALLENGES FROM INDRANI

This section takes as its starting point the exploration of increasingly open performance texts, as in Zimmerman's case, and extends our interest in White Snake performances into the digital. The focus here is an award-winning short digital video, *The Legend of Lady White Snake*, created by the India-born photographer and filmmaker Indrani Pal-Chaudhuri in 2013 and released as a film in 2015 in the United States.[73] I analyze the digitization of the Chinese legend in a transnational context and question the relationship between digital-ness and plasticity, between subject-making and metamorphosis, and between queer mentality and intermedial experimentation. A graduate of Princeton University with a major in cultural anthropology, Indrani, as she is mononymously known, has worked with popular music stars such as David Bowie, Beyoncé, and Lady Gaga, among others. In her debut film, Indrani refashions the White Snake legend through poetry, photography, and, most importantly, fashion. She and her celebrity-filled production team, including socialite and fashion icon Daphne Guinness, designer and producer GK Reid, and Indrani's own photographer duo Markus Klinko and Indrani, were initially commissioned to shoot a portrait for *The London Sunday Times*. Indrani incorporated in the piece a wide range of poetic fragments from, or inspired by, authors such as Neil Gaiman, Samuel Taylor Coleridge, Edgar Allan Poe, J. Robert Oppenheimer, Rabindranath Tagore, Ralph Waldo Emerson, and William Shakespeare. The result is a hauntingly spectacular, sensual experience that is digitally produced, transmitted, and consumed and offered as a tribute to the late designer Alexander McQueen. We, as viewers of this digital performance, are invited to contemplate the central themes of women's empowerment, LGBTQ+ rights, and environmental sustainability, as embodied by Guinness's expressive portrayal of the White Snake through poetry fragments inspired by Chinese and Indian thought, GK Reid and McQueen's flamboyantly Orientalist designs, and Klinko and Indrani's iconic photographs.

The iconographies central to this digital performance include ghosts and demon-lovers, visions and dreams, pleasure domes and romantic chasms. All have been represented throughout our explorations of the White Snake repertoire throughout this study. In Indrani's work, they are designed to evoke broad appreciation from viewers speaking different languages and of disparate backgrounds. "A meditation on obsession, gender and metamorphosis, inspired by an ancient Chinese legend," Indrani's "experimental labor of love" enriches the White Snake repertoire in revealing ways.[74] At the same time, it proves to be a great challenge to anyone intent on holding on to any "original" or "authentic" flavor of the legend. Consequently, the short film also lays bare a number of potential problems in our previous conceptions of transmigration and metamorphosis. This section aims to examine what might be lost and found in digitally performing a Chinese legend for the high fashion world and beyond and how that might contribute renewed understanding to the White Snake repertoire we have been building throughout this study.

Indrani was brought to my attention by an undergraduate student at the University of Kentucky, when I first taught my *White Snake* seminar in the spring of 2017. The student had been doing a series of weekly reflections on the Green Snake figure in the White Snake repertoire. Although a supporting character in most versions of the legend, Green Snake has been transformed into the leading protagonist in many recent renditions since the late 1970s.[75] These renditions emphasize transgender themes and homosexual tensions between the four protagonists: White Snake, Green Snake, the human husband Xu Xian, and the Buddhist abbot Fahai. With this background, the student proposed to analyze a short fashion film for her final creative project, and she started with an in-class screening of the film. It was a shocking experience for the whole class. This took place at the end of the semester, after we had read various prototypes of the White Snake legend written in the eleventh, fourteenth, and seventeenth centuries and as rendered in the late nineteenth-century missionary and diplomatic accounts. We had also been introduced to the versions centered on the "lust, caution" theme as well as recent romanticizing and humanizing adaptations of the legend throughout the twentieth century. However, we had never seen anything like Indrani's film.

There are obvious inaccuracies in this eight-minute work. For one, there is no source to support Indrani's claim that the legend of the White Snake is "three thousand years old." Moreover, the idea that "love" is central to the story is perhaps best considered a reconceptualization from the last few centuries and a result of the snake spirit's humanization; "love" is certainly not to be found in the legend's early versions. However, like any other form of transculturation, this short fashion film not only takes on the name of the Chinese White Snake legend and pushes some of its central themes to an extreme but also challenges both the White Snake repertoire and its aesthetic conventions in revealing ways. Things "traditionally Chinese" may have been lost in this digital reproduction, but other less culturally specific and contextually situated meanings are also found and recreated, albeit in fragments and without the narrative structure that we have seen at the center of the White Snake repertoire. However, the three keywords structuring my discussion of Indrani—poetry, photography, fashion—should be taken seriously in the context of digitally performing a Chinese legend for the world of high fashion. In particular, when such a mediated performance has been transmitted worldwide via digital media as the debut film of a celebrity photographer and when it has won prizes at multiple film festivals, including Los Angeles, London, Paris, Kolkata, San Diego, and Princeton, it deserves our critical reflection and careful analysis.

The film's female voiceover narration borrows heavily from Coleridge's 1816 poem "Kubla Khan," known as "an opium-induced, Orientalizing fantasia of the unconscious."[76] In fact, the following fragments from the famous poem are pieced together, seemingly at random, and woven into quotations from other poems in the film "script":

> The sacred river, ran . . . through caverns measureless to man, . . . that deep romantic chasm which slanted . . . down the green hill, . . . a waning moon was haunted . . . by a woman wailing for her demon-lover! . . . from this chasm, with ceaseless turmoil seething, . . . ancestral voices prophesying war! . . . weave a circle round him thrice . . . and close your eyes, . . . his flashing eyes, his floating hair! . . . And all should cry, Beware! Beware! . . . For he on honey-dew hath fed . . . and drunk the milk of Paradise.[77]

This narration pays little attention to the original flow of Coleridge's poem. It disregards the poem's insistence on the relationship between a woman and her "demon-lover," but also diverges from the Chinese White Snake legend's focus on the female protagonist being a "demoness-lover" herself. Instead, in Indrani's film the "demon-lover" and the "he" merge into an androgynous, hybrid figure, at whom White Snake's enthralling gaze is directed. The overlapping digital images of floating water, coiling snakes, twisting bodies, and the shining metallic pieces of foil resembling the clear and almost transparent scales of snake skins, stitch the poetry fragments together, if only on the level of the visual surface (fig. 51).

In addition to "Kubla Khan," Neil Gaiman's 2005 poem "The Hidden Chamber" was reportedly suggested to Indrani as an inspiration by Gaiman himself, after he saw an early cut of the film.[78] It was said to have set the keynote for the film "script," although the narrative is no more than stitched-together poetry fragments from a generally Eastern-inspired canon in an unapologetically Orientalist fashion: "Do not fear the ghosts in this house. They are the least of your worries"; "Cupped my hands around her (the butterfly's) fluttering self, feeling her wings kiss my palms so gentle, and put her out."[79] Two Emerson poems, both inspired by Indian thought, each offered a fragment as well: "When me they fly, I am the wings; I am the doubter and the doubt, I am the hymn the Brahmin sings" ("Brahma");[80] "ILLUSION works impenetrable, weaving webs innumerable," and "Charmer who will be believed, by man who thirsts to be deceived" ("Maia").[81] Fragments of two Tagore poems are also included: "Time is endless in your hands . . . ages bloom and fade like flowers" ("Endless Time");[82] and "I seem to have loved you in numberless forms, numberless times . . . in life after life, in age after age, forever" ("Unending Love").[83] In addition, *A Midsummer Night's Dream* offers a fragment, "I am a spirit of

Figure 51: Daphne Guinness as Lady White Snake. Still from the film *Legend of Lady White Snake*, directed and written by Indrani Pal-Chaudhuri, produced by and costume design by GK Reid. New York: Double Exposure Studios, Meta GK, [2013] 2015. Fully accessible at https://vimeopro.com/indranipc/indrani-pal-chaudhuri/video/259596618, 2:11. Screenshot by author, courtesy of Indrani.

no common rate," spoken by Oberon in Shakespeare's play, while a phrase from the Indian classic *Bhagavad Gita*, "I have become death, devourer of worlds"[84] emphasizes White Snake's vampirism, a familiar image in Western snake woman lore, thanks to the Lamia myth.[85] Edgar Allan Poe's "A Dream within a Dream" is also cited in the film's ending credits, but I have had a hard time locating identifiable quotations from it in the truly fragmented and often hard-to-comprehend female voiceover narration tinged with British and Irish accents.[86]

In the end, only the film title and its opening and ending credits suggest, in textual form, the film's debt to the Chinese legend. The female narration was purportedly partly written on set, in the spur of the moment, by French philosopher Bernard-Henri Lévy for his lover, the legendary socialite and fashion icon Daphne Guinness, who performed the title character, Lady White Snake (fig. 52).[87] The narration mentions nothing of either the plot or the four central characters in the Chinese legend. The visual feast, on top of that, is hardly Chinese. If poetry here is reduced to digital fragments, digital photographs have taken over as the main agents of storytelling. The film was

Figure 52: Daphne Guinness as Lady White Snake with shining snake scales highlighted. In *Legend of Lady White Snake*, directed and written by Indrani Pal-Chaudhuri, produced by and costume design by GK Reid. New York: Double Exposure Studios, Meta GK, [2013] 2015, 07:19. Fully accessible at https://vimeopro.com/indranipc/indrani-pal-chaudhuri/video/259596618. Screenshot by author. Courtesy of Indrani.

produced by Markus + Indrani (her photography partnership) with stylist GK Reid, and spectacular iconic fashion photographs are sprinkled throughout it. Still, the film could be said to be somewhat "Chinese" in its taste, as a Chinese composer was involved in the creation of the digital soundtrack. In addition, the music was performed by the Viva Girls (*Nüzi shi'er yuefang* 女子十二樂坊), a twelve-girl instrumental group specializing in traditional Chinese music, which took China, Japan, and the world by storm in the early 2000s.[88]

The themes reflected in the short digital video, and expressed particularly by the fragments from "Kubla Khan" and "The Hidden Chamber," are more widely applicable than China-specific: dreams and fragments, visions and illusions, ghosts and demon-lovers, pleasure domes and savage places, endless time and unending love. How can one resist such enchanted and enchanting subject matters? The film is presented as a "postmodern collage of an ancient Chinese tragedy" and "a meditation on obsession, identity, metamorphosis, changing gender and time, through cross-cultural poetry perspectives."[89] It is, at the same time, a music video–style commercial for its sponsor MAC Cosmetics, a presentation of a new fashion line, the "Genghis Khan" collection designed by GK Reid, alongside other avant-garde designers, but, more importantly, a tribute to the late fashion designer Alexander McQueen, whose suicide at age forty shocked the fashion world in 2010.[90]

The visionary and iconoclastic McQueen was an openly gay designer who not only revolutionized the world of high fashion but also constantly wrestled with his own inner demons. He was known for his signature "manta" dresses featuring "digitally enhanced, mirror-image-style prints, resembling giant manta rays, sea-serpents and other strange or imagined denizens of the deep,"[91] and in his last and most enigmatic runway show during Paris Fashion Week in 2009, he "told the story of women morphing into creatures of the deep as the seas slowly reclaimed planet earth." The show featured models with sculpted dresses, "digitally enhanced prints of fantastical fish, snakes, praying mantis, moths, beetles and giant squid," with some gleaming in golden, fish-scale 'armor' like warrior-mermaids.[92] In its abundant use and flamboyant celebration of snake women figures and related sea creatures, McQueen's avant-gardist final performance for the world provides visual testimony of his feminist and environmentalist message to his fellow artists and human beings.

In their 2018 documentary *McQueen*, Ian Bonhôte and Peter Ettedgui feature clips from McQueen's iconic runway shows, home videos of McQueen with his friends, and intimate interviews with family members and friends to offer a multidimensional portrayal of this enigmatic figure. McQueen's explorations of the tensions between humans, animals, and machines; his inquiries into death, beauty, and rebirth; and his reputation as poet and commerce united, to paraphrase designer Tom Ford,[93] bring us back to the central issues surrounding the White Snake legends and their contemporary metamorphoses. Most importantly, McQueen's at once deeply personal and highly experimental approach to combining the digital and the emotional, the feminist and the environmentalist, in his final runway show, foreshadows Indrani's inspired tribute to him in the form of a short fashion film drawing on the White Snake legend. *The Legend of Lady White Snake* turns out to be a most fitting commemorative act for the late fashion designer whose life and career have been punctuated by relentless inquiries into the transient nature of human existence.

Through the intertwining of poetry, photography, and fashion in the digital video, we see the themes of gender and species, media and politics coming together, in director Indrani's insistence on using digital media to foster queer subjectivity and to celebrate the life and work of a queer designer, whose inspired and tortured existence has left lingering echoes and extensive legacies in our contemporary moment and for our ongoing struggles for women's empowerment, LGBTQ+ rights, and environmental justice.[94] The changing genders, from male to female, of the White Snake's lover in Indrani's film; the gender doubling in the images of the human lover, which is the embodiment of queer subject-making; and the power of the transgressive human/nonhuman hybrid—these are extravagantly stitched together in *The Legend of Lady White Snake* through digital technology and the superimposition of digital images, accentuating the plasticity, the shape-shifting, and the transformative qualities of metamorphosis tales that are at the center of the White Snake legends.

CONCLUDING REMARKS

Inspired by the Chinese White Snake legend, the three Anglophone White Snake projects introduced here energetically engage with issues relevant to minority activism in the United States, enriching our understanding of contemporary White Snake repertoire as vigorously multivalent, constantly regenerating, contemplative and empowering. These three cases demonstrate the range of interpretative possibilities the White Snake legend has to offer, especially in regard to the image of the snake women and their power of minority representation. Living as "aliens" in the "Human Realm," the snake women have always been treated with suspicion, fear, exclusion, and violent suppression/exorcism. They are immigrants to the human world, whose serpentine identity made them "resident aliens," the legal category given to immigrants in the United States before they receive their "Green Cards" and become "permanent residents." The implication of being a snake woman in the human world took on new meanings when the Covid-19 pandemic worsened the existing xenophobia, fear, and suspicion toward minority populations in contemporary United States and throughout the world.

The Covid-19 pandemic also posed a unique challenge to any performance company. The White Snake Projects confronted these challenges head on and used Cerise Lim Jacob's vision of minority activism as the direction to which online events have been initiated and organized. "Sing Out Strong: Decolonized Voices" was unveiled in May 2020 amid the pandemic. It is one of the events in the White Snake Projects' "Sing Out Strong" series, which livestreams short pieces of operatic performances based on poems written by immigrant high school students in Boston. It was empowering not only for many of the students who were writing in their second or third languages, but also for all involved: the immigrant composers, the minority singers, the sound engineers, the whole cast and crew, and all the audience members. White Snake Projects' most recent online performances took place in December 2020 and May 2021. It is the newest installment of "Sing Out Strong" series, with all librettos of the short opera pieces based on interviews of essential workers in the current pandemic. The latter is a virtual opera titled "Death by Life," conceived as a monument of support for the Black Lives Matter movement. For me, this series of online events orchestrated by Cerise Lim Jacobs at the White Snake Projects showcases the audacities of and the possibilities created by this Asian American activist opera company.

In the case of Mary Zimmerman's play *The White Snake*, as the written text itself leaves room for alternative interpretations, its many performances throughout the world have formed an exciting chorus in demonstrating how this "Romeo and Juliet–style" love story is able to transcend the barrier between the human and the nonhuman. Again, in Zimmerman's own words, deep down, the play is about how "you can be loved for who you truly are," regardless of your identity and difference.

Similarly, McQueen's contemplation on the transient nature of human existence, on LGBTQ+ rights and environmental justice, became central themes for Indrani's inspired tribute to him in her short digital video and continues to inform her activism today. As a minority female director, in dedicating her debut film to McQueen, Indrani consolidated the connection between the Chinese legend, its powerfully hybrid snake woman, and the snake woman's ability to continuingly inspire and incite activist projects in our shared fight for minority rights and social justice. Indrani continues to evoke the White Snake film in her activist teaching, filmmaking, and outreach efforts. As a guest lecturer at Princeton University in the fall of 2020, she offered a course on how film can inspire millions into social action.

The Anglophone White Snake works discussed in this chapter offer a radical new reading of the White Snake legend as surprisingly activist and revolutionary. It highlights a spirit of persistent anti-authoritarianism and tolerance for the strange and the unusual. It shows how Lady White Snake travels through adaptations across cultures, time, geography and media. Her story bending and twisting in meaning, always on the move and in mediation. This ability to travel and transform is what keeps any legend, any tradition, and any culture alive, as they shed skin after skin to reach new stages of life and afterlife.

CHAPTER 8

The Eternal Bodies of the White Snake

KOREAN WEBTOON LADY WHITE AND HER AFTERLIFE IN CHINESE

A Korean webtoon by writer Chang Hŭi 장희 and award-winning artist Ju Homin 주호민, best known for his phenomenally successful 2010 webtoon *With Gods* (*Shin'gwa hamkke* 신과함께),[1] started its serialization on Naver Webtoon in April 2017 and concluded its 170 weekly episodes by June 2020.[2] The webtoon is set in Southern Song dynasty China (1127–1279), depicted as a land of ghosts and goblins, and it features as its monster-hunting protagonists a Daoist by the name of Gui'an 귀안 and a young girl by the name of Yeo Yeon 여연, who both possess magic powers.[3] Lady White (Paek Nangcha 백낭자), presented as from the Chinese White Snake legend, directly appears in episodes 42, 43, and 70, and she is mentioned indirectly in a number of other episodes throughout the latter half of the webtoon's serialization.

In the first of her three direct appearances, a one-eyed guru named Paek Yŏm 백염 and a tiger ghost named Pun-un 분운, the webtoon's two leading antagonists, call Lady White out from inside a jar buried under a pagoda. She emerges from her prison cell as a small white snake, then transforms into a python; she then turns into a beautiful girl with a snake tail stretching out from under her pinkish dress, both her tail and her neck visibly covered with snake scales. The villains have summoned her hoping that, if they free her and lead her to her human lover, she will use her magic power (*shint'ongnyŏk* 신통력) to aid them in their evil pursuits. Indeed, as soon as she emerges, Lady White inquires about Hŏ Sŏn's (Xu Xian) whereabouts. This figure is unmistakably the White Snake from the Chinese legend, trapped under the pagoda by the Buddhist abbot Pŏp'ae (법해, Fahai), and for the benefit of the webtoon's Korean readers, her identity is also clearly stated in a footnote (fig. 53).

By Lady White's third appearance in episode 70, however, she is betrayed by Paek Yŏm and Pun-un and killed. Although they had promised to free her and lead her to Hŏ Sŏn, the evil duo devises a different plan. Encouraged by Paek Yŏm the one-eyed guru, the tiger ghost Pun-un devours the physical body (*yukshin* 육신) of Lady White, while she is still trapped in the pagoda, seeking to absorb her power into himself. This abrupt and violent ending to

Figure 53: Lady White (Paek Nangcha). In *Pingt'ang huru* (*Bingtang hulu*), by Chang Hŭi and Ju Homin. Episode 42, January 29, 2018. Korean webtoon series on Naver Webtoon: https://comic.naver.com/webtoon/list.nhn?titleId=695321.

Lady White's physical presence in the Korean webtoon provoked many discussions in the comment section on its homepage. One of the most popular comments expressed deep sympathy for Lady White, who, according to the commentator, loved a human male, was caught and imprisoned by a male monk, and finally in this incarnation, was cheated by an evil guru and eaten alive by a tiger ghost.[4]

I begin this final chapter with the violent and abrupt disappearance of Lady White's physical body in a recent Korean webtoon for a number of reasons. First, even after her physical body is consumed, readers like me keep waiting and hoping for Lady White's reappearance, possibly in a different form. Second, although Lady White has not reappeared in this Korean webtoon, there has been one particularly intriguing reincarnation. In January 2019, she appeared on Dongman Manhua 咚漫漫畫, a popular Chinese web comics platform partnered with Naver, in a Chinese adaptation.[5] It appears that a rearranged (*chongzhi* 重置) version of the Korean webtoon in Chinese has been serialized on this platform since February 2018, less than a year after the webtoon's first episode appeared in Korean in April 2017. Calling the Chinese version a rearranged version rather than a translation, the Chinese webtoon artist by the obvious pseudonym of Mr. Tomato (Fanqie jun 番茄君) has redrawn every frame of the cartoon, in addition to translating all Korean captions into Chinese (fig. 54).[6]

As a result, the image of Lady White as reimagined in this Chinese version differs significantly from her "original" appearance in the Korean webtoon. Although her hairstyle still somewhat reminiscent of the Japanese-inspired Korean webtoon, she has been transformed from a cute girl with a disproportionally large head to a charming woman, who appears tall and slim and wears an elaborately decorated long dress. The pink outer layer of her dress has changed to a more characteristically white outer layer; the purple undergarment has changed to light blue, diluting the prominent colors in the Korean webtoon and adding many intricate details in the Chinese version. Most significantly, Lady White's conspicuous snake attributes, her noticeable snake tail and bare neck, both highlighted in proportion to her child-like height and covered with snake scales in the Korean webtoon, have disappeared in the Chinese recasting. The Chinese webtoon presents Lady White's tail in such an insignificant manner that it could simply be ignored by viewers. The skin of her bare neck is like that of an ordinary woman, with no snake scales in sight.

Lady White's symbolic travel from Song dynasty to contemporary China, as mediated through her reemergence in the Chinese webtoon after her physical death in the Korean webtoon, serves as a recent example and a fitting metaphor for the global travels of the White Snake as depicted throughout this study, both historically and geopolitically. The reimagined Chinese Lady White appears more human-like and more elaborately made-up than her Korean counterpart, reflecting subtle but significant differences in the recasting of her image by two East Asian neighbors in contemporary times. The main body of this concluding chapter follows the lead of this introductory case study to analyze three ways of reimagining the White Snake in contemporary China, tracing three case studies from 2019 back to 2016, and connecting them to new developments in 2020. It begins with the most recent internet drama series, which premiered in April 2019; followed by the US-China coproduced animation film, which opened in January of the same year; and ends with the 2016 White Snake mini-TV series with an all-child cast, itself a reimagining of the 1992 Taiwanese White Snake TV series. Together, these final case studies reveal deeper historical and geopolitical

Figure 54: Bai Niangzi. In *Yiwen zhi Bingtang hulu*, adapted by Mr. Tomato, No. 50, January 29, 2019, Chinese webtoon on Dongman Manhua: https://www.dongmanmanhua.cn/ANCIENTCHINESE/bingtanghulu/list?title_no=1233&page=2.

connections with many White Snake cases examined throughout this study and highlight the antiauthoritarian spirit and nonbinary, queer sensibilities as exemplified by the snake women's eternal bodies in their child, female, hybrid, and "alien" forms.

THE RETURN OF THE POWERFUL HYBRID

On April 3, 2019, a thirty-six-episode internet drama series, *New Legend of Madame White Snake* (*Xin Bainiangzi chuanqi*), began airing on one of the most influential Chinese-language video portals and one of the largest video sites in the world, iQiyi 愛奇藝. The series, which played both in Mainland China and in Taiwan, was scheduled to air three days a week, two episodes per day, ending its first run on May 10, 2019. Within days (if not hours) of its going live online, multiple internet platforms outside of the Chinese-speaking worlds, including licensed sites such as Viki and often unauthorized uploads on YouTube, started to circulate already-aired episodes of the series; fully subtitled, in English and other languages, they attracted viewers from all over the world.[7]

Opening with a *Bambi*-like, albeit computer-generated, animation sequence, the new White Snake series blends live action with animation on multiple levels, with both characterizations and landscapes resembling video game sequences even when they are live acted and shot on location. Advertised as the only authorized remake of the 1992 Taiwanese series,[8] the new internet series not only uses the same set of highly recognizable theme songs to punctuate key emotional moments but also features cameo appearances by actors from twenty-seven years ago: Cecilia Yip Tung (Ye Tong 葉童), the actress who cross-dressed to play Xu Xian, appears as Xu Xian's mother; and Maggie Chan Mei Kei (Chen Meiqi 陳美琪), the actress who played Green Snake, is now Green Snake's mother. The producers of the new series claim to pay tribute to the now canonical 1992 series through the revival of songs and actors, while at the same time breaking new ground in this new incarnation of the White Snake legend.[9]

Indeed, critical features of the 1992 series, such as the musical style and the martial arts elements, have been preserved. However, the 2019 series also absorbs many other influences, including Green Snake's ambiguous gender identity and sexual attraction to the White Snake, which are prominent in the Sichuan opera version, in Lilian Lee's reinvented Green Snake, and in Zhou Long and Cerise Lim Jacobs's *Madame White Snake* opera, which casts a male soprano in the role. In the 2019 series, Green Snake chooses to be a girl in order to be able to keep the White Snake company. In making that choice, Green Snake effectively negates its soon-to-become male body, which apparently is considered superior to the female body and thus requires a higher level of self-cultivation. In effect, the iconic love story between the nonhuman White Snake and the human male Xu Xian is queered by means of Green Snake's voluntary sex change, which results from her absolute devotion to the White Snake. On the other hand, it could be argued that in maintaining Green Snake's supporting role in the heterosexual narrative between the White Snake and her male lover, such a gesture may indeed function only as "queerbaiting,"[10] hinting at homoeroticism without carrying it through.

However, one of the most remarkable additions in the new series is the double-voiced figure Madame Wu (Wu furen 吳夫人), in effect "Madame Centipede" (Wugong furen 蜈蚣夫人), as the surname Wu 吳 sounds exactly like the first character of centipede (*wu* 蜈). This hybrid figure is the result of a merger of two souls, one belonging to a monstrous centipede, the other to a heartbroken mother whose daughter was killed by that centipede three thousand years ago. They converge in a most unlikely hybrid of human and nonhuman, love and hate, speaking in both female and male voices, with the female voice representing the mother and the male voice representing the centipede. They appear only in the physical form of the beautiful mother, with the disembodied voice of the centipede originating from outside the female body. A transparent centipede, seemingly drawn as an ink painting but most likely computer-generated, appears from its female shell as the evil force to be eradicated, and the human mother fights with the monstrous centipede in order to reclaim the soul of her dead child. Such a figure eerily echoes the half-human, half-gem title character Steven in the popular Cartoon Network short animation series *Steven Universe*,[11] in which nonbinary characters fuse into new, imaginative forms through synchronized dances. Moreover, such an ambiguous monster-woman hybrid as Madame Centipede, with its embodied internal struggle between good and evil, brings the White Snake theme's enduring attraction into sharper relief: the alluring nature of something that is physically or culturally transgressive, which simultaneously repels and compels.[12]

Another key addition to the 2019 internet drama series is the creation of the nine-tailed Fox Spirit in the image of a famed courtesan surnamed Hu 胡, a name that gestures toward her fox (*hu* 狐) identity as the ultimate seductress. These homophonic names could indeed be considered as another aspect of metamorphosis. When the Fox Spirit is cornered by Fahai the Buddhist monk, she vows to kill everyone present, with her vengeful spirit materializing as poison snowflakes. After the Fox Spirit disintegrates under the pressure of Fahai's divine power, one of the snowflakes enters the monk's body, accompanied by the disembodied voice of the Fox Spirit, claiming: "You will not be able to kill me; I am you and you are me."[13] This moment marks the emergence of a new human/nonhuman hybrid, created through the infiltration of Fahai's cultivated male body by the seductive, feminine power of the Fox Spirit.

This emphasis on the embodied internal struggle between good and evil is also vividly illustrated in the renewed characterization of Fahai himself, in particular, in his gradual transformation from believing such orthodoxies as "demon is demon, Buddha is Buddha" to adopting the views of his more enlightened teacher, who believes that "those who have a kind heart may attain Nirvana even if they are demons."[14] Fahai dreams that he himself "becomes a demon" and is praised by his teacher, who considers the dream evidence that he is "beginning to understand compassion based on empathy with the suffering [of others]."[15] In addition to interacting with his teacher and becoming more empathetic spiritually, Fahai also closely interacts with the now female-bodied Green Snake physically, including fighting side by side with her against the monstrous centipede, allowing a drunken Green Snake to vomit into his demon-suppressing divine weapon—an alms bowl—and even letting her sleep with his magic staff, which his teacher had bestowed on him as another demon-suppressing divine weapon.[16]

With the gradual deconstruction of Fahai's authoritarianism, which makes him more humane, the new series also revamps the Xu Xian figure and brings greater clarity to the characterization of the human male lover as intellectually cultivated, more understanding, more daring, and more heroic. When the White Snake attempts to leave him due to a misunderstanding, Xu offers to go with her. When the White Snake is framed for a murder she did not commit, Xu goes to jail in her place. The fortification of Xu's character is accompanied by the revamping of the White Snake as child-like and innocent. She is fittingly oblivious of the way things work in the human world, as her newly acquired humanity conditions her genuine curiosity and lack of experience. With such a devoted male lover worthy of the pure and innocent White Snake's love, the new series caters to young internet users and their youthful desire to witness and experience eternal love in the familiar setting of the 1992 classic, through which most of them were first introduced to romantic love on-screen. Nevertheless, compared to the 1992 series, the 2019 series comes with revealing updates and surprises better suited to the tastes and values of a new generation increasingly influenced by nonbinary, queer sensibilities in their everyday life. Such queer sensibilities, somewhat ironically, receive their most revealing manifestations not so much in the image of the White Snake herself, but in the previously marginalized and freshly revamped human-nonhuman hybrids and in the reinvention of traditionally-accepted characterizations of other leading characters of the legend.

QUEERING AN ICON, BECOMING A DEMON

The animation *White Snake: The Legend Begins* (*Baishe: yuanqi*), coproduced by Beijing-based Light Chaser Animation and Warner Bros., premiered on January 11, 2019, throughout China.[17] It opens with a sequence in an ink painting animation style (fig. 55). During the one-minute sequence, it outlines the snake women and their surrounding environment in beautiful brush strokes, exhibiting a distinctive aesthetic style that is reminiscent of traditional landscape paintings in China, Japan, Korea, and India, as well as of Mizoguchi Kenji's reinvention of such a style for the 1953 film *Ugetsu*. White Snake and Green Snake, two snakes turned female beauties, are portrayed together in an intimate manner, the ambiguous nature of their relationship accentuated by close bodily contact. Thus, this animation queers the iconic romantic narrative between a snake woman and a human male from the very beginning. Immediately after the opening sequence, however, the animation style quickly changes to the industry standard of 3D animation, largely resembling contemporary Disney and other Warner Bros. productions.

The new animation is presented as a prequel to the White Snake legend. The key antagonist is the Imperial Priest (Guoshi), who forces the people of Snake-Catcher Village (Bushe cun) to catch snakes in order to aid his secret pursuit of immortality.[18] The story opens as the Green Snake helps the White Snake retrieve her memories that are sealed in a jade hairpin. The hairpin eventually leads viewers to the Fox Spirit character, the ultimate enabler of many key transgressions between the human and the nonhuman in the story. However, the most revolutionary development in the 2019 animation appears when the human male lover Ah Xuan 阿宣 (Xu Xuan, Xu Xian) declares that he will become a demon in order to be together with Xiao Bai 小白 (White Snake), making him not only a worthy object of White Snake's love but also the most daring and the most heroic lover to date, surpassing even the male lover's characterization as a Disney-style Prince Charming in the 1958 Japanese animation *Hakujaden*. The ingenious addition of Du Dou 肚兜 the

Figure 55: White Snake struggles to battle dark forces in her memory at the ending of a one-minute sequence highlighting the ink painting animation style, 2:17. In *White Snake: The Legend Begins* (dir. Amp Wong and Zhao Ji, 2019). Screenshot by author, courtesy of Light Chaser Animation.

talking dog echoes the anthropomorphic animal "sidekicks" in the 1958 Japanese animation, in which the giant panda and a duck character, which may call to mind Kungfu Panda and Donald Duck, humanize the nonhuman in significant ways. It also reminds us of the abundance of animal characters in the 1926 Chinese cigarette cards that were based on the first White Snake feature film series, discussed in chapter 2.

Additional ways of deconstructing the canon are introduced, lightheartedly, to bring some comic relief to the seriousness of the situation. When White Snake asks Ah Xuan why his secret mountaintop hideout includes a plaque with the name Bao'an Tang 保安堂, a reference to Baohe Tang where Xu Xuan (more widely known as Xu Xian) practices medicine in some previous versions of the legend, the man simply replies, "I picked it up on the street."[19] Nothing meaningful in the name, the animators seem to suggest here. However, these efforts at deconstruction seem half-hearted at certain points. For example, the umbrella lent by the human lover to the White Snake in the original story, as the key instrument of enchantment, still occupies an important position in the 2019 animation. It is simply used more ingeniously, functioning as a flying device that rescues the lovers as they fall through the air, bringing them safely back to earth. It aids Ah Xuan's theory of "living freely" (*huode zizai* 活得自在), allowing the lovers to ride the wind and roam the sky. Another moment of comic relief comes when the White Snake and Ah Xuan both sneeze while flying with the umbrella, possibly because of an allergic reaction: the rosy flower petals filling the air around them may not only have served as a romantic background for the unlikely lovers' first physical contact but also have entered the scene, triggering an allergic reaction.[20]

The story introduces White Snake as she wakes up in Snake-Catcher Village. Having lost her memory after being saved by Ah Xuan, White Snake gradually recovers her memories and the mystery of the jade hairpin unravels. Ah Xuan declares early on to White Snake, "You are not an evil person" (*ni bushi e'ren* 你不是惡人).[21] For the viewer, Ah Xuan's seemingly innocent comment may be read in multiple layers: White Snake is not human, so she cannot be an evil person; White Snake is good, so she cannot be evil. Later, when they share a boat together, Ah Xuan sings a beautiful song and teaches the White Snake to sing. The whole sequence, though animated and in color, resembles the iconic boat scene in Mizoguchi's live-acted *Ugetsu* in monochrome, where a female (rather than the male) singing voice accentuates the transient nature of life, just as Ah Xuan sings here: "Our floating life seems to be a dream" (*fusheng rumeng* 浮生如夢). Here we reach a high point in the story that often takes much longer to reach in earlier versions of the White Snake legend, where the human lover declares the irrelevance of White Snake's nonhuman identity: "Yes you are a demon spirit, so what?" (*jiusuan shiyao you zenmeyang* 就算是妖又怎麼樣). Du Dou the dog comes in handy for Ah Xuan to make a useful comparison here: "Even if Du Dou is a demon spirit, I still will like him, and he still will like me."[22]

Memory loss becomes an ingenious plot device in this White Snake animation, as in many TV dramas popular in East Asia.[23] The White Snake has no memory of her own demon identity, to the extent that she is shocked by her own giant snake tail: "Think about that tail, I am really a demon." The most surprising moment comes, however, when Ah Xuan responds to this revelation with total nonchalance: "If you are, you are." He reasons: "There are so many evil humans with two legs. What if you have a tail?" (*renjian duode shi zhangle liangzhijiao de e'ren, zhangle tiao weiba you zenme yang* 人間多的是長了兩隻腳的惡人, 長了條尾巴又怎麼樣), to which the White Snake responds, "You are not an evil person," repeating Ah Xuan's earlier reply to the White Snake, that she is not evil, even though she is not human.[24]

Here, the dividing line between good and evil overrides the rift between human and nonhuman: an evil human is demonic, while a kind demon can be full of humanity. This good versus evil, human versus nonhuman paradox in effect suggests that we should revise our definitions of "humanity" and "the demonic." If demons are as capable of love and empathy as humans, why should we characterize love and empathy as "humane" qualities? If humans are as capable of evil behavior as demons, why should we characterize evil behavior as "demonic?" In this sense, the humanity of the nonhuman actually becomes an inverted contradiction in terms: not because the nonhuman is incapable of "humanity," but because the very idea of "humanity" is inadequate.

The jade hairpin eventually leads the pair of human and nonhuman protagonists to Bao Qing Fang 寶青坊, the workshop where the enigmatic piece was made, thus introducing the Fox Spirit character and the role she and her establishment play in propelling key plot developments. As mentioned earlier, foxes play a major role in the Chinese literary and cultural imagination and have a long history in Chinese legends and folktales. In this new White Snake animation, the image of the Fox Spirit gains a new life as a powerful enabler of many transgressions. The film grants the Fox Spirit, a flamboyantly dressed femme fatale figure with the head of a beautiful woman in front and the head of a white fox in the back, the ultimate authority to enable these transgressions. This two-headed Fox Spirit, as she calls herself, could "transplant flowers and trees, change heaven and earth, transform humans into demons, and convert demons into humans" (*yihua jiemu gaibian qiankun huaren weiyao huayao weiren* 移花接木 改變乾坤 化人為妖 化妖為人).[25] She is able to discern that Ah Xuan and the White Snake have had intimate bodily contact just by observing Ah Xuan's appearance (in an earlier scene, Ah Xuan warmed the frozen White Snake with his own body), which she describes as "giving out the air of a demon even when he is a human."[26] This comment comically echoes the rhetoric used by the White Snake to sexually monopolize her human husband in the 1978 *Love of the White Snake*; in that film, the supposedly more demon-like Green Snake's bodily contact with the human husband will surely pollute him and give him the air of a demon.

The White Snake's memory is finally activated when she encounters the Green Snake, who seems to also hold the key to solving the White Snake's many problems, including her self-discovery. They address each other as "Little White" (Xiao Bai) and "Little Green" (Xiao Qing), and that is how the White Snake is known to Ah Xuan and the audience from that point on.[27] Through the viewpoint of the Green Snake, who is the primary female narrator in many contemporary renditions of the White Snake legend, the Imperial Priest becomes the "stinking Daoist" (*chou daoshi* 臭道士) who plots to harvest the snakes' feminine (*yin*) essence to boost his own evil power. Little Green also conveys the views of the similarly evil female leader of the snake tribe (*shezu* 蛇族), whose verdict is that "humans are evil," although Little White insists that Ah Xuan is different from other humans.[28]

As is appropriate to the theme of forbidden love and sexual liaison, the animators portray the climactic kissing and bed scenes between Ah Xuan and

Little White in a truly realistic fashion with vivid details.[29] This decision was met with raised eyebrows both in China and abroad, since sex and animation are still widely perceived as incompatible. Hong Kong–based reporter Josh Ye called for the whole family to avoid the 2019 animation, branding it "*Frozen* with sex."[30] The tension between the highly sexual content of the White Snake legend and the choice of animation, traditionally a genre for children and families, is a matter of course. In 1958 in Japan, the producers of *Hakujaden* had had to deal with a similar set of contradictions when packaging and marketing their film as "family friendly" and suitable for children, as discussed in chapter 4.

As a result of the sexual rendezvous as well as the lovers' emotional attachment, Ah Xuan declares that he will become a demon in order to be with Little White.[31] This is the most revolutionary change in the history of the legend's many plot variations, making the male lover not only worthy of White Snake's love, but also the most daring, the most heroic figure to date. With the help of the Fox Spirit, Ah Xuan exchanges his male essence for the chance to become a demon. He grows a tail and transforms into a demon, and in the process, Du Dou the dog loses its tail to Ah Xuan. Thus, as Ah Xuan becomes nonhuman, Du Dou becomes non-dog, making both of them comically "demonic." Indeed, earlier in the animation, when White Snake gives Du Dou the power of speech, its newly acquired ability already cements Du Dou's inclusion in the long genealogy of anthropomorphic animals, whose designations were often more comical than demonic. Therein lies the comical and radical ingredients largely responsible for the new animation's success: the talking animal and the sacrificial male lover in service of the female lead, a snake woman.

Formalistically, the 2019 Sino-US coproduction contains multiple traces of Miyazaki Hayao's animated worlds of dragons and spirits. In particular, the dragon-like giant python into which the White Snake transforms in the new animation brings to mind Haku, the white dragon in Miyazaki's *Spirited Away* from 2001. Given Miyazaki's fascination with the 1958 Japanese White Snake animation, such formal legacies seem to suggest that White Snake animations are just like the White Snake theme itself, metamorphosing into an eternally circulating body of work in the style of the tail-eating Ouroboros.

EVERLASTING BODILY MEMORY

New Legend of Madame White Snake (*Xin Bainiangzi chuanqi*), the fifty-episode Taiwanese 1992 television drama on which the 2019 internet drama was based, has enchanted audiences throughout the Chinese-speaking world since its initial broadcast and has been etched into the collective memory of Chinese-speaking populations around the world, especially for the generations born after the 1970s. During the Chinese National Day holiday season in early October 2016, *Star of Tomorrow: Legend of the White Snake* (*Xiaoxigu: Baishe zhuan*), a retelling of that television drama in the form of a five-episode mini television series starring actors eight to ten years old, went viral online.[32] The series is praised as a "divine restoration" (*shen huanyuan* 神還原) of the Taiwanese television drama, and for that very reason, it successfully tapped into the emotionally receptive generations of Mainland Chinese who had grown up watching the 1992 series and who are also the majority of internet users today. How did the 2016 retelling of the fantastic White Snake legend, with its cast of child actors, generate such sensational popularity online?

A close reading of some of the tens of thousands of online reviews clearly demonstrates *Star of Tomorrow*'s strong affective power.[33] Many post-80s female viewers mention their childhood experience of impersonating the White Snake of the 1992 series, played by the star actress Angie Chiu Ngar Chi (Zhao Yazhi 趙雅芝; fig. 56). In particular, they describe how they used white bed sheets and other props to imitate her white dresses and unique hairstyle. Such vivid depictions, cited by many reviewers and frequently heard in conversations about the series, demonstrate the deep emotional impact the 1992 television drama had on the viewers and their coming-of-age experience.

Amid the profusion of glowing reviews, two types of experiences emerge. They can be summarized in two sets of keywords and are worth analyzing as such. The first set of keywords are "bodily memory" (*shenti de jiyi* 身體的記憶) and "affective identification" (*qingdong de rentong* 情動的認同). The reviews demonstrate how bodily memory and affective identification took hold of that generation of receptive audiences, with many even reporting a sort of "wild" bodily reaction similar to the experience of "being drugged."[34] By recounting in 2016 their own youthful experience of watching the 1992 series, their voluntary emotional identification is aroused. It could be argued that the 2016 short series served as a "time machine," helping them to relive their childhood memories, which by 2016 had become objects of nostalgia.

How can this experience of bodily memory and affective identification be realized? The reviewers claim that the 2016 short series achieved this by "planting divine music into the brain" (*shenqu runao* 神曲入腦).[35] Indeed, *Star of Tomorrow* faithfully reenacted many popular songs from the 1992 television series; these songs have since become canonical, achieving the status of "divine music" in the Chinese popular imagination. When those much-

Figure 56: (left) Angie Chiu (Zhao Yazhi) as White Snake, in *New Legend of Madame White Snake* (*Xin Bainiangzi chuanqi*), directed by Tsu-hui Hsia (Xia Zuhui) and Chi Ho (He Qi). Taiwan Television, November 5, 1992 to January 13, 1993. Fifty episodes. Image: http://k.sina.com.cn/article_6434497003_17f86a1eb00100f4j6.html?cre=tianyi&mod=pcpager_focus&loc=2&r=9&doct=0&rfunc=4&tj=none&tr=9&wm=, accessed June 17, 2020; (right) Tao Yixi as White Snake, in *Star of Tomorrow: Legend of the White Snake* (*Xiaoxigu: Baishe zhuan*), directed by Pan Liping, Lu Jianmei, and Liu Yujie. Hunan Satellite TV, October 2, 2016. Five 20-min. episodes. Image: http://k.sina.com.cn/article_6734750577_1916c237100100chwe.html, accessed June 17, 2020.

loved songs, such as "Waiting for a Thousand Years" (*Qiannian deng yihui* 千年等一回), accompany the child actors' skillful performances in the 2016 short series, the audience receives an instant emotional cue specific to their earlier experience with the 1992 television drama, which is itself designed to evoke positive emotional and physical reactions. With such powerfully "divine" music invading their brains, these receptive audiences are able to ignore the production's in-your-face make-believe quality, which results from the combination of the White Snake legend's famously "adult" content and the extreme youth of the actors, whose average age is under ten. The music helped the audience enter the world of the story and maintained its hold on the audience throughout; as a result, the audience came to appreciate the child actors as "spirits of the times" (*shiguang de jingling* 時光的精靈) and were moved by their "sincere attitude" (*renzhen de taidu* 認真的態度) in performing something beyond their personal experience.[36]

The keywords in the second set are "relying on acting skills" (*kao yanji* 靠演技) and "relying on appearance" (*kaolian* 靠臉). Similar to the experience of "having divine music invading their brain," the more receptive groups of audiences came to react affectively to the "divine acting skills" (*shen yiban de yanji* 神一般的演技) of the child actors, especially their extraordinary performance during scenes in which they were required to show intense grief. The two girl actors who cross-dressed and performed the roles of Xu Xian, the husband of the White Snake, and Xu Shilin 許仕林, the son of the White Snake, became the focal points of audience affection. Most claimed to be tired of Chinese adult actors, disparagingly termed "little flowers" (*xiaohua* 小花) and "little fresh meats" (*xiao xianrou* 小鮮肉), who have little acting skill and build their careers instead by flaunting their good looks and relying on their appearance. Through an affective identification with the "authentic" child actors' superb acting skills and their sincere devotion to their art, these receptive audiences were able to vent their dissatisfaction toward adult actors who seem to suffer from "facial paralysis" (*miantan* 面癱),[37] a common criticism referring to their lack of facial expression and acting skill.

The verbal abuse expressed in the repeated use of such phrases as "face-slapping" (dalian 打臉), "hanging and beating" (*diaoda* 吊打), "instant kill" (*miaosha* 秒殺), and "complete victory over little fresh meat" (*wanbao xiao xianrou* 完爆小鮮肉) speak to audience members' frustration with those adult actors at which the criticisms are aimed; at the same time, it enacts the use and abuse of those same actors, figuratively "chewing them up and spitting them out," ironically consuming the beautiful faces and bodies of these ostensibly reviled actors yet again. Moreover, these comments had a likely trigger and target. Precisely at the moment when *Star of Tomorrow* became an internet sensation, two actors who were named best supporting actor and actress at the "Hundred Flowers Awards" (Baihua jiang 百花獎), one of the most prestigious acting awards in China, became prime targets of such criticism. The two actors, considered by some audience members to have won the awards for their dashing good looks rather than their acting skills, were explicitly attacked in the online reviews of the 2016 White Snake mini TV series.[38]

The 2016 *Star of Tomorrow* succeeded in developing the theme of family love through the child actors' devotion to acting beyond their age. The power of such make-believe performance in retelling the White Snake legend was firmly established in the Taiwanese series in the early 1990s, when Hong Kong actress Cecilia Yip, cross-dressed as male to impersonate both the husband and the son of the White Snake. Yip's exuberant performance, aided by the constantly evocative power of the musical score, had planted in the audience's hearts a fantastically androgynous image of the male protagonist. The husband's female body and the actress Cecilia Yip's gender-bending performance had, to a certain extent, diluted the "lust, caution" theme prominent in the Feng Menglong version of the White Snake legend from the seventeenth century and even "purified" the theme of lust that had been amplified in the White Snake genealogy in the Japanese recreations in terms of heterosexual relationships. At the same time, it reconnected with old traditions as well as opened up new ones for the possibilities of homosexual expressions. This expurgation of in-your-face sexuality (in this case, really only heterosexuality) and the child-friendly reconfiguring of the story have much to do with how the 1992 television series became a contemporary classic, which was considered befitting both the young and the old throughout the Chinese-speaking world and beyond.

The love story contained within the tale of seduction and sexual indulgence, consequently, evolved to encompass a much larger sphere of meaning. This, in turn, provided a solid foundation for the transformation of the heterosexual relationship between young lovers to reflect a range of multivalent possibilities regarding love between family members, friends, and others in the 2016 series. In this context, we come to a better understanding of the audience members' affective identification with the two girl actors' superb crying scenes as they embody the male roles of the two Xus, White Snake's husband and son. It is through this all-child version of the White Snake legend and its peeling away of the layers of "sexual desire" (often taken for granted as "heterosexual desire") that we come to understand the secret ingredients for the success of the 1992 television drama. Its focus on family, children, youth, memory, and audience identification, rather than on narrowly defined (hetero)sexual desires, must have provided some of the main impetuses for its emergence as a contemporary classic in the 1990s and its continued popularity thereafter.

In fact, neither the 1992 television drama nor the 2016 retelling of the series initiated the trend of focusing on child-like love and innocence and using families and children as target audiences for the retelling of the White Snake legend. The 1958 Japanese animation *Hakujaden* had already packaged the White Snake legend as suitable for families and children.[39] In order to understand the significance of such a thematic revision, we need to revisit the White Snake theme in Japanese literary and cinematic traditions, as analyzed in chapter 4. In the 1920s, early Japanese film already highlighted the eroticism of the White Snake. Mizoguchi Kenji's 1953 enigmatic *Ugetsu* and Toyoda Shirō's 1956 costume film starring the Manchuria-born Japanese actress Yamaguchi Yoshiko continued the trend, creating explicit scenes of kissing and bedroom intimacy rarely seen in the 1950s Asian context.[40]

Against this backdrop, how might the Japanese have marketed the 1958 animation as a popular film for family and children? This was indeed a challenging endeavor. The 1958 animation ingeniously introduced animals as supporting characters, and the talking animals were rather successful in putting the legend's overflowing human (hetero)sexuality on a leash. The adorable animals shifted away from the focus on lust, seen in White Snake legend retellings in Japanese literary traditions; the expressive heterosexual love between White Snake and Xu Xian was transferred instead into a love between family and friends, especially as expressed between Xu Xian and his animal friends (Panda and Mimi) and between White Snake, Green Fish (as in the Feng Menglong version), and her piscine companions.[41] These inter-species intimacy and more inclusive forms of love and emotional bounds are important clues for the animation's successful repackaging as child- and family-friendly.

Introducing pandas to the White snake legend is a seemingly absurd maneuver, but it may well represent a very deliberate strategy of the animation's Japanese creators. In the mid- to late 1950s, when Japan was barely out of the shadow of the US Occupation, choosing a Chinese legend to tell a story of Japanese postwar cultural reincarnation could only have resulted from meticulous planning. Tōei Animation, producer of the 1958 work, wanted to use the White Snake legend to perform a politics of reconciliation in East Asia. More importantly, by adopting Fordist means of production,[42] the company also hoped to construct the postwar Japanese animation industry as a rival to Disney in cultural, economic, and international influence. The cuteness of the pandas, the use of the Chinese musical instrument *erhu*, and the inclusion of many other prominent Chinese elements all served as means to generate an affective power that would help mend Japan's relationship with East Asian countries and rival Disney (and hence America) economically and culturally, at a crucial moment in Japan's postwar national rebuilding.

TRACKING THE MEDIATED BODIES IN THE WHITE SNAKE LEGENDS

The 1958 Japanese animation *Hakujaden* was not the first visual retelling of the White Snake legend to highlight the affective power of supporting animal characters. As early as 1926, *The Righteous Snake,* the first Chinese feature film adaptation of the White Snake legend already employed a large number of supporting animal characters in its promotional materials.[43] Although the work, both the 1926 two-part feature film and its 1927 third part, is no longer extant, we can still catch glimpses of its fascinating employment of animal bodies through the cheaply printed colorful cigarette cards used to promote the film, which were discussed in chapter 3. The first four cards predictably feature the four protagonists—the White Snake, Little Green, Xu Xian, and Abbot Fahai. The protagonists wear typical theatrical costumes, as if they had simply walked off a traditional Chinese opera stage, where the White Snake legend had been so popular for so long.

It is the other cards, which feature a wide range of supporting animal characters, that preserved visual evidence of the 1926 film and its promotional activities as creative revampings of the White Snake legend. The cards feature the nearly naked bodies of women and children.[44] Those depicting the spirits of a dragonfly, scorpion, and bat are most striking: all appear as female nudes, with only a belt of silk covering their private parts. The spirits of the clam and spider appear as children. The clam spirit takes the form of a little girl wearing only a red scarf to cover her belly and private parts, while the spider spirit appears as a completely naked little boy. As shown earlier in this chapter, these hybrid human-animal bodies would come to be activated and animated in recent internet television drama and animation film, both from 2019, demonstrating the lasting attraction of such transgressive experiments in representing hybrid bodies in the White Snake legends. Transgressing human boundaries in the name of animals is indeed the eternal theme of the White Snake legend. In this context, our historicizing and contextualizing the White Snake theme, aided by the "nonhuman turn" in the studies of humanities in Western academia, further articulates the political potential and affective power of the "alien" bodies of animals, children, and women to resist the hegemonies of the human, the adult, and the male.[45]

Throughout the last few centuries, the White Snake legends were subjected to multiple interpretations in myriad forms of folk literature and literati arts. However, a widely accepted image of the White Snake gradually emerged: a powerful nonhuman character that transforms into a woman, marries a human male, bears a human son, and becomes virtually human herself. Beginning in the seventeenth century, the White Snake further transformed herself into a divine physician, Madame White, and in some eighteenth-century and almost all nineteenth-century versions, she would eventually be saved by her human son. Under Communist China's state feminism, however, she was saved by her maid/sister Green Snake, who returns as the leader of all water creatures (the "proletariat") to destroy the symbol of "feudal" oppression, the Thunder Peak Pagoda, thus articulating the feminist and class politics of grassroots revolution and its "anti-feudal" message. Thus, the snake body, the female body, and the maternal body of the White Snake evolved and transformed over time. Bodily transformation and divine transformation, identity and belonging, and the human and the nonhuman intersected in the White Snake legend's metamorphoses. In these shifting narratives, the pursuit of humanity, womanhood, and motherhood remain at the center.

In the context of contemporary China, the humanization of the White Snake went hand in hand with the maintenance of the animal nature of the Green Snake. While the White Snake, to a great extent, successfully transformed into a maternal body that Abbot Fahai deemed unattainable, the snake body and snake nature at the center of the legend needed an outlet. The body of the Green Snake and her rebellions and indulgences gave expression to these aspects of the legend. The so-called "Green Snake" tradition in the White Snake legend became a favored trope in the contexts of China's revolutionary tradition and of postmodernity in China and beyond. This is precisely because such a transgressive energy fit well with the anti-traditional spirit and experimental quality of both the revolutionary and the postmodern conditions.

Examining the many textual and visual reconstructions of the image of the Green Snake, one cannot help but notice how Green Snake has developed from a supporting character in the White Snake legend to a more prominent and radically transgressive subject. Hong Kong writer Lilian Lee has often been considered the initiator of this series of textual and visual recreations. Her novel, *Green Snake*, written in the late 1980s and revised in the early 1990s, became the base text for Tsui Hark's 1993 film of the same name and Tian Qinxin's experimental stage performance, which served as the opening play for the Wuzhen Theatre Festival in 2014. This series of textual and visual reconstructions emphasized Green Snake's relentless pursuit of "freedom," her dismissal of revolutions as "theatrics" and "games," and her ambiguous gender and sexual reorientations.

However, long before Lilian Lee, the bodies of Green Snake had already acquired their androgynous quality through Green Snake's transformation from male to female in Sichuan opera, among other theatrical traditions. Green Snake's previous life, as lodged in a male body, provided rich material for latter-day writers and directors to mold the image of the Green Snake as a combination of both masculine and feminine characteristics. This resulted in a more radical and more powerful Green Snake. For example, such attributes are foregrounded in Zhou Long's 2011 Pulitzer–Prize winning opera Madame White Snake, analyzed in chapter 7, in which Green Snake was performed by a male soprano. In that production, Green Snake's high notes soared above those of female singers, while his male body may have been considered as adding androgynous charm in the visual embodiment of the Green Snake.[46] More recently, in the internet drama series released in April 2019, *New Legend of Madame White Snake*, the Green Snake gave up its soon-to-become-male body in order to be able to stay close to the White Snake. Such postmodern narratives centered on the Green Snake highlight the complicated four-way relationship between Green Snake, Abbot Fahai, White Snake, and Xu Xian, and further explore the relationship between animal nature and humanity, love and desire, emotion and rationality.

Similarly, as examined in chapter 6, in Geling Yan's 1998 novella *White Snake*, the vicissitudes in a White Snake dancer's life between the late 1950s and the early 1980s in Mainland China became a metaphor for the affective power of the body. The political trauma of the Cultural Revolution became a personal memory of the female protagonist's bodily awakening in a female same-sex relationship, with a cross-dressing female fan performing the role of the androgynous Green Snake. Continuing Lilian Lee's and Geling Yan's recreations, Li Rui and Jiang Yun's 2007 novel *The Human Realm* accentuated sexual and identity transgressions. Here, Green Snake welcomed its identity as nonhuman and non-demon, or between human and demon, for the very reason that it brought her freedom. The novel's title points to the "pure" human realm that Abbot Fahai had attempted so eagerly to maintain in the seventeenth-century Feng Menglong version, and the narrative celebrated a hybrid existence between the human and the nonhuman.

From the early 1990s onwards, the Taiwanese television drama *New Legend of Madame White Snake* flooded Mainland China, resurrected the White Snake legend as a household name and cemented its own position as a modern classic in contemporary China. Angie Chiu, the actress who performed the White Snake in that series, became the face of the White Snake. Her body became the body of the White snake. Her image, gestures, and smile, all became integral to the coming-of-age memories of generations of Mainland Chinese born in the post-70s moment. Consequently, the White Snake legend became known in the Chinese social media as its "national people's intellectual property," mainly referring to its power to constantly generate new and financially profitable reproductions.[47] Well into the twenty-first century, entertainment programs on Chinese-language television continue to pay tribute to the 1992 Taiwanese television series. The series was also influential in queering the legend. Actress Cecilia Yip, who cross-dressed to perform White Snake's husband Xu Xian and son Xu Shilin in the series, opened up possibilities for latter-day stage and screen experimentation with gender and sexual transgression.

The last decade has seen the image of the White Snake becoming even more popular in contemporary China through a wide array of traditional and online media. In July 2012 Hunan Satellite TV premiered *Your Face Sounds Familiar* (*Baibian dakaxiu* 百變大咖秀), a reality TV series that continually used the White Snake legend as its featured promotional strategy. Xie Na 謝娜, its star hostess, consecutively transformed herself into the 1992 Angie Chiu version of the White Snake as well as the 1993 Maggie Cheung Man-yuk (Zhang Manyu 張曼玉) version of the Green Snake, from Tsui Hark's film.[48] Not coincidentally, the first season of *Keep Running* (*Benpaoba xiongdi* 奔跑吧兄弟), the Chinese version of the popular South Korean entertainment program *Running Men* 런닝맨, also used the White Snake trope to open its season, and it continued to bring up the Green Snake and the White Snake as topics of conversation.[49]

Angie Chiu, the star of the 1992 Taiwan series, now in her sixties, continues to be extremely popular and was considered the leading "goddess" in a 2016 popular reality television show, *Here Come the Goddesses* (*Nüshen laile* 女神來了), evidence of the White Snake legend's tremendous impact in contemporary popular culture throughout the Chinese-speaking world. Mentioned in chapter 1 as one of the recent live-action adaptations of the legend, the 2018 sixty-episode internet drama series *The Destiny of White Snake* (*Tianji zhi Baishe chuanshuo*),[50] cashed in on Angie Chiu's star power from twenty-six years earlier and invited her to perform the role of Guanyin, the Goddess of Mercy, in the new series.

The profound influence of the 1992 Taiwan series lives on, most expressively through its beloved theme songs. Most recently, those songs were lovingly reenacted in episode 8 of *Lady Land* (*Jiejie de aiyue zhicheng* 姐姐的愛樂之程), shot on location in Hangzhou and broadcasted on December 25, 2020, on Hunan Satellite TV.[51] *Lady Land* is a popular spinoff reality TV program of the phenomenally successful *Siters Make Waves* (*Chengfeng polang de jiejie* 乘風破浪的姐姐), where thirty celebrity women over thirty compete for seven spots to form a "girl group," now known as X-Sisters.[52] The new show *Lady Land* features the seven X-Sisters on tour through some of the most scenic cities in China.

Episode 8 of *Lady Land* opens with X-Sisters arriving in Hangzhou, the city famous for its West Lake and deeply associated with the White Snake legend. Opening with three of the X-Sisters spontaneously bursting into singing "Ferrying Love" (*Duqing* 渡情), the ending theme song of the 1992 Taiwan series, the episode goes on to feature rehearsals and performances of the many theme songs of the same series. Dressing up in costumes resembling characters from the series (the snake women sisters and the human lover Xu Xian), the X-Sisters and two celebrity male actors and singers who made guest appearances in this episode, put up an on-site live music performance atop a traditional-style touring boat on the West Lake, with visitors standing on the Broken Bridge as audiences. The impressive longevity and affective power of the theme songs and the magical romantic ambience produced by the White Snake lagend and the sight of the beautiful West Lake were brought into full play, when the X-Sisters and their audiences join together in a huge chorus singing their hearts out amid a most enchanting view of the "evening illuminations over Thunder Peak."[53]

However, the provocative and controversial collaborations between the German "New Chinese Art Music" (*zhongguo xin yishu yinyue* 中國新藝術音樂) composer, Robert Zollitsch (Lao Luo 老鑼, or Old Gong, as he is known in Chinese), and the leading voice in Chinese art music today, Gong Linna 龔琳娜, must be included in these vibrant popular reenactments of the White Snake themes and better understood in the genealogy of the dynamic interactions between the avant-garde and the popular. Lao Luo, who grew up playing the zither in the classical Bavarian folk music tradition, was trained at Hochschule für Musik Hanns Eisler Berlin before venturing to Shanghai to study the Chinese zither (*guqin* 古琴) in 1993;[54] while Gong Linna was trained at the China Conservatory of Music (Zhongguo yinyue xueyuan 中國音樂學院) in Beijing specializing in folk style singing (with additional trainings in Chinese opera) and became increasingly known as a Chinese fusion singer worldwide. Their experimental music partnership (the two married in 2004 and often collaborate as co-composer and co-performer) has produced a series of phenomenally popular pieces, known as "divine music" (*shenqu*) in Chinese, starting with Gong's breakthrough in performing "Uneasy" (*Tante* 忐忑) at the 2010 new year concert in Beijing and on Hunan Satellite TV on the new year's eve of 2011, and after the video of her flamboyant performance went viral online.[55]

Two years later, Gong Linna's exuberant embodiment of the White Snake in "Fahai, You don't understand love" (*Fahai, ni budong ai* 法海，你不懂愛), a piece conceived, written and composed, and produced by Lao Luo, and co-performed by Gong and himself (as Xu Xian) on the new year's eve of 2013 on Hunan Satellite TV, created a second "divine music" sensation and aroused a new wave of viral following.[56] According to interviews with Gong and Lao Luo, the song was conceived by Lao Luo to celebrate the year of snake in 2013 out of his infatuation with the legend of the White Snake. The German composer approached the household Chinese legend with a focus on the Buddhist abbot Fahai, who, according to Lao Luo, "followed his own reasoning and rules to intervene into the love of the White Snake and Xu Xian, but the power of true love would eventually topple the Thunder Peak Pagoda." For Gong Linna in particular, the song speaks to her interracial and transnational love and marriage with Lao Luo and how her parents could not understand such a love, similar to Fahai's not understanding the love between a snake spirit and a human male in the White Snake legend.[57]

Stylistically, Lao Luo's lyrics and composition of "Fahai, you don't understand love" seemed to contain a "viral" rhythm, easy to remember, recite, and reenact. The repeated hand gestures and dance movements performed by the couple to accompany the highlights of the lyrics are simple enough for anyone to follow along, another reason for the video of their live performance on Hunan Satellite TV to instantly go viral online. Lao Luo has articulated his own take on the globalization of Chinese music in a Chinese article, arguing that reproducing Western music is not how Chinese music can be globalized. He highlighted how such richly multivalent Chinese music practices can only be globalized through multiple channels, with keen attention to not only the elite, but also the popular audiences. At the same time, ethnomusicologists have studied the couple's music experiments as academic discourses, with special focus on their use of traditional Chinese musical elements.[58] A final twist of this fascinating story of traversing the boundaries of the experimental and the commercial came about when a wide range of actors, from Buddhist establishment, academics, student groups, and the general public, started to harshly criticize the song and its performance and hold Gong Linna and Lao Luo responsible for defaming a respectable Buddhist master (as Fahai is based on a real life figure) and for their "vulgar" attempt at producing entertainment at the expense of morality,[59] a far cry from the couple's attempt at bringing new Chinese art music to the world but unwittingly attested to the power and presence of the White Snake legend in energizing contemporary cultural debates.

The contemporary popularity of the White Snake legends reminds us how folk legends and literary classics have entered contemporary popular culture via the spread of new media and digital technologies.[60] However, being at the center of popular culture does not necessarily reduce the White Snake legends to "empty signs" in a postmodern pastiche. Throughout this study, we have benefited from venturing beyond an elitist position and focusing on how folk culture can generate creative energies in the process of popularization. The exploration has illuminated how collaboration between old stories and new media can powerfully intervene and reshape realities and engender new affective power and creative cultural expressions.

CONCLUDING REMARKS

In the context of East Asia, the White Snake legend has been metamorphosing for hundreds of years, constantly renewing the challenges it invokes—the nonhuman bodies of the Green Snake and the White Snake challenge the boundary of humanity; folk legends persist amid emerging senses of modernity and inclusivity; and the central theme of hybridity challenges authoritarianism and binary identities. Since the Ming dynasty and under disparate social conditions, the body of the snake women has variously been used to promote radical trends, including "free love," feminism, grassroots revolution, homosexual love, transgender identities, and nonbinary sensibilities. Many of these trends were considered revolutionary and avant-gardist during their own time, and many are ever more relevant for our contemporary times.

Today, the legend of the White Snake continues to exert influence through its pervasive presences at scenic spots and theme parks, on performance stages, across screens, and in cyberspace. It has become a prominent thread connecting folk cultures as well as literary and artistic canons with a neoliberal global economy, and its discontents, throughout Chinese-speaking worlds and beyond. The complexities and contradictions within the transformations of the White Snake legend are apparent in these unlikely intersections, but with the increasing complexity of technological development and the constant renewal of media and political forms, they also demonstrate a deeper connection between humans, animals, machines, and polities. On September 4, 2016, at the G20 economic summit, the fantastic metamorphosis tales of the White Snake and the Butterfly Lovers (among other narratives) were presented as a high-tech spectacle to demonstrate the soft power as well as cultural flourishing of the PRC under the new leadership of Xi Jinping.[61]

The internet drama series *New Legend of Madame White Snake* that premiered on April 3, 2019, the Sino-US coproduced animation film *White Snake: The Legend Begins* that opened on January 11, 2019, and the all-child mini television series *Star of Tomorrow* that emerged as a viral internet phenomenon in October 2016 all lay bare a series of key observations at the center of this study. The 2019 drama series and the 2019 animation film both queered a heteronormative romance and presented a radical celebration of the humanity of the nonhuman, and the 2016 mini television series used images of children and females to challenge a world dominated by adults and males. These characteristics lead us to the following observations: these queer, seemingly monstrous bodies, so prominent in the new adaptations, may serve as renewed expressions of the humanity of the nonhuman in our time. These new White Snake adaptions suggest that we, in this male-dominated, adult-centered human world, must face the challenges presented by the bodies of children, animals, and women, and in so doing, they remind us of a similar need to engage with the challenges of machines and artificial intelligence, indicated by the recent rise of Chinese science fiction in English-speaking worlds.[62] We need to harvest the energies of the constant renewal and constant regeneration harbored in the White Snake legends. The archetype of the White Snake, as seen in folk legends, traditional art forms, revolutionary propaganda, and contemporary popular culture, could also provide useful cultural lessons for the field of humanities in general and comparative and East Asian literary and cultural studies in particular. White Snake legend's purported status as "national people's intellectual property" in China, and its power to constantly generate new expressions in the spheres of gender, species, media, and politics, could bring much-needed attention and moral support to the "nonhuman," the subaltern, and underprivileged groups, including animals, children, women, minorities, persons with disabilities, and immigrants.

In the Chinese and Asian studies fields and in the field of world literature, the travels of the White Snake legends connect a range of multivalent antiauthoritarian discourses and, more importantly, make explicit their subtle differences. The Mainland Chinese interpretation of the legend that follows the modernist and Maoist class struggle rhetoric has provided a key foundation for these antiauthoritarian narratives, in which the fight between the snake women and the Buddhist abbot has been framed as a story of "anti-feudal" struggle leading to the "liberation" of the White Snake from under the Thunder Peak Pagoda. The language of communism provided an entire political grammar for such affective, antiauthoritarian storytelling, from "speaking bitterness" against landlords to anti-corruption campaigns in contemporary China. This interpretative tradition has had a lasting impact on the legend's contemporary reiterations in the Sinophone worlds, although the focus on class struggle may have shifted to a focus on grassroots revolutionary energies. Similarly, in the Japanese and Korean traditions, the White Snake legends have often come to speak for the members of minority groups, of the hybrid, the marginal, the nontraditional, or the nonmainstream. It is in this sense of articulating the oppressed voices of these underrepresented and disenfranchised groups of people that the White Snake legends continue to serve as antiauthoritarian narratives in the Japanese, Korean, contemporary Sinophone, and Anglophone renditions.

In such renditions, the celebration of sexual and racial minorities and the embracing of bi, trans, and other nonbinary identities more familiar to Western readers shares a strong affinity with the modernist quest for human love and personal freedom and with the Maoist antiauthoritarian rhetoric of revolution from the bottom up. However, when the secular modernist rhetoric and the populist Maoist narrative against "feudalism," Buddhism, and any other "reactionary" elements were transplanted into the context of Japanese, Korean, and contemporary Sinophone and Anglophone renditions of the White Snake legend, the resulting linguistic and cultural translations and adaptations created subtle but significant political differences. Sexual dissidents are still dissidents, but they are rather different from political dissidents. In particular, when award-winning Anglophone White Snake narratives made in the United States are reimported into China in the twenty-first century, they gesture toward the significant roles that Japanese, Korean, and contemporary Sinophone and Anglophone agents have played in reshaping the White Snake narratives to serve continually renewed purposes of dissent.

Studies of the metamorphosis of a text and a theme require the vision and perspective of comparative and cultural history and must be situated in the diachronic context of historical development as well as in the synchronic context of its cultural matrix. The legends of the White Snake have served various political, cultural, and economic purposes historically and are still fulfilling many such functions. The bodies of the White Snake and Green Snake, in their animal, child, female, and hybrid forms, and expressed in myriad artistic genres and spanning hundreds of years, suggest that the multiplicity and openness of such narratives will continue to challenge our essentialist views on animality, humanity, gender and identify formations and transformations.

Notes

Chapter 1

1. See Grimm, Grimm, and Hunt, "The White Snake."

2. Whitesnake was active since the late 1970s. It is still active today and has a global following. Their newest album, *The Rock Album*, containing remixed and remastered versions of the band's best rock songs, was released in June 2020. For more on the band, see Popoff, *Sail Away*, and visit Whitesnake's official website, accessed April 28, 2019, https://fleshandblood.whitesnake.com/

3. The Whitesnake figure appeared in the 2000 Japanese manga series *JoJo's Bizarre Adventure* and in *JoJo's Bizarre Adventure: All Star Battle,* a fighting game based on the manga released for Playstation 3 in 2013. See "Whitesnake," *JoJo's Bizarre Encyclopedia*, accessed April 28, 2019, https://jojo.fandom.com/wiki/Whitesnake

4. The earliest Western-language rendition of the White Snake legend is a French translation titled *Blanche et Bleue, ou Les deux couleuvres-fées; roman chinois.* It was translated by the French sinologist Stanislas Julien and published in Paris in 1834. Julien's rendition was introduced to the English-speaking world later in the same year, by the *Journal of the Royal Asiatic Society* in London. It is beyond the scope of this book to delve into Julien's version, but it is worth mentioning its likely influence on the later Anglophone renditions discussed in this book, including an English translation by a certain H. C., serialized in *The Chinese and Japanese Repository* throughout 1864, Wong Chin Foo's short story published in *The Cosmopolitan* in 1888, as well as American missionary Samuel I. Woodbridge's rendition published in Shanghai in 1896. See Julien, *Blanche et Bleue*; "White and Blue"; H. C., "Lüi-fung Tă," in *The Chinese and Japanese Repository*, vol. X; Wong Chin Foo, "Poh Yuin Ko, The Serpent Princess," and Woodbridge, *The Mystery of the White Snake.*

5. I thank Mary Zimmerman for her help in articulating my argument here.

6. A fascinating case in point for White Snake's global travel in the Anglophone sphere is the 2017 Singaporean production *Mama White Snake*, on stage at Drama Centre Theatre from November 24 to December 16, 2017, and recently streamed online from May 22 to June 7, 2020, as part of Wild Rice's Wild@Home program during the Covid-19 pandemic. Visit Wild Rice's official website for more information on *Mama White Snake*, accessed June 28, 2020, https://www.wildrice.com.sg/event/11785-wild home-mama-white-snake/

7. For a recent study on the uses of legendary discourses to convey wide-ranging,

transgressive meanings in contemporary East Africa and beyond, see Katrina Thompson, *Popobawa*.

8. See Sun Chang, "Guomin IP de fanpai he shangyehua: 'Xin Bainiangzi chuanqi' geile women zheyang de qishi" [The adaptation and commercialization of 'national people's intellectual property': Illuminations from the April 2019 TV series *New Legend of Madame White Snake*], *IP jiazhiguan* [IP valuer] WeChat official account, April 24, 2019.

9. See Rolston, "Performance Review: Two Decades of Selling Peking Opera White Snakes to Foreigners." I was able to attend performances of both productions, on March 30, 2014, at the Kennedy Center in Washington, DC, for the avant-gardist *Green Snake* performance, and on September 2, 2015, at Lincoln Center in New York City for Zhang Huoding's *jingyu* performance of *Legend of the White Snake*. The Zhang Huoding performance was prefaced on the day of the performance by a lecture by Professor David Der-wei Wang of Harvard University. Both performances were widely reported in Chinese- and English-language news media. The prominence of both avant-garde and traditional-style performances of the White Snake legend attests to its enduring popularity and power to transcend genre limitations.

10. See, for example, *Legend of the White Snake* (*Baishe zhuan*), an experimental dance performance created by Lin Hwai-min (Lin Huaimin) for Cloud Gate Dance Theatre (Yunmen wuji) and premiered in Singapore in 1975; *White Water* (*Baishui*), written by Tien Chi-yuan (Tian Qiyuan) and premiered in Taiwan in 1993; and *White Snake Spectacular* (*Chaoxuan Baishe zhuan*) performed by Ming Hwa Yuan (Ming Hua Yuan) Taiwanese opera troupe and premiered in Taiwan in 2004.

11. Sun Wukong of *Xiyou ji*. For an introduction to the supernatural in Chinese literature, including contextualization of terms such as *shen* 神, *gui* 鬼, *yao* 妖 in Chinese literary history, see Huntington, "The Supernatural," esp. 112–14.

12. Celebrated on the fifth day of the fifth month of the lunar calendar, which is near midsummer and during one of the hottest times of the year, the Dragon Boat Festival (more commonly known in Chinese as Duanwu jie 端午節) has long come to be associated with poisonous reptiles and insects such as snakes, centipedes, and scorpions in the Chinese tradition. People would drink realgar wine (*xionghuangjiu* 雄黃酒) to fend off poisonous creatures and keep diseases away. Such a practice became an important plot element in many versions of the White Snake legend, highlighting the conflict between White Snake's identity as a *sheyao* 蛇妖 (snake demoness) and her ritual duty to drink realgar wine with her human husband at the Dragon Boat Festival.

13. The Chinese character *qing* 青, although often translated as green in the name of the Green Snake, could actually refer to one of three colors: blue, green, or black. When forced to choose, stage productions and translators tend to go with green, although blue is also a common choice, especially in earlier renditions; rarely was black used in this specific reference.

14. See, for example, Feng, "Bai niangzi yongzhen Leifengta"; Fang Chengpei, *Leifengta chuanqi*; and Idema, *The White Snake and Her Son*.

15. White Snake is a rather unique goddess or a bit of an outlier character. She is a demoness (*yao*) that breaks from the celestial hierarchy, only to be subjugated and reinstated as a god with a specific position. This is a common framework in late imperial narratives, as in the case of Sun Wukong (*The Monkey*, aka *Journey to the West*) and the many gods of *Fengshen yanyi* (*Investiture of the Gods*). Unlike other gods, however, there is hardly any evidence that White Snake was actually worshipped, and her path to becoming an immortal (*xian* 仙) was much more humane; in some cases, she earns merit through her son's sacrifice, rather than gaining worshippers.

16. This ambivalence in the representation of the White Snake, different from that of the snake in the Garden of Eden as always evil (though Milton saw it a bit differently, as purveyor of knowledge and ethics), invites associations with Gloria Anzaldúa's take on La Malinche, the serpent's forked tongue and its relationship to language and translation, and what she calls "the new mestiza" (the new hybridity) in the Chicano experience. See Anzaldúa, *Borderlands/La Frontera.*

17. See Tarryn Li-Min Chun's discussion of *Impression West Lake* (*Yinxiang Xihu*) produced by film director Zhang Yimou as a spectacular outdoor performance on site at West Lake in Hangzhou, part of the *Impressions Series* at popular tourist destinations throughout the PRC; Chun, "Mediated Transgression and Madame White," esp. 315–25.

18. For an exciting new study on the use of love in neoliberal China, see Charlie Yi Zhang, *Dreadful Desires.*

19. See Xia and He, *Xin Bainiangzi chuanqi.*

20. See, for example, "Yang Zi Ren Jialun + Liu Jialing Zhao Yazhi: *Tianji zhi Baishe chuanshuo* weibo xianre" [Yang Zi and Ren Jialun, Carina Lau and Angie Chiu: *The Destiny of White Snake* goes popular before broadcasting], accessed February 20, 2018, https://baike.baidu.com/tashuo/browse/content?id=84a16c8985fd4b4bf93dde74; and "Ru Fuo wangju yi xiajia" [Internet drama offensive to Buddhism has been shelved], accessed August 8, 2018, https://mp.weixin.qq.com/s/_qq1s3cYzkkHuXZmez1hog

21. Amp Wong and Zhao Ji, *Baishe: yuanqi.* See the animation film's homepage on Douban dianying, the leading film review site in China, accessed January 19, 2019, https://movie.douban.com/subject/30331149/

22. In Mainland China, see the internet drama on iQiyi in Mandarin with subtitles in simplified Chinese, accessed April 14, 2019, https://www.iqiyi.com/a_19rrgxjest.html; and in Taiwan, see it on iQiyi Taiwan with subtitles in traditional Chinese, accessed April 14, 2019, https://tw.iqiyi.com/v_19rshn0ljc.html. The Mainland Chinese site was no longer accessible on June 6, 2020. However, the series was fully accessible on June 6, 2020, outside China, with multiple subtitles, for example, on Viki, https://www.viki.com/tv/36277c-the-legend-of-white-snake, and on Netflix, https://www.netflix.com/title/81108281

23. See Constellation Theatre Company's website for more information on *The White Snake*, accessed April 14, 2019, https://www.constellationtheatre.org/white-snake; also see Luo, "Performance Review: *The White Snake*."

24. See Kroeber, *Retelling/Rereading*, 3–4.

25. I thank David Rolston for this insight. *Journey to the West* (*Xiyou ji*) is full of all three kinds of *jing* 精. The "demonology" of this novel has been written about by Campany, "Demons, Gods, and Pilgrims."

26. Moreover, in traditional Chinese literature, women in general are regarded as an alien and polluting species. Buddhism presents reincarnation as a male a reward but reincarnation as a female a punishment. It also blames women for creating pollution in the act of procreation, for which they must atone in the Blood Pond Hell. See, for example, Idema and Grant, *Escape from Blood Pond Hell*. For more on pollution, containment, male anxiety over female sexual powers in Late Imperial Chinese literature, see McMahon, *Causality and Containment*; Epstein, *Competing Discourses*; and Barr, "Disarming Intruders."

27. See, for example, Grusin, *The Nonhuman Turn*.

28. See Miyazaki, *Starting Point*, 19.

29. See "The Snake Charmer's Birthday Gift: Cerise Jacobs at TEDxBeacon Street," video imbedded in the official website of White Snake Projects, accessed February 20, 2018, http://www.whitesnakeprojects.org/about/cerise-jacobs, 1:37–2:02.

30. See Sophia Nguyen, "The Lawyer Librettist," *Harvard Magazine*, January–February 2017, accessed February 20, 2018, https://harvardmagazine.com/2017/01/lawyer-librettist

31. See Zhou, *Madame White Snake*.

32. See Zhou, *Madame White Snake*; and Zimmerman, *The White Snake*.

33. For more on recent debates regarding the concept of the "Sinophone," see Shih, Tsai, and Bernards, *Sinophone Studies*; and Ng Kim Chew (Huang Jinshu), "Zheyang de 'huayu yuxi' lun keyi xiuyi" [Let's stop using "Sinophone" in this sense], *Shuoshu*, accessed January 3, 2018, https://sobooks.tw/sinophone-literature-review/. The above link became inaccessible in June 2020, but the same content can be found on Douban, accessed June 6, 2020, https://www.douban.com/note/651722776/

34. For more on the 1956 film and its Japanese context, see Ueda, *Ugetsu monogatari*; Tanizaki, "Jasei no in"; Mizoguchi, *Ugetsu*; and Hu, "The Animated Resurrection." The 1978 film's complex coproduction history is still open to further inquiry.

35. The other three legends are *The Cowherd and the Weaving Girl* (*Niulang zhinü*), *The Butterfly Lovers* (*Liang Zhu*), and *Lady Mengjiang* (*Mengjiang nü*).

36. See Li et al., "Li Huang." For earlier stories from Tang and Song dynasties about such amorous encounters, there might be some connections between these stories and male scholar officials' courtship at brothels. As often appeared in Tang tales, the term *zhenren* 真人 or *xianren* 仙人 ("immortals") are euphemisms for courtesans. Therefore, some scholars (including Chen Yinque) argue that *Yingying zhuan*, also titled *Huizhen ji* (*Encountering immortals*), is based upon this kind of experience, while others (such as Qian Zhongshu) disagree with using literature to support historical research. See, for example, Wu Guo, "Qian Zhongshu."

37. See Idema, *The White Snake and Her Son*, 115. Translation slightly modified.

38. *Fifteen Strings of Cash* (*Shiwu guan*) is the title of a hit 1956 *kunqu* (often translated as Kun opera) play from Mainland China based on one of the vernacular tales from Feng Menglong's *Stories to Awaken the World* (*Xingshi hengyan*, 1627). This popular play from the 1950s may not have a direct connection to the "fifteen strings of cash" mentioned in the "Li Huang" story, which likely dates to the tenth century, but the emphasis on the transactional nature of human relations and, in particular, the exchange value of women's bodies, are perfectly highlighted in the continued relevance of the contemporary play. For more on the 1956 play, see Rebull, "Locating Theatricality."

39. There are important differences between "Li Huang" and later versions as well. The woman in blue in "Li Huang" is old and says she is the aunt of the woman in white, whereas Green Snake is typically presented as younger than White Snake. Further, Li Huang seems to be interested in the unnamed woman in white only sexually; he is also already married. He gives the woman a sizeable sum of money, whereas in later versions, the woman gives money to the man.

40. See Hong Mai, *Yijian zhi*, 1062–63, 1755–56; also see Inglis, *Hong Mai's Record of the Listener*.

41. This bath taboo may remind readers of the legends of the serpent/fish woman Melusine in European traditions, which emerged around the same time as this late twelfth-century tale. For a comparative study of Melusine and the White Snake, see Zifeng Zhao, "Metamorphoses of Snake Women."

42. For translations of both, see Idema, *The White Snake and Her Son*, 117–18.

43. The seductresses could be transformed from animals, ghosts, or even objects. For more on animals and their transformations into demonic spirits in the Buddhist literature in medieval China, see Huaiyu Chen, "Cong shi'er shishou dao shi'er jingmei," esp. 329; for a Chinese Buddhist's classification of animals and plants in the seventh century, see Huaiyu Chen, "A Buddhist Classification of Animals and Plants in Early Tang Times." Both spirits and exorcists can be from Daoist, Buddhist, or hybrid traditions.

44. See Hong Pian, "Xihu santaji." The story appears in the collection *Qingping shantang huaben*, whose title is a made-up and misleading one: not all of the stories are *huaben*, or vernacular stories, and the original title of the collection was *Liushi jia xiaoshuo* (*Stories from sixty authors*). Patrick Hanan dates "Xihu santaji" to "probably early Ming." He also mentions an early Ming play using the same material. See Hanan, *The Chinese Short Story*, 234.

45. The Xuanzan in Xi's name is short for Xuanzan sheren, an official title. Often in vernacular tales from the Song and Yuan dynasties, official titles were used as an honorific way to refer to a commoner, many of them artisans. The most common example is the use of the title Shizhao in Feng, "Cui Shizhao shengsi yuanjia."

46. Idema, *The White Snake and Her Son*, 129.

47. Idema, *The White Snake and Her Son*, 121–34.

48. For a modern rendition of this trope, see Ang Lee, *Lust, Caution* (*Se, jie*), which

is based on a short story of the same name by Eileen Chang (Zhang Ailing). In addition, the image of Thunder Peak Pagoda and its cultural and symbolic implications are very relevant to Chang's life and writing. Chang finished a semiautobiographical novel, *The Fall of the Pagoda*, originally published in English in the United States in 1963 but published posthumously in Hong Kong only in 2010. The publication of *The Fall of the Pagoda* coincided with Chang's decade-long revision process for "Lust, Caution," from the late 1950s to the late 1970s. See Eileen Chang, *The Fall of the Pagoda*. For an illuminating essay exploring the central importance of the White Snake figure and the serpentine motif in Chang's creative resistance of any and all pagodas as symbols of oppression, see David Der-wei Wang, "Eileen Chang and *The Fall of the Pagoda*."

49. Feng, "Madam White is Kept Forever," 474–505. An earlier translation by H. C. Chang is worth noting here, see "Madam White," in Kang-i Sun Chang and Owen, *The Cambridge History of Chinese Literature*, 216–61.

50. In a Western narrative from this period (or almost any period), a woman proposing marriage would be a startling detail. It might even raise suspicion concerning her background. This is also the case in China, and such an action is clearly "out of this world," so to speak.

51. Feng, "Madam White Is Kept Forever," 474–505.

52. Huang Tubi, "Leifengta"; see the translation of Huang's preface in Idema, *The White Snake and Her Son*, 141; and Balivet, "The Many Transformations of White Snake," 25–26.

53. Fang Chengpei, *Leifengta chuanqi*; Yushan zhuren, *Leifengta qizhuan*; and Chen Yuqian, *Xiuxiang yiyao quanzhuan*. *Chuanqi* is a southern theatrical tradition, literally "spreading the strange" and often translated as "legend," which can be misleading as it does not reflect the geographical implication of the genre, better reflected in the translation "southern dramas." *Tanci* is a diverse group of professional storytelling styles with stringed musical accompaniment, and one of the main storytelling conventions for White Snake stories over the years. Given the diversity within the *tanci* genre, from short ballads to epic-length narratives, and with their varying performance styles and local variations, it has been variously translated as "string ballad," "story-singing," "chantefable," "plucking rhyme," and "prosimetric narrative," among other renderings. I am leaving these terms untranslated in the text to pay respect to the internal diversity of the genres.

54. Actors (presumably representing the tastes of their audiences to some extend) did also have some input in how Huang's version of the play became Fang's version between 1738 and 1777, see Guo Yingde, *Ming Qing chuanqi zonglu*, 935; and Kang-i Sun Chang and Owen, *The Cambridge History of Chinese Literature*, 317–18.

55. While some elite authors might have objected, the majority took such happy endings involving grand unions (*da tuanyuan* 大團圓) for granted. A related modern text with a focus on the voice of the people, first collected in Dingxian in the 1920s and reprinted in Taiwan in the 1970s, is the legend's "rice-sprout song" (*yangge* 秧歌)

version; see "Baishe zhuan," Li ed., *Dingxian yangge xuan*, 958–1049. For an English translation, see Gamble, "The White Snake."

56. These factors become more important when the performance tradition switches from full play to *zhezi xi* 折子戲, or excerpted highlights, and anthologies such as *Red Coral Ballads* (*Yuefu hongshan*) sort the *zhezi xi* into functional categories that match the kind of social events where corresponding highlights were performed. See Wang C. K., "Yuefu hongshan kao."

57. See Kristopher Tapley, "Oscars: Guillermo del Toro Sends Message to Young Filmmakers as 'Shape of Water' Wins Best Picture," *Variety*, March 4, 2018, http://variety.com/2018/film/awards/shape-of-water-wins-oscar-best-picture-1202716095/; Matthew Jacobs, "How Weird, A Movie About Fish Sex Became Awards Season's Consensus Vote," *Huffington Post*, March 5, 2018, https://www.huffingtonpost.com/entry/the-shape-of-water-best-picture-oscars_us_5a9cd003e4b089ec353bfdad

58. Gilbert Cruz, "10 Questions for Guillermo del Toro," *Time*, September 5, 2011, http://content.time.com/time/magazine/article/0,9171,2090370,00.html; Molly Freeman, "The Shape of Water Review: A Monstrous Fairy Tale for the Ages," *Screen Rant*, December 1, 2017, https://screenrant.com/shape-water-movie-reviews/

59. In this context, White Snake's connection with water is worthy of deeper exploration. Not all snakes are connected with water. There is something to be said about snakes in Southern China and their cultural and symbolic meanings in this comparative context. Water creatures, because of their environment, do tend to be streamlined in ways land creatures do not, intensifying their sexual appeal and exotic attraction. In fact, many more snake stories occur in southern regions; see, for example, the story about a young girl, Li Ji, slaying a giant snake, in Gan Bao's *Soushen ji* (*Anecdotes about Spirits and Immortals*), chap. 19, 195–200. Another example is the Taiwanese folktale "She langjun" (*Snake husband*), where a transgressive love between human and nonhuman also occurs, but with interesting twists: the snake is a handsome gentleman and the marriage is happy, although the older sister tried to destroy it out of jealousy. See, for example, Jin, "'Shelang' tanyuan."

60. Some might argue that because of the tendency to humanize and beautify the image of the White Snake throughout the retelling processes, she was not allowed to be snaky or alien in human society and instead had to accommodate societal prescriptions for women that denied many fundamental aspects of her nature and otherness. This line of argument is valid in many instances. However, this does not negate my core argument of an increasing cultural syncretism and a tendency toward greater tolerance of any differences, as recent retellings of the White Snake legend made explicit. In some of the most recent film versions, characters openly celebrate their hybrid identities, some even desiring to become demons. See, for example, Ching, *Baishe chuanshuo;* and Amp Wong and Zhao Ji, *Baishe: yuanqi.*

61. In the Chinese literary tradition, there are many examples of successful alien-human transmigration in human society (what happens in heaven is different because

the rules are different there); the writer who probably produced the most examples is Pu Songling. Again, such "successes" are defined as the near complete domestication of the fox spirits, ghosts, and other supernatural figures, who are predominantly female; while they are allowed to retain something that indicates their unusual origins (to those in the know), they become even more ideal wives and loving mothers than humans. See, for example, Pu, "Hongyu," 269–75.

62. In the Chinese philosophical tradition, everything is made of *qi* 氣, or energy, and differs only in level or refinement. For more on the cultivation of internal energy and on the source of demons' and immortals' power, see, for example, Campany, "Cosmogony and Self-Cultivation."

63. See Pei-yi Wu, "'The White Snake,' The Evolution of a Myth in China"; and Idema, *The White Snake and Her Son.* Wu's dissertation provides a solid foundation for future research, with summaries, translations, and scene-by-scene analysis of important White Snake texts. Idema's book includes translations of sources relevant to the development of the legend, as well as a detailed scholarly introduction, and annotations and notes. Also see Chang 2004 and Balivet 2020.

64. See, for example, Taniguchi, "Feng Menglong to Huang Tubi no aida"; and Yang Hoiseok, "Zhongguo xiqu gaige yundong yanjiu." For a recent semiotic study on the use of the White Snake narrative in post–World War II East Asian "nation-state" films, see Choi and Moon, "Chŏnhu shigi Tongashia maech'esŏsaŭi rok'ŏllit'i."

65. See Zhang Lianhong, *Lilian jinghun.*

66. See, for example, Alvin Ka Hin Wong, "Transgenderism as a Heuristic Device."

67. See Arrighi, *The Long Twentieth Century.*

68. The cigarette cards could be compared to another way images of White Snake circulated very broadly, through *nianhua*, or New Year paintings; see Bai, "Qingdai Baishe zhuan nianhua."

69. Marshall Berman's formulation that modernity is living in two worlds simultaneously and Mary Gluck's connecting emerging modern artists and modernist aesthetics to the changing forms of popular culture have inspired my previous work and are very relevant here, see Berman, *All That Is Solid Melts into Air*; Gluck, *Popular Bohemia*; and Luo, *The Avant-Garde and the Popular.*

70. "Worn shoes" (*poxie*) is a derogatory reference to women deemed sexually promiscuous.

71. See Li Bihua, *Qingshe.*

72. See Luo, "The Experimental and the Popular in Chinese Socialist Theater of the 1950s."

73. See, for example, Dirlik and Zhang, *Postmodernism & China*; Xiaobin Yang, *The Chinese Postmodern*; Ho, *The Transition Study of Postsocialist China*; and Fung, "Postcolonial Hong Kong Identity."

74. For a number of deeply reflexive accounts on gender and sexuality from the perspective of women who grew up in the Mao era, see Zhong, Wang, and Bai, *Some of Us.*

75. Yiman Wang's rigorous study on Shanghai and Hong Kong remakes of Holly-

wood genre films and Hong Kong remakes of both Shanghai and Hollywood films provides a good example for combining the study of adaptation and migration in specific local contexts, see Yiman Wang, *Remaking Chinese Cinema.*

76. See Geertz, "Thick Description."

77. See Moretti, "Conjectures on World Literature"; Moretti, *Distant Reading*; and Damrosch, *What Is World Literature?* In addition, Beecroft's formulation of the six phases of "world literature" can be instructive here. See Beecroft, *Authorship and Cultural Identity*, 5.

78. See Propp, *Morphology of the Folktale*; Lévi-Strauss, *The Raw and the Cooked*; Campbell, *The Hero with a Thousand Faces*; and Stith Thompson, *The Folktale.*

Chapter 2

1. Woodbridge's version was first serialized starting September 4, 1896, and was then collected as a single volume and published later in 1896. See Woodbridge, "The Mystery of the White Snake," 410; and Woodbridge, *The Mystery of the White Snake*, "Introduction," 1.

2. Le Bon, *Psychologie des Foules.*

3. According to a contemporary account, the Chinese *yuan* was introduced at par with the Mexican *peso* and was divided into 100 cents. See "Currency of China," *The Banking Law Journal* (Knickerbocker Print Company) 15 (1898): 150; also see Ulrich Theobald, "Qing Period Money," April 13, 2016, http://www.chinaknowledge.de/History/Terms/cash-qing.html

4. See Woodbridge, "The Mystery of the White Snake," 4.

5. The May Fourth new cultural movement, from the mid-1910s to the mid-1920s, ushered in a secular, scientific, democratic, and romantic tradition in modern Chinese cultural history during Woodbridge's residency in China. For more on the May Fourth movement, see Tse-tsung Chow, *The May Fourth Movement*; Leo Ou-fan Lee, *The Romantic Generation*; Yusheng Lin, *The Crisis of Chinese Consciousness*; and Doležlová-Velingerová and Sanders, *The Appropriation of Cultural Capital.*

6. Roel Sterckx is the Joseph Needham Professor of Chinese History, Science and Civilization at the University of Cambridge. His scholarship focuses on forms of knowledge about the natural world in premodern China, including cultural ecology. See Sterckx, *The Animal and the Daemon.*

7. See Mo Yan, *Shengsi pilao.*

8. Mo Yan also opened his novel to the impermanence of self even within a lifetime and emphasized the novel's antiauthoritarian function. For relevant analysis, see Yiju Huang, "A Buddhist Perspective," 224; and Haiyan Lee, *The Stranger and the Chinese Moral Imagination*, 99–100.

9. See Woodbridge, *The Mystery of the White Snake*, front page.

10. See English Revised Version of the Bible, 1885, accessed June 28, 2018, http://biblehub.com/erv/romans/1.htm

11. See Edkins, *Shijiao zhengmiu*, 4.

12. See Woodbridge, *The Mystery of the White Snake*, 10.

13. Woodbridge, *The Mystery of the White Snake*, 2.

14. "Woodbridge Reading Response," MCL 595: Topics in Folklore and Mythology: The White Snake, University of Kentucky, April 18, 2017, https://uk.instructure.com/courses/1884673/discussion_topics/11908174

15. For a recent Chinese-language study linking Woodbridge's 1896 White Snake rendition to his missionary objectives, see Yao, "Shuyi yu chuanjiao."

16. The formation and transmission of the White Snake legend can be intimately connected to the geographical, economic, and cultural background of the Grand Canal. See Wang Jue, "Cong 'Baishe zhuan' gushi tanjiu Ming Qing Jiangnan Da Yunhe"; and Zou Xiaohua, "Cong Da Yunhe wenhua beijing kan *Baishe zhuan* de xingcheng he chuanbo" [Examining the formation and transmission of the *Legend of the White Snake* from the cultural background of the Grand Canal], *Jiangsu difangzhi* [Jiangsu provincial gazetteer], no. 5 (2019), accessed May 30, 2020, http://jssdfz.jiangsu.gov.cn/art/2019/10/28/art_57405_8745672.html

17. Woodbridge, "The Mystery of the White Snake," 410.

18. Woodbridge, "The Mystery of the White Snake," 410.

19. Dillery, "The First Egyptian Narrative History."

20. See Julien, *Blanche et Bleue*, "Avertissement," xi-xii. Julien cited a Chinese version from 1807 and credited it to "*Iu-chân-tchu-jîn*."

21. "White and Blue," 307, 315–21.

22. H. C., "Lüi-fung Tă," in *The Chinese and Japanese Repository,* vol. 1, 357–65, 401–10, 429–35, 461–68, 503–13; vol. 2, 11–19, 89–97; Wong Chin Foo, "Poh Yuin Ko, The Serpent Princess," in *The Cosmopolitan* 6, no. 2 (December 1888): 180–90. I am grateful for Ping Zhu for bringing Wong's fascinating text to my attention. For more on Wong's writing in the context of his activism as "the first Chinese American," see Ping Zhu, "Chinese Literature at Large."

23. See Buck, *Fighting Angel*, 66. On the other hand, missionaries recognized that the theater was very influential among common people, hence Arthur Smith devoted a chapter to village theater in his 1899 book; still, for all of that, he did not show much interest in the plays themselves. See Arthur Smith, *Village Life in China*, 54–69.

24. See Chen Yuqian, *Xiuxiang yiyao quanzhuan.*

25. See Woodbridge, *The Mystery of the White Snake*, 3; also see Julien, *Blanche et Bleue*, 15.

26. Woodbridge, *The Mystery of the White Snake*, 4.

27. Woodbridge, *The Mystery of the White Snake*, 5.

28. By contrast, the English translation serialized through 1864 has White Snake (Pĭ chen-niang) confess her love to her human lover (Hăn-wan), as in all other versions, with the exception of Wong Chin Foo's 1888 short story, in which Whey Goon, the male protagonist, confessed his love to the serpent-princess first. See H. C., "Lüi-fung Tă," in *The Chinese and Japanese Repository*, vol. 1, 401; Wong Chin Foo, "Poh Yuin Ko, The Serpent-Princess," 187.

29. See Woodbridge, *The Mystery of the White Snake*, 10.

30. Woodbridge, *The Mystery of the White Snake*, 15. Woodbridge may be influenced by Ovid or Virgil here.

31. This plot already exists in the 1806 Chinese version, *Leifengta qizhuan,* attributed to Yushan zhuren. Woodbridge was likely influenced by the 1864 English translation based on that Chinese version; see H. C., "Lüi-fung Tǎ," in *The Chinese and Japanese Repository*, vol. 1, 359.

32. Here Woodbridge's demonstration of White Snake's human vulnerability could also have been influenced by the 1864 English translation, where she similarly "fell to the earth" under attack. See H. C., "Lüi-fung Tǎ," in *The Chinese and Japanese Repository*, vol. 1, 463.

33. See Woodbridge, *The Mystery of the White Snake*, 17.

34. Both the White Snake and the female Guanyin in the Chinese tradition may well have derived from snake cults in the Jiangnan region during the Tang dynasty. See Yü, *Kuan-yin*; Fan Pen Li Chen, "Cloud-Transcending Crossing"; and Fan Pen Li Chen, *Journey of a Goddess.* In addition, this plot fits well with the very common nineteenth-century Western preoccupation with official corruption and the contemporary critique of Chinese modes of *guanxi* in doing business.

35. See Woodbridge, *The Mystery of the White Snake*, 20.

36. Woodbridge had resided in Zhenjiang for well over a decade by the time of his writing in 1896. Traces of the 1864 English translation can still be detected here in the act of cross-dressing; see H. C., "Lüi-fung Tǎ," in *The Chinese and Japanese Repository*, vol. 1, 510.

37. See Woodbridge, *The Mystery of the White Snake*, 24.

38. Woodbridge, *The Mystery of the White Snake*, 24.

39. Woodbridge, *The Mystery of the White Snake*, 27. This can be read as Woodbridge's critique of Buddhist practice as "unnatural" for human relations.

40. Woodbridge, *The Mystery of the White Snake*, 28.

41. Woodbridge, *The Mystery of the White Snake*, 29.

42. A contemporary reviewer, in a short book review published in *The North-China Herald* on November 27, 1896, discovered "a fascinating little romance" in Woodbridge's rendition. See J. W. P., "Review of *The Mystery of the White Snake: A Legend of Thunder Peak Tower*," *N.-C. Herald and S. C. & C. Gazette*, November 27, 1896, 916.

43. Haiyan Lee, in her review of Lynn Pan's *When True Love Came to China*, cautions against such divisions between China and the West, and traditional love and modern true love. She urges scholars to engage with the growing and truly multidisciplinary scholarship on emotion, "to situate love in a larger affective terrain and map out its relationship to other emotions, attachments, loyalties, values, and ideals." See Haiyan Lee, "How the Chinese Fell in Love with Love."

44. Woodbridge, *The Golden-Horned Dragon King.*

45. Legge, *The Chinese Classics*, 55.

46. Woodbridge, *The Golden-Horned Dragon King*, "Translator's Preface," 1.

47. Woodbridge, *The Golden-Horned Dragon King*, "Translator's Preface," 1. This

particular dragon king is the one executed by Wei Zheng after Emperor Taizong had promised to protect him. There is a rather fragmentary Dunhuang manuscript of the story, extant and translated by Arthur Waley. A less satirical version was copied into *Yongle Encyclopedia* (*Yongle dadian*), and it was finally used in *Journey to the West* to set up Taizong holding a grand mass for the dead. For a recent Chinese-language study on Woodbridge's 1895 translation, see Wu Xiaofang, "'Buchong yongsheng Shangdi zhirong.'"

48. Woodbridge, *China's Only Hope*, "Translator's Note," 8; and quoted in *China's Only Hope*, "Introduction" [by Griffith John], 17.

49. See Chang Chih-tung (Zhang Zhidong), *Quanxue pian*.

50. Griffith John, having translated the Bible into Chinese, wrote an introduction to Woodbridge's *China's Only Hope*, since Zhang's promotion of Western learning as a means of strengthening the Chinese "body politic" and its insistence on "religious toleration," though it stopped short of openly promoting Christianity, still fitted well with the larger missionary goals in China at the time.

51. See Woodbridge, *Fifty Years in China*, 41.

52. Woodbridge, *Fifty Years in China*, 41–42.

53. Woodbridge, *Fifty Years in China*, 166.

54. Woodbridge, *Fifty Years in China*, 166.

55. See Cloud, *Hangchow*, 73–102. This is comparable to earlier Anglophone renditions of the White Snake legend, almost exclusively embedded in publications intended to spread useful information and introduce empirical knowledge. See "White and Blue"; and H. C., "Lüi-fung Tă," in *The Chinese and Japanese Repository*, vols. 1 and 2.

56. See Cloud, *Hangchow*, front page.

57. See Cloud, foreword to *Hangchow*, unpaginated; and Cloud, "The Legend of the White Snake," *Hangchow*, 73n1.

58. See Cloud, *Hangchow*, 41.

59. Cloud, *Hangchow*, 43.

60. Cloud, *Hangchow*, 44.

61. Cloud, *Hangchow*, 73.

62. The sixteen installments are: "Traces of the Immortal" (*Xianzong*), "Encounter at the Lake" (*Youhu*), "Match-making" (*Shuoqin*), "Sent into Exile" (*Fanpei*), "Beauty Recovered" (*Fuyan*), "Shop Opened" (*Kaidian*), "Magic Competition" (*Doufa*), "Dragon Boat Festival" (*Duanyang*), "The Immortal Herb" (*Xiancao*), "Treasure Stolen" (*Daobao*), "Becoming a Monk" (*Tanxiang*), "The Flood" (*Shuiman*), "Giving Birth" (*Chanzi*), "Suppressed by the Alms Bowl" (*Hebo*), "Schoolroom" (*Xuetang*), and "Making Sacrifice at the Pagoda" (*Jita*). See Chen Yuqian, *Xiuxiang yiyao quanzhuan*.

63. See Cloud, *Hangchow*, 79.

64. Cloud, *Hangchow*, 79.

65. Cloud, *Hangchow*, 76.

66. See Mittler, *A Newspaper for China?*, 85–86.

67. For more on the *yamen* in the making of Chinese cities, see Friedmann, "Reflections on Place and Place-Making in the Cities of China," 61–73.

68. See Cloud, *Hangchow*, after page 16, unpaginated.

69. See Cloud, *Hangchow*, after page 24, unpaginated. Hangzhou Bore is a world-famous tidal bore on Qiantang River and at Hangzhou Bay, and a major attraction for tourists visiting Hangzhou.

70. See Cloud, *Hangchow*, "The Lake, Viewed from American Consulate," after page 38, unpaginated.

71. See Cloud, *Hangchow*, before page 77, unpaginated.

72. See Cloud, *Hangchow*, 77.

73. See Cloud, *A Digest of the Treaty, Laws, and Regulations.*

74. These performances are called "colorful lantern shows" (*dengcai xi*). For general background, see Jin Yaozhang and Luan Guanhua, "Dengcai," in *Zhongguo da baike quanshu, xiqu quyi* (Beijing: Zhongguo dabaike quanshu chubanshe; Shanghai: Xinhua shudian, 1983), 59. On the history of the kind of lanterns used on stage in Shanghai and how to make them, see Kong and Wang, *Shanghai dengcai.*

75. See *Shenbao* (Shanghai edition), May 31, 1875, 5; June 2, 1875, 6; January 3, 1880, 6; and August 1, 1880, 5.

76. See, for example, *Shenbao* (Shanghai edition), February 16, 1895, 6.

77. From what I can trace throughout the lifespan of the daily, the series' first installment appeared on page 8 of issue 229, and the last installment of the series appeared on page 6 of issue 404, the last issue published. See *Tuhua ribao*, vols. 5–8.

78. *Shenbao* (Shanghai edition), June 7, 1905, 7; and June 8, 1910, 7.

79. See Li Wei, *Ershi shiji xiqu gaige de sanda fanshi*, chap. 1; see Liang Luo, "Review of Li Wei, *Three Paradigms of Reforming Traditional Theatre in the Twentieth Century*," *CHINOPERL: Journal of Chinese Oral and Performing Literature* 36, no. 2 (2017): 139–44.

80. See Goldstein, *Drama Kings*, 76–77.

81. See, for example, a cartoon titled "New Legend of White Snake [Xin Baishe zhuan] portrays the Tanaka Cabinet of Japan as a monstrous serpent scaring a man to death," *Sanxing* [*Three Stars*], June 22, 1928, 2. Another cartoon titled "A Wonderful Scene from New Legend of White Snake" [Xin Baishe zhuan jingcai yimu] portrays a giant serpent rising from a sack of rice and devouring a starving man; it is likely commenting on starvation raging at the time of the civil war. See *Dongfang ribao* [*Eastern Daily*], June 29, 1947, 1. Although almost twenty years apart, both cartoons were published around the Dragon Boat Festival (fifth day of the fifth months in the lunar calendar), a date when White Snake plays were ritually performed.

82. *Shenbao*, January 1, 1911, 8.

83. *Shenbao*, January 15, 1912, 4; and January 16, 1912, 4.

84. *Shenbao*, June 9, 1913, 9.

85. *Shenbao*, May 4, 1915, 12.

86. Woodbridge, *Fifty Years in China*, 42.

87. *Shenbao*, June 16, 1915, 9; and June 17, 1915, 9.

88. Cai, "Yi meiyu dai zongjiao."

89. Here Woodbridge is building upon a cluster of texts that include the 1806 Chinese, 1834 French, and the 1864 and 1888 English versions. More importantly, Woodbridge's Westernization of the White Snake legend and his Christian missionary work, though converging with the anti-Buddhist rhetoric of many Chinese modern intellectuals, still departed from their tendency toward secularization. Woodbridge upheld Christianity as the only salvation to China's problems.

90. *Shenbao*, November 21, 1914, 9. The troupe that presented the mixed-cast performances, Minxing She, is rather unusual for adopting this casting practice. Shanghai, with its concessions, led the way for such experimentation, while Beijing was far more conservative. It should also be noted that the use of "fiction" (*xiaoshuo*) in referring to the storytelling performance here is rather liberal. For example, *tanci* texts at the time used speech prefixes that identified speakers/singers by role type, as would happen in scripts of a play.

91. *Shenbao*, November 20, 1914, 12.

92. *Shenbao*, June 2, 1917, 16.

93. The White Snake performances were also variously known as a "famous farce" (*zhuming quju*) and a "festival farce" (*yingshi quju*). See *Shenbao*, April 29, 1917, 16; June 14, 1918, 8; July 21, 1918, 8; December 18, 1918, 8; June 2, 1919, 5; and December 27, 1920, 8.

94. *Shenbao*, May 30, 1926, 23.

95. Attempts to perform the entire White Snake story theatrically, known as *quanben xi*, tended to be relatively rare compared to excerpts, known as *zhezi xi*. Moreover, White Snake was not chosen for performance in a lengthy serialized version in either the Qing palace or in Shanghai, eventually the home of serial plays.

96. The White Snake plays were certainly part of the repertoire of *yingjie xi*, or festival plays, most prominently for the Dragon Boat Festival, on the fifth day of the fifth month in the lunar calendar. The seventh day of the seventh month in the lunar calendar is more frequently associated with the legend of the Cowherd and the Weaving Girl (*Niulang zhinü*). In one of his "White Snake" films made in 1960, Korean filmmaker Shin Sang-ok combined the two legends in the film plot, see Shin, *Paeksa buin,* and chapter 5 for more details.

97. The rise of Cantonese opera, as well as many other regional operas using local dialects, has been narrated as a response to *jingju*'s presumptive cultural dominance. The story of Cantonese opera's popularity in Republican Shanghai and its far-reaching impact in East and Southeast Asia and in Cantonese-speaking diasporic communities all over the world enriches our understanding of the importance of the genre and the intertwined cultural history between the local, the national, and the transnational. For more on the rise of the three genres of *jingju*, *tanci*, and *yueju*, and their illustrious history and development throughout the past centuries, see, for example, Ruru Li, *The Soul of Beijing Opera*; Li Guo, *Women's Tanci Fiction*; and Wing Chung Ng, *The Rise of Cantonese Opera*.

98. *Shenbao*, November 13, 1913, 12.

99. *Shenbao*, December 20, 1914, 9.

100. *Shenbao*, February 13, 1917, 16.

101. *Shenbao*, March 13, 1918, 8.

102. See, for example, Yunlu, "Viewing Fen Juhua's Performances" [Fen Juhua zhi juguan], *Da shijie* [Grand world], May 14, 1920, 3; Xinfo, "A Brief Biography of Fen Juhua" [Fen Juhua xiaozhuan], *Da shijie*, June 9, 1920, 3.

103. *Shenbao*, March 22, 1916, 9.

104. *Shenbao*, May 19, 1934, 11; and July 8, 1942, 7. As a narrative storytelling (*shuochang*) genre, *tanci* does not require props, scenery, or elaborate costume, and this may have contributed to its mobility and adaptability. *Tanci* was joined by *pinghua* in its development, and they collectively formed the hybrid and even more robust storytelling genre of *pingtan* 評彈 throughout its development in twentieth-century China. Suzhou *pingtan* was among the first group of representative works designated as National Intangible Cultural Heritage (*Guojiaji feiwuzhi wenhua yichan*). The current Suzhou Pingtan Group (*Suzhou pingtan tuan*, founded in 1951) is located on the historical site of Guangyu Guild (*Guangyu she*) and claims lineage from the guild's founding in 1776. See http://www.szsptt.com/page.php?id=1. Generations of *pingtan* artists have contributed memorable performances in the development of White Snake storytelling, with Jiang Yuequan's 1961 and 1984 recorded performances as representative examples. A thirty-episode televised *pingtan* series *Legend of the White Snake* (*Baishe zhuan*) made in 2017 can be found on the YouTube channel Y. Yu, which is "devoted to the promotion and preservation of Suzhou pingtan." For links to representative *pingtan* performances, see "Selected Chronological List of White Snake Texts" in the back matter.

105. *Shenbao*, November 30, 1919, 8.

106. See Luo, "The Experimental and the Popular in Chinese Socialist Theater of the 1950s."

107. Kang signed his name as Kang Nanhai, as he is popularly known for his birthplace in Nanhai, Canton (Guangdong) Province. See *Shenbao*, October 28, 1920, 17.

108. *Shenbao*, December 22, 1924, 8.

109. *Shenbao* (Shanghai version), July 20, 1882, 2.

110. *Shenbao* (Shanghai version), May 1, 1883, 2.

111. *Shenbao*, December 18, 1878, 6; May 19, 1895, 6; May 27, 1918, 15; May 27, 1915; July 6, 1921, 19; and June 3, 1923, 5.

112. *Shenbao*, July 13, 1916, 14.

113. *Shenbao*, February 6, 1917, 17.

114. Shu questioned the use of time-marking signage such as "Seven Years Later" or "Eighteen Years Later" during a performance of the White Snake on the *jingju* stage; see Shu Sheyu, "Guanju zhiyi" [Doubts after watching the performance], *Shenbao*, June 27, 1921, 18.

115. Lin Ren, "Duanwujie de mixin" [The superstition of Dragon Boat Festival], *Shenbao*, June 1, 1941, 11.

116. Zhang Huang, "Duanwu suoji" [Random thoughts at Dragon Boat Festival], *Shenbao*, June 10, 1921, 14; and Zhuoran, "Guan Shanghai xixiao zhi Jinshan si" [After viewing 'Golden Mountain Monastery' by Shanghai Theater School], *Shenbao*, May 23, 1942, 7.

117. Cloud, *Hangchow*, 68–71.

118. *Shenbao*, June 1, 1922, 9; and June 21, 1922, 11.

119. For *tanci*'s contemporary transformations and popular cultural influence, see Jiang Yuequan, *Baishe: shang Jinshan*; Jiang Yuequan and Liu Yunru, *Baishe: penfu*; and Wang Peijun and Xia Xiyan, *Baishe zhuan*.

120. *Shenbao*, January 9, 1923, 18.

121. *Shenbao*, March 13, 1924, local supplement, 18.

122. See Liu Xiaohai and Wang, "Jindai Suzhou pingtan."

123. *Shenbao*, June 8, 1929, 33.

124. *Shenbao*, June 8, 1929, 33.

125. Wenzhi, "Shubao jieshao: *Baishe yu Xu Xian*" [Book report: *White Snake and Xu Xian*], *Shenbao*, August 25, 1930, 23.

126. *Shenbao*, February 17, 1933, 7.

127. *Shenbao*, February 15, 1933, 8.

128. *Shenbao*, December 5, 1933, 20.

129. *Shenbao*, April 11, 1926, 20; January 11, 1934, 20; January 15, 1934, 12; May 19, 1934, 11; June 16, 1934, 13; June 10, 1939, 11; and February 23, 1941, 1. These cigarette cards are further discussed in chapter 3.

130. *Shenbao*, May 19, 1933, 25; and May 9, 1936, 12.

131. *Shenbao*, June 11, 1934, 10.

132. *Shenbao*, June 15, 1934, 27.

133. *Shenbao*, June 17, 1934, 27.

134. *Shenbao* (Shanghai version), July 20, 1882, 2.

135. Woodbridge, *Fifty Years in China*, 42.

136. Shenbao, June 17, 1934, 27.

137. Sanduo, "Yiwu guanggao" [Voluntary advertisement], *Shenbao*, June 20, 1934, 1.

138. *Shenbao*, July 28, 1934, 28.

139. *Shenbao*, May 27, 1949, 2.

140. *Shenbao*, May 16, 1935, 29; May 17, 1935, 25; May 18, 1935, 27; and May 19, 1935, 27.

141. *Shenbao*, May 16, 1935, 29.

142. Yang Xiaozhong, *Baishe zhuan* (aka *Huangta chenyuan*).

143. *Shenbao*, May 17, 1935, 25.

144. *Shenbao*, May 18, 1935, 27.

145. This echoes what Colin Mackerras emphasizes in his discussion on Yangzhou local theater from the late eighteenth century onwards. He notes especially the resilience and longevity of popular local theater (*huabu* 花部) compared to more elite forms (*yabu* 雅部) and, as a result, the importance of younger female roles and clowns. See Mackerras, "Yangzhou Local Theatre," 208–10.

146. It is unclear whether *Tarzan, the Ape Man* reached Shanghai or not. For more on the global influence of *King Kong*, see Erb, *Tracking King Kong*.

147. *Shenbao*, May 19, 1935, 27.

148. *Shenbao*, June 5, 1935, 27.

149. *Shenbao*, July 10, 1935, 24.

150. *Shenbao*, June 21, 1939, 16.

151. *Shenbao*, June 13, 1942, 5.

152. *Shenbao*, August 19, 1944, 3; *Shenbao*, May 27, 1949, 2.

153. Qiren, "Shang Xiaoyun biaoyan si jutou" [Shang Xiaoyun performs the openings of four plays], *Shibao* [*Eastern times*], special issue on theater, August 1, 1934, 1, with a photo showcasing Shang made up as Bai Suzhen.

154. For photos featuring the "dream scene" of the Newer Stage (Gengxin wutai) White Snake performance in the order of their appearance in the news, see the Shanghai local supplement of *Xinwen bao* [*Daily news*], November 14, 1928, 2; *Longbao* [*Dragon news*], November 22, 1928, 3; *Fu'ermosi* [*Charlotte Holmes*], May 29, 1929, 2; and *Xiaobao* [*News for laughter*], June 19, 1929, 2. For photos featuring the "water battle" (*shuidou*) scene, also in the order of appearance, see the Shanghai local supplement of *Xinwen bao*, November 13, 1928, 1; and *Longbao*, November 19, 1928, 3.

155. *Shenbao*, June 9, 1940, 11.

156. *Shenbao*, September 29, 1924, 16.

157. *Shenbao*, April 18, 1948, 7. This is likely a critique of the ongoing civil war in real life.

158. Lu Xun's and other intellectual and popular responses to the fall of Thunder Peak Pagoda form the central concern of the first part of chapter 3. See Lu Xun, "Lun Leifengta de daodiao" [On the fall of Thunder Peak Pagoda], *Yusi* 1 (November 17, 1924).

159. *Shenbao*, June 15, 1948, 8.

160. "Former Star Returns to Footlights," *South China Morning Post*, July 9, 1950, 5.

Chapter 3

1. Quzhai (Yu Pingbo), "Xiguan zhuanta tazhuan ge" [Songs on the bricks from the Xiguan Brick Pagoda], in *Women de liuyue* [*Our June*], ed. Zhu Ziqing (Shanghai: Shanghai shehui kexue chubanshe, [1925] 1994). For more on the iconography of the Thunder Peak Pagoda in Chinese art and intellectual history, see Eugene Wang, "Tope and Topos"; and Wu Xueshan, "Leifeng xizhao."

2. Yu Pingbo, "Ji Xihu Leifengta faxian de tazhuan yu cangjing" [On the bricks and scriptures found at Thunder Peak Pagoda], *Xiaoshuo yuebao* 16, no. 1 (1925): 147–56; and Yu Pingbo, *Za ban'er* [*Miscellany*] (Shanghai: Kaiming shudian, 1928), 63.

3. See Yu Pingbo, *Za ban'er*, 64 (see chap. 3, n. 2).

4. Founded in 1904, *Dongfang zazhi* had become the most widely circulated magazine in China in the 1910s and continued to thrive in the 1920s; it even survived the warlord period and war with Japan and lasted until 1948. It is comparable to the

influential newspaper *Shenbao*, whose advertisements and reports were examined in chapter 2.

5. Chunfeng, "Jiehou Leifengta ji" [A record of Thunder Peak Pagoda after its catastrophic fall], *Dongfang zazhi* 21, no. 18 (September 1924): 48.

6. Though *Shibao* was cited as the source of the September 25, 1924, piece by Chunfeng in *Dongfang zazhi*, this was probably an error, as no article concerning the fall of the Thunder Peak Pagoda appeared in *Shibao* on that date.

7. Sun Jinglu, "Leifengta dejing ji" [On retrieving scriptures from Thunder Peak Pagoda], in *Dongfang zazhi* 21, no. 18 (September 25, 1924): 120. Here the relevant Chinese text "jin youde sijing sanjuan" (now I again received another three volumes of the same sutra) does not specify whether he retrieved them from the collapsed Thunder Peak Pagoda or received them from somewhere else, after the collapse.

8. Contemporary reports in *Shenbao* demonstrate the public's general fascination with scriptures, bricks, and the Thunder Peak Pagoda itself. Guansheng Yuan, a newly established food company, promoted its products by handing out scriptures collected from the wreckage and sets of "before and after" photos of the pagoda. One article reported that, for the preceding three days, the company had handed out about one thousand scripture fragments and photo sets each day. See *Shenbao* (Shanghai local supplement), December 23, 1924, 1.

9. Yu Pingbo, "Yu Pingbo zhi Gu Jiegang han" [Yu Pingbo's letter to Gu Jiegang], *Beijing daxue rikan*, October 30, 1924, 2.

10. For more on the Buddhist influence on modern Chinese literature, see, for example, Tan, "Minguo Fojiao wenxue dui xiandai Zhongguo wenxueshi chonggou de yiyi"; and Tan, "Qingmo Minchu Zhongguo de Fojiao wenxue yu qimeng sichao."

11. Huaiyu Chen, "Honoring the Dead," 102.

12. Huaiyu Chen, "Honoring the Dead," 104–5.

13. Yu published these two pieces following the death of his uncle and father-in-law and his own relocation from Hangzhou to Beijing. In addition to the two pieces cited above, Yu also wrote and published the following: "A Brief Study of the Thunder Peak Pagoda" [Leifengta kaolüe], January 30, 1928, Beijing, originally published in Yu Pingbo, *Za ban'er* (see chap. 3, n. 2), included in Wang Guoping, *Xihu wenxian jicheng*, 570–76; and "Xiguan zhuanta cang Baoqieyintuoluonijing ge," February 5, 1928, Beijing, included in Yu Pingbo, *Yanzhi cao* (Beijing: Zhongguo wenlian chuban gongsi, [1930] 1998), 31–32.

14. Some of these accounts were framed humorously. One particular telegraph-style short report recounts Sun Chuanfang's inviting a Buddhist lama to Hangzhou in order to suppress the likely ascension of the White Snake. See *Xinwen bao*, March 25, 1924, 5.

15. *Tuhua zhoukan* took the alternative name of *Tuhua shibao* on February 17, 1924, and briefly ceased printing after the Japanese invasion of Manchuria on September 18, 1931; it then resumed printing until 1937, right before the outbreak of the Second Sino-Japanese War. More than a thousand total issues were published. See Liu Min,

"Ge Gongzhen yu baozhi 'Tuhua zhoukan' yanjiu," 15–16; for more on *Shibao*, see Judge, *"Shibao" and the Culture of Reform in Late Qing China.*

16. See *Shibao tuhua zhoukan*, no. 220, October 5, 1924.

17. See Wu Xueshan, "Leifeng xizhao," 76.

18. This ideal "lyrical beauty" has much to do with the geographical location of West Lake and its association with the cities of Hangzhou, Suzhou, and Zhenjiang to the north along the Grand Canal, and Mount Emei and the city of Chengdu to the west along the Yangtze River. More importantly, it is imbued with cultural and symbolic meanings in relation to the legend of the White Snake, as these specific locales are endowed with particular significance as important locations for the development and spread of the legend throughout the last few centuries.

19. See *Tu C. Y. sheyingji.*

20. *Tu C. Y. sheyingji*, 13, 76. For more on the histories and poetics of photography in early twentieth-century China, see Shengqing Wu, *Photo Poetics*; *Lüxing de tuxiang yu wenben*, chap. 4.

21. See Quzhai (Yu Pingbo), "Xiguan zhuanta tazhuan ge," 244 (see chap. 3, n. 1); and Ningboshi dang'anguan, "Pan Guogang diyong qingxing," 2445.

22. This type of serial illustration came to be recognized as comic strips in the first decade of the twentieth century. See Chen Zhiming, *Zhongguo lianhuanhua shi kaolüe*, 79.

23. Yimei, "Hu Yaguang xiansheng xiaozhuan" [A brief biography of Mr. Hu Yaguang], *Mei*, no. 7 (1947): 2; Xu Guowei, *Chumo lishi*, 564–65; and Huang Ke, *Manhua Haipai manhua*, 11.

24. Liu Dabai, "Leifengta daohou" [After the collapse of Thunder Peak Pagoda], *Fudan* 1, no. 2 (1925): 125–34.

25. Ding Huikang, "Youhang riji" [Hangzhou travel diary], *Tongji zazhi*, no. 19 (1923): 9.

26. Such as in "Evening Illuminations over Thunder Peak," one of the famous "Ten Great Views of the West Lake."

27. See Cloud, *Hangchow*, after 40, unpaginated.

28. See Le, *Buddhist Architecture*, 183.

29. See "Leifeng yiying," *Banyue* 4, no. 3 (1925): 1; and "Leifeng boying," *Nanfang huabao*, no. 9 (1925): unpaginated.

30. Liu Gonglu, "Leifeng jiujing" [An old view of Thunder Peak Pagoda], *Taipingyang huabao* 1, no. 1 (1926): 32.

31. Zheng Yimei, "Ji Liu Gonglu xiansheng ruogan shi" [On various deeds of Mr. Liu Gonglu], *Yong'an yuekan* 113 (1948): 17–18.

32. See "Chen Baoyi *Leifeng xizhao* youhua" [Chen Baoyi's oil painting *Evening Illuminations over Thunder Peak*," *Sanjiao zhiguang* [*Light of the triangle*] 2, no. 7 (1926): 2.

33. Using the name of Shu Sheyu, Lao She published a piece in the "Free Talk" column of *Shenbao*, criticizing the use of modern signage to mark time on *jingju* stage; this is discussed in chapter 2.

34. Sheyu, "Leifengta paizhao ji" [On photographing the Thunder Peak Pagoda], *Taipingyang huabao* 1, no. 1 (1926): 4.

35. Lu Yin, "Leifengta xia" [Under the Thunder Peak Pagoda], *Gucheng zhoukan* 1, no. 1 (1927): 1–3.

36. "Benkan tougao jianzhang" [Brief submission guidelines for our journal], *Foshan jingwu yuekan* 3 (1925): 56.

37. Yu Shaochang, "Leifeng xizhao" [Evening illuminations over Thunder Peak], *Foshan jingwu yuekan* 2, no. 3 (1927): 11.

38. See Gao Jianfu, "Leifeng wanzhao" [Evening illuminations over Thunder Peak], *Dongfang zazhi* 23, no. 7 (April 1926): unpaginated.

39. See, for example, "Leifeng wanzhao," *Liangyou*, no. 22 (December 30, 1927): frontispiece; and "Leifeng wanzhao," *Yifeng* [*Artistic wind*] 1, no. 5 (1933): unpaginated. For more on the links between photography, calligraphy, and painting in Republican China, see Shengqing Wu, *Photo Poetics*.

40. Xu Beihong, "Tan Gao Jianfu xiansheng hua" [On Mr. Gao Jianfu's painting], *Yifeng* 3, no. 7 (1935): 95. Xu Beihong refers to Lin Liang as the founder of the Canton school of painting and compares the richness of Cantonese language to the Canton school, which was said to have influenced Mizoguchi Kenji's filmmaking, especially his signature monochrome films, discussed in detail in chapter 4.

41. Wang Jingwei later emerged as the leader of the collaborationist government with Japan during World War II. For more on Wang Jingwei and the relationship between poetry, painting, and politics during his time, see Zhiyi Yang, "The Road to Lyric Martyrdom"; and Zhiyi Yang, "A Humanist in France."

42. Xu, "Tan Gao Jianfu xiansheng hua," 95 (see chap. 3, n. 40). For more on Gao Jianfu in particular and the rise of national-style painting in modern China in general, see Aida Yuen Wong, "Gao Jianfu shuhua de canpomei yu beixue de guanxi"; and Aida Yuen Wong, *Parting the Mists*.

43. Xu Zhimo, "Xihu ji" [West Lake travel diary], in *Aimei xiaozha: Zhimo riji, shuxin ji* (Beijing: Zhongyang bianyi chubanshe, [1923] 2013), 92–93. Translation is my own.

44. Xu Zhimo, "Yuexia Leifeng yingpian" [The shadow of the moon-lit Thunder Peak Pagoda], in *Zhimo de shi* (Harbin: Beifang wenyi chubanshe, [1923] 2014), 113. Translation is my own.

45. The composer Tianhe is unmistakably Chen Tianhe, as Chen's name is listed in full, together with He Lüting's, as one of the contributors to the *Music Education* journal, which published both compositions. See "Zhuangao zhe" [Contributors], *Yinyue jiaoyu* 2, no. 2 (1934): 8. For more on Chen's important contribution in composing art songs (*yishu gequ*) from the 1930s to the 1940s, see Ju, "Lun Chen Tianhe ershi shiji sanshi zhi sishi niandai de yishu gequ chuangzuo."

46. See published sheet music for "Shadow of the Thunder Peak Pagoda" [Leifeng taying], poem by Xu Zhimo, composed by Hu Lüting, in *Yinyue jiaoyu* 3, no. 1 (1935): 26–27.

47. See Luo, *The Avant-Garde and the Popular*, 159.

48. For a new composition and new rendition of Xu's "Yuexia Leifeng yingpian" from Taiwan in the 1980s, see a recording of the song composed by Cheng Hua Jiuan

(Zheng Huajuan 鄭華娟) and performed by Samson Shih (Shi Xiaorong 施孝榮), accessed June 22, 2020, https://youtu.be/sDo0kwsw0l4

49. *Red Roses* was a popular magazine famous for its serialization of *Legend of Fantastic Knights of the Martial Arts World* (*Jianghu qixiazhuan*), which was later adapted as the extremely popular *Burning of the Red Lotus Temple* (*Huoshao hongliansi*) film series. See Yingchuan qiushui, "Bai Niangniang fandui chongjian Leifengta lun" [On how Madame White would be against rebuilding Thunder Peak Pagoda], *Hong meigui* 1, no. 22 (Dec. 27, 1924): 1–2; for a recent study on the author of *Jianghu qixiazhuan*, see Hamm, *The Unworthy Scholar from Pingjiang*.

50. The Thunder Peak Pagoda was eventually rebuilt anyway, albeit only in 2002.

51. This is a rather Westernized, modern conception later analyzed in art historian Wu Hung's 2012 study on the presence and absence of ruins in Chinese art and visual culture. See Wu Hung, *A Story of Ruins*.

52. Yingchuan qiushui, "Bai Niangniang fandui chongjian Leifengta lun" (see chap. 3, n. 49).

53. Lu Xun, "Lun Leifengta de daodiao," 3–4 (see chap. 2, n. 158).

54. I agree with Aaron Balivet's interpretation that the link made by Lu Xun (and his contemporaries) between the fall of the pagoda with the rise of the White Snake was related to the relative popularity of excerpt scenes over complete versions of the White Snake story. This explains why even though many versions of the story in fact ended with the White Snake's release, the general public still closely associated the liberation of the White Snake with the pagoda's fall. See Balivet, "The Many Transformations of White Snake," 3.

55. Lu Xun, "Lun Leifengta de daodiao," 3 (see chap. 2, n. 158).

56. Lu Xun, "Lun Leifengta de daodiao," 4 (see chap. 2, n. 158).

57. For more on the Shaw Brothers, see Poshek Fu, *China Forever*.

58. See "Synopsis," 1–8.

59. Due to the archaic nature of the romanizations in the original text, pinyin transcriptions are provided to identify the proper nouns in the story.

60. "Synopsis," 3–4.

61. In the 1806 version attributed to Yushan zhuren, there is an important hint of Green Snake's likely "sharing" in the sexual indulgences (*fenrun chunguang*) of the newly wedded couple. This anticipates the rise of the sexually aggressive Green Snake in later renditions. See Yushan zhuren, *Leifengta qizhuan*, 16.

62. "Synopsis," 5.

63. "Synopsis," 5.

64. "Synopsis," 5–6.

65. "Synopsis," 1.

66. "Synopsis," 8.

67. See "Lingering Shadow of the Thunder Peak Pagoda," in *Tianyi tekan diliuqi Yiyao Baishe zhuan*, July 1, 1926, unpaginated; and "Pe Su-cheng of The Righteous Snake," in *Tianyi tekan diliuqi Yiyao Baishe zhuan*.

68. "Zimu" [Intertitles], in *Tianyi tekan diliuqi Yiyao Baishe zhuan*, 24 (see chap. 3, n. 67).

69. "Ben gongsi chupin yilan" [A full list of film productions from our company], in *Tianyi tekan diliuqi Yiyao Baishe zhuan* (see chap. 3, n. 67).

70. Hong Hong Shui, "Baishe Zhuan shiying ji" [On test screening *The Righteous Snake*], in *Tianyi tekan diliuqi Yiyao Baishe zhuan*," 1 (see chap. 3, n. 67).

71. See Li Han-hsiang, *The Love Eterne* [sic]. For a recent study of the Butterfly Lovers story in China and Korea, see Cho, *Transforming Gender and Emotion*.

72. See "Fuchang wudie pai xiangyan changxiao" [Fuchang Five Butterfly Brand cigarette in great demand], *Shenbao*, April 11, 1926, 20. Zhou died in 1922, so it is rather unlikely that he was the painter of the White Snake cards, which were based specifically on the 1926 films featuring the actress Hu Die and used as promotional tools for both *The Righteous Snake* film and the Five Butterfly Brand cigarettes. For more on calendar posters and visual culture in Shanghai at the time, see Laing, *Selling Happiness*.

73. "Wudie pai" [Five Butterfly Brand], in *Shenbao*, July 13, 1926, 13.

74. For more on Huang Chujiu and his innovative promotional strategies, see Li Chunmei, "Huang Chujiu de pinpai yingxiao zhidao," 62–63.

75. See Huang Xiaoyin, "Xinqi de *Baishe zhuan* yanhuapian."

76. See Liang Luo, "Baishe de nüti yu tongti" [The female body and the child body of the White Snake], in *Wenxue yu wenhua* 2 (2017), 63–69.

77. Images accessed June 9, 2018, https://tieba.baidu.com/p/4338420505; when accessed again on June 11, 2020, only the four images of the four protagonists were on the same site.

78. See Zhu Ping, "'Shizhuang guxi' yu Zhongguo dianying de diyici shangye langchao" ['Ancient stories dressed in contemporary costumes' and the first commercial wave of Chinese cinema], *Dangdai dianying* 8 (2017): 146.

79. It is also possible that the shooting of *The Righteous Snake* was already underway when the company was confronted with criticisms of the use of modern costumes in *The Butterfly Lovers*. The more important point is that Unique Film and other companies did see market success in spite of such criticisms.

80. See Zhu, "'Shizhuang guxi,'" 147.

81. See Bu, *Hubian chunmeng*; and Luo, *The Avant-Garde and the Popular*, 89–91.

82. See Luo, *The Avant-Garde and the Popular*, 89–91.

83. See Anonymous folklorists, *Leifengta; Bai niangniang*, 43.

84. For more information, see Suryadinata, *Prominent Indonesian Chinese*.

85. See "Guoyun xinglong zai Leifengta" [The prosperity of the nation depends on Thunder Peak Pagoda], *Chahua*, no. 29 (1948): 13.

86. See "Tianxia xingwang Leifengta youze" [Thunder Peak Pagoda is responsible for the fate of the nation], *Shibao* 60 (1948): 6.

87. When Thunder Peak Pagoda was finally rebuilt many decades later, in 2002, it was designated "a major historical and cultural site protected at the national level" (*quanguo zhongdian wenwu baohu danwei*) by China's National Administration of Cultural Heritage in 2013.

Chapter 4

1. Ueda, *Ugetsu monogatari.*

2. Tanizaki, *Jasei no in.*

3. Tian Han, "Nü yu she"; and Kawata, "Hakujaden ni miru gendai no taidō."

4. See Tian Han, *Jinbo ji*; Tian Han, "Baishe zhuan."

5. See Luo, "The Experimental and the Popular in Chinese Socialist Theater of the 1950s"; and Luo, *The Avant-Garde and the Popular*, chap. 5.

6. See Dower, *Embracing Defeat.*

7. See Le Fanu, "Mizoguchi, the Great Triptych," 300.

8. For a high-quality, fully accessible version of the original Japanese text of the two tales from Ueda's collection, see Ueda, *Ugetsu Monogatari*, vols. 1, 3, Waseda University Library: http://www.wul.waseda.ac.jp/kotenseki/html/he13/he13_04376/index.html

9. See Luo, *The Avant-Garde and the Popular*, 207–12.

10. See Feng, "Bai niangzi yongzhen Leifengta"; and Feng, *Stories to Caution the World*, chap. 28.

11. See Ueda, *Tales of Moonlight and Rain.* Edited and translated by Anthony H. Chambers, 157–58.

12. See Roddy, "In Praise of Jeweled Streams," 16. The association of water with the feminine principle has far-ranging resonance in various world cultures, including in Celtic mythology.

13. See Luo, "The White Snake in Hong Kong Horror Cinema," 36–37. Although in Mizoguchi's film, the wife welcomes the husband home even after she turns into a ghost (as in "The House in the Thicket"), which compliments the femme fatale image of female ghost (as in "The Lust of the Serpent").

14. *Rashomon* is Kurosawa Akira's 1950 film, which won Japan its first major international film prize, the Golden Lion, at the 1951 Venice International Film Festival.

15. See Mizoguchi, *Ugetsu*, opening intertitles. Often praised as one of Mizoguchi's three best productions, *Ugetsu* brought its director the Silver Lion award at the 1953 Venice Film Festival (no Golden Lion awarded that year). *The Life of Oharu* (1952) won the International Award and *Sansho the Bailiff* (1954) garnered the Silver Lion at the same festival. See Le Fanu, "Mizoguchi, the Great Triptych," 289.

16. See interview of Miyagawa in Shindō, *Aru eiga-kantoku no shōgai*, 1:44:00–1:45:00.

17. As quoted in Miyao, *The Aesthetics of Shadow*, 257.

18. See Aida Yuen Wong, *Parting the Mists.*

19. See Aida Yuen Wong, "Gao Jianfu shuhua de canpomei yu beixue de guanxi."

20. See Gordon, *Postwar Japan as History*, "Conclusion," 449.

21. See Miyao, *The Aesthetics of Shadow*, 267–68.

22. Miyao, *The Aesthetics of Shadow*, 267.

23. The first color film in Japan, *Carmen Goes Home* (*Karumen kokyo ni kaeru*), was made at Shōchiku by Kinoshita Keisuke in 1951.

24. The other color film was *Princess Yang Kwei-fei* (*Yōkihi*), also in 1955, an adap-

tation of a Chinese story and Mizoguchi's first collaboration with a major Hong Kong studio.

25. See Tanizaki, "Jasei no in"; and Chiba, *Eiga to Tanizaki.* As discussed at the beginning of this chapter, Tian Han introduced Tanizaki's film scenario *The Lust of the Serpent* to his friend Migishi in 1926 as an experimental cinematic rendition of the Ueda story in *Tales of Moonlight and Rain.* Film techniques such as the "close-up" shot entered Tanizaki's film scenario to dramatize the psychological world of its female protagonist, Manago. The film gave full expression to the serpent's titular "lust," as shown in the movements and facial expressions of the human wife whom it had possessed.

26. See Tanizaki, "In'ei raisan," esp. 73, 84–87, 93–97. For an English translation of Tanizaki's essay by Thomas Harper and Edward Seidensticker, see Tanizaki, *In Praise of Shadows.*

27. See Miyao, *The Aesthetics of Shadow*, 1–2.

28. Both Thomas Kurihara, director of *Jasei no in*, and Tanizaki were inspired by *The Cabinet of Dr. Caligari*, which opened in Tokyo in 1921. See Luo, *The Avant-Garde and the Popular*, 49–51.

29. See Miyao, *The Aesthetics of Shadow*, 258.

30. Miyao, *The Aesthetics of Shadow*, 280–81.

31. See Sang and Huang, *Liang Shanbo yu Zhu Yingtai.*

32. See Lanjun Xu, "The Lure of Sadness."

33. See Jacoby, "Mizoguchi Kenji."

34. Yoko Ima-Izumi calls Lady Wakasa "a well-developed femme fatale figure" that emerged under a new wave of Americanization. See Ima-Izumi, "A Land Where Femmes Fatales Fear to Tread," 131.

35. Some consider the two couples related by blood, treating Ohama as Genjūrō's younger sister. I am more inclined to read their relationship as a "fictive kinship," as they appear to me more like close neighbors and good friends.

36. See Sterckx, *The Animal and the Daemon*, 209.

37. In her notes to the Criterion Collection, Keiko McDonald points out that this scene, with Mizoguchi's deft, suggestive touches, is in a way "reminiscent of the supernatural moods created by Japanese *suiboku-ga*," also known as *sumi-e*, linking Chinese ink painting, developed during the Song dynasty, to the Japanese monochrome ink painting taken back to Japan by Zen Buddhist monks from China in the mid-fourteenth century. See Keiko McDonald, "Ugetsu," December 29, 1993, https://www.criterion.com/current/posts/966-ugetsu; and "Suiboku-ga," *Encyclopaedia Britannica*, February 16, 2011, https://www.britannica.com/art/suiboku-ga

38. See Le Fanu, "Mizoguchi, the Great Triptych," 301.

39. See Le Fanu, "Mizoguchi, the Great Triptych," 303.

40. See Chris Chang, "Ghost Tones," 16.

41. See Ima-Izumi, "A Land Where Femmes Fatales Fear to Tread," 131.

42. See Le Fanu, "Mizoguchi, the Great Triptych," 299–300.

43. See Mak, *Xianggang dianying yu xinjiapo*, 84; and Sangjoon Lee, "The Transnational Asian Studio System," 113–14.

44. See Anderson and Richie, *The Japanese Film*, 248–49.

45. See Toyoda, *Byaku fujin no yōren.*

46. See Hayashi, *Byaku fujin no yōjutsu.*

47. For more on the Takarazuka Revue as a historical and anthropological phenomenon in modern Japan, see Robertson, *Takarazuka*; and Yamanashi, *A History of the Takarazuka Revue Since 1914.*

48. See Katsuyama, "Kindai Nihon ni okeru Chūgoku hakuwa shōsetsu shū."

49. See Hayashi, Karashima, and Yasumi, *Byaku fujin no yōren.*

50. See Karashima, *Chūgoku no shingeki*, 4–5.

51. See Yau, *Japanese and Hong Kong Film Industries.*

52. See Henry D. Smith, *Japan's First Student Radicals.*

53. See Freeman, *Tokyo in Transit*; and Luo, *The Avant-Garde and the Popular.*

54. See Freeman, *Tokyo in Transit*, 152–53; and Long, "The Japanese Literati and the 'China Incident,'" 29.

55. See Long, "The Japanese Literati and the 'China Incident.'"

56. See Harootunian, *Overcome by Modernity*; and Calichman, *Overcoming Modernity.*

57. See Calichman, *Overcoming Modernity*, 92–110.

58. See Yau, *Honkon, Nihon eiga kōryūshi*, 185.

59. Quoted in Liu Yunchao, "Nihon eiga ni okeru Chūgoku koten."

60. As mentioned in chapter 1, *qing*, which appears in the Chinese name for the White Snake's companion Qingshe, may be translated both as "green" and "blue" (and rarely also as "black"). In this 1956 Japanese film rendition, she is shown dressed in both green and blue.

61. See a description of the creator deities in de Bary, *Sources of Japanese Tradition*, 13–20.

62. Luo, *The Avant-Garde and the Popular*, 90–92, 191–93.

63. Quoted in Liu Yunchao, "Nihon eiga ni okeru Chūgoku koten," 134.

64. For more on state feminism in Communist China, see Wang Zheng, "'State Feminism'?"; and Wang Zheng, *Finding Women in the State.*

65. Quoted in Liu Yunchao, "Nihon eiga ni okeru Chūgoku koten," 136. However, given the heavy censorship of Chinese movies and plays during the 1950s, which deprived Chinese audiences of choice, such reasoning may not reflect the historical realities of the time.

66. For a discussion of the pearl (and the moon) as cosmic expressions of the female principle, see Schaffer, *The Divine Woman*, 7–8, 21.

67. Similar to earlier versions, Xu was arrested because the silver given to him by White Snake had been stolen.

68. Tsui Hark's *Green Snake* is another example.

69. See Ragone, *Eiji Tsuburaya, Master of Monsters*, 50.

70. See Al Taylor, "The Man Who Made Godzilla Famous," 19.

71. Also see figure 8 in this book.

72. See Ragone, *Eiji Tsuburaya, Master of Monsters.*

73. See Tanaka, *Tōhō tokusatsu eiga zenshi.*

74. See Lin Qinghua, "Huangmeixi dianying zai Xianggang ji Taiwan de fazhan," 74–82.

75. "Japanese Film Success, Most Effective Use of Its Color, Berlin Festival," *South China Morning Post*, June 26, 1956.

76. This color poster can be found on China's most popular movie review website, Douban dianying, together with close to a dozen other posters for the 1956 *Madame White Snake*, accessed June 13, 2020, https://movie.douban.com/subject/1302094/photos?type=R. It is labeled a "preview poster for Hong Kong," but additional printed information on the right side of the poster identifies this particular poster as for the Lido-Ipoh premiere in Malaysia on March 21, 1957. For a brief discussion of how Shaw Brothers' benefited technically from the coproduction with Tōhō on *Madame White Snake*, see Wang Gang, "Qianxi zaoqi Riben Dongbao yu Xianggang Shaoshi hezuo dianying *Baishe zhuan* de meishu sheji" [A preliminary discussion of the art design of early Japanese Tōhō and Hong Kong Shaw Brothers coproduction *Madame White Snake*], *Yishu keji*, September 15, 2016, 129. For a detailed textual and visual archive of the history of Shaw Brothers from 1920s Shanghai to 2018 Singapore, including images for Shaw Brothers' theaters in postwar Malaysia, see the Shaw Theatre's website, accessed June 13, 2020, https://www.shaw.sg/About/aboutshaw.html

77. See the Douban website, accessed June 13, 2020, https://movie.douban.com/subject/1302094/photos?type=R

78. This color poster, labeled "Official Poster for Thailand," can also be located on Douban dianying, accessed June 13, 2020, https://movie.douban.com/subject/1302094/photos?type=R

79. See Yabushita, *Hakujaden.*

80. See Ruh, "Early Japanese Animation in the United States," 215; and Phil Hall, "The Bootleg Files: *Hakujaden*," *Film Threat*, last updated November 5, 2004, http://filmthreat.com/uncategorized/the-bootleg-files-hakujaden/

81. See also, Hu, "The Animated Resurrection," 43–61.

82. Napier, *Anime from Akira to Howl's Moving Castle*, 152, quoted in Condry, *The Soul of Anime*, 148.

83. I thank Jinying Li for her help framing the issue here. See also, Sangjoon Lee, "The Transnational Asian Studio System."

84. See Lamarre, *The Anime Machine*, 66–68.

85. Lamarre, *The Anime Machine*, 67–68.

86. See Daisy Yan Du, *Animated Encounters*, 62–63.

87. Daisy Yan Du, *Animated Encounters*, 183. Like generations of Chinese children born in the 1970s and after, I grew up watching and loving *Tetsuwan Atomu (Iron-armed Atom; Tiebi Atongmu* 鐵臂阿童木), after it was translated into Chinese and

imported by Chinese Central Television (CCTV) in the early 1980s for the mainland Chinese market.

88. See Roquet, "A Blue Cat on the Galactic Railroad," 126.

89. Roquet, "A Blue Cat on the Galactic Railroad," 126.

90. Bai-Niang's self-sacrifice for love brings to mind the sacrifice of the Little Mermaid in her pursuit of human love. For a recent study of the transformation of "The Little Mermaid" tale in Japanese and English, see Fraser, *The Pleasures of Metamorphosis.*

91. See Roquet, "A Blue Cat on the Galactic Railroad," 146.

92. See Condry, *The Soul of Anime*, 89.

93. Condry, *The Soul of Anime*, 89.

94. See Daisy Yan Du, *Animated Encounters*, 55–58.

95. As Daisy Yan Du argues in her book, Mochinaga Tadahito's approach to making puppet animation in the 1950s represented an alternative tradition to cel or two-dimensional animation, represented by Tōei Animation, Tezuka Osamu, and later Miyazaki Hayao. See Daisy Yan Du, *Animated Encounters*, 105.

96. Dubbed the "Chinese Romeo and Juliet," *The Butterfly Lovers* triumphed at the 1954 Geneva Conference. The film also won best picture in the musical category at the Eighth International Film Festival at Czechoslovakia in 1955 and traveled to Paris, Hong Kong, and Southeast Asia. For more on the film's international impact, see Lanjun Xu, "The Lure of Sadness"; and Cho, *Transforming Gender and Emotion.* For a study of another widely influential legend and its adaptation history, see Idema, *The Metamorphosis of Tianxian pei.*

97. See Hans Christian Anderson, *Den lille Havfrue*, H. C. Anderson Centret, accessed June 20, 2020, https://andersen.sdu.dk/vaerk/havfrue/; Jean Hersholt, trans., *The Little Mermaid*, https://andersen.sdu.dk/vaerk/hersholt/TheLittleMermaid_e.html; and Fraser, *The Pleasures of Metamorphosis.* For more on the power of the mermaid to positively inspire women in contemporary Asian societies, see Jonathan DeHart, "Mermaids of Asia: Dugongs, Dragon Wives and the Deep," *The Diplomat*, September 19, 2013, https://thediplomat.com/2013/09/mermaids-of-asia-dugongs-dragon-wives-and-the-deep/

98. The *erhu* serves as an instrument of enchantment controlled by the White Snake in the animation.

Chapter 5

1. Salome's suggestive "Dance of the Seven Veils" became the ultimate embodiment of an emerging modern female sexuality in the early decades of twentieth century. See Luo, *The Avant-Garde and the Popular*, 99.

2. For more on Nanguo she, see Lo, "Yishu de shehuizhuyi."

3. See Suzuki, *Sanghae ui Chosŏn-in yŏnghwa hwangje*; and Pak, *Xunzhao wode waigong.*

4. See Berry, "Sino-Korea Screen Connections."

5. See Hye Seung Chung, “The Korean Valentino.”

6. See Luo, *The Avant-Garde and the Popular*, 38–43.

7. Luo, *The Avant-Garde and the Popular*, 28.

8. See Poshek Fu, *Between Shanghai and Hong Kong*.

9. See Shin, *Paeksa buin;* and Shin, *Sanyŏ*. For more on Shin's life as a leading filmmaker in South Korea, North Korea, and Hollywood, see Lee Sŏngsu, *Han'guk yŏnghwa ŭi p'unguna*; and Korean Film Archive, “A Life More Movie-Like than a Movie: Film Director Shin Sang-ok, 1926–2006,” accessed July 24, 2018, https://artsandculture.google.com/exhibit/wQyurtEV

10. *Romantic Papa*, Shin's 1960 box office hit, drew one hundred thousand patrons as recorded by the Korean Film Archive. See Sangjoon Lee, “The Transnational Asian Studio System,” 245; and Shin, *Romaensŭ ppappa*.

11. See Shin, *Sanyŏ*. My thanks to Goeun Lee for informing the KMDB of this mistake on my behalf. The translation of the film title has now changed from “Dead Woman” to “Snake Woman,” accessed January 6, 2021, https://www.kmdb.or.kr/db/kor/detail/movie/K/01842

12. See Shin, *Naeshi*.

13. See Shin, *Ijo yŏin chanhoksa*.

14. The number is 21,179, which is suspiciously small and may speak to the limited release of a Korean-dubbed version in Korea, as the film is listed as a domestically made Korean-language film in the database.

15. See Choi and Lee, *Paeksajŏn*; and Sangjoon Lee, “The Transnational Asian Studio System,” 267–70.

16. See Korean Film Archive, “A Life More Movie-Like than a Movie” (see chap. 5, n. 9).

17. See Steven Chung, *Split Screen Korea*, 110. This mistranslation has been corrected in the KMDB record (see chap. 5, no. 11).

18. Shaw Brothers' new Clearwater Studio was completed and began to operate in full swing in 1961.

19. See Sangjoon Lee, “The Transnational Asian Studio System,” 245.

20. See Sangjoon Lee, *Cinema and the Cultural Cold War*, 140–45; Korean Film Archive, “A Life More Movie-Like than a Movie” (see chap. 5, n. 9); and Shin Sang-ok filmography in Steven Chung, *Split Screen Korea*, appendix.

21. See Sangjoon Lee, *Cinema and the Cultural Cold War*, 148–49.

22. See Korean Film Archive, “A Life More Movie-Like than a Movie” (see chap. 5, n. 9).

23. Korean Film Archive, “A Life More Movie-like than a Movie” (see chap. 5, n. 9).

24. It is generally believed that Ch'oe Ŭn-hŭi was kidnapped. However, it is still an open question whether Shin Sang-ok was kidnapped or went to the North voluntarily.

25. Quoted in Schonherr, *North Korean Cinema*, 75; also see Kim, *Illusive Utopia*, 19–20. For more on Shin Sang-ok and Ch'oe Ŭn-hŭi in North Korea, see Sebo, “A Study on the Impact of Shin Sang-ok.”

26. The pharmacist theme emerges as an important one throughout the White Snake legends over time. This pattern brings to mind Derrida's work on pharmakon, a connection made explicit in the 2017 Wild Rice (Singapore) recreation of the White Snake legend. See Derrida, "Plato's Pharmacy"; and Oei, *Wild@Home—Mama White Snake.*

27. See Shin, *Paeksa buin*; the synopsis has been edited.

28. The Japanese have celebrated the Tanabata Festival on July 7 since the Meiji Restoration. In China, the seventh day of the seventh month in the lunar calendar is considered to be a day for lovers, restyled in contemporary popular culture as the Chinese Valentine's Day.

29. When Shin made the film, Chinese characters were still widely used in Korean society; later, a new tide of nationalism promoted the sole use of *hangul* to maintain a distinctive Korean cultural identity. For more on the evolving history of and debate over the use of Chinese characters in the Korean language, see Insup Taylor and M. Martin Taylor, *Writing and Literacy in Chinese, Korean, and Japanese*, 203–10.

30. In *Ugetsu,* however, Lady Wakasa does hold Genjūrō's hand and leads him to sit down, some 43 minutes into the film. See Mizoguchi, *Ugetsu.*

31. See Tian, *Jinbo ji*; and Tian, *Baishe zhuan.*

32. See "Japanese Film Success, Most Effective Use of Its Color, Berlin Festival" (see chap. 4, n. 75); and Ching, *Baishe chuanshuo.*

33. As discussed in chapter 2, such devices as artificial rainfall onstage had been used as a promotional strategy for the Shanghai performances of the White Snake legend.

34. See "Kang Sŏng-pŏm," Korean Movie Database, accessed July 26, 2018, http://www.kmdb.or.kr/db/per/00004850

35. Yi was later known for setting a record for broadcasting an anti-Communist radio drama up to 5,500 times beginning in 1964. See "Yi Sang-man," Korean Movie Database, accessed July 26, 2018, http://www.kmdb.or.kr/db/per/00004712

36. See "Chŏn Tae-chun," in Korean Movie Database, accessed July 26, 2018, http://www.kmdb.or.kr/db/per/00004851

37. The discovery of the 1962 film *Chastity Gate* (*Yeolnyeo mun*) preserved in Taipei Archives served as an illustration of Shin Films' reach in the region. See Berry, "Sino-Korea Screen Connections."

38. These collaborations bear traces of Mizoguchi's pioneering collaboration with Hong Kong in the 1954 *Princess Yang Kwei-fei* and the coproduction efforts between Japan's Tōhō film company and Shaw Brothers in Hong Kong, resulting in the 1956 live action *Madame White Snake.* Both films feature enchanting seductresses.

39. See Shin Sang-ok's filmography in Steven Chung, *Split Screen Korea*, appendix. According to Sangjoon Lee, although Shin advertised this film as a coproduction, it is actually not a coproduction with Shaw but one of those "counterfeit coproductions."

40. The Demon King in Shin's film may have been devised with the King of Hell in mind. The King of Hell originated from the Indian god Yamarāja, or Yama (also

known as God of Death). The image of Yama was introduced through Buddhism to China, where it metamorphosed, under the influence of Chinese folk belief in ghosts and deities and Chinese political and bureaucratic systems. Representations of the King of Hell have been found from Chosŏn Korea (1392–1910), among many other time periods and locations throughout East and Southeast Asia. For a representation from seventeenth-century Korea, see the painting *King of Hell* in the Philadelphia Museum of Art Collection, PMA_.1970-259-3.

41. There are, in fact, many precedents linking the figure of the White Snake with that of the Buddhist Goddess of Mercy, known in Chinese as Guanyin and in Japanese as Kannon. In American missionary Samuel I. Woodbridge's English-language retelling of the White Snake legend, the White Snake impersonates Guanyin; Woodbridge likely borrowed this plot point from his sources, including previous Chinese versions of the legend, such as the 1806 version attributed to Yushan zhuren. The Goddess of Mercy has also been depicted as Virgin Mary in some cases because of their similar iconographies. More interestingly, White Snake's power to control water and the Goddess of Mercy's ability to heal with the pure water in her vase bring to mind Mazu, the Goddess of the Sea, and some even have come to believe Mazu as a manifestation of the Goddess of Mercy. For an intriguing case study in the Philippines, see Dy, "The Virgin Mary as Mazu or Guanyin."

42. There are echoes of the story of Pygmalion, who fell in love with a statue he had carved, a tale best known from Ovid's narrative poem *Metamorphoses*. *Snake Woman* is also reminiscent of Gerhart Hauptmann's *The Sunken Bell*, in which a bell maker seeks to make a perfect-sounding bell, and of Oscar Wilde's *The Picture of Dorian Gray*, in which there is an enigmatic and deadly transference between the figure in the painting and the real person. The relationship between the sculptor and his model and the importance of the craftsman's hands also bring to mind Mira Nair's 1996 film *Kama Sutra*. These connections are beyond the scope of this chapter but could be starting points for fascinating future research.

43. See Idema, *The White Snake and Her Son*; and Woodbridge, *The Mystery of the White Snake*.

44. The dialectic between comedy and horror has fascinated moviegoers and researchers throughout the world. See, for example, Hallenbeck, *Comedy-Horror Films: A Chronological History, 1914–2008*. Given the prominence of both horror and comedy in Asian (and Hong Kong) film industries in particular, recent studies have focused on the generic interrelationships over time, see Martin and Bettinson, *Hong Kong Horror Cinema*, "Part II: Genre Hybridity: Comedy and Kong-Fu in the Hong Kong Horror."

45. The white hair ornament, in particular, which replaces the flower decoration seen in both the 1956 Japanese live-action film and the 1958 animation, serves as an elegant and alluring marker of the snake woman's charms.

46. The Goddess of Mercy's impersonation of the abbot is intriguing here, as it speaks to the power of transformation and its ability to reconnect and reconcile. The abbot, in this case, also embodies a range of qualities from Buddhism, Daoism, to

Confucianism, from meditation and enlightenment, exorcism, to the idea of harmony and unity.

47. See Choi and Lee, *Paeksajŏn*.

48. See Choe and Si-ma, *Zhen Baishe zhuan*.

49. See Li Han-hsiang, *Zhen Baishe zhuan*.

50. For a short biography of Nishimoto with an emphasis on his contribution to film technology in Hong Kong, see Hong Kong Film Archive, accessed June 15, 2020, https://www.filmarchive.gov.hk/documents/2005525/10069133/Nishimoto%2BTadashi_e.pdf

51. This promotional language is used on a color poster for *Love of the White Snake*, followed by the following description: "The countless special effects created by superb craftsmanship brings out the ultimate in audiovisual entertainment, costing millions of dollars" (*teji qianbian wanhua guifu shengong ji shiting zhiyu haozi shu qianwan* 特技千變萬化鬼斧神工極視聽之娛耗資數千萬). This poster, together with other posters for the same film, can be located on Douban dianying, accessed June 15, 2020, https://movie.douban.com/subject/1307346/photos?type=R. The mention of Japanese experts may directly refer to Nishimoto's special effects company and the experts he brought from Japan to make the film.

52. For more on Li Han-hsiang's film career connecting Hong Kong and Taiwan, see Yeh, "From Shaw Brothers to Grand Motion Picture." Li's phenomenally successful *The Love Eterne*, also shot by Nishimoto, is discussed later in this chapter as another prominent example of the connections that arose between Hong Kong and Taiwan through Li's market success.

53. See Szema and Chen, *Love of the White Snake*.

54. The hardness of the rocks and softness of the leaves suggest a stereotypical, almost comical association with what is conventionally perceived as masculine and feminine in these magical transformations. In *Story of the Stone* (*Shitou ji* 石頭記), better known as *Dream of the Red Chamber* (*Honglou meng*), it is Baoyu the male protagonist who is born with a precious jade in his mouth and embodies the converging, androgynous qualities of both rocks and leaves, both masculine and feminine.

55. See "Lin Qingxia bei Chen Zixing zhuidao Hanguo" [Lin Ching Hsia was followed by an Indonesian merchant Mr. Chen Tzu Hsing to Korea], *Yinse shijie* 96 (December 1977).

56. See "Xin Wutai jumu," *Taiwan nichinichi shinpō* [*Taiwan riri xinbao*] (Chinese version), July 29, 1921, 6.

57. See Mak, *Xianggang dianying yu xinjiapo*, 36.

58. Loke's Singaporean background is likely why *The Kingdom and the Beauty* was entered as a Singaporean entry for the Academy Awards. MP & GI was renamed as Cathay Organization (*Guotai zuzhi*) in 1965. See Mak, *Xianggang dianying yu xinjiapo*, 90–91.

59. For rare historical footage and detailed accounts of the festival, as well as information on the four Taiwan representatives, see the Chinese Taipei Film Archive web-

site, especially its page devoted to the festival, http://www.ctfa.org.tw/tai_image/film-b.html. For more on digital preservation and restoration of Taiwanese cinema, visit the Taiwan Film and Audiovisual Institute website, https://www.tfi.org.tw/, and its YouTube channel, https://www.youtube.com/user/TWCTFA/featured. All accessed June 15, 2020.

60. Mak, *Xianggang dianying yu xinjiapo*, 15–17.

61. Lin Qinghua, "Huangmeixi dianying zai Xianggang ji Taiwan de fazhan," 79–82. For example, the prologue in *Madam White Snake*, titled "Xianxiang" (Home of the immortal), directly borrowed lyrics and instrumental arrangements from a song in *Heavenly Match,* "Tiangong suiyue lengqingqing" 天宮歲月冷清清 ("Lonely times in the heavenly palace"); see especially page 80 in Lin Qinhua's article.

62. See "Chia Ling," Hong Kong Movie Database, accessed January 14, 2019, http://hkmdb.com/db/people/view.mhtml?id=3866

63. See Luo, "The Experimental and the Popular in Chinese Socialist Theater of the 1950s."

64. Such a derogative designation of Hong Kong's lack of culture was said to have originated on February 27, 1927, during Lu Xun's second visit to Hong Kong. Asked by a group of young Hong Kong writers themselves, "Is Hong Kong a cultural desert?" Lu Xun responded, "No, such a designation is too dispirited. Even if it is a desert, it can be changed." Such a critical exchange, however, was lost in transmission over time, and the dismissive label of "cultural desert" stayed with Hong Kong throughout the twentieth century.

65. See Glosser, *Li Fengjin.*

66. See Luo, *The Avant-Garde and the Popular*, chap. 5.

Chapter 6

1. See Luo, *The Avant-Garde and the Popular*, chap. 5.

2. See LaMothe, *Between Dancing and Writing*, 4–5; and Chen Yang, *Yueshu*, vol. 67, 1.

3. LaMothe, *Between Dancing and Writing*, 4–5.

4. See King, *Writing in Motion*, xiii–xiv.

5. King, *Writing in Motion*, 1–2, 4; italics in the original.

6. Cited in Knafo, *Dancing with the Unconscious*, xvii.

7. See Knafo, *Dancing with the Unconscious*, 18–23. The 1895 Basic Books English edition of *Studies on Hysteria* is available in full text on archive.org.

8. Anthropological studies of trance, spirit possession, and embodiment are relevant here too. See, for example, Lock and Farquhar, *Beyond the Body Proper.*

9. See Halprin, *The Expressive Body in Life, Art and Therapy*, 14–15.

10. Halprin, *The Expressive Body in Life, Art and Therapy*, 18–20. Also see Levine and Frederick, *Waking the Tiger.*

11. The dialectics of writing/dancing or text/body and the history of poetry-

singing-dancing-music as a unified set remind us of a similarity to the Nāṭyaśāstra in the Indian tradition. This classic Sanskrit text on performing arts is at the same time connected to the architecture of the playhouse, in addition to acting, dancing, poetry, and music, among other things. For a full English translation, accessed June 1, 2020, see https://www.wisdomlib.org/hinduism/book/the-natyashastra

12. See Ruan, *Shisanjing zhushu: Zhouli*, 356; and Chen Yunlu, *Ting Zhu Guangqian jiang meixue*. The Chinese translation of aesthetics, *meixue*, literally means "study of beauty." For a general introduction of the term in twentieth-century Chinese context, see Jiang and Cai, "Aesthetics," *Oxford Bibliographies*, last modified September 25, 2018, https://doi.org/10.1093/OBO/9780199920082-0160

13. Mao, Zheng, and Kong, *Maoshi zhushu*, 12–19. The translation is my own.

14. See Du Fu, "Guan Gongsun daniang dizi wu jianqi xing, bingxu," in Owen, *The Poetry of Du Fu*, 332. Du Fu's poem on viewing the sword dance was highlighted in a recent BBC documentary through reenactments. See the "Sword Dance" clip in *Du Fu, China's Greatest Poet*, presented by Michael Wood, broadcast on BBC Four, April 6–7, 2020, accessed June 1, 2020, https://www.bbc.co.uk/programmes/p0885c3t. For a complete English translation of Du Fu's poems published in a Chinese-English bilingual version as part of the Library of Chinese Humanities, both in print and with open-access, see Stephen Owen, *The Poetry of Du Fu*, Berlin: De Gruyter, 2016, accessed June 1, 2020, https://www.degruyter.com/view/title/319782. For an excellent contemporary Singaporean novel on Du Fu, see Cheng, *Gull Between Heaven and Earth*.

15. See, for example, "Seeking the Herb" (*Qiucao*) in Fang Chengpei, *Leifengta chuanqi*.

16. The most popular form of Southern martial arts from China, Wing Chun claims disciples such as Bruce Lee, Jackie Chan, and Donnie Yen. It has also been featured widely in both Sinophone and Anglophone popular cultures, including a recent series of big-budget films on its legendary master Ip Man. See *Ip Man 1* (2008), *Ip Man 2* (2010), *The Grandmaster* (2013), *Ip Man 3* (2015), and *Ip Man 4: The Finale* (2019).

17. See, for example, Longxi Zhang's discussion on the power of Chinese writing and its relationship with inscription in *The Tao and the Logos*, 33. Also see, Billeter, *The Chinese Art of Writing*. There are other contexts where movement, writing, and ritual intersect significantly, such as in the context of Islamic calligraphy, see Blair, *Islamic Calligraphy*. However, according to Joseph R. Allen, the power of Chinese calligraphy extends far beyond reflecting personal character to the arenas of historical, cultural, and national representation, and its weight endures today. See Joseph Allen, "The Babel Fallacy," 137–40.

18. For the importance of the Chinese script in East Asia, see, for example, Kornicki, *Language, Scripts, and Chinese Texts in East Asia*; Handel, *Sinography: The Borrowing and Adaptation of the Chinese Script*; Denecke, "Worlds without Translation: Premodern East Asia and the Power of Character Scripts"; Insup Taylor and M. Martin Taylor, *Writing and Literacy in Chinese, Korean and Japanese*; and Qian, Smith, and Zhang eds., *Reexamining the Sinosphere* and *Rethinking the Sinosphere*.

19. For another version featuring Green Snake (Blue Snake) in a Sichuan shadow play, see Fan Pen Li Chen, "Cloud-Transcending Crossing."

20. For a recent study complicating this representation, see Hershatter, *The Gender of Memory*.

21. See Tang, "Chuanju Baishe zhuan tanwei," 56–58.

22. Li Bihua, *Qingshe*, 31–32.

23. A November 18, 1993, performance of *White Water* in Kaohsiung is available on YouTube, accessed June 27, 2020, https://youtu.be/_NxxKbiZ9Jk. More recently, Taiwanese artist Su Hui-Yu created a live theatrical work *The White Waters* for the Performa 19 Biennial in New York City to explore the spirit of Tian Qiyuan and to pay homage to Tian's *White Water*. Tian was Taiwan's first openly gay and HIV-positive student and was cofounder of the experimental theater group Critical Point Theatre Phenomenon (Linjiedian juxianglu 臨界點劇象錄) in the 1980s. Information on Su Hui-Yu's work, which ran from November 15 to 16, 2019, can be found on Performa 19's website, accessed May 28, 2020, http://performa19.org/tickets/the-white-waters

24. All translations, unless otherwise noted, are my own; for the Chinese original, see Li Bihua, *Qingshe*, 101–2.

25. See Cruz, "10 Questions for Guillermo del Toro" (see chap. 1, n. 58).

26. Chaos is an important Greek mytheme. Its relevance to the Chinese texts discussed here promises intriguing comparative research, which is beyond the scope of this study but worthy of future investigation. For an introduction on "the war against chaos" in a global religious context, see Margo Kitts, "Cosmic War and Cosmic Conflict," in *Encyclopedia of Global Religion*, ed. Mark Juergensmeyer and Wade Clark Roof (Los Angeles: Sage, 2012), vol. 1, 258–62.

27. See Menghua guanzhu, *Baishe quanzhuan*, 90–93.

28. For more on how *jingju* master Mei Lanfang, during a visit to Russia, inspired a range of modernist artists in their formal experiments, see Saussy, "Mei Lanfang in Moscow, 1935."

29. For a nuanced Chinese study on Guan Liang's "double identity" and his ability to synthesize "tradition" and "modernity," see Hang, "Guan Liang de shuangchong shenfen jiqi xingshi yuyan."

30. According to Aaron Balivet, the use of male role types for Green Snake goes back at least to the time of Fang Chengpei's play in the late eighteenth century. Fang's play uses a *chou* role type to depict Green Snake in the scenes "Subduing Green" and "Suppressed by the Alms Bowl," The "Subduing Green" scene was a popular excerpt in both *pihuang* and *kunqu* traditions up to the late nineteenth century, although the detail of Green Snake's hope to win White Snake's hand in marriage may be unique to Sichuan opera. See Balivet, "The Many Transformations of White Snake," 73–80; Tang, "Chuanju Baishe zhuan tanwei," 58; and Du Jianhua, *Chuanju biaoxian shoufa tonglan*, 86–87.

31. Jiang, *Wudong Baishe zhuan*, 110–11.

32. Chung, "Tian Qiyuan biandao fengge yanjiu"; Wang, "The body that can(not) represent us."

33. Idema and Grant, *The Red Brush*; Widmer and Chang, *Writing Women in Late Imperial China*; Dooling and Torgeson, *Writing Women in Modern China*; and Fiss and Guo, "Women, Writing and Visuality in Contemporary China." Also see Mann, *Precious Records*; and the online digital archive of Ming-Qing women's writing directed by Grace Fong at McGill University: https://digital.library.mcgill.ca/mingqing/chinese/introduction.php

34. See "Li Bihua fangwen—Qingshe zhihou," accessed September 8, 2015, http://www.cosmosbooks.com.hk/topic_3/page_2.asp?docid=9

35. Yan, *White Snake and Other Stories,* 3–4; Yan, *Baishe,* 5.

36. See, for example, Ding and Wang, "Shiqinian wenxue: 'ren' he 'ziwo' de shiluo." Emily Wilcox's excellent work complicates such representations and contributes significantly to studies of the Seventeen Years in general and dance studies in China in particular; see Wilcox, *Revolutionary Bodies.*

37. See Chen, *Wo shicong gu'eryuan laide,* 35.

38. English-language publications originating from China at the time translated the title of the piece as "Maid of the Sea." See Chang Sen, "Maid of the Sea," *Peking Review*, no. 52 (1959): 20.

39. Lawrence Walker, translator of Yan's *White Snake*, interpreted "this question" as referring to the next sentence; hence he used a colon to connect the two sentences and did not capitalize the first word of the following sentence. I, however, read "this question" as referring to the previous sentence, hence changed the colon to a period and capitalized the first word of the next sentence.

40. Yan, *White Snake and Other Stories,* 17; Yan, *Baishe,* 22–23.

41. Yan, *White Snake and Other Stories,* 17; Yan, *Baishe,* 22–23. It is possible that Yan here is alluding to Yu Hua's 1993 novel *To Live* (*Huozhe*) and Zhang Yimou's 1994 film adaptation, suggesting a response to a new individualism linked with existentialist ideas circulating at the time.

42. Rey Chow, *Primitive Passions,* 22–23.

43. Yan, *White Snake and Other Stories,* 33. The use of the word "concrete" paired with "obtuse" here is a bit odd. Normally, the opposition would be between abstract and concrete, with dance being a concrete form of expression; "language, emotion, knowledge" would be considered abstract by comparison. However, to pair "obtuse" with "concrete" as if they are antonyms seems strange. The original Chinese refers to the established knowledge categories, such as wisdom and defined emotions, as literally "too clumsy and heavy," what Walker has translated as "too obtuse," and "too concrete," meaning it is too defined to convey the kind of "precision" embodied by the dancer's body. However, it is also possible that Walker, in using the term "obtuse," has indeed interpreted the point of differentiation between undefined kinetic expression (dance) and knowledge and defined emotion (language-based expression) as precision or lack thereof. For the Chinese original, see Yan, *Baishe,* 44.

44. Yan, *White Snake and Other Stories,* 27; Yan, *Baishe,* 36–37.

45. Yan, *White Snake and Other Stories,* 27.

46. Walker translates Qingshe as Blue Snake. He might have been influenced by

Donald Chang and William Packard's rendering of the character's name in their translation of the Tian Han version of the White Snake legend, included in Mitchell, *The Red Pear Garden.* I have changed "Blue Snake" to "Green Snake" in all quotations, as translations since the 1990s, including of Lilian Lee's novel and Tsui Hark's film, have established Green Snake as the standard translation of Qingshe. See Yan, *White Snake and Other Stories*, 29; Yan, *Baishe*, 38–39.

47. Yan, *White Snake and Other Stories*, 30; for the Chinese original, see Yan, *Baishe*, 40–41. This passage brings to mind *Silk Stockings*, a 1957 Hollywood remake of Ernst Lubitsch's 1939 *Ninotchka*, with its mix of dance, sexuality, and politics as seen from an American point of view that equated Communism with sexual repression and dance with sexual liberation and therefore political freedom. See Mamoulian, *Silk Stockings*.

48. See Li Bihua, *Qingshe*, https://www.kanunu8.com/book/3516/34587.html, accessed February 12, 2018.

49. Yan's eight years dancing in Chengdu, from age twelve to age twenty, was an experience that inevitably left deep traces in this allegorical story about the dancing White Snake and writing Green Snake.

50. Yan, "Wo wenshenme xie *Fanghua*?," accessed February 12, 2018, http://www.chinesepen.org/blog/archives/95788

51. Yan, *White Snake and Other Stories*, 30-31; Yan, *Baishe*, 40–41.

52. Yan, *White Snake and Other Stories*, 35–36; Yan, *Baishe*, 47–49.

53. Derrida, Foucault, Lyotard, and their fellow postmodernists were all deeply interested in realpolitik. See, for example, Derrida's "ten plagues" in *Specters of Marx*; Foucault on prisoner's rights, penal systems; and Deleuze and Guattari on asylums. In this sense, the "postmodern" is best articulated as the postings between different modernities or claims for modernities as they replace and contest one another; or the several modern aspirations that vie for traction (for example, mass media and consumption versus building welfare states, including the US New Deal) either geographically (modernity as seen from Beijing in 1949 versus New York or New Delhi) or the paradox of modernities we identify in the Cultural Revolution in this chapter: the "typical" puritanical-patriarchal revolutionary comradeship—true of German social democrats in the 1920s, of the civil rights movement in the United States—to transform the realpolitik and political economies from underdevelopment to global player, and sexual liberation to overthrow fossilizing authorities from an earlier period. Personal communications with Michael Fischer, May 16–May 26, 2020.

54. Yan, *White Snake and Other Stories*, 37; Yan, *Baishe*, 50.

55. Yan, *White Snake and Other Stories*, 38; Yan, *Baishe*, 51.

56. Yan, *White Snake and Other Stories*, 46–47; Yan, *Baishe*, 63–66.

57. Yan, *White Snake and Other Stories*, 54; Yan, *Baishe*, 74.

58. Yan, *White Snake and Other Stories*, 56; Yan, *Baishe*, 77.

59. See Wan and Hung, "The Iron Girl"; and Wen, "Good Daughter of the Party."

60. The project was conceived in 1999 by the owner of the Scottish publisher Canongate Books, and the first three titles in the series were published in October

2005. The website has been revamped and "The Myths" is now part of the "About" section on the website, accessed August 14, 2018, https://canongate.co.uk/about/

61. This is inspired by personal communications with Michael Fischer, May 16–May 26, 2020.

62. See Li Rui and Jiang Yun, *Renjian.*

63. Thorpe, "Modern Theatre for the Twenty-First Century?"

64. Yang, "Duoyuan yu baorong."

65. Lin Huaimin, *Yuhuo chongsheng*, 2013; Ming Hwa Yuan, *Chaoxuan Baishe zhuan*, 2013.

66. Ming Hwa Yuan, *Chaoxuan Baishe zhuan*, 2007. For an excellent analysis on the use of media and technology in *White Snake Spectacular*, see Chun, "Mediated Transgression and Madame White." Here is a case where working back from the present to the past seems more vivid than a chronological account. White Snake performances in early twentieth-century Shanghai (as discussed in chapter 2) seem to resemble so many other shows of that era, so it is hard to get a feel of the sensual rush that might have been involved—like going to a Wild West show in Berlin or Vienna at the time. For readers of this book, moving backwards or nonlinearly through the chapters might also produce a different dramatic effect.

67. For an insightful new study of the memories of the Mao era through a wide range of commemorative media, see Jie Li, *Utopian Ruins.*

Chapter 7

1. See the composer's note in Zhou Long, *Madame White Snake*, unpaginated.

2. The study score is published in an English-Chinese bilingual version.

3. See the composer's note in Zhou Long, *Madame White Snake*, unpaginated.

4. Haiyan Lee, "How the Chinese Fell in Love with Love."

5. "Premiere of the Opera *Madame White Snake* in Boston," accessed August 10, 2018, https://www.youtube.com/watch?v=lE6QvuSvVIg

6. "Michael Maniaci as Xiao Qing," accessed August 10, 2018, http://ouroborostrilogy.org/featuring/view/Michael-Maniaci. As discussed in chapter 6, in Sichuan opera and other theatrical traditions in China, Green Snake can be performed in the role types of a "secondary female" (*tiedan*), a "clown" (*chou*), a "mighty male" (*jing*), or a "martial male" (*wusheng*), among others.

7. For more on the genre convention of the relationship between a young scholar and a beautiful girl in Chinese literature, see McMahon, "The Classic 'Beauty-Scholar' Romance and the Superiority of the Talented Woman."

8. Zhou Long, *Madame White Snake*, unpaginated.

9. See official website of The Pulitzer Prizes, accessed August 5, 2018, http://www.pulitzer.org/winners/zhou-long

10. This is likely an echo of the 2009 Shanghai production of the symphonic-style *jingju* performance *Madame White Snake: Seasons of Love* (*Bai niangzi: aiqing siji*). It is also entirely possible that Jacobs and Zhou came to this structure inde-

pendently, as the seasonal metaphor is commonly used to symbolize the ebb and flow of love.

11. "Ouroboros Trilogy: About," accessed August 5, 2018, http://ouroborostrilogy.org/about

12. Zhou Long, *Madame White Snake*, 4–8.

13. See, for example, discussions in chapter 2 on *jingju* and other forms of local operas and storytelling genres, including the extremely popular *tanci* storytelling.

14. By "limitation and difficulty," Zhou is talking about a specific problem, the need to deal with the pitch contours of Chinese syllables when setting words to music, something that does not apply to English. By "exoticism," he talks about the differences between Western and Chinese audiences of the play, and he attributes the idea of a male Green Snake to his wife, fellow composer Chen Yi; see "Madame White Snake," WQXR blog, New York Public Radio, accessed August 11, 2018, https://www.wqxr.org/story/13971-madame-white-snake/

15. "Madame White Snake," WQXR blog (see chap. 7, n. 14).

16. Zhou Long, *Madame White Snake*, 86–93.

17. Zhou Long, *Madame White Snake*, 99–101.

18. Zhou Long, *Madame White Snake*, 213–24.

19. Zhou Long, *Madame White Snake*, 223–25.

20. Zhou Long, *Madame White Snake*, 262-63.

21. Zhou Long, *Madame White Snake*, 291.

22. Zhou Long, *Madame White Snake*, 316.

23. See Shengold, "Madame White Snake Worthwhile Effort from Opera Boston," accessed August 11, 2018, https://www.classical-scene.com/2010/03/03/madame-white-snake-worthwhile-effort-from-opera-boston/

24. See another article by Shengold on the *Ouroboros Trilogy* and *Madame White Snake*, September 29, 2016, https://www.gaycitynews.com/snake-oil/

25. Personal interview with Cerise Lim Jacobs, July 11, 2020. Jacobs specifically mentioned the festive and ritualistic atmosphere of watching Wayang-style outdoor White Snake performances as a child. She recalled that the performance language was Cantonese or Teochew (Chaozhou), but never Mandarin. In addition to outdoor performances, she fondly remembered endlessly watching *Madam White Snake*, the 1962 Shaw Brothers film starring Lin Dai, on the black-and-white TV at her grandparents' house in her early teens. The film changed from her "favorite" to "the worst" when she watched it again while researching for *Madame White Snake* in 2010. Its conservatism and prescription of traditional feminine virtues clashed harshly with Jacobs's conviction of the White Snake image's empowering possibilities and its potential for minority expressions at our contemporary moment.

26. See Fang Bo, "Lin Xiaoying tan geju *Baishe zhuan*," 54–55.

27. This is adapted from Cerise Lim Jacobs's biographical statement on the White Snake Projects official website, accessed August 11, 2018, http://www.whitesnakeprojects.org/bios/cerise/

28. See Mizoguchi, *Ugetsu*; and Ozu, *Tōkyō monogatari.*

29. See Caldwell Titcomb, "Opera Review: 'Madame White Snake,'" *The Arts Fuse*, March 4, 2010, http://artsfuse.org/5644/opera-review-madame-white-snake/

30. See Fang Bo, "Lin Xiaoying tan geju *Baishe zhuan*," 56–57. For more up-to-date information on the activist White Snake Projects, including new and timely productions such as "Alice in the Pandemic," "Cosmic Cowboy," "I Am A Dreamer Who No Longer Dreams," "Monkey, A Kung Fu Parable," as well as community-based projects "Sing Out Strong: Immigrant Voices," "Sing Out Strong: Decolonized Voices", and "Sing Out Strong: Essential Voices," among other titles, see the White Snake Projects website, accessed December 19, 2020, https://www.whitesnakeprojects.org/

31. See Mo Zhou's foreword in Zimmerman, *The White Snake: A Play*, xi.

32. As quoted in Mo Zhou's foreword in Zimmerman, *The White Snake: A Play*, xi. Zhou may have misattributed the source as the preface to the *baojuan* version, as I have not been able to locate the exact English translation from Idema's book, nor is there a preface to the *baojuan* version in Chinese.

33. "Writer/Director Mary Zimmerman Discusses 'The White Snake,'" *Chicago Sun-Times*, May 16, 2014, https://www.youtube.com/watch?v=l6ivlrWSUSU

34. "The White Snake: Behind the Scenes," Goodman Theatre, May 9, 2014, https://www.youtube.com/watch?v=DsYCCNKiVi8

35. "The Story of *The White Snake*," Oregon Shakespeare Festival, October 5, 2011, https://www.youtube.com/watch?v=SEwhtOwkKfk

36. As I watched the play only once, on November 7, 2014, during the Wuzhen Theatre Festival, I will refrain from commenting on other performances of the original production directed by Zimmerman. It played at six venues, in addition to Wuzhen: Oregon Shakespeare Festival (premiere), Berkeley Repertory Theatre, Goodman Theatre in Chicago, The Old Globe in San Diego, McCarter Theatre Center in Princeton, and Guthrie Theatre in Minneapolis. See written feedback from Mary Zimmerman via email communication with Christopher Dreyer, June 3, 2020.

37. Personal communications with Mary Zimmerman, June 30, 2020.

38. "Interview with Mary Zimmerman," Association for Theatre in Higher Education, August 13, 2015, https://www.youtube.com/watch?v=RRLKOrr776o

39. I saw Tian Qinxin's *Green Snake* performed by the National Theatre of China during its premiere at the Eisenhower Theater at the Kennedy Center in Washington, DC, on March 28, 2014. I saw it a second time at the opening of the Wuzhen Theatre Festival in Wuzhen's outdoor Water Theatre (*Shui juchang*) on October 30, 2014. A three-hour version of Tian's play, longer than both versions I saw live, is available on YouTube, accessed May 28, 2020, https://youtu.be/PzR9PB06ERA?t=1

40. See Haiyan Lee, "The Revolutionary Structure of Feeling."

41. See written feedback from Mary Zimmerman via email communication with Christopher Dreyer, received on June 3, 2020.

42. See Andrew Jewell, Willa Cather Archive, University of Nebraska-Lincoln, accessed March 26, 2019, http://cather.unl.edu.

43. "*The White Snake* Part 2: The Writing Process," Oregon Shakespeare Festival, October 5, 2011, https://www.youtube.com/watch?v=9ucVQk-974g

44. "'White Snake' and the Playground of Live Theatre," KPBS, April 9, 2015, https://www.youtube.com/watch?v=Xi-_phQa12A. This philosophy is reminiscent of the ideas famously articulated in the "muse of fire" speech that opens Shakespeare's *Henry V*.

45. "Tony Award Winner Mary Zimmerman to Present White Snake at Wuzhen Theatre Festival in China," news provided by Wuzhen Tourism Co., *PR Newswire*, October 3, 2014, https://www.prnewswire.com/news-releases/tony-award-winner-mary-zimmerman-to-present-white-snake-at-wuzhen-theater-festival-in-china-278010891.html

46. Zimmerman's play *The White Snake* was most recently on stage at the Constellation Theatre Company (CTC) in Washington, DC, under the direction of Allison Arkell Stockman, from April 25 to May 26, 2019. I saw the CTC production twice, at 2 p.m. and 8 p.m. on May 11, 2019. On that same day, at 4 p.m., I participated in a post-performance discussion and Q&A with Stockman, with most of the cast and crew members in the audience.

47. It is such a privilege to count Professor Liana Chen of Georgetown University, Professor Ke Ren of the College of the Holy Cross and his wife Ms. Mimi Tang, a specialist in refashioning historical architecture in China, Professor Hongmei Sun of George Mason University, and Professor Claire Chen, then at St. Mary's College of Maryland, as my fellow theatergoers for the two performances of *The White Snake* at the CTC on May 11, 2019. Professor Liana Chen recorded my full conversation with Director Stockman after the 2 p.m. performance, and Professor Ren asked thought-provoking questions during the Q&A. Sitting among such a wonderful group of China specialists and watching *The White Snake* together in the audience was a once-in-a-lifetime experience. Our shared tears and laughter, as well as our immediate and sustained conservations about the performance informed my thinking, and I thank them for their contributions to this discussion.

48. See Zung, *Secrets of the Chinese Drama*, cited by Mo Zhou in her foreword to Zimmerman, *The White Snake*, xi.

49. See Julia Arbutus, "Food, Family, and Memories: A Spotlight on Eunice Bae," *The Retriever*, March 14, 2018, https://retriever.umbc.edu/2018/03/remembering-red-bean-mochi-squares-and-late-night-cup-noodles/

50. See Zimmerman, *The White Snake*, 125.

51. See Zimmerman, *The White Snake*, 51. For a relevant discussion on the contemporary political implications of such a seemingly contradictory figure, see Liana Chen, "Post Performance Q&A, Director's Vision," Constellation Theatre Company, Director's Vision on the White Snake, May 11, 2019, https://www.youtube.com/watch?v=x5GcVJVNRfM, 21:40–22:45.

52. See "Ryan Sellers," in *About the Artists*, accessed October 18, 2019, http://www.abouttheartists.com/artists/273731-ryan-sellers

53. See Liana Chen, "Post Performance Q&A, Director's Vision," 17:30–18:30 (see chap. 7, n. 51).

54. See Zimmerman, *The White Snake*, 138.

55. I watched the CTC performance of Zimmerman's *Journey to the West* on April 30, 2016, with colleagues who are Chinese literature and theater specialists in the DC area.

56. For more on Dong Xi's *Out of the Blue*, see Tom Teasley's website, accessed October 18, 2019, http://www.tomteasley.com/store/cds/out-blue/

57. Personal communications with Tian and Teasley, May 11 and October 18, 2019, and via Dong Xi Music's Facebook page, https://www.facebook.com/dongximusic/

58. Zimmerman, *The White Snake*, 51.

59. "Zimmerman Reading Response," MCL 595: Topics in Folklore and Mythology: The White Snake, University of Kentucky, Spring 2017, accessed January 18, 2019, https://uk.instructure.com/courses/1884673/discussion_topics/11877979

60. For a fascinating new study on how the pharmacy can serve as a persuasive and entertaining guide to major transformations in the conceptualization and production of knowledge in early modern China, see Bian, *Know Your Remedies*.

61. Zimmerman, *The White Snake*, 60–61.

62. Zhao Qingge, foreword (written in January 1956) to *The Legend of White Snake*, unpaginated. A similar process took place in the rewriting of *Tianxian pei*; see Idema, *The Metamorphosis of Tianxian pei*.

63. See Haiyan Lee, "The Revolutionary Structure of Feeling."

64. Zhao Qingge, preface (written on October 30, 1997) to *The Legend of White Snake*, unpaginated.

65. Zhao Qingge, *The Legend of White Snake*, 2.

66. Zhao Qingge, *The Legend of White Snake*, 76.

67. As discussed in chapter 5 regarding Shin Sang-ok's Korean films, the White Snake and Guanyin (in female form) are, however, also closely related or even occasionally mistaken for one another in early Chinese and missionary accounts and in modern cinematic adaptations.

68. Zhao Qingge, *The Legend of White Snake*, 191.

69. Zhao Qingge, *The Legend of White Snake*, 78.

70. See, for example, Nedostup, *Superstitious Regimes*. See also the characters of Third Fairy (San xiangu) and Liu the Sage (Er zhuge), symbols of "feudal remnants" in Zhao Shuli's famous 1943 story, written in the Communist base during the Second Sino-Japanese War; Zhao Shuli, *Xiao erhei jiehun*.

71. Zhao Qingge, *The Legend of White Snake*, 222, 242.

72. Idema, *The White Snake and Her Son*, 6.

73. Indrani, *The Legend of Lady White Snake*.

74. See Indrani's official website, accessed January 18, 2019, https://www.indrani.com/films

75. Quite remarkably, Little Green (Green Snake) is now the "Wonder Woman of China" in the DC Universe, see Gene Luen Yang et al., *New Super-Man*.

76. "Samuel Taylor Coleridge," accessed May 28, 2020, https://www.poetryfoundation.org/poets/samuel-taylor-coleridge

77. Samuel Taylor Coleridge, "Kubla Khan," accessed March 20, 2018, https://www.poetryfoundation.org/poems/43991/kubla-khan

78. "Daphne Guinness and 'The Legend of Lady White Snake,'" accessed March 20, 2018, http://wwd.com/fashion-news/fashion-scoops/look-out-kevin-bacon-5619421/

79. Gaiman, *Fragile Things*, 45–48.

80. Ralph Waldo Emerson, "Brahma," accessed March 20, 2018, https://www.poetryfoundation.org/poems/45868/brahma-56d225936127b

81. Ralph Waldo Emerson, "Maia," accessed March 20, 2018, https://quod.lib.umich.edu/a/amverse/BAD1982.0001.001/1:9.2.11?rgn=div3;view=fulltext

82. Tagore, "Endless Time," accessed March 20, 2018, https://allpoetry.com/Endless-Time

83. Tagore, "Unending Love," accessed March 20, 2018, https://allpoetry.com/Unending-Love

84. This particular line was made famous by J. Robert Oppenheimer, developer of the atomic bomb.

85. See Keats, *Lamia*.

86. The internet availability and keyword searchability of all of these cited texts could have partly enabled Indrani to stitch together these texts in this fashion.

87. See "Daphne Guinness and 'The Legend of Lady White Snake'" (see chap. 7, n. 78); and "Biography," website of Bernard-Henri Lévy, accessed April 17, 2019, http://www.bernard-henri-levy.com/en/category/biography

88. See Su Chunmin, "Zhongguo chuantong minyue fazhan zoushi de gouxiang—you 'nüzi shi'er yuefang' yinyue xianxiang yinfa de sikao" [Some thoughts about the trends of Chinese traditional folk music—triggered by the performance of the music team of 12 female instrumentalists], *Suzhou keji xueyuan xuebao, shehui kexue ban* 23, no. 2 (August 2006): 136–38.

89. See a plot summary on IMDB, accessed March 20, 2018, http://www.imdb.com/title/tt2250164/plotsummary?ref_=tt_ov_pl

90. For a moving documentary on McQueen, see Bonhôte and Ettedgui, *McQueen*. For more information on the documentary, visit its official website, accessed April 17, 2019, https://bleeckerstreetmedia.com/mcqueen

91. "Deep Sea Devotion," accessed April 17, 2019, http://fashion.telegraph.co.uk/news-features/TMG7449042/Deep-Sea-Devotion-Alexander-McQueens-Manta-Designs.html

92. "Paris Fashion Week," accessed April 17, 2019, https://www.telegraph.co.uk/news/6267046/Paris-Fashion-Week-Alexander-McQueen.html

93. See Bonhôte and Ettedgui, *McQueen*, esp. 95:00–96:00.

94. Savage Beauty, the McQueen retrospective at the Metropolitan Museum of Art in New York, was a blockbuster and the most popular exhibition in the museum's history. A petition for the retrospective to tour the world resulted in another

record-breaking run in the Victoria & Albert Museum in London. Lady Gaga claims that McQueen inspired her to write "Born this Way," and a stage play about McQueen ran in 2015 at the St. James Theatre in London. Along with the aforementioned 2018 documentary, these are among the many recent tributes to the late designer. See "Alexander McQueen: Savage Beauty," accessed April 17, 2019, https://brooklynrail.org/2011/07/artseen/alexander-mcqueen-savage-beauty

Chapter 8

1. For more on Ju Homin's *With God* and its cross-platform impact from Korea to China, see Keane, Yecies, and Flew, *Willing Collaborators*, 129–30.

2. Titled *Pingt'ang huru* 빙탕후루 (*Bingtang hulu*), after a Chinese snack featuring sugar-coated haws on a stick, the Korean webtoon series can be found on Naver Webtoon, accessed June 29, 2020: https://comic.naver.com/webtoon/list.nhn?titleId=695321

3. Such a plot resembles the popular Chinese "monster-hunting" films that have emerged in recent years, including the 3D fantasy action comedy *Zhuoyao ji* (Monster Hunt, 2015) and *Zhuoyao ji 2* (Monster Hunt 2, 2018), both directed by Hong Kong animator and film director Raman Hui Shing-Ngai; both broke box office records.

4. See one of the top-ranking reader comments to episode 70 of *Pingt'ang huru* on Naver Webtoon: https://comic.naver.com/webtoon/detail.nhn?titleId=695321&seq=70. The comments are located at the bottom of the page. The specific comment is ranked seventh among all comments, with some 2,400 likes as of June 29, 2020.

5. The corresponding Chinese version to episode 42 of *Pingt'ang huru* can be located on Dongman Manhua, no. 50 of *Yiwen zhi Bingtang hulu* 異聞之冰糖葫蘆, accessed June 29, 2020: https://www.dongmanmanhua.cn/ANCIENTCHINESE/bingtanghulu/list?title_no=1233&page=2

6. For a recent study on the Chinese transcreators of Korean webtoons, who are often volunteering fans, and the cultural and economic implications of such collective fan labor, see Yecies, Shim, and Yang, "Chinese Transcreators, Webtoons and the Korean Digital Wave."

7. See the internet drama on iQiyi in Mandarin with Chinese subtitles: https://www.iqiyi.com/a_19rrgxjest.html; and on Viki in Mandarin with subtitles in twelve languages, including Bulgarian, English, French, German, Greek, Hungarian, Italian, Polish, Portuguese, Spanish, Turkish, and Vietnamese. See the English-subtitled version, accessed April 14, 2019, https://www.viki.com/tv/36277c-the-legend-of-white-snake

8. See Xia and He, *Xin Bainiangzi chuanqi*.

9. See Wang, "Old Tale Resonates with a Modern Audience," *China Daily*, updated April 10, 2019, http://en.chinaculture.org/2019-04/10/content_1375011.htm

10. See Brennan, "Queerbaiting."

11. *Steven Universe*, an animated short series created by Rebecca Sugar, premiered on

Cartoon Network in 2013 and ended in 2020. In *Steven Universe,* the bodies of the gem forms are merely holograms with mass; their literal form is simply a gemstone. Thus, Steven's gemstone in his belly button is his mother, even though her body does not exist. Throughout the series this is emphasized, as many of Steven's mother's friends/enemies still think that his mother, Rose Quartz, exists, and that Steven is just a shapeshifted version of her that has forgotten her true self. In addition, there is actually a minor caterpillar/centipede character in *Steven Universe* that is a fusion of several gems, with an interesting backstory. The Thirtieth Annual GLAAD Media Awards recognized and honored the series as an Outstanding Kids & Family Program, for its "fair, accurate and inclusive representations of the lesbian, gay, bisexual, transgender and queer (LGBTQ) community and the issues that affect their lives," accessed April 10, 2019, https://www.glaad.org/mediaawards/30. For more on the series, see McDonnell, *Steven Universe.*

12. The story of Math fab Mathonwy in the Welsh story-cycle Mabinogion comes to mind as an example of gender queering in early narratives, especially connected with the idea of forced gender swapping as punishment or consequence. See also Tiresias in Greek mythology, probably the best-known Western example of this trope.

13. See episode 12 of *New Legend of Madame White Snake,* accessed April 14, 2019, https://www.viki.com/videos/1148639v-the-legend-of-white-snake-episode-12, 1:40–4:05. The nine-tailed fox (*jiuwei hu* 九尾狐) is a mythical creature that appears in *The Classic of Mountains and Seas* (*Shanhai jing*), with the following description: "It takes the shape of a fox but has nine tails, it has the voice of a baby, and it can eat people" (*qizhuang ruhu er jiuwei, qiyin ru ying'er, neng shiren* 其狀如狐而九尾, 其音如嬰兒, 能食人). See *Shanhai jing,* 4. For an English translation, see Birrell, *The Classic of Mountains and Seas.* Similar to the White Snake, a hybrid of snake and beautiful woman, the nine-tailed fox, as a hybrid of a fox and a beauty, has generated a long tradition of adaptations in Japanese, Korean, and Vietnamese literati and popular cultures. There is a Pokémon called Ninetales that is a nine-tailed fox, for example; multiple Korean dramas have featured the nine-tailed fox, with the most recent hit visualizing the fox as a beautiful man, see the 2020 *Tale of the Nine-Tailed* (*Kumihodyŏn* 구미호뎐), available on Viki with 45-language subtitles, accessed December 28, 2020: https://www.viki.com/tv/37373c. For more on foxes in Chinese literature, see Huntington, *Alien Kind*; Kang, *The Cult of the Fox*; and Kang, "The Fox (*hu* 狐) and the Barbarian (*hu* 胡)."

14. See episode 1 of *New Legend of Madame White Snake,* accessed April 14, 2019, https://www.viki.com/videos/1148628v-the-legend-of-white-snake-episode-1, 18:10–18:25.

15. See episode 5 of *New Legend of Madame White Snake,* accessed April 14, 2019, https://www.viki.com/videos/1148632v-the-legend-of-white-snake-episode-5, 29:07–29:19.

16. See episode 9 of *New Legend of Madame White Snake,* accessed April 14, 2019, https://www.viki.com/videos/1148636v-the-legend-of-white-snake-episode-9, 26–26:19, and 30:16–31:16.

17. Amp Wong and Zhao Ji, *Baishe: yuanqi.* A sequel headlining Green Snake is planned by Light Chaser for 2021.

18. According to a published interview with the directors of the animation on its opening day, the plot of the new animation was partially inspired by “On Snake Catchers” (*Bushezhe shuo*) by Liu Zongyuan (773–819) of the Tang dynasty. The creators intended to revamp a traditional story for contemporary young audiences. See Sanwenyu, “Light Chaser for the Young: Interviewing *White Snake* director Amp Wong and Zhao Ji” [Mianxiang nianqingren de Zhuiguang: zhuanfang *Baishe yuanqi* daoyan Huang Jiakang, Zhao Ji], January 11, 2019, https://user.guancha.cn/main/content?id=71132

19. See Amp Wong and Zhao Ji, *Baishe: yuanqi*, 11:16–11:23.

20. See Amp Wong and Zhao Ji, *Baishe: yuanqi*, 13:27–13:42.

21. See Amp Wong and Zhao Ji, *Baishe: yuanqi*, 16:33–16:45.

22. See Amp Wong and Zhao Ji, *Baishe: yuanqi*, 22:25–25:14.

23. Memory loss can be connected to the trope of amnesia in relation to political and personal trauma. A prominent theme in contemporary Chinese literature is amnesia of the Cultural Revolution. See, for example, Chan, *The Fat Years*.

24. See Amp Wong and Zhao Ji, *Baishe: yuanqi*, 30:26–30:58.

25. See Amp Wong and Zhao Ji, *Baishe: yuanqi*, 36:10–36:20.

26. See Amp Wong and Zhao Ji, *Baishe: yuanqi*, 33:00–33:15.

27. See Amp Wong and Zhao Ji, *Baishe: yuanqi*, 37:20–38:15.

28. See Amp Wong and Zhao Ji, *Baishe: yuanqi*, 38:30–38:58.

29. See Amp Wong and Zhao Ji, *Baishe: yuanqi*, 45:00–46:10.

30. See Josh Ye, “*White Snake* Review: *Frozen* with Sex is One for the Whole Family to Avoid,” accessed April 5, 2019, https://www.abacusnews.com/reviewed/white-snake-review-frozen-sex-one-whole-family-avoid/article/3000534

31. See Amp Wong and Zhao Ji, *Baishe: yuanqi*, 51:35–52:22.

32. See Pan, Lu, and Liu, *Xiaoxigu: Baishe zhuan*.

33. By May 8, 2017, there were 10,536 reviews on *Star of Tomorrow: Legend of the White Snake* on Douban. The film was given a score of 8.4, better than 97 percent of other costume dramas reviewed on the same site, accessed May 8, 2017, https://movie.douban.com/subject/26887890/

34. This suggests a connection with the psychotherapeutic modality known as somatic recreation, mentioned in chapter 6.

35. See Bingshui hunhewu, “*Star of Tomorrow*: What Made You So Popular among My WeChat Friend Circles?” [*Xiaoxigu: Baishe zhuan:* niping shenme huobao pengyouquan], accessed May 8, 2017, https://movie.douban.com/review/8198809/

36. Wushu, “Thank You, Spirits of the Times” [Ganxie nimen, shiguang de jingling], accessed May 8, 2017, https://movie.douban.com/review/8126307/. Bertolt Brecht, in his theatrical experiments from the 1930s, similarly used popular music to achieve such persuasive affective power. Between stage performance used as political propaganda historically and popular TV series becoming a viral internet phenomenon today, we can begin to appreciate the power of music as an ingredient of popularity in disparate contexts.

37. Gudong yu, "How Do I know How Many Flowers Bloomed in My Dream" [Mengli 'huakai' zhi duoshao], accessed May 8, 2017, https://movie.douban.com/review/8132995/

38. Jiaomujun jiang, "They Are the Best Slap in the Face for the Giddy Adult World" [Tamen, shi gei zhe fuzao chengren shijie zuihao de dalian], accessed May 8, 2017, https://movie.douban.com/review/8136550/

39. Hu, "The Animated Resurrection."

40. Toyoda, *Byaku fujin no yōren.*

41. Yabushita, *Hakujaden.*

42. See, for example, Condry, *The Soul of Anime.* A Japanese-language trailer for the film available online shows desk after desk of animators at work in the company's studio, a segment that seems less aimed at viewers than future purchasers or backers of animation projects; accessed May 28, 2020, https://www.youtube.com/watch?v=cN0i8v9VTWE

43. Tianyi, *Yiyao Baishe zhuan*, parts I and II.

44. See cigarette cards promoting the 1926 film, accessed May 8, 2017, https://tieba.baidu.com/p/4338420505

45. The use of female nudity in the 1927 silent film *The Cave of the Silken Web* (*Pansi dong*), featuring the spider spirits taking a bath, is a comparable case here. A very damaged copy of the film was found in Norway recently and is available at the National Library of Norway, with Chinese and Norwegian intertitles, accessed June 16, 2020, https://youtu.be/a3Da8JIP3QQ

46. According to Wilt Idema, who was at the premiere of the Boston Opera production of *Madame White Snake*, this line of reasoning may be plausible theoretically, but it is not so much the case in his personal experience. Personal communication via email.

47. The whole repository of White Snake legends has been repeatedly referred to as a "national people's intellectual property" in Chinese-language discourses, emphasizing its regenerative powers and highly marketable qualities. Such a profit-driven, neoliberal take on the commercial and nationalistic usages of the legends is pervasive in contemporary media coverage of the White Snake legends in the PRC.

48. Xie Na impersonated the Angie Chiu version of the White Snake in the episode that aired on July 19, 2012, https://www.mgtv.com/b/7257/3169414.html, and she performed the Maggie Chuang version of the Green Snake in the episode the aired on November 1, 2012, https://www.mgtv.com/b/290476/3169348.html; both accessed April 14, 2019.

49. *Keep Running* (*Benpaoba xiongdi*), the Chinese version of the Korean entertainment program *Running Men,* premiered on October 10, 2014, with members of the full cast gathering at the Thunder Peak Pagoda in order to "activate" the legend of the White Snake; accessed April 14, 2019, https://www.iqiyi.com/v_19rrn5m8gw.html

50. Yin Tao and Liu Guohui, *Tianji zhi Baishe chuanshuo.*

51. Episode 8 of *Lady Land* (*Jiejie de aiyue zhicheng*) premiered on Youtube via China Hunan TV Official Channel on December 26, 2020, accessed December 30, 2020: https://youtu.be/EggiJlzcliI

52. *Sisters Make Waves* (*Chengfeng polang de jiejie*) became phenomenally successful throughout its broadcasting on Hunan Satellite TV from June 12 to September 4, 2020. Its focus on female celebrities over thirty distinguished itself from other reality TV programs exclusively based on the dominant "youth economy" of contemporary entertainment TV. The full series with English subtitles is available on Youtube via China Hunan TV Official Channel, accessed December 30, 2020: https://youtu.be/4QnMPcKgwkc

53. Both on site at the Broken Bridge looking over the Thunder Peak Pagoda and the West Lake and in cyberspace, Chinese audiences have echoed their love for "Ferrying Love" (*Duqing*) and other theme songs of the 1992 Taiwanese TV series, as expressed in the tens of thousands of views and hundreds of comments posted only hours after the official Weibo account of CCTV TV Series channel posted a video of "Ferrying Love" with highlights from the 1992 series with the hashtag *xuanlü li de zhongguo* (China through songs), accessed December 30, 2020: https://m.weibo.cn/status/4587855324381311

54. See personal homepage of Robert Zollitsch (Lao Luo), accessed December 30, 2020: http://www.zollitsch.com/index.html

55. Two versions of "Uneasy" (*Tante*) can be found on Gong Linna's Youtube channel, one from a May 2011 concert in Beijing when she sang the viral song together with audience members during the concert's encore, the other "upgraded" version of the song combining five highlights from five Chinese operatic traditions, first performed on *Celebrity Battle* (*Quanneng xingzhan*) in November 2013 on Jiangu Satellite TV, accessed December 30, 2020: https://www.youtube.com/watch?v=zI5g6MBmfP4 and https://www.youtube.com/watch?v=8SCfJwNv8N4

56. Gong Linna's performance of "Fahai, you don't understand love" (*Fahai, ni budong ai*) on December 31, 2012 is available from her Youtube channel, accessed December 30, 2020: https://www.youtube.com/watch?v=DEnf409CsgU

57. See "'Tante' zhihou Gong Linna zaichang shenqu," *Hangzhou ribao*, December 30, 2012, https://hzdaily.hangzhou.com.cn/hzrb/html/2012-12/30/content_1408445.htm; and He Xi, "'Shenqu' Gong Linna: xunzhao zhenshi de shengyin," *Nanfeng chuang*, October 4, 2016, no. 20, 95–97.

58. See Lao Luo, "Fuzhi xifang yinyue bushi guojihua," *Yishu bao*, April 17, 2015, 3; and Dai Hong, "Gong Linna 'xin yishu yinyue' zhong de chuantong yinyue yuansu," *Gehai*, 2019, no. 4, 68–73.

59. Yuan Jian in his article instead asks the Chinese public to think independently regarding the "vulgar" label affixed on Gong Linna and Lao Luo's music, see Yuan Jian, "Jiedu Gong Linna zhi shenqu 'Fahai, ni budong ai'—you 'Fahai shijian' kan minzhong de zizhu sikao," *Shidai wenxue*, January 2015, no 2, 197–98.

60. As the White Snake legend has been popular especially in the big cities of the Jiangnan area and has always appealed not only to broad urban audiences but also to intellectuals, it has always combined the folk and the intellectual in its long history of adaptation and circulation.

61. See Chun, "Mediated Transgression and Madame White"; and Raymond Zhou, "Classical Tales from East and West Converge in Lake Extravaganza," *China Daily*, updated September 5, 2016: http://www.chinadaily.com.cn/china/2016-09/05/content_26697237.htm

62. Liu Cixin, Han Song, and Hao Jingfang are just three of the better-known Chinese science fiction writers in the English-speaking world. For an excellent recent selection, see Song and Huters, *The Reincarnated Giant*.

Selected Chronological List of White Snake Texts

Li Fang 李昉 et al., ed. *Taiping guangji* 太平廣記 [Extensive record of the Taiping era; **977–984**]. Shanghai: Saoye shanfang, 1926, juan [vol.] 458, snake story 3, "Li Huang" 李黃 [Li Huang].

Hong Mai 洪邁, ed. *Yijian zhi* 夷堅志 [Records of the listener, **1162–1202**]. Edited with commentary by He Zhuo 何卓. Beijing: Zhonghua shuju, 1981. "Sun zhixian qi" 孫知縣妻 [Wife of county magistrate Sun], 1062–63; "Qian Yan shusheng" 錢炎書生 [Student Qian Yan], 1755–56.

Hong Pian 洪楩, ed. *Qingping shantang huaben* 清平山堂話本 [Vernacular stories from Qingping mountain studio; **1541–1551**]. Beijing: Wenxue guji kanxingshe, 1955. "Xihu santaji" 西湖三塔記 [West Lake's three stupas]. The title of the collection used here is a made-up and misleading one: not all of the stories are *huaben*, or vernacular stories; the original title was *Liushi jia xiaoshuo* 六十家小說 [Stories from sixty authors].

Feng Menglong 馮夢龍, ed. *Jingshi tongyan* 警世通言 [Stories to caution the world; **1624**]. Beijing: Renmin wenxue chubanshe, 1956, chapter 28, "Bai niangzi yongzhen Leifengta" 白娘子永鎮雷峰塔 [Lady White is imprisoned forever under Thunder Peak Pagoda].

Mo Langzi 墨浪子, ed. *Xihu jiahua* 西湖佳話 [Beautiful tales of West Lake; **1673**]. Beijing: Gudian wenxue chubanshe, 1956, no. 15, "Leifeng guaiji" 雷峰怪跡 [Strange happenings at the Thunder Peak].

Huang Tubi 黃圖珌. "Leifengta" 雷峰塔 [Thunder Peak Pagoda; **1738**]. In *Baishe zhuan ji* 白蛇傳集 [A collection of White Snake stories], ed. Fu Xihua 傅惜華, 282–338. Shanghai: Shanghai chuban gongsi, 1955.

Fang Chengpei 方成培, ed. *Leifengta chuanqi* 雷峰塔傳奇 [Legend of Thunder Peak Pagoda; **1771**]. Shanghai: Shanghai guji chubanshe, 1995.

Ueda Akinari 上田秋成. "Jasei no in" 蛇性の婬 [Lust of the serpent]. In *Ugetsu monogatari* 雨月物語 [Tales of moonlight and rain; **1776**]. Included in *Ueda Akinari shū* 上田秋成集 [Collected works of Ueda Akinari], 285–310. Tokyo: Yūhōdō, 1911.

Ueda Akinari. "Jasei no in" [Lust of the serpent]. In *Ugetsu monogatari.* 4th ed. 3 vols. Osaka: Bun'eidō, n.d. Full-text available at Waseda University library: http://www.wul.waseda.ac.jp/kotenseki/html/he13/he13_04376/index.html

Yushan zhuren 玉山主人. *Leifengta qizhuan* 雷峰塔奇傳 [Strange tale of the Thunder

Peak Pagoda; **1806**]. Beijing: Huaxia chubanshe, 1995. Full text available at Chinese Text Project: https://ctext.org/wiki.pl?if=gb&res=906942&remap=gb

Chen Yuqian 陳遇乾, ed. *Xiuxiang yiyao quanzhuan* 繡像義妖全傳 [The complete illustrated righteous snake]. Edited by Chen Shiqi and Yu Xiushan. Preface dated **1809**. Full text available at Waseda University Archive: http://archive.wul.waseda.ac.jp/kosho/he19/he19_03304/

Julien, Stanislas, trans. *Blanche et Bleue, ou Les deux couleuvres-fées; roman chinois / Baishe jingji* 白蛇精記 [Legend of the White Snake femme fatale]. Paris: Gosselin, **1834**.

"White and Blue; or the Serpent Fairies." In "Analysis of Works" [a summary of Stanislas Julien's *Blanche et Bleue, ou Les deux couleuvres-fées; roman chinois*], *The Journal of the Royal Asiatic Society of Great Britain and Ireland* 1, no. 2, 307, 315–21. London: John W. Parker, West Strand, **1834**.

H. C., "Lüi-fung Tă, 'Thunder Peak Pagoda,' or 'The Story of Han-wăn and the White Serpent." In Vol. 1 (July 1863–June 1864), *The Chinese and Japanese Repository of Facts and Events in Science, History, and Art, Relating to Eastern Asia*, ed. Rev. James Summers, 357–65, 401–10, 429–35, 461–68, 503–13. London: W. H. Allen and Co.; Paris: Benjamin Duprat; and London: The Office of the Chinese and Japanese Repository, **1864**.

[H. C.], "Luo-fung Ta, 'Thunder Peak Pagoda,' or 'The Story of Han-wan and the White Serpent." In Vol. 2 (August 1864–December 1864), *The Chinese and Japanese Repository of Facts and Events in Science, History, and Art, Relating to Eastern Asia*, ed. Rev. James Summers, 11–19, 89–97. Nendeln, Liechtenstein: Kraus Reprint Limited, **1864**; Tokyo: reprinted by Yushodo Booksellers Ltd., 1967.

Lim Ho Hin. *Baishejingji* 白蛇精記 [The story of Xu Hanwen 許漢文 and the White Serpent; **1883**]. Reprinted in 1908 and 1917. Malay translation published in Indonesia.

Wong Chin Foo 王清福. "Poh Yuin Ko, The Serpent Princess." *The Cosmopolitan* 6, no. 2 (December **1888**): 180–90.

Tan Beng Teck 陳明德. *Ini lah buku bernama Lwee Hong Thak* 雷峰塔*, charita dulu kala dari pasal Oh Pek Chua* 黑白蛇 *sama Kho Hun Boon* 許漢文*, di turon-kan dari surat China, di Jaman Guan Teow* 元朝*, di Chnee Tong Quan* 錢塘縣*, dalam prentaan Chat Kang Hoo* 浙江口 [This is an ancient story translated from the Chinese and entitled *Leifeng ta* or 'The Thunder Peak Pagoda'; it deals with the Black and White Serpents and Xu Hanwen, during the Yuan Dynasty, in the District of Qianjiang [sic] in the Province of Zhejiang]. Singapore: Poh Wah Hean Press, **1889**. Translation in Romanized Malay.

Woodbridge, Samuel I. "The Mystery of the White Snake: A Legend of the Thunder Peak Tower, from the Chinese." *N.-C. Herald and S. C. & C. Gazette*, September 4, **1896**–October 16, 1896.

Woodbridge, Samuel I. *The Mystery of the White Snake: A Legend of the Thunder Peak Tower*. Shanghai: printed at the office of the North-China Herald, **1896**.

Cloud, Frederick D. "The Legend of the White Snake." In Cloud, *Hangchow, the "City of Heaven," with a Brief Historical Sketch of Soochow*, 73–102. Shanghai: Presbyterian Mission Press, **1906.**

Pang Teck Joon 馮德潤. *Hikayat ini bernama 'Lwee Hong Thak'* 雷峰塔 *cherita yang ajahep dari hal 'Oh Pek Chua'* 黑白蛇 *sama Kho Han Boon* 許漢文 *di zaman Guan Tiaw raja 'Guan Si Cho'* 元世祖 [Story entitled *Leifeng ta*, 'Thunder Peak Pagoda'; an amazing story about *Heibai she*, the Black and White Snakes and Xu Hanwen, during Yuan Dynasty at the time of the reign of emperor . . .]. 2 volumes. Singapore: Kim Seck Chye Press, **1911**. Translation in Romanized Malay.

Menghua guanzhu 夢花館主, ed. *Baishe quanzhuan* 白蛇全傳 [Complete legend of the White Snake; first printed in the **1920s**]. Changsha: Yuelu shushe, 2011.

Tanizaki Jun'ichirō 谷崎潤一郎, script writer. *Jasei no in* 蛇性の婬 [Lust of the serpent]. Directed by Kurihara Kisaburō 栗原喜三郎. Yokohama: Taishō katsuei, **1921**. Nonextant.

Tanizaki Jun'ichirō. "Jasei no in" [Lust of the serpent]. *Shufu no tomo*, April **1922**.

Shaw Runje 邵醉翁, dir. *Yiyao Baishe zhuan* 義妖白蛇傳 [Righteous snake], Parts I and II. Shanghai: Tianyi [Unique], **1926**. Nonextant.

"Synopsis," in "Yiyao baishe zhuan" 義妖白蛇傳 [Righteous snake], in *Tianyi tekan diliuqi Yiyao Baishe zhuan,* July 1, **1926**, 1–8.

Bu Wancang 卜萬倉, dir. *Hubian chunmeng* 湖邊春夢 [Lakeshore spring dream]. Story and intertitles by Tian Han 田漢. Shanghai: Mingxing dianying gongsi, **1927**. Nonextant.

"Baishe zhuan" 白蛇傳 [Legend of the White Snake]. In *Dingxian yangge xuan* 定縣秧歌選 [Selected folk plays of Dingxian; **1920s**], ed. Li Jinghan 李景漢. Folklore and Folk Literature Series of National Peking University and Chinese Association for Folklore, vol. 40, 958–1049. Taipei: Dongfang shuju, 1971.

Anonymous folklorists. *Leifeng ta; Bai niangniang* 雷峰塔·白娘娘 [Thunder Peak Pagoda; Madame White Snake: Collection of myths about Madame White Snake; **late 1920s**]. Folklore and Folk Literature Series of National Peking University and Chinese Association for Folklore, vol. 135. Taipei: Dongfang shuju, 1970.

Shao Runje and Li Pingqian 李萍倩, dirs. *Shilin jita* 仕林祭塔 [Memorial at the Pagoda]. Hong Kong: Naam Yuet Movie Co., **1934**. Black-and-white film in Cantonese.

Yang Xiaozhong 楊小仲, dir. *Baishe zhuan* 白蛇傳 [Legend of the White Snake]. Alternate title: *Huangta chenyuan* 荒塔沉冤 [All quiet in the pagoda]. Shanghai: Huaxin yingpian gongsi, **1939**. Black-and-white film in Mandarin Chinese.

Tian Han 田漢. *Jinbo ji* 金缽記 [Tale of the golden bowl; **1943**]. Shanghai: Zhonghua shuju, 1951.

Hayashi Fusao 林房雄. *Byaku fujin no yōjutsu* 白夫人の妖術 [Witchcraft of Madame White Snake]. Tokyo: Fusō shobō, **1948**.

Chen Ping 陳平, dir. *Yeji leifengta* 夜祭雷峰塔 [Nocturnal sacrifice at Lui Fung Tower]. Hong Kong, **1949**. Black-and-white film in Cantonese.

Wang Tianlin 王天林 and Hong Shuyun 洪叔雲, dirs. *Baishe zhuan* 白蛇傳 [Legend of the White Snake]. Hong Kong: Fuhua gongsi, **1952**. Black-and-white film in Mandarin Chinese.

Waley, Arthur, trans. "Mrs. White." In *The Real Tripitaka and Other Pieces*, 183–213. London: George Allen and Unwin, **1952**.

Tian Han. "Baishe zhuan" [Legend of the White Snake]. *Juben*, no. 8 (**1953**): 5–34.

Mizoguchi Kenji 溝口健二, dir. *Ugetsu* 雨月物語 [Tales of moonlight and rain]. Tokyo: Daiei, **1953**. Black-and-white film in Japanese.

Zhang Henshui 張恨水. *Baishe zhuan* 白蛇傳 [Legend of the White Snake]. Beijing: Tongsu wenyi chubanshe, **1955**.

Fu Xihua, ed. *Baishe zhuan ji* [A collection of White Snake stories]. Shanghai: Shanghai chuban gongsi, **1955**.

Chow See Luk 周詩祿, dir. *Baishe zhuan* 白蛇傳 [Legend of the White Snake]. Hong Kong: Taishan yingpian gongsi, **1955**. Black-and-white film in Cantonese.

Toyoda Shirō 豊田四郎, dir. *Byaku fujin no yōren* 白夫人の妖恋 [(Bewitching love of) Madame White Snake]. Starring Yamaguchi Yoshiko 山口淑子, or Li Xianglan (Ri Kōran 李香蘭). Coproduced by Toho and Shaw Brothers, **1956**. Color film in Japanese.

Hayashi Fusao, Karashima Takeshi 辛島驍, and Yasumi Toshio 八住利雄. *Byaku fujin no yōren: Shōsetsu, gensaku, shinario* 白夫人の妖恋: 小説・原作・シナリオ [Bewitching love of Madame White Snake: The novel, the original work, and scenarios]. Tokyo: Dainihon yūbenkai kōdansha, **1956**.

Zhao Qingge 趙清閣. *Baishe zhuan* 白蛇傳 [The legend of the White Snake]. Shanghai: Shanghai wenhua chubanshe, **1956**.

The White Snake, A Peking Opera by Tien Han. Translated by Yang Hsien-yi and Gladys Yang. Peking: Foreign Languages Press, **1957**.

Yabushita Taiji 薮下泰司, dir. *Hakujaden* 白蛇伝 [Tale of the White Serpent]. Tokyo: Tōei Animation, **1958**. Color film in Japanese.

Wong Fung 王風, dir. *Bai niangniang jieshi huanhun* 白娘娘借屍還魂 [Lady White's Reincarnation]. Hong Kong: **1959**. Color film in Cantonese.

Shin Sang-ok 申相玉 신상옥, dir. *Paeksa buin* 白蛇夫人 백사부인 [Madam White Snake]. Seoul: Shin Films, **1960**. Black-and-white film in Korean.

Jiang Yuequan 蔣月泉. *Baishe: shang Jinshan* 白蛇: 上金山 [White Snake: Going up the Golden Mountain]. Suzhou *pingtan* 評彈 storytelling performance. Recorded at Shanghai Music Hall, **1961**. Last updated by Y. Yu, December 20, 2016, https://youtu.be/uD22vkff5pI

Yueh Feng 岳楓, dir. *Baishe zhuan* 白蛇傳 [Madam White Snake]. Hong Kong: Shaw Brothers, **1962**. Color film in Mandarin Chinese.

Wong Fung, dir. *Duanqiao chanzi* 斷橋產子 [Giving birth on the Bridge]. Hong Kong: Chiu Ming, **1962**. Black-and-white film in Cantonese.

Chan Pei 陳皮, dir. *Gechang Shilin jita* 歌唱仕林祭塔 [Till death do we part]. Hong Kong: Hing Fat Film Co., **1962**. Black-and-white film in Cantonese.

Zhang Henshui and Zhao Qingge. *Baishe zhuan: Zhang Zhao ben* 白蛇傳: 張趙本 [Legend of the White Snake: The Zhang Henshui and Zhao Qingge versions]. Xingzhou: Shijie shuju, **1965**.

Shin Sang-ok, dir. *Sanyŏ* 蛇女 사녀 [Snake woman]. Seoul: Shin Films, **1969**. Color film in Korean.

Gamble, Sidney D., ed. "The White Snake." In *Chinese Village Plays from the Ting Hsien Region*, 703–62. Amsterdam: Philo Press, **1970**.

Chang, H. C., trans. "Madam White." Translation of Feng Menglong's version. In *Chinese Literature: Popular Fiction and Drama*, 216–61. Edinburgh: Edinburgh University Press, **1973**.

Chang, Donald, and William Packard, trans. "The White Snake." Translation of Tian Han's version. In *The Red Pear Garden: Three Great Dramas of Revolutionary China, ed.* John Dietrich Mitchell, 20–120. Boston: D. R. Godine, **1973**.

Lin Hwai-Min 林懷民, dir. *Baishe zhuan* 白蛇傳 [Legend of the White Snake]. Premiered by Taiwan's Cloud Gate Dance Theatre 雲門舞集 at the National Theatre of Singapore, **1975**. Dance drama.

Choe Dong-joon 崔東俊 and Si-ma Ke 司馬克, dirs. *Zhen Baishe zhuan* 真白蛇傳 [Love of the White Snake]. Hong Kong: First Films, **1978**. Color film in Mandarin Chinese; Choi Dong-joon and Lee Han-sang, dirs. *Paeksajŏn* 백사전 [Story of the White Snake]. South Korea, 1978. Color film in Korean; Li Han-hsiang 李翰祥, dir. *Zhen Baishe zhuan* [Love of the White Snake]. Taiwan, Hong Kong, and South Korea, 1978. Color film in Mandarin Chinese.

Li Qiao 李喬. *Qingtian wuhen: Baishe xinzhuan* 情天無恨: 白蛇新傳 [A new legend of the White Snake]. Taipei: Qianwei chubanshe, **1983**.

Jiang Yuequan and Liu Yunruo 劉韻若. *Baishe: penfu* 白蛇: 噴符 [White Snake: Puffing out water talisman]. Suzhou *pingtan* 評彈 performance in commemoration of Jiang Yuequan's fifty-year career, **1984**. Last updated by Y. Yu, June 2, 2017, https://youtu.be/GWeaakB5LAk

Li Bihua 李碧華. *Qingshe* 青蛇 [Green Snake]. Hong Kong: Tiandi tushu youxian gongsi, **1986**.

Chin, San Sooi. *Lady White: A Tale from the Chinese Opera Re-told*. Kuala Lumpur: Five Arts Centre, **1986**.

Xia Zuhui 夏祖輝 and He Qi 何麒, dirs. *Xin Bainiangzi chuanqi* 新白娘子傳奇 [New legend of Madame White Snake]. Starring Angie Chiu 趙雅芝 as the White Snake and Cecilia Yip 葉童 as Xu Xian. Taiwan: Taiwan Television, November 5, **1992** to January 13, 1993. Television series in Mandarin Chinese, 50 episodes.

Li Bihua. *Qingshe: quanxinban* 青蛇: 全新版 [Green Snake: A completely new edition]. Taipei: Huangguan, **1993**.

Tsui Hark 徐克, dir. *Qingshe* 青蛇 [Green Snake]. Hong Kong: Mei Ah Entertainment, **1993**. Color film in Cantonese.

Lim, Joyce, and Marcus A. S. *Legenda Ular Putih* [Legend of the White Snake]. Jakarta: Elex Media Komputindo, **1994**.

Zhao, Qingge. *The Legend of White Snake*. Translated by Paul White. Beijing: New World Press, **1998**. Chinese-English bilingual version.

Yan Geling 嚴歌苓. "Baishe" 白蛇 [White Snake], in *Shiyue* 十月 [October], **1998**, no. 5.

Yan Geling. *Baishe* [White Snake]. Taipei: Jiuge chubanshe, **1999**.

Yan, Geling. *White Snake and Other Stories*. Translated by Lawrence A. Walker. San Francisco: Aunt Lute Books, **1999**.

Yeh Ching 葉青 Taiwanese opera troupe. *Baishe zhuan* 白蛇傳 [Legend of the White Snake]. Taiwan: Chinese Television, November 5, **1999** to December 31, 1999. TV series in Taiwanese, 20 episodes.

Shepard, Aaron, ed. *A Lady White Snake Bookshelf*. **1999**–2003, 2012, 2014. http://www.aaronshep.com/bookshelves/WhiteSnake.html

Yin Chi 尹祺. *Baishe* 白蛇 [White Snake]. Winner of best film scripts of 2000, no. 6. Taipei: Government Information Office, Executive Yuan, **2000**. Film script based on Geling Yan's novella *White Snake*.

Li Bihua. *Qingshe* 青蛇 [Green Snake]. Beijing: Renmin wenxue chubanshe, **2000**.

Liu Yi 劉翼, dir. *Baishe zhuan* 白蛇傳 [Legend of the White Snake]. Chinese Central Television, Sichuan Television, and Chengdu Sichuan Opera Theater, **2003**. Sichuan opera television series in Sichuanese, 12 episodes.

Feng Menglong, ed. "Madam White Is Kept Forever under the Thunder Peak Tower." In *Stories to Caution the World: A Ming Dynasty Collection*, translated by Shuhui Yang and Yunqin Yang, vol. 2, chapter 28, 474–505. Seattle: University of Washington Press, **2005**.

Watanabe Senshū 渡辺仙州 (editor) and Isa Emon 石原依門 (illustrator). *Hakujaden* 白蛇伝 [Legend of the White Snake]. Tokyo: Kaishesha, **2005**. Illustrated fiction in Japanese.

Tsai Chih Chung 蔡志忠. *Madam White Snake*, translated by Joyce Lim. Taipei: Modern Publishing House, **2006**. English-Chinese bilingual Cartoon.

Wu Jiatai 吳家駘, dir. *Baishe zhuan* 白蛇傳 [Legend of the White Snake]. Starring Liu Tao 劉濤 as the White Snake. Chinese Central Television, **2006**. Television series in Mandarin Chinese, 30 episodes.

Li Rui 李銳 and Jiang Yun 蔣韻. *Renjian: chongshu baishe zhuan* 人間: 重述白蛇傳 [The human realm: the legend of the White Snake retold]. Chongqing: Chongqing chubanshe, **2007**.

Ueda Akinari. "A Serpent's Lust." In *Tales of Moonlight and Rain*, edited and translated by Anthony H. Chambers, 155–85. New York: Columbia University Press, **2007**.

Ming Hwa Yuan 明華園. *Chaoxuan Baishe zhuan* 超炫白蛇傳 [White Snake spectacular]. Taiwanese opera, **2008**. DVD. Live recording of 2007 performance in Taipei in Taiwanese.

Lady White Snake: A Tale from Chinese Opera. Retold by Aaron Shepard. Illustrated by Song Nan Zhang. Chinese translation by Isabella Chen. Union City: Pan Asian Publications, **2008**. Animated Chinese Classic Story on DVD.

Idema, Wilt. *The White Snake and Her Son: A Translation of "The Precious Scroll of Thunder Peak" with Related Texts*. Indianapolis: Hackett Publishing Company, **2009**.

Bai niangzi: aiqing siji 白娘子: 愛情四季 [Madame White Snake: Seasons of love]. Shanghai: Shanghai Conservatory of Music, **2009**. Symphonic-style Peking opera performance in Mandarin Chinese.

Wichmann-Walczak, Elizabeth, dir. *The White Snake*. University of Hawai'i at Manoa. Performed in English at the Kennedy Theatre, February 5–14, **2010**. Peking opera based on Tian Han's script.

Zhou Long 周龍. *Madame White Snake: An Opera in Four Acts*. Libretto by Cerise Lim Jacobs. Oxford: Oxford University Press, **2011**.

Ching Sui-tung 程小東, dir. *Baishe chuanshuo* 白蛇傳說 [The sorcerer and the White Snake, or it's love]. Starring Jet Li as Fahai. China Juli Entertainment Media, **2011**. Film in Mandarin Chinese.

Dagui 大鬼, dir. *Chaoji xin Bainiangzi chuanqi zhi youdian xian* 超級新白娘子傳奇之有碘鹹 [Super new legend of the White Snake, with a grain of salt]. Beijing: Xiha Crosstalk Group, May 18, **2011**–July 3, 2011. Crosstalk Theatre in Mandarin Chinese.

Guo Guang Opera Company 國光劇團. *Baishe zhuan* 白蛇傳 [The legend of White Snake]. Taipei: New Melody from the National Palace Museum, **2011**. A joint performance of Peking and Kunqu operas. Performance DVD.

Gu Qing 顧青 and Zhang Jiankang 張建康, dirs. *Shuiman Jinshan* 水漫金山 [The flooding of Jinshan Temple]. Nanjing: Hongbai yingshi. Chinese Central Television, premiered March 13, **2012**. Animation series, 52 episodes.

Gong Linna 龔琳娜 and Lao Luo 老鑼 (Robert Zollitsch). *Fahai, ni budong ai* 法海，你不懂愛 [Fahai, You don't understand love]. Changsha: Hunan Satellite TV, December 31, 2012. https://www.youtube.com/watch?v=DEnf409CsgU

Zimmerman, Mary. *The White Snake: A Play*. Evanston, IL: Northwestern University Press, **2013**.

Pal-Chaudhuri, Indrani, dir. *The Legend of Lady White Snake*. New York: Double Exposure Studios, Meta GK, [**2013**] 2015. Short film in English.

Chen, Fan Pen Li. "'Cloud-Transcending Crossing' ('Lingyun du') or 'The Great Revenge of Blue Snake' ('Qingshe da baochou'), the Second and Final Installment of a Chengdu Shadow Play Script, *Thunder Peak Pagoda* (Leifeng ta)." *CHINOPERL: Journal of Chinese Oral and Performing Literature* 32, no. 1 (**2013**): 30–71.

Yang Xiao-ming, trans. *The Legend of a White Snake—A Beijing Opera*. Beijing: Foreign Language Teaching and Research Press, **2013**.

Tian Qinxin 田沁鑫, dir. *Qingshe* 青蛇 [Green Snake], National Theatre of China. Eisenhower Theater, Kennedy Center, Washington DC, March 30, **2014**. In Chinese with English subtitles.

Tian Qinxin, dir. *Qingshe* [Green Snake], National Theatre of China. Wuzhen Theatre Festival, Water Theatre, Wuzhen, China, October 30, **2014**.

Zimmerman, Mary, dir. *The White Snake*. Wuzhen Theatre Festival, Wuzhen Grand Theatre, Wuzhen, China, November 7, **2014**. In English with Chinese subtitles.

Chen Qiufan 陳秋帆 (rewriting), Lin Baochun 林保淳 (reading guide), and Lan Fuyuan 藍傳源 (illustration). *Baishe zhuan* 白蛇傳 [Legend of the White Snake]. Based on the 1806 version attributed to Yushan zhuren, rewritten into modern Chinese. Classic Novels for All Ages. Taipei: Eastern Publishing Company, **2014**.

Zhang Huoding 張火丁, as White Snake, in *Baishe zhuan* 白蛇傳 [Legend of the White Snake]. Peking opera, performed by National Academy of Chinese Theatre Arts, presented by China Arts and Entertainment Group. David H. Koch Theater, Lincoln Center, New York City, NY, September 2, **2015**. In Chinese with English subtitles.

Jacobs, Cerise Lim. *Ouroboros Trilogy: Madame White Snake*. Composed by Zhou Long, libretto by Cerise Lim Jacobs. World premiere, Cutler Majestic Theatre, Boston, September 10, **2016**, performance recording courtesy of Cerise Lim Jacobs.

Pan Liping 潘禮平, Lu Jianmei 陸劍梅, and Liu Yujie 劉玉潔, dirs. *Xiaoxigu: baishe zhuan* 小戲骨白蛇傳 [Star of tomorrow: Legend of White Snake]. Hunan Satellite TV, October 2, **2016**. Television series in Mandarin Chinese, five 20-min. episodes.

Wang Peijun 王培君 and Xia Xiyan 夏夕燕. *Baishe zhuan* 白蛇傳 [Legend of the White Snake]. Suzhou dianshi shuchang, **2017**, August 10, 2018, https://www.youtube.com/playlist?list=PLhbYKZKr81efuYzNB-rS7CUHX_de301dt. Full-length Suzhou *pingtan* storytelling performance, 30 televised episodes with Chinese subtitles.

Yin Tao 尹濤 and Liu Guohui 劉國輝, dirs. *Tianji zhi baishe chuanshuo* 天乩之白蛇傳說 [The destiny of White Snake]. Starring Yang Zi 楊紫 as the White Snake. H&R Century Pictures, Innovation Media Power, and Shanghai New Culture, original release on iQiyi on July 9, **2018**. Internet drama series in Mandarin Chinese, 60 episodes.

Wong, Amp 黃家康, and Zhao Ji 趙霽, dirs. *Baishe: yuanqi* 白蛇: 緣起 [White Snake: The legend begins]. Light Chaser Animation Studios and Warner Bros., January 11, **2019**. Animation in Mandarin Chinese and dubbed in English, with multiple subtitles.

Zhi Lei 智磊, dir. *Xin Bainiangzi chuanqi* 新白娘子傳奇 [The legend of White Snake]. Starring Ju Jingyi 鞠婧禕 as the White Snake. iQiyi: https://www.iqiyi.com/a_19rrgxjest.html, April 3 to May 10, **2019**. Internet drama series in Mandarin Chinese, 36 episodes. The link has been deactivated likely due to music copyright disputes.

Zhi Lei, dir. *Xin Bainiangzi chuanqi* [The legend of White Snake]. Viki: https://www.viki.com/tv/36277c-the-legend-of-white-snake, **2019**. Internet drama series in Mandarin Chinese, 36 episodes, subtitled in eleven languages.

Zhi Lei, dir. *Xin Bainiangzi chuanqi* [The legend of White Snake]. Netflix: https://www.netflix.com/title/81108281, **2019**. Internet drama series in Mandarin Chinese, 36 episodes, subtitled in English, French, Spanish, and Simplified and Traditional Chinese.

Stockman, Allison Arkell, dir. *The White Snake*. Written and originally directed by Mary Zimmerman. With live music by Tom Teasley and Chao Tian. Constellation Theatre Company, Washington, DC, April 25 to May 26, **2019**.

Oei, Pam, dir. *Wild@Home—Mama White Snake*, a Wild Rice production. Book and lyrics by Alfian Sa'at. Music by Elaine Chan. Recorded live on December 8, 2017, Singapore: Drama Centre Theatre. Streamed May 22 to June 7, **2020**, https://www.wildrice.com.sg/event/11785-wildhome-mama-white-snake/

Ju Homin 주호민 周浩旻 (artist) and Chang Hŭi 장희 (writer). *Pingt'ang huru* 빙탕후루 [*Bingtang hulu* 冰糖葫蘆]. Webtoon in Korean, serialized on Naver from April 2017 and completed at 170 episodes in June **2020**. Lady White (Paek Nangcha 백낭자 白娘子) featured in episodes 42, 43, and 70. https://comic.naver.com/webtoon/list.nhn?titleId=695321.

Zhang Xianfeng 張險峰, dir. *Baishe zhuan · qing* 白蛇傳 • 情 [*White Snake, or Snake White: Love Endures*]. Starring Zeng Xiaomin 曾小敏 as the White Snake. Produced by Pearl River Film Group, Guangdong Cantonese Opera Institute, and Foshan Cultural Investment and Management Co., Ltd., 2019. Cantonese opera fantasy film, 4K Dolby Atmos. Premiered in mainland China on May 20, **2021** to sensational followings and critical acclaim.

Selected Bibliography

For brief references to terms, images, websites, and newspaper and magazine pages, see corresponding notes and captions.

A Ying 阿英. *Leifengta chuanqi xulu* 雷峰塔傳奇敘錄 [Commentaries on the southern dramas of *Thunder Peak Pagoda*]. Shanghai: Zhonghua shuju, 1960.

Alaimo, Stacy. *Exposed: Environmental Politics and Pleasures in Posthuman Times.* Minneapolis: University of Minnesota Press, 2016.

Allen, Joseph R. "The Babel Fallacy: When Translation Does Not Matter." *Cultural Critique* 102 (2019): 117–50.

Allen, Sarah M. *Shifting Stories: History, Gossip, and Love in Narratives from Tang Dynasty China.* Cambridge, MA: Harvard University Asia Center, 2014.

Altenburger, Roland. *The Sword and the Needle: The Female Knight-Errant (xia) in Traditional Chinese Narrative.* Bern: Peter Lang, 2009.

An, Jinsoo. *Parameters of Disavowal: Colonial Representation in South Korean Cinema.* Oakland: University of California Press, 2018.

Anderson, Joseph L., and Donald Richie. *The Japanese Film: Art and Industry.* Expanded ed. Princeton: Princeton University Press, 2018.

Anobile, Richard J., ed. *Ernst Lubitsch's Ninotchka, Starring Greta Garbo, Melvyn Douglas.* New York: Universe Books, 1975.

Anzaldúa, Gloria. *Borderlands/La Frontera: The New Mestiza.* Fourth ed. San Francisco: Aunt Lute Books, 2012.

Appadurai, Arjun. *Modernity at Large: Cultural Dimensions of Globalization.* Minneapolis: University of Minnesota Press, 1996.

Arrighi, Giovanni. *The Long Twentieth Century: Money, Power, and the Origins of Our Times.* London: Verso, 1994.

Bacchilega, Cristina. *Postmodern Fairy Tales: Gender and Narrative Strategies.* Philadelphia: University of Pennsylvania Press, 1999.

Bai Fan 白帆. "Qingdai Baishe zhuan nianhua yu shenü gushi—minjian meishu zhongde minjian xushi shuxie guankui" 清代白蛇傳年畫與蛇女故事—民間美術中的民間敘事書寫管窺 [White Snake New Year paintings and snake women tales in the Qing dynasty—A preliminary look at folk narratives in folk art]. *Meishu guancha* 292 (December 2019): 45–50.

Balivet, Aaron. "The Many Transformations of White Snake: Gender, Ritual, and Performance in Late Imperial China." PhD diss., University of Wisconsin-Madison, 2020.

Barr, Allan. "Disarming Intruders: Alien Women in *Liaozhai zhiyi*." *Harvard Journal of Asiatic Studies* 49, no. 2 (December 1989): 501–17.

Beecroft, Alexander. *Authorship and Cultural Identity in Early Greece and China: Patterns of Literary Circulation*. Cambridge: Cambridge University Press, 2010.

Beecroft, Alexander. *An Ecology of World Literature: From Antiquity to the Present Day*. London: Verso, 2015.

Berman, Marshall. *All That Is Solid Melts into Air: The Experience of Modernity*. New York: Penguin Books, 1988.

Berry, Chris. "Sino-Korea Screen Connections: Towards a History of Fragments." *Journal of Chinese Cinemas* 10, no. 3 (2016): 247–64.

Bian, He. *Know Your Remedies: Pharmacy and Culture in Early Modern China*. Princeton: Princeton University Press, 2020.

Billeter, Jean François. *The Chinese Art of Writing*. New York: Skira/Rizzoli,1990.

Birrell, Anne, trans. *The Classic of Mountains and Seas*. London: Penguin Classics, 2000.

Blair, Sheila S. *Islamic Calligraphy*. Edinburgh: Edinburgh University Press, 2006.

Bonhôte, Ian, and Peter Ettedgui, dirs. *McQueen*. New York: Bleecker Street Media, 2018. Documentary.

Børdahl, Vibeke. *The Oral Tradition of Yangzhou Storytelling*. London: Curzon Press, 1996.

Børdahl, Vibeke, and Margaret B. Wan, eds. *The Interplay of the Oral and the Written in Chinese Popular Literature*. Copenhagen: NIAS Press, 2010.

Bordo, Susan, M. Cristina Alcalde, and Ellen Rosenman, eds. *Provocations: A Transnational Reader in the History of Feminist Thought*. Oakland: University of California Press, 2015.

Brennan, Joseph. "Queerbaiting: The 'Playful' Possibilities of Homoeroticism." *International Journal of Cultural Studies* 21, no. 2 (March 2016): 189–206.

Brooks, Peter. *Body Work: Objects of Desire in Modern Narrative*. Cambridge, MA: Harvard University Press, 1993.

Buck, Pearl S. *Fighting Angel: Portrait of a Soul*. New York: Reynal & Hitchcock, 1936.

Buck, Pearl S. *My Several Worlds: A Personal Record*. New York: The John Day Company, 1954.

Cai Yuanpei 蔡元培. "Yi meiyu dai zongjiao" 以美育代宗教 [Using aesthetic education as a substitute for religion]. *Xin qingnian* 3, no. 6 (1917). Included in *Xin qingnian jiben duben*, edited by Wang Yaohua, 266–71. Shanghai: Shanghai shudian, 2015.

Calichman, Richard, ed. and trans. *Overcoming Modernity: Cultural Identity in Wartime Japan*. New York: Columbia University Press, 2008.

Campany, Rob. "Cosmogony and Self-Cultivation: The Demonic and the Ethical in Two Chinese Novels." *The Journal of Religious Ethics* 14, no. 1 (Spring, 1986): 81–112.

Campany, Rob. "Demons, Gods, and Pilgrims: The Demonology of the *Hsi-yu Chi*." *Chinese Literature: Essays, Articles, Reviews* 7, no. 1/2 (July 1985): 95–115.

Campany, Rob. *Strange Writing: Anomaly Accounts in Early Medieval China*. Albany: SUNY Press, 1996.

Campbell, Joseph. *The Hero with a Thousand Faces*. 3rd ed. Novato: New World Library, 2008.

Chan, Koonchung 陳冠中. *The Fat Years*. Translated by Michael S. Duke. New York: First Anchor Books Edition, 2013.

Chang, Chia-Ju. "The Chinese Snake Woman: Mythology, Culture, and Female Expression." PhD diss., Rutgers University, 2004.

Chang Chih-tung 張之洞. *Quanxue pian* 勸學篇 [An exhortation to study]. Beijing: Tongwenguan, 1898.

Chang, Chris. "Ghost Tones." *Film Comment* (March–April 2006): 16.

Chang, Eileen. *The Fall of the Pagoda*. Hong Kong: Hong Kong University Press, 2010.

Chang, Kang-i Sun, and Stephen Owen, eds. *The Cambridge History of Chinese Literature: From 1375*. New York: Cambridge University Press, 2010.

Chen Ailian 陳愛蓮. *Wo shicong gu'eryuan laide* 我是從孤兒院來的 [I came from an orphanage). Beijing: Sanlian shudian, 1982.

Chen Fang-ying 陳芳英. *Xiqu lunji: shuqing yu xushi de duihua* 戲曲論集: 抒情與敘事的對話 [A collection of essays on *xiqu*: dialogues between the lyrical and the narrative]. Taipei: Taipei National University of the Arts Press, 2009.

Chen, Fan Pen Li. *Journey of a Goddess: Chen Jinggu Subdues the Snake Demon*. Albany: SUNY Press, 2017.

Chen, Huaiyu 陳懷宇. "A Buddhist Classification of Animals and Plants in Early Tang Times." *Journal of Asian History* 43, no. 1 (2009): 31–51.

Chen Huaiyu. "Cong shi'er shishou dao shi'er jingmei: Nanbeichao Sui Tang Fojiao wenxian zhongde shi'er shengxiao" 從十二時獸到十二精魅：南北朝隋唐佛教文獻中的十二生肖 [From twelve calendrical beasts to twelve demonic spirits: Changing image of twelve animals in medieval Chinese Buddhist literature]. *Tang yanjiu* 13 (2007): 301–45.

Chen, Huaiyu. "Honoring the Dead: The Buddhist Reinvention of Commemorative Literature, Ritual, and Material Culture in Early Medieval China." In *Old Society, New Belief: Religious Transformation of China and Rome, ca. 1st–6th Centuries*, ed. Mu-chou Poo, Harold Drake, and Lisa Raphals, 91–105. New York: Oxford University Press, 2017.

Chen Jianxian 陳建憲. "Cong yindang de sheyao dao aiyumei de huashen—lun Dongxifang *Baishe zhuan* zhong renwu xingxiangde yanhua" 從淫蕩的蛇妖到愛與美的化身—論東西方《白蛇傳》中人物形象的演化 [From a lewd snake spirit to an embodiment of love and beauty—on character evolution in Eastern and Western versions of *Legend of White Snake*]. *Huazhong shifan daxue xuebao* 2 (1987): 101–5.

Chen, Xiaomei, Tarryn Li-Min Chun, and Siyuan Liu, eds. *Rethinking Chinese Socialist Theaters of Reform: Performance Practice and Debate in the Mao Era*. Ann Arbor: University of Michigan Press, 2021.

Chen Yang 陳暘. *Yueshu* 樂書 [Book of music, 12th century]. Reprint of Wenyuange edition, vol. 67. Taipei: The Commercial Press, 1979.

Chen Yunlu 陳雲路. *Ting Zhu Guangqian jiang meixue* 聽朱光潛講美學 [Listening to Zhu Guangqian's lectures on aesthetics]. Xi'an: Shaanxi shifan daxue chubanshe, 2009.

Chen Zhiming 陳志明. *Zhongguo lianhuanhua shi kaolüe* 中國連環畫史考略 [A brief history of Chinese lianhuanhua]. Hangzhou: Zhejiang renmin meishu chubanshe, 2015.

Cheng, Boey Kim. *Gull Between Heaven and Earth.* Singapore: Epigram Books, 2017.

Chiang, Howard, ed. *Sexuality in China: Histories of Power and Pleasure.* Seattle: University of Washington Press, 2018.

Chiba Nobuo. *Eiga to Tanizaki.* Tokyo: Seiabō, 1989.

Cho, Sookja. *Transforming Gender and Emotion: The Butterfly Lovers Story in China and Korea.* Ann Arbor: University of Michigan Press, 2018.

Choi Young Hee 최영희 崔栄姬 and Moon Hyun Sun 문현선 文炫善. "Chŏnhu shigi Tongashia maech'esŏsaŭi rok'ŏllit'i—Hanjungil samguk yŏnghwaesŏŭi chungguk kojŏnsŏsa Paeksajŏn suyongŭl chungshimŭro" 전후 시기 동아시아 매체서사의 로컬리티— 한중일 삼국 영화에서의 중국 고전서사 <백사전 (白蛇傳)> 수용을 중심으로 [Locality of East Asian media narratives after World War II — Focusing on the acceptance of the Chinese classical narrative 'Bai-she-zhuan (白蛇傳)' in the nation-state films of Japan, Korea, and China]. *Chungguk sosŏl lonch'ong* 55 (2018): 245–72.

Chow, Rey. *Primitive Passions: Visuality, Sexuality, Ethnography, and Contemporary Chinese Cinema.* New York: Columbia University Press, 1995.

Chow Sing Chi (Stephen Chow 周星馳), dir. *Meiren yu* 美人魚 [The Mermaid]. Beijing: China Film Group, 2016.

Chow, Tse-tsung. *The May Fourth Movement: Intellectual Revolution in Modern China.* Cambridge, MA: Harvard University Press, 1960.

Chun, Tarryn Li-Min. "Mediated Transgression and Madame White: Technology and the Nonhuman in Contemporary Stagings of a Chinese Folktale." *Theatre Journal* 71, no. 3 (September 2019): 307–26.

Chun, Tarryn Li-Min. "Resurrecting a Postlapsarian Pagoda in a Postrevolutionary World." In *A New Literary History of Modern China*, ed. David Der-wei Wang, 883–88. Cambridge, MA: Harvard University Press, 2017.

Chung, Hye Seung. "The Korean Valentino: Jin Yan (Kim Yŏm), Sino-Korean Unity, and Shanghai Films of the 1930s." *Korean Studies* 37 (2013): 150–70.

Chung, Steven. *Split Screen Korea: Shin Sang-ok and Postwar Cinema.* Minneapolis: University of Minnesota Press, 2014.

Chung Te-Fan 鍾德凡. "Tian Qiyuan biandao fengge yanjiu—yi *Baishui* weili" 田啟元編導風格研究—以《白水》為例" [An Analysis of the Playwriting and Directing Style of Tien Chi-Yuan as Demonstrated in *White Water*]. MA thesis, National Taiwan University of Arts, 2007.

Clark, Paul. *Youth Culture in China: From Red Guards to Netizens.* Cambridge: Cambridge University Press, 2012.

Cloud, Frederick D. *A Digest of the Treaty, Laws, and Regulations Governing the Admission of Chinese*. Washington, DC: Government Printing Office, 1908.

Cloud, Frederick D. *Hangchow, the "City of Heaven," with a Brief Historical Sketch of Soochow*. Shanghai: Presbyterian Mission Press, 1906.

Cohen, Jeffrey Jerome, ed. *Monster Theory: Reading Culture*. Minneapolis: University of Minnesota Press, 1996.

Cohen, Paul A. *Speaking to History: The Story of King Goujian in Twentieth-Century China*. Berkeley: University of California Press, 2009.

Condry, Ian. *The Soul of Anime: Collaborative Creativity and Japan's Media Success Story*. Durham, NC: Duke University Press. 2013.

Cote, Jennifer. "The White Snake." In *China's Magical Creatures*, a student-authored textbook, ed. Tineke D'Haeseleer. Pressbooks, 2020. Https://open.muhlenberg.pub/chinasmagicalcreatures/chapter/the-white-snake/

Crossley, Pamela. *What Is Global History?* Cambridge, UK: Polity, 2008.

Cullen, Christopher. "Patients and Healers in Late Imperial China: Evidence from 'Jinpingmei.'" *History of Science* 31, no. 2 (June 1993): 99–150.

Dai Bufan 戴不凡, et al. *Mingjia tan Baishe zhuan* 名家談白蛇傳 [Famous critics on *The White Snake*]. Beijing: Wenhua yishu chubanshe, 2006.

Damrosch, David. *What Is World Literature?* Princeton: Princeton University Press, 2003.

Davis, Richard M. "Imaginary Conquests: Folktales, Film, and the Japanese Empire in Asia." *Ex-position*, no. 42 (December 2019): 5–27.

Denecke, Wiebke. "Worlds without Translation: Premodern East Asia and the Power of Character Scripts." In *A Companion to Translation Studies*, ed. Sandra Bermann and Catherine Porter, 204–16. Chichester: Wiley, 2014.

Derrida, Jacques. "Plato's Pharmacy." In *Dissemination*, trans. Barbara Johnson, 63–171. Chicago: University of Chicago Press, 1981.

Derrida, Jacques. *Specters of Marx: The State of the Debt, the Work of Mourning and the New International*, translated by Peggy Kamuf. New York and London: Routledge, 1994.

Dhaliwal, Aminder. *Woman World*. Montreal: Drawn & Quarterly, 2018. Graphic novel.

Dillery, John. "The First Egyptian Narrative History: Manetho and Greek Historiography." *Zeitschrift für Papyrologie und Epigraphik* 127 (1999): 93–116.

Ding Fan 丁帆 and Wang Shicheng 王世城, "Shiqinian wenxue: 'ren' yu 'ziwo' de shiluo" 十七年文學："人"與"自我"的失落 [Literature of the seventeen years: the loss of "human" and "self"]. Zhengzhou: Henan daxue chubanshe, 1999.

Dirlik, Arif, and Xudong Zhang, eds. *Postmodernism & China*. Durham, NC: Duke University Press, 2000.

Ditter, Alexei, Jessey Choo, and Sarah M. Allen, eds. *Tales from Tang Dynasty China: Selections from the Taiping Guangji*. Indianapolis: Hackett Publishing, 2017.

Doležlová-Velingerová, Milena, and Graham Martin Sanders, eds. *The Appropriation of Cultural Capital: China's May Fourth Project*. Cambridge, MA: Harvard University Press, 2001.

Dooling, Amy D., and Kristina M. Torgeson, eds. *Writing Women in Modern China: An Anthology of Women's Literature from the Early Twentieth Century*. New York: Columbia University Press, 1998.

Dower, John W. *Embracing Defeat: Japan in the Wake of World War II*. New York: W. W. Norton & Company, 1999.

Du, Daisy Yan. *Animated Encounters: Transnational Movements of Chinese Animation, 1940s–1970s*. Honolulu: University of Hawai'i Press, 2018.

Du Jianhua 杜建華, ed. *Chuanju biaoxian shoufa tonglan* 川劇表現手法通覽 [An overview of the performance techniques of Sichuan opera]. Chengdu: Sichuan wenyi chubanshe, 2002.

Duan, Xiaolin. *The Rise of West Lake: A Cultural Landmark in the Song Dynasty*. Seattle: University of Washington Press, 2020.

Dy, Aristotle C. "The Virgin Mary as Mazu or Guanyin: The Syncretic Nature of Chinese Religion in the Philippines." *Philippine Sociological Review* 62 (2014): 41–63. Special issue on sociology of religion.

Edkins, Joseph. *Shijiao zhengmiu* 釋教正謬 [Correcting the mistakes in Buddhism], translated by Sanyan Jushi. Shanghai: Mohai shuguan, 1857.

Epstein, Maram. *Competing Discourses: Orthodoxy, Authenticity, and Engendered Meanings in Late Imperial Chinese Fiction*. Cambridge, MA: Harvard University Asia Center, 2001.

Erb, Cynthia Marie. *Tracking King Kong: A Hollywood Icon in World Culture*. Detroit: Wayne State University Press, 2009.

Fang Bo 方博. "Lin Xiaoying tan geju *Baishe zhuan*" 林曉英談歌劇《白蛇傳》 [An interview with Cerise Lim Jacobs on *Madame White Snake*]. *Geju* 4 (2019): 52–57.

Feng Menglong 馮夢龍, ed. "Artisan Cui's Love is Cursed in Life and in Death." In *Stories to Caution the World: A Ming Dynasty Collection*, translated by Shuhui Yang and Yunqin Yang, vol. 2, chapter 8, 109–23. Seattle: University of Washington Press, 2005.

Feng Menglong, ed. "Cui Shizhao shengsi yuanjia" 崔待詔生死冤家 [Artisan Cui's love is cursed in life and in death). In *Jingshi tongyan*, chapter 8. Beijing: Renmin wenxue chubanshe, 1956.

Fischer, Michael M. J. *Anthropological Futures*. Durham, NC: Duke University Press, 2009. Https://archive.org/details/anthropologicalf01fisc/page/n9/mode/2up

Fischer, Paul, trans. and ed. "Fragments." In *Shizi: China's First Syncretist*, 120–72. New York: Columbia University Press, 2012.

Fiss, Géraldine and Li Guo, eds. "Women, Writing and Visuality in Contemporary China." Special issue, *Frontiers of Literary Studies in China* 11, no. 1 (May 2017).

Fogel, Joshua A. *Articulating the Sinosphere: Sino-Japanese Relations in Space and Time*. Cambridge, MA: Harvard University Press, 2009.

Foucault, Michel. *The Birth of the Clinic: An Archaeology of Medical Perception*. New York: Vintage, 1994.

Fraser, Lucy. *The Pleasures of Metamorphosis: Japanese and English Fairy Tale Transformations of "The Little Mermaid."* Detroit: Wayne State University Press, 2017.

Freeman, Alisa. *Tokyo in Transit: Japanese Culture on the Rails and Road.* Stanford: Stanford University Press, 2010.

Friedmann, John. "Reflections on Place and Place-Making in the Cities of China." *International Journal of Urban and Regional Research* 31, no. 2 (June 2007): 257–79.

Fu Jin 傅謹. *Jingju lishi wenxian huibian Qingdai juan* 京劇歷史文獻匯編清代卷 [A collection of historical records on Peking opera from the Qing dynasty], 10 vols. Nanjing: Fenghuang chubanshe, 2013.

Fu Jin. "Xiulian: 'Baishe zhuan' de renxing biaoda" 修煉:《白蛇傳》的人性表達 [Self-cultivation: on the humanistic expressions of *Legend of White Snake*]. *Xiju: Journal of Chinese Central Academy of Drama* 1 (2017): 53–62.

Fu Jin. *Zhongguo xiju shi* 中國戲劇史 [A history of Chinese theater]. Beijing: Peking University Press, 2014.

Fu, Poshek. *Between Shanghai and Hong Kong: The Politics of Chinese Cinemas.* Stanford: Stanford University Press, 2008.

Fu, Poshek, ed. *China Forever: The Shaw Brothers and Diasporic Cinema.* Champaign: University of Illinois Press, 2008.

Fu, Poshek, and David Desser, eds. *The Cinema of Hong Kong: History, Arts, Identity.* Cambridge: Cambridge University Press, 2000.

Fung, Anthony. "Postcolonial Hong Kong Identity: Hybridizing the Local and the National." *Social Identities* 10, no. 3 (2004): 399–414. https://doi.org/10.1080/1350463042000230854

Gaiman, Neil. *Fragile Things: Short Fictions and Wonders.* New York: HarperCollins, 2006.

Gan Bao 干宝. *Soushen ji* 搜神記 [Anecdotes about spirits and immortals], chapter 19, 195–200. Prague: e-artnow s.r.o., 2018.

Gao, James Z. *The Communist Takeover of Hangzhou: The Transformation of City and Cadre, 1949–1954.* Honolulu: University of Hawai'i Press, 2004.

Gao Yanfang 高豔芳. "Baishe zhuan yanjiu de bainian huigu yu fansi" 白蛇傳研究的百年回顧與反思 [Reflections on the research on the White Snake legend in the past hundred years]. *Guangxi shifan daxue xuebao: zhexue shehui kexue ban* 49, no. 6 (2003): 51–57.

Ge, Liangyan. *The Scholar and the State: Fiction as Political Discourse in Late Imperial China.* Seattle: University of Washington Press, 2014.

Geertz, Clifford. "Thick Description: Toward an Interpretive Theory of Culture." In *The Interpretation of Cultures: Selected Essays*, 3–30. New York: Basic Books, 1973.

Glosser, Susan L., ed. and trans. *Li Fengjin: How the New Marriage Law Helped Chinese Women Stand Up.* Portland, OR: Opal Mogus Books, 2005.

Gluck, Mary. *Popular Bohemia: Modernism and Urban Culture in Nineteenth-Century Paris.* Cambridge, MA: Harvard University Press, 2005.

Goldstein, Joshua. *Drama Kings: Players and Publics in the Re-creation of Peking Opera, 1870–1937*. Berkeley: University of California Press, 2007.

Gordon, Andrew, ed. *Postwar Japan as History*. Berkeley: University of California Press, 1993.

Greene, Maggie. *Resisting Spirits: Drama Reform and Cultural Transformation in the People's Republic of China*. Ann Arbor: University of Michigan Press, 2019.

Grimm, Jacob, Wilhelm Grimm, and Margaret Hunt. "The White Snake." In *Household Tales by the Brothers Grimm*. Auckland: Floating Press, 1812.

Grusin, Richard, ed. *The Nonhuman Turn*. Minneapolis: University of Minnesota Press, 2015.

Gu Dong 古棟. "Han'guk yŏnghwa Paeksabuinŭi Paeksajŏne taehan pyŏnyong yangsang" 한국 영화〈 백사부인〉의 '백사전(白蛇傳)' 에 대한 변용 양상 [Study on the variation of the movie *Paeksa buin* from folklore *Madam White Snake*]. *Chungguk munhak* 97 (2018): 145–72.

Guo, Li. *Women's Tanci Fiction in Late Imperial and Early Twentieth-Century China*. West Lafayette: Purdue University Press, 2015.

Guo Yingde 郭英德. *Ming Qing chuanqi zonglu* 明清傳奇綜錄 [A Comprehensive record of Ming and Qing *chuanqi*]. Shijiazhuang: Hebei jiaoyu chubanshe, 1997.

Hallenbeck, Bruce G. *Comedy-Horror Films: A Chronological History, 1914–2008*. Jefferson: McFarland, 2009.

Halprin, Daria. *The Expressive Body in Life, Art, and Therapy: Working with Movement, Metaphor, and Meaning*. London: Jessica Kingsley Publishers, 2003.

Hamm, John Christopher. *The Unworthy Scholar from Pingjiang: Republican Era Martial Arts Fiction*. New York: Columbia University Press, 2019.

Hanan, Patrick. *The Chinese Short Story: Studies in Dating, Authorship, and Composition*. Cambridge, MA: Harvard University Press, 1973.

Handel, Zev. *Sinography: The Borrowing and Adaptation of the Chinese Script*. Leiden: Brill, 2019.

Hang Chunxiao 杭春曉. "Guan Liang de 'shuangchong shenfen' jiqi xingshi yuyan—ershi shiji 'chuantong', 'xiandai' de yizhong renzhi jizhi" 關良的 "雙重身份" 及其形式語言—20世紀 '傳統'、'現代' 的一種認知機制 [Guan Liang's "double identity" and formalistic language—A mechanism to cognize "tradition" and "modernity" in the twentieth century]. *Wenyi yanjiu* 5 (2017): 118–37.

Harootunian, Harry. *Overcome by Modernity: History, Culture, and Community in Interwar Japan*. Princeton: Princeton University Press, 2000.

Hershatter, Gail. *The Gender of Memory: Rural Women and China's Collective Past*. Oakland: University of California Press, 2014.

Hershatter, Gail. *Women in China's Long Twentieth Century*. Berkeley: University of California Press, 2007.

Ho, Engseng. "Inter-Asian Concepts for Mobile Societies." *The Journal of Asian Studies* 76, no. 4 (November 2017): 907–28.

Ho, Wing-Chung. *Transition Study of Postsocialist China: An Ethnographic Study of a Model Community*. Singapore: World Scientific Publishing Co., 2010.

Hobsbawm, Eric, and Terence Ranger, eds. *The Invention of Tradition*. Cambridge: Cambridge University Press, 1983.

Holcombe, Charles. *The Genesis of East Asia, 221 B.C.–A.D. 907*. Asian Interactions and Comparisons. Honolulu: University of Hawai'i Press, 2001.

Hong Shu-Ling 洪淑苓. "Xushixue guandian xiade Baishe gushi—1771–1927 nianjian de liuge wenben de xushi fenxi yu bijiao" 敘事學觀點下的白蛇故事—1771–1927年間的六個文本的敘事分析與比較 [Narrative discussions on the White Snake story—analyses and comparisons of 6 texts during 1771–1927]. *Dong Hwa Journal of Chinese Studies* (Donghua hanxue) 8 (December 2008): 63–105.

Hsu Lemei 徐樂眉. *Bainian Taiwan dianyingshi* 百年台灣電影史 [A century of Taiwan movie history]. New Taipei City: Yang-Chih Book Co., 2012.

Hsu, Wen-hung. "The Evolution of the Legend of the White Serpent." *Tamkang Review* 4, no. 1 (1973): 109–27; no. 2 (1973): 121–56.

Hsu Ya-Hsiang 徐亞湘. *Rizhi shiqi Zhongguo xiban zai Taiwan* 日治時期中國戲班在台灣 [Chinese theater troupes in colonial Taiwan]. Taipei: Nantian shuju, 2000.

Hu, Tze-yue G. "The Animated Resurrection of the *Legend of the White Snake* in Japan." *Animation* 2, no. 1 (2007): 43–61.

Huang Ke 黃可. *Manhua haipai manhua* 漫話海派漫畫 [Random thoughts on Shanghai school cartoons]. Shanghai: Wenhui chubanshe, 2015.

Huang Xiaoyin 黃曉音. "Xinqi de *Baishe zhuan* yanhuapian" 新奇的《白蛇傳》煙畫片 [Novel cigarette cards from *The Righteous Snake*]. *Yangzi wanbao*, August 19, 2004.

Huang, Yiju. "A Buddhist Perspective: Trauma and Reincarnation in Mo Yan's *Life and Death Are Wearing Me Out*." *Modern Chinese Literature and Culture* 28, no. 2 (Fall 2016): 201–28.

Hughes, Theodore. *Literature and Film in Cold War South Korea: Freedom's Frontier*. New York: Columbia University Press, 2012.

Huntington, Rania. *Alien Kind: Foxes and Late Imperial Chinese Narrative*. Cambridge, MA: Harvard University Press, 2004.

Huntington, Rania. "The Supernatural." In *The Columbia History of Chinese Literature*, ed. Victor Mair, 110–31. New York: Columbia University Press, 2001.

Huss, Ann Louise. "Old Tales Retold: Contemporary Chinese Fiction and the Classical Tradition." PhD diss., Columbia University, 2000.

Idema, Wilt L. *The Metamorphosis of Tianxian pei: Local Opera under the Revolution (1949–1956)*. Hong Kong: The Chinese University Press, 2015.

Idema, Wilt L. *The White Snake and Her Son: A Translation of "The Precious Scroll of Thunder Peak" with Related Texts*. Indianapolis: Hackett Publishing Company, 2009.

Idema, Wilt L., and Beata Grant. *Escape from Blood Pond Hell: The Tales of Mulian and Woman Huang*. Seattle: University of Washington Press, 2011.

Idema, Wilt L., and Beata Grant. *The Red Brush: Writing Women of Imperial China*. Cambridge, MA: Harvard University Asia Center, 2004.

Ima-Izumi, Yoko. "A Land Where Femmes Fatales Fear to Tread: Eroticism and Japanese Cinema." *Japan Review* 10 (1998): 123–50.

Inglis, Alister David. *Hong Mai's Record of the Listener and Its Song Dynasty Context.* Albany: State University of New York Press, 2006.

Jacoby, Alexander. "Mizoguchi Kenji." *Senses of Cinema*, Great Directors, no. 22 (October 2002), http://sensesofcinema.com/2002/great-directors/mizoguchi/.

Jiang Xun 蔣勳. *Wudong Baishe zhuan* 舞動白蛇傳 [Dancing White Snake]. Taipei: Yuanliu, 2004.

Jin Ronghua 金榮華. "'Shelang' tanyuan" '蛇郎'探源 [Examining the origins of the 'Snake Husband'], in *2009 Haixia liang'an minsu ji minjian wenxue xueshu yantaohui lunwenxuan*, 19–24. Taipei: Zhongguo kouchuan wenxuehui, 2009.

John, Griffith 楊格非. *Xinyue shengshu* 新約聖書 [The new testament]. Hankou: National Bible Society of Scotland, 1884.

Johns, Andrew F. *Circuit Listening: Chinese Popular Music in the Global 1960s.* Minneapolis: University of Minnesota Press, 2020.

Ju Qihong 居其宏. "Lun Chen Tianhe ershi shiji sanshi zhi sishi niandai de yishu gequ chuangzuo" 論陳田鶴二十世紀30–40年代的藝術歌曲創作 [On Chen Tianhe's composition of art songs from the 1930s to the 1940s]. *Yinyue yanjiu* 5 (September 2011): 25–39, 57.

Judge, Joan. *"Shibao" and the Culture of Reform in Late Qing China.* Stanford: Stanford University Press, 1996.

Jung Sun-Kyung 정선경 鄭宣景. *Shenxian de shikong:* Taiping guangji *shenxian gushi yanjiu* 神仙的時空—《太平廣記》神仙故事研究 [The chronotope of immortals: on stories of immortals in *Taiping guangji*]. Beijing: Zhongyang minzu daxue chubanshe, 2007.

Kang, Xiaofei. *The Cult of the Fox: Power, Gender, and Popular Religion in Late Imperial and Modern China.* New York: Columbia University Press, 2006.

Kang, Xiaofei. "The Fox (*hu* 狐) and the Barbarian (*hu* 胡): Unraveling Representations of the Other in Late Tang Tales." *Journal of Chinese Religions* 27 (1999): 35–67.

Karashima Takeshi 辛島驍. *Chūgoku no shingeki* 中国の新劇 [The new theater of China]. Tokyo: Shōheidō, 1948.

Katsuyama Minoru 勝山稔. "Kindai Nihon ni okeru Chūgoku hakuwa shōsetsu shū 'Sanyan' shoshū hen no juyō ni tsuite: Kamiya Kōhei to Hayashi Fusao no yakugyō o chūshin to shite" 近代日本に於ける中国白話小説集「三言」所収篇の受容について: 神谷衡平と林房雄の訳業を中心として [On the reception of the Chinese vernacular fiction collection "Sanyan" in modern Japan: With a focus on translations by Kamiya Kōhei and Hayashi Fusao]. *Kokusai bunka kenkyūka ronshū* 17 (December 2009): 35-53.

Kawata Kō 川田耕. "*Hakujaden* ni miru gendai no taidō" 「白蛇伝」にみる近代の胎動 [Some sociopsychological considerations on the *Legend of the White Snake*]. *Journal of the Faculty of Economics* (Kyoto Gakuen University) 23, no. 2 (March 2014): 35–57.

Keats, John. *Lamia*, with illustrative designs by Will H. Low. Philadelphia: J. B. Lippincott Company, 1885.

Khor, Neil. "Lady White: The Literary Migration of a Chinese Tale." *Indonesia and the Malay World* 42, no. 123 (2014): 286–303.

Kim, Suk-Young. *Illusive Utopia: Theater, Film, and Everyday Performance in North Korea*. Ann Arbor: University of Michigan Press, 2010.

Kimizuka Shō 君塚祥. *Shanhai hakujatei kidan 1* 上海白蛇亭奇譚 1 [Strange tales at Shanghai White Snake Pavilion, no. 1]. Bunch Comics. Tokyo: Shinchōsha, 2015.

King, Kenneth. *Writing in Motion: Body—Language—Technology*. Middletown: Wesleyan University Press, 2010.

Klein, Lucas. "Mediation is Our Authenticity: *Dagong* Poetry and the *Shijing* in Translation." In *Chinese Poetry and Translation: Rights and Wrongs*, ed. Maghiel van Crevel and Lucas Klein, 201–22. Amsterdam: Amsterdam University Press, 2019.

Knafo, Danielle. *Dancing with the Unconscious: The Art of Psychoanalysis and the Psychoanalysis of Art*. New York: Routledge, 2012.

Ko Chai Cian 高嘉謙 and Cheng Yu-yu 鄭毓瑜, eds. *Cong Moluo dao Nuobei'er: wenxue, jingdian, xiandai yishi* 從摩羅到諾貝爾: 文學·經典·現代意識 [From Mara poet to Nobel laureate: literature, canonicity, and modernity]. Taipei: Rye Field Publications, 2015.

Komatsu, Hiroshi. "The Foundation of Modernism: Japanese Cinema in the Year 1927." *Film History* 17, nos. 2/3, (2005): 363–75.

Kong Xiaomin 孔曉敏 and Wang Juan 王娟, eds. *Shanghai dengcai: jiaoke shu* 上海燈彩: 教科書 [Shanghai lanterns: a textbook]. Shanghai: Shanghai guji chubanshe, 2013.

Kornicki, Peter. *Language, Scripts, and Chinese Texts in East Asia*. Oxford: Oxford University Press, 2018.

Kroeber, Karl. *Retelling/Rereading: The Fate of Storytelling in Modern Times*. New Brunswick: Rutgers University Press, 1992.

Kubo Tsugunari and Yuyama Akira, trans. "Chapter XII Devadatta." In *The Lotus Sutra*, translated from the Chinese of Kumārajiva, 179–85. BDK English Tripiṭaka Series. Berkeley: Numata Center for Buddhist Translation and Research, 2007.

Kuhn, Philip A. *Chinese Among Others: Emigration in Modern Times*. State & Society in East Asia. Lanham: Rowman & Littlefield, 2009.

Kuriyama, Shigehisa. *The Expressiveness of the Body and the Divergence of Greek and Chinese Medicine*. New York: Zone Books, 1999.

Kwa Chong Guan and Kua Bak Lim, eds. *A General History of the Chinese in Singapore*. Singapore: Singapore Federation of Chinese Clan Associations; World Scientific, 2019.

Lai, Larissa. *Salt Fish Girl: A Novel*. Markham: Thomas Allen Publishers, 2002.

Lai, Whalen. "From Folklore to Literate Theater: Unpacking 'Madame White Snake.'" *Asian Folklore Studies* 50, no. 1 (1992): 51–66.

Laing, Ellen Johnston. *Selling Happiness: Calendar Posters and Visual Culture in Early Twentieth-Century Shanghai*. Honolulu: University of Hawai'i Press, 2004.

Lamarre, Thomas. *The Anime Machine: A Media Theory of Animation*. Minneapolis: University of Minnesota Press, 2009.

Lamarre, Thomas. *Shadows on the Screen: Tanizaki Jun'ichirō on Cinema and "Oriental" Aesthetics*. Ann Arbor: Center for Japanese Studies, University of Michigan, 2005.

LaMothe, Kimerer L. *Between Dancing and Writing: The Practice of Religious Studies*. New York: Fordham University Press, 2004.

Lau Yin-ping 劉燕萍. *Nüxing yu mingyun: yueju · yueyu xiqu dianying lunji* 女性與命運: 粵劇·粵語戲曲電影論集 [Females and fate: a collection of articles on Cantonese operas and films]. Literature and Cinema Series. Hong Kong: Open University of Hong Kong Press, 2010.

Lavin, Maud, Ling Yang, and Jing Jamie Zhao, eds. *Boy's Love, Cosplay, and Androgynous Idols: Queer Fan Cultures in Mainland China, Hong Kong, and Taiwan*. Hong Kong: Hong Kong University Press, 2017.

Le Bon, Gustave. *Psychologie des Foules* [The crowd: a study of the popular mind, 1895]. Édition Félix Alcan, 9th ed. 1905.

Le Fanu, Mark. "Mizoguchi, the Great Triptych." *Cambridge Quarterly* 26, no. 4 (1997): 289–313.

Le, Huu Phuoc. *Buddhist Architecture*. Lakeville, MN: Grafikol, 2010.

Lears, T. J. Jackson. *No Place of Grace: Antimodernism and the Transformation of American Culture, 1880–1920*. New York: Pantheon, 1981.

Lee, Ang 李安, dir. *Lust, Caution* [*Se, jie* 色·戒]. Universal City, CA: Focus Features, 2007. DVD.

Lee, Haiyan. "How the Chinese Fell in Love with Love, Caveats and All: Review of *When True Love Came to China* by Lynn Pan." MCLC Resource Center. 2017. http://u.osu.edu/mclc/book-reviews/haiyanlee/

Lee, Haiyan. "The Revolutionary Structure of Feeling." In *Revolution of the Heart: A Genealogy of Love in China, 1900–1950*. Stanford: Stanford University Press, 2006.

Lee, Haiyan. *The Stranger and the Chinese Moral Imagination*. Stanford: Stanford University Press, 2014.

Lee, Leo Ou-fan. *Shanghai Modern: The Flowering of a New Urban Culture in China, 1930–1945*. Cambridge, MA: Harvard University Press, 1999.

Lee, Leo Ou-fan. *The Romantic Generation of Modern Chinese Writers*. Cambridge, MA: Harvard University Press, 1973.

Lee, Sangjoon. *Cinema and the Cultural Cold War: US Diplomacy and the Origins of the Asian Cinema Network*. Ithaca: Cornell University Press, 2020.

Lee, Sangjoon. "The Transnational Asian Studio System: Cinema, Nation-State, and Globalization in Cold War Asia." PhD diss., University of Chicago, 2011.

Lee Sŏngsu 이성수, dir. *Han'guk yŏnghwa ŭi p'unguna: yŏnghwa kamdok Shin sang-ok* 한국 영화의 풍운아: 영화 감독 신상옥 [Director Shin Sang-ok: The hero of Korean cinema]. 1999. Documentary, https://www.kmdb.or.kr/db/kor/detail/movie/A/03172

Lee, Tong King. "Mobility as Method: Distributed Literatures and Semiotic Repertoires." MCLC Resource Center Publication, March 2019, https://u.osu.edu/mclc/online-series/tong-king-lee/

Legge, James, trans. *The Chinese Classics*, vol. 1. Hong Kong: The London Missionary Society, 1861.

Levine, Peter A., and Ann Frederick. *Waking the Tiger: Healing Trauma*. Berkeley: North Atlantic Books, 1997.

Lévi-Strauss, Claude. *The Raw and the Cooked*. Mythologiques, vol. 1. Translated from the French by John and Doreen Weightman. Chicago: University of Chicago Press, 1983.

Li Chunmei 李春梅. "Huang Chujiu de pinpai yingxiao zhidao: yi Bailing ji weili" 黃楚九的品牌營銷之道: 以百齡機為例 [Huang Chujiu's method of brand promotion: Centered on the case of 'Hundred-Year-Machine']. *Chuanmei guancha* (December 2011): 62–63.

Li Han-hsiang 李翰祥, dir. *Liang Shanbo yu Zhu Yingtai* 梁山伯與祝英台 [The Love eterne]. Hong Kong: Shaw Brothers Studio, 1963.

Li, Jie. *Utopian Ruins: A Memorial Museum of the Mao Era*. Durham: Duke University Press, 2020.

Li, Ruru. *The Soul of Beijing Opera: Theatrical Creativity and Continuity in the Changing World*. Hong Kong: Hong Kong University Press, 2010.

Li Wei 李偉. *Ershi shiji xiqu gaige de sanda fanshi* 20 世紀戲曲改革的三大範式 [Three paradigms of *xiqu* reform in the twentieth century]. Beijing: Zhonghua shuju, 2014.

Li Zigui 李紫貴. *Yi Jiangnan: Li Zigui koushushi* 憶江南: 李紫貴口述史 [Remembering Jiangnan: An oral History of Li Zigui]. Beijing: Zhongguo xiju chubanshe, 2011.

Lin Qinghua 林青華. "Huangmeixi dianying zai Xianggang ji Taiwan de fazhan" 黃梅戲電影在香港及台灣的發展 [The development of huangmei opera film in Hong Kong and Taiwan]. *Zhongyang yinyue xueyuan xuebao* 115, no. 2 (2009): 74–82, 120.

Lin, Yu-sheng. *The Crisis of Chinese Consciousness: Radical Antitraditionalism in the May Fourth Era*. Madison: University of Wisconsin Press, 1979.

Lippit, Akira Mizuta. *Electric Animal: Toward a Rhetoric of Wildlife*. Minneapolis: University of Minnesota Press, 2008.

Liu, Lydia H. *Translingual Practice: Literature, National Culture, and Translated Modernity—China, 1900–1937*. Stanford: Stanford University Press, 1995.

Liu, Lydia H., Rebecca E. Karl, and Dorothy Ko, eds. *The Birth of Chinese Feminism: Essential Texts in Transnational Theory*. New York: Columbia University Press, 2013.

Liu Min 劉敏. "Ge Gongzhen yu baozhi 'tuhua zhoukan' yanjiu" 戈公振與報紙 "圖畫週刊" 研究 [An investigation of Ge Gongzhen and 'The Pictorial Weekly of Eastern Times']. MA thesis, Nanchang University, 2014.

Liu, Petrus. *Queer Marxism in Two Chinas*. Durham, NC: Duke University Press, 2015.

Liu Xiaohai 劉曉海 and Wang Shuwen 王書文. "Jindai Suzhou pingtan chuancheng tixi de goujian—yi Guangyu she wei zhongxin" 近代蘇州評彈傳承體系的構建—以光裕社為中心 [The construction of a system of inheritance for Suzhou *pingtan* in modern times—Centered on *Guangyu she*]. *Difang wenhua yanjiu* 1 (2017): 21–26.

Liu Yunchao 劉韻超. "Nihon eiga ni okeru Chūgoku koten no juyō to hen'yō: Eiga 'Byaku fujin no yōren' to 'Hakujaden' o chūshin ni" 日本映画における中国古典の受容と変容: 映画『白夫人の妖恋』と『白蛇伝』を中心に [The reception and transformation of Chinese classics in Japanese cinema: With a focus on *Byaku fujin no yōren* and *Hakujaden*." *Kokusai bunka kenkyū* 21 (2015): 129–40.

Lo Man Chi 盧敏芝. "'Yishu de shehuizhuyi'—Tian Han, Nanguo yundong yu zuoyi shijie zhuyi shiyexia de weimei zhuyi yishu shijian" 「藝術的社會主義」—田漢、南國運動與左翼世界主義視野下的唯美主義藝術實踐 ['The Artistic Socialism': Tian Han, Nanguo movement, and the practice of aestheticism in the vision of leftist cosmopolitanism]. *Zhongguo wenhua yanjiusuo xuebao* 68 (January 2019): 109–35.

Lock, Margaret, and Judith Farquhar. *Beyond the Body Proper: Reading the Anthropology of Material Life*. Durham, NC: Duke University Press, 2007.

Long, Jeff E. "The Japanese Literati and the 'China Incident': Hayashi Fusao Reporting the Battle of Shanghai." *Sino-Japanese Studies* 15 (April 2003), 27–44.

Lufkin, Felicity. *Folk Art and Modern Culture in Republican China*. Lanham, MD: Lexington Books, 2016.

Luo, Liang. "Dancing White Snake, Writing Green Snake, and the Cultural Revolution as Memory and Imagination." *Frontiers of Literary Studies in China* 11, no. 1 (March 2017): 7–37.

Luo, Liang. "Performance Review: *The White Snake*, Constellation Theatre Company, Washington, DC, April 25-May 26, 2019." *CHINOPERL: Journal of Chinese Oral and Performing Literature*, vol. 39, no. 2 (December 2020), 182–97.

Luo, Liang. *The Avant-Garde and the Popular in Modern China: Tian Han and the Intersection of Performance and Politics*. Ann Arbor: University of Michigan Press, 2014.

Luo, Liang. "The Experimental and the Popular in Chinese Socialist Theater of the 1950s." In *Rethinking Chinese Socialist Theaters of Reform: Performance Practice and Debate in the Mao Era*, ed. Xiaomei Chen, Tarryn Li-Min Chun, and Siyuan Liu, 135–61. Ann Arbor: University of Michigan Press, 2021.

Luo, Liang. "The White Snake in Hong Kong Horror Cinema." In *Hong Kong Horror Cinema*, ed. Daniel Martin and Garry Bettinson, 34–51. Edinburgh: Edinburgh University Press, 2018.

Ma, Lan. "Dancing into Modernity and Socialism: Kinesthesia, Narrative, and Revolutions in China (1900–1978)." PhD diss., University of Wisconsin Madison, 2015.

Ma, Lan. *When Words Are Inadequate: Modern Dance and Transnationalism in China*. New York: Oxford University Press, forthcoming.

Macdonald, Sean. "Notes on the Fantastic in Chinese Literature and Film." *Frontiers of Literary Studies in China* 13, no. 1 (2019): 1–24.

Mackerras, Colin, "Yangzhou Local Theatre in the Second Half of the Qing." In *Lifestyle and Entertainment in Yangzhou*, ed. Lucie Olivová and Vibeke Børdahl, 207–24. Copenhagen: NIAS Press, 2009.

Mak Yan Yan Grace 麥欣恩. *Xianggang dianying yu xinjiapo* 香港電影與新加坡 [Hong Kong film and Singapore]. Hong Kong: Hong Kong University Press, 2018.

Mamoulian, Rouben, dir. *Silk Stockings*, 1957. Culver City: MGM/UA Home Video, 1985. DVD.

Man Kit-wah 文潔華, ed. *Yueyu de zhengzhi* 粵語的政治 [The politics of the Cantonese language in Hong Kong]. Bordertown Thinker Series. Hong Kong: The Chinese University Press, 2014.

Mann, Susan. *Precious Records: Women in China's Long Eighteenth Century.* Stanford: Stanford University Press, 1997.

Mao Heng 毛亨, Zheng Xuan 鄭玄, and Kong Yinda 孔穎達. *Maoshi zhushu* 毛詩註疏 [Annotated edition of the *Classic of Poetry* with a preface by Mao], vol. 1. Taipei: Yiwen yinshuguan, 1979.

Martin, Daniel, and Garry Bettinson, eds. *Hong Kong Horror Cinema.* Edinburgh: Edinburgh University Press, 2018.

McDonald, Keiko I, ed. *Ugetsu: Kenji Mizoguchi, Director*. Rutgers Films in Print 17. New Brunswick, NJ: Rutgers University Press, 1993.

McDonnell, Chris. *Steven Universe: Art & Origins.* New York: Abrams Books, 2017.

McMahon, Keith. *Causality and Containment in Seventeenth-Century Chinese Fiction.* Leiden: Brill, 1988.

McMahon, Keith. "The Classic 'Beauty-Scholar' Romance and the Superiority of the Talented Woman." In *Body, Subject & Power in China*, ed. Angela Zito and Tani E. Barlow, 227–52. Chicago: University of Chicago Press, 1994.

Meyer-Fong, Tobie. *Building Culture in Early Qing Yangzhou.* Stanford: Stanford University Press, 2003.

Meyer-Fong, Tobie. *What Remains: Coming to Terms with Civil War in 19th-Century China.* Stanford: Stanford University Press, 2013.

Mitchell, John Dietrich, ed. *The Red Pear Garden: Three Great Dramas of Revolutionary China.* Boston: D. R. Godine, 1973.

Mittler, Barbara. *A Newspaper for China? Power, Identity, and Change in Shanghai's News Media, 1872–1912.* Cambridge, MA: Harvard University Asia Center, 2004.

Miyao, Daisuke. *The Aesthetics of Shadow: Lighting and Japanese Cinema.* Durham, NC: Duke University Press, 2013.

Miyazaki, Hayao. *Starting Point, 1979–1996.* San Francisco: Viz Media, 2014.

Mo Yan 莫言. *Shengsi pilao* 生死疲勞 [Life and death are wearing me out]. Beijing: Zuojia chubanshe, 2006.

Molina, J. Michelle, and Donald K. Swearer, with Susan Lloyd McGarry. *Rethinking the Human.* Cambridge, MA: Center for the Study of World Religions, Harvard Divinity School, 2010.

Moretti, Franco. "Conjectures on World Literature." *New Left Review* 1 (Jan/Feb 2000): 54–68.

Moretti, Franco. *Distant Reading.* London: Verso, 2013.

Nadel, Alan. "Lady and (or) the Tramp: Sexual Containment and the Domestic Playboy." *Containment Culture: American Narratives, Post-Modernism, and the Atomic Age*, 117–54. Durham, NC: Duke University Press, 1995.

Napier, Susan. *Anime from Akira to Howl's Moving Castle: Experiencing Contemporary Japanese Animation.* 2nd ed. New York: St. Martin's Press, 2005.

Nedostup, Rebecca. *Superstitious Regimes: Religion and the Politics of Chinese Modernity.* Cambridge, MA: Harvard University Asia Center, 2010.

Ng, Kenny Kwok-Kwan. "Censorship at Work: Cold War Paranoia and Purgation of Chinese Ghost Stories." In *Hong Kong Culture and Society in the New Millennium: Hong Kong as Method*, ed. Yiu-Wai Chu, 111–28. Singapore: Springer, 2017.

Ng, Kenny Kwok-Kwan. "The Eternal Return of Mythology: The White (Green) Snake Legend in Maoist China and Colonial Hong Kong." In *Chinese Shock of the Anthropocene: Image, Music and Text in the Age of Climate Change*, ed. Kwai-Cheung Lo and Jessica Yeung, 83–107. Singapore: Palgrave Macmillan, 2019.

Ng, Wing Chung. *The Rise of Cantonese Opera.* Urbana: University of Illinois Press, 2015.

Ningboshi Dang'anguan 寧波市檔案館, ed. "Pan Guogang diyong qingxing" 潘國綱抵甬情形 [On Pan Guogang's arrival in Ningbo]. *Shenbao Ningbo shiliaoji, vol.* 5, 2445. Ningbo: Ningbo chubanshe, 2013.

Olivová, Lucie, and Vibeke Børdahl, eds. *Lifestyle and Entertainment in Yangzhou.* Copenhagen: NIAS Press, 2009.

Ozu Yasujirō 小津安二郎. *Tōkyō monogatari* 東京物語 [Tokyo story]. Tokyo: Shōchiku, 1953.

Pak Kyu-wŏn 朴圭媛. *Xunzhao wode waigong: Zhongguo dianying huangdi Jin Yan* 尋找我的外公: 中國电影皇帝金焰 [Looking for my grandfather: Jin Yan (Kim Yŏm), the King of Chinese Movie]. Translated from the Korean by Shi Meiyu and Zhao Xuemei. Shanghai: Shanghai wenyi chubanshe, 2006.

Pan Jiangdong 潘江東. *Baishe gushi yanjiu* 白蛇故事研究 [Research on the White Snake tales]. 3 vols. Taipei: Xuesheng shuju, 1981.

Popoff, Martin. *Sail Away: Whitesnake's Fantastic Voyage.* London: Soundcheck Books LLP, 2015.

Propp, Vladimir. *Morphology of the Folktale.* Revised and edited with a preface by Louis A. Wagner, with a new introduction by Alan Dundes. 2nd ed. Austin: University of Texas Press, 1968.

Pu Songling 蒲松齡. "Hongyu" 红玉. In *Quanben xinzhu Liaozhai zhiyi* 全本新注聊齋誌異 [Complete and newly annotated *Strange Tales from a Make-Do Studio*], ed. Zhu Qikai, 269–275. Beijing: Renmin wenxue chubanshe, 1989.

Puett, Michael. "Economies of Ghosts, Gods, and Goods: The History and Anthropology of Chinese Temple Networks." In *Radical Egalitarianism: Local Realities, Global Relations*, ed. Miriam Goheen, Stanley Tambiah, Michael Fischer, and Felicity Aulino, 91–100. New York: Fordham University Press, 2013.

Puett, Michael. "The Haunted World of Humanity: Ritual Theory from Early China." In *Rethinking the Human*, ed. J. Michelle Molina and Donald K. Swearer, with Susan Lloyd McGarry. Cambridge, MA: Center for the Study of World Religions, Harvard Divinity School, 2010.

Puett, Michael. *To Become a God: Cosmology, Sacrifice, and Self-Divinization in Early China.* Cambridge, MA: Harvard University Asia Center, 2002.

Qian, Nanxiu, Richard J. Smith, and Bowei Zhang eds. *Reexamining the Sinosphere: Cultural Transmissions and Transformations in East Asia.* Amherst: Cambria Press, 2020.

Qian, Nanxiu, Richard J. Smith, and Bowei Zhang eds. *Rethinking the Sinosphere: Poetics, Aesthetics, and Identity Formation.* Amherst: Cambria Press, 2020.

Ragone, August. *Eiji Tsuburaya, Master of Monsters: Defending the Earth with Ultraman, Godzilla, and Friends in the Golden Age of Japanese Science Fiction Film.* San Francisco: Chronicle Books, 2014.

Rebull, Anne. "Locating Theatricality on Stage and Screen: Rescuing Performance Practice and the Phenomenon of *Fifteen Strings of Cash* (*Shiwu guan*; 1956)." *CHINOPERL: Journal of Chinese Oral and Performing Literature* 36, no. 1 (2017): 46–71.

Rebull, Anne. "Reconstructing the Repertoire from the Stage, Screen, and Page: Xiqu Reform 1937–1959." PhD diss., University of Chicago, 2017.

Reed, Christopher A. *Gutenberg in Shanghai: Chinese Print Capitalism, 1876–1937.* Vancouver: UBC Press, 2004.

Reveal Books 果力文化, ed. *Dakai yunmen—jiemi Yunmen de jishu meixue yu jianchi* 打開雲門—解密雲門的技術美學與堅持 [The making of Cloud Gate]. Taipei: Reveal Books, 2013.

Robertson, Jennifer Ellen. *Takarazuka: Sexual Politics and Popular Culture in Modern Japan.* Berkeley: University of California Press, 1998.

Roddy, Stephen J. "In Praise of Jeweled Streams: 'Ugetsu monogatari,' Nativism, and Tea." *Japanese Literatures and Culture* 49, no. 1 (April 2015): 16.

Rojas, Carlos ed., *Method as Method*, special issue of *Prism: Theory and Modern Chinese Literature* 16, no. 2 (October 2019).

Rolston, David. "Performance Review: Two Decades of Selling Peking Opera White Snake to Foreigners: From Tourist Peking Opera in Beijing (1996) to Zhang Huoding at Lincoln Center (2015)." *CHINOPERL: Journal of Chinese Oral and Performing Literature* 37, no. 1 (November 2018), 57–74.

Roquet, Paul. "A Blue Cat on the Galactic Railroad: Anime and Cosmic Subjectivity." *Representations* 128, no. 1 (Fall 2014): 124–58.

Ruan Yuan 阮元 ed., *Shisanjing zhushu: Zhouli* 十三經註疏 周禮 [Annotated edition of the thirteen classics: Ritual of Zhou], vol. 12. Taipei: Yiwen yinshuguan, 1985.

Ruh, Brian. "Early Japanese Animation in the United States: Changing Tetsuwan Atomu to Astro Boy." In *The Japanification of Children's Popular Culture: From Godzilla to Miyazaki*, ed. Mark I. West, 215. Lanham, MD: Scarecrow Press, 2008.

Salmon, Claudine, ed. *Literary Migrations: Traditional Chinese Fiction in Asia (17th–20th Centuries).* Reprint of 1987 edition. Singapore: Institute of Southeast Asian Studies, 2013.

Sang Hu 桑弧 and Huang Sha 黃沙, dirs. *Liang Shanbo yu Zhu Yingtai* 梁山伯與祝英台 [The Butterfly lovers]. Shanghai: Shanghai dianying zhipianchang, 1953. Film.

Sato Tadao 佐藤忠男. *Kenji Mizoguchi and the Art of Japanese Cinema.* Translated by Brij Tankha. Edited by Aruna Vasudev and Latika Padgaonkar. Oxford: Berg, 2008.

Sato Tadao. *Mizoguchi Kenji no sekai* 溝口健二の世界 [The world of Mizoguchi Kenji]. Tokyo: Heibonsha, 2006.

Saussy, Haun. "Mei Lanfang in Moscow, 1935: Familiar, Unfamiliar, Defamiliar." *Modern Chinese Literature and Culture* 18, no. 1, special issue on Modernisms' Chinas (Spring 2006): 8–29.

Saussy, Haun. "The Comparative History of East Asian Literatures: A Sort of Manifesto." *Modern Languages Open* 1 (2018): 20. Https://doi.org/10.3828/mlo.v0i0.206.

Saussy, Haun. *Translation as Citation: Zhuangzi Inside Out*. New York: Oxford UniversityPress, 2017.

Saussy, Haun, ed. *Texts and Transformations: Essays in Honor of the 75th Birthday of Victor H. Mair*. Amherst, MA: Cambria Press, 2018.

Schaffer, Edward H. *The Divine Woman: Dragon Ladies and Rain Maidens in Tang Literature*. Berkeley: California University Press, 1973.

Schmalzer, Sigrid. *The People's Peking Man: Popular Science and Human Identity in Twentieth-Century China*. Chicago: University of Chicago Press, 2008.

Schonherr, Johannes. *North Korean Cinema: A History*. Jefferson, NC: McFarland, 2012.

Sebo, Gabor. "A Study on the Impact of Shin Sang-ok on North Korean Cinema." PhD diss., Korea University, 2018.

Sen, Sharmila. *Not Quite Not White: Losing and Finding Race in America*. New York: Penguin Books, 2018.

Shanhai jing 山海經 [The classic of mountains and seas]. Edited and annotated by Zhou Mingchu. Hangzhou: Zhejiang wenyi chubanshe, 2016.

Shaw Runje 邵醉翁, dir. *Liangzhu tongshi* 梁祝痛史 [The butterfly lovers]. Shanghai: Tianyi, 1926. Film. Nonextant.

Shenbao (Shun Pao, Shen-pao 申報) [Shanghai news]. Founded by Earnest Major. Shanghai: Shen Bao she, April 30, 1872–May 27, 1949.

Shih, Chih-yu. "A Rising Unknown: Rediscovering China in Japan's East Asia." *China Review* 11, no. 1 (Spring 2011): 1–26.

Shih, Shu-mei, Chien-hsin Tsai, and Brian Bernards, eds. *Sinophone Studies: A Critical Reader*. New York: Columbia University Press, 2013.

Shin Sang-ok 신상옥 申相玉, dir. *Lomaenseu ppappa* 로맨스빠빠 [A romantic papa]. South Korea, 1960. Film.

Shin Sang-ok, dir. *Ijo yŏin chanhoksa* 이조 여인 잔혹사 [Women of the Yi dynasty]. South Korea, 1969. Film.

Shin Sang-ok, dir. *Naesi* 내시 [Eunuch]. South Korea, 1968. Film, 90 min.

Shindō Kaneto 新藤兼人. *Aru eiga-kantoku no shōgai: Mizoguchi Kenji no kiroku* ある映画監督の生涯：溝口健二の記録 [Kenji Mizoguchi: The life of a film director]. Tokyo: Kindai Eiga Kyokai, 1975. Film.

Simpson, David. *Romanticism and the Question of the Stranger*. Chicago: University of Chicago Press, 2013.

Siu, Wang-Ngai and Peter Lovrick. *Chinese Opera: Images and Stories*. Vancouver: UBC Press, 1997.

Smith, Arthur H. *Village Life in China: A Study in Sociology*. Edinburgh: Oliphant, Anderson & Ferrier, 1899.

Smith, Henry DeWitt. *Japan's First Student Radicals*. Cambridge, MA: Harvard University Press, 1972.

Son Wan I 손완이 孫晥怡. "Paeksajŏn sogŭi tongsŏngae yangsang yŏn'gu" 『白蛇傳』 속의 동성애 양상 연구 [A study on *Legend of the White Snake* from the perspective of homosexual love]. *Chungguk sosŏl lonch'ong* 16 (2002): 127–46.

Son Wan I. "Paeksajŏnŭi sŏngŭishik koch'al" 『백사전』의 성의식 고찰 [An Investigation into sexual consciousness in *Legend of the White Snake*]. *Chungŏ chungmunhak* 31 (2002): 371–92.

Son Wan I. "Shilun *Baishe zhuan* de dianshiju gaibian" 試論白蛇傳的電視劇改編 [A tentative discussion of the TV adaptations of *Legend of the White Snake*], in *Chungguk inmun'gwahak* 42 (2009): 455–70.

Song, Mingwei, and Theodore Huters, eds. *The Reincarnated Giant: Twenty-First-Century Chinese Science Fiction*. New York: Columbia University Press, 2018.

Sterckx, Roel. *The Animal and the Daemon in Early China*. Albany: SUNY Press, 2002.

Sterckx, Roel, Martina Siebert, and Dagmar Schäfer eds. *Animals Through Chinese History: Earliest Times to 1911*. Cambridge: Cambridge University Press, 2019. https://doi.org/10.1017/9781108551571

Stiegler, Bernard. *What Makes Life Worth Living: On Pharmacology*. Translated by Daniel Ross. Cambridge, UK: Polity, 2010.

Sun, Hongmei. *Transforming Monkey: Adaptation and Representation of a Chinese Epic*. Seattle: University of Washington Press, 2018.

Sun Jing 孫競. "Jin shijinian *Baishe zhuan* yanjiu wenxian zongshu" 近十幾年白蛇傳研究文獻綜述 [A summary of research documents on the White Snake legend from the last decade or so]. *Kaifeng jiaoyu xueyuan xuebao* 36, no. 2 (2016): 21–23.

Suryadinata, Leo. *Prominent Indonesian Chinese: Biographical Sketches*. 4th ed. Singapore: Institute of Southeast Asian Studies, 2015.

Suzuki Tsunekatsu 鈴木常勝. *Sanghae ui Chosŏn-in yŏnghwa hwangje* 상해의 조선인 영화 황제 [The Korean movie emperor in Shanghai]. Translated from the Japanese by Yi Sang. Seoul: Silch'ŏn munhwasa, 1996.

Suzuki Tsunekatsu. *Tārū: Chōsenjin no Shanhai den'ei kōtei* 大路: 朝鮮人の上海電影皇帝 [The Big Road: the Korean movie emperor in Shanghai]. Tokyo: Shinsensha, 1994.

Tan Guilin 譚桂林. "Minguo Fojiao wenxue dui xiandai Zhongguo wenxueshi chonggou de yiyi" 民國佛教文學對現代中國文學史重構的意義 [Republican Buddhist literature and its contribution to the reconstruction of modern Chinese literary history]. *Jianghan luntan* 6 (2014): 71–74.

Tan Guilin. "Qingmo Minchu Zhongguo de Fojiao wenxue yu qimeng sichao" 清末民初中國的佛教文學與啟蒙思潮 [Buddhist literature and Enlightenment thought in Late Qing and Early Republican China]. *Zhongguo shehui kexue* 3 (2010): 158–71, 223–24.

Tanaka Tomoyuki 田中友幸, ed. *Tōhō tokusatsu eiga zenshi* 東宝特撮映画全史 [A complete history of films made by Tōhō]. Tokyo: Tōhō kabushiki kaisha shuppan jigyōshitsu, 1983.

Tang Simin 唐思敏. "Chuanju *Baishe zhuan* tanwei" 川劇白蛇傳探微 [A preliminary discussion of Sichuan opera *White Snake*]. *Zhongguo xiju* 4 (2013): 56–58.

Taniguchi Yoshisuke 谷口義介. "Feng Menglong to Huang Tubi no aida: *Hakujaden*, shōsetsu kara gikyoku e" 馮夢龍と黄圖珌のあいだ: 白蛇傳·小説から戲曲へ [Between Feng Menglong and Huang Tubi: *The White Snake* from fiction to theater]. *Gakurin* 58 (March 2014): 78–103.

Tanizaki Jun'ichirō 谷崎潤一郎. "In'ei raisan" 陰翳礼讃 [In praise of shadows]. In *In'ei raisan*, 57–121. Tokyo: Sogensha, 1939. National Diet Library Digital Collections: https://dl.ndl.go.jp/info:ndljp/pid/1684256?__lang=en

Tanizaki Jun'ichirō. *In Praise of Shadows*, translated by Thomas Harper and Edward Seidensticker. Sedgwick, ME: Leete's Island Books, 1977.

Tansman, Alan M. "Mournful Tears and Sake: The Postwar Myth of Misora Hibari." In *Contemporary Japan and Popular Culture*, ed. John Whittier Treat, 103–33. Honolulu: University of Hawai'i Press, 1996.

Taylor, Al. "The Man Who Made Godzilla Famous." *Fantastic Films and Other Imaginative Media* (January 1980): 17-20.

Taylor, Insup, and M. Martin Taylor. *Writing and Literacy in Chinese, Korean, and Japanese*. Amsterdam: John Benjamins Publishing Company, 2014.

Thompson, Katrina Daly. *Popobawa: Tanzanian Talk, Global Misreadings*. Bloomington: Indiana University Press, 2017.

Thompson, Stith. *The Folktale*. New York: The Dryden Press, 1946.

Thorpe, Ashley. "Modern Theatre for the Twenty-First Century? Shanghai Conservatory of Music's Staging of *The White Goddess* (2009)." *Asian Theatre Journal* 28, no. 2 (Fall 2011): 483–504.

Tian Han 田漢. "Nü yu she" 女與蛇 (Women and the Snake, 1927). In *Tian Han sanwen ji*, 90-96. Shanghai: Jindai shudian, 1936.

Ting, Nai-tung 丁乃通. *A Type Index of Chinese Folktales: in the Oral Tradition and Major Works of Non-Religious Classical Literature*. Helsinki: Suomalainen Tiedeakatemia Academia Scientiarum Fennica, 1978.

Ting, Nai-tung. "The Holy Man and the Snake–Woman: A Study of a Lamia Story in Asian and European Literature." *Fabula* 1 (1966): 145–91.

Treat, John Whittier. *The Rise and Fall of Modern Japanese Literature*. Chicago: University of Chicago Press, 2018.

Treat, John Whittier, ed. *Contemporary Japan and Popular Culture*. Honolulu: University of Hawai'i Press, 1996.

Tsai, Hsiu-chih. "Female Sexuality: Its Allurement and Repression in Geling Yan's 'White Snake.'" *American Journal of Semiotics* 23, no. 1 (2007): 123–46.

Tu C. Y. 屠哲隱. *Tu C. Y. sheyingji* 屠哲隱攝影集 [A collection of photographs by Tu C. Y.]. Shanghai: Wenhua meishu tushu yinshua gongsi, 1930.

Tu, Weiming. "The Continuity of Being: Chinese Visions of Nature." In *Nature in Asian Traditions of Thought: Essays in Environmental Philosophy*, ed. J. Baird Callicott and Roger T. Ames. SUNY Series in Philosophy and Biology. Albany: SUNY Press, 1989.

Tuhua jubao 圖畫劇報 [Theater illustrated]. Founded by Zheng Zhengqiu. Shanghai: Tuhua jubao faxingsuo, 1912–1917.

Tuhua ribao 圖畫日報 [Illustrated daily, 1909–1910], 8 vols., ed. Huanqiu she bianji bu 環球社編輯部. Shanghai: Shanghai guji chubanshe, 1999.

Turgeon, Carolyn. "Neither Fish nor Flesh." *The New Inquiry*, August 1, 2013, https://thenewinquiry.com/neither-fish-nor-flesh/

Ueda Akinari 上田秋成. *Tales of Moonlight and Rain*. Edited and translated by Anthony H. Chambers. New York: Columbia University Press, 2007.

Ueda, Akinari. *Ugetsu monogatari*. 4th ed. 3 vols. Osaka: Bun'eidō, n.d. Waseda University Library Digital Collections: http://www.wul.waseda.ac.jp/kotenseki/html/he13/he13_04376/index.html

Wan, Shan-hung and Hung Tieh-shan. "The Iron Girl." *Chinese Literature* 5 (1971): 59–66.

Wang An-chi 王安祈. *Xingbie, zhengzhi yu jingju biaoyan wenhua* 性別、政治與京劇表演文化 [Gender, politics and *jingju* performance culture]. Taipei: National Taiwan University Press, 2011.

Wang, Ban, ed. *Chinese Visions of World Order: Tianxia, Culture, and World Politics*. Durham, NC: Duke University Press, 2017.

Wang C. K. 王秋桂. "Yuefu hongshan kao" 樂府紅珊考 [On 'Red Coral Ballads']. *Zhongwai wenxue* 4, no. 9 (February 1976): 116–42.

Wang, David Der-wei. "Eileen Chang and The Fall of the Pagoda." *Chinese Literature Today* (Summer 2010): 94–100.

Wang, David Der-wei. "The Literary Mind and the Carving of Modernities." *Journal of Chinese Literature and Culture* 3, no. 2 (November 2016): 203–14.

Wang, David Der-wei. *The Lyrical in Epic Time: Chinese Intellectuals and Artists through the 1949 Crisis*. New York: Columbia University Press, 2015.

Wang Dewei 王德威 and Ji Jin 季進, eds. *Shijie zhuyi de renwen shijing* 世界主義的人文視景 [Humanistic vistas of cosmopolitanism]. Zhenjiang: Jiangsu University Press, 2019.

Wang, Eugene Y. "Tope and Topos: The Leifeng Pagoda and the Discourse of the Demonic." In *Writing and Materiality in China: Essays in Honor of Patrick Hanan*, ed. Judith T. Zeitlin, Lydia H. Liu, with Ellen Widmer, 489–552. Cambridge, MA: Harvard University Asia Center, 2003.

Wang, Gungwu. *The Chinese Overseas: From Earthbound China to the Quest for Autonomy*. The Edwin D. Reischauer Lectures, 1997. Cambridge, MA: Harvard University Press, 2000.

Wang Guoping 王國平, ed. *Xihu wenxian jicheng* 西湖文獻集成 [A collection of writings about West Lake]. Hangzhou: Hangzhou chubanshe, 2004.

Wang Jue 王珏. "Cong 'Baishe zhuan' gushi tanjiu Ming Qing Jiangnan Da Yunhe liang'an chengzhen de shehui shenghuo" 從'白蛇傳'故事探究明清江南大運河兩岸城鎮的社會生活 [Examining social life along the Great Canal during the Ming and Qing dynasties through the 'White Snake' story]. *Ming Qing xiaoshuo yanjiu* 5 (2019): 45–55.

Wang Shih-pe 汪詩珮. "Qianji yu mingzong: Qing zhongye 'Leifengta' chuanqi yanbian xinlun" 潛跡與明蹤: 清中葉《雷峰塔》傳奇演變新論 [The underlain footprints and revealed route: a re-examination of the development of Thunder Peak Pagoda in Mid-Qing]. *Minsu quyi* 199 (March 2018): 263–327.

Wang Tiantian 汪田田, "Wu Banqiao yingyi 'Baishejing ji: Leifengta chuanqi' yanjiu" 吳板橋英譯《白蛇精記：雷峰塔傳奇》研究 [A study of Samuel I. Woodbridge's English translation of *The Mystery of The White Snake: A Legend of Thunder Tower*]. *Yanshan daxue xuebao, zhexue shehui kexue ban* 20, no. 1 (January 2019): 26–31.

Wang, Wei-Chih. "The body that can(not) represent us—Tian Chi-Yuan's *White Water* and modern Taiwanese theatre," *Inter-Asia Cultural Studies*, 19:4 (December 2018), 578–96, DOI: 10.1080/14649373.2018.1543373

Wang, Yiman. *Remaking Chinese Cinema Through the Prism of Shanghai, Hong Kong, and Hollywood*. Honolulu: University of Hawai'i Press, 2013.

Wang, Zheng. *Finding Women in the State: A Socialist Feminist Revolution in the People's Republic of China, 1949–1964*. Berkeley: University of California Press, 2016.

Wang, Zheng. "'State Feminism'? Gender and Socialist State Formation in Maoist China." *Feminist Studies* 31, no. 3 (Fall 2005): 519–51.

Warner, W. Lloyd. *The Family of God: A Symbolic Study of Christian Life in America*. New Haven: Yale University Press, 1961.

Weinstock, Jeffrey Andrew, ed. *The Monster Theory Reader*. Minneapolis: University of Minnesota Press, 2020. https://doi.org/10.5749/j.ctvtv937f

Wen, Tzu-pien. "Good Daughter of the Party." *Chinese Literature* 3 (1971): 3–30.

Widdis, Emma. *Socialist Senses: Film, Feeling, and the Soviet Subject, 1917–1940*. Bloomington: Indiana University Press, 2017.

Widmer, Ellen, and Kang-i Sun Chang, eds. *Writing Women in Late Imperial China*. Stanford: Stanford University Press, 1997.

Wilcox, Emily. *Revolutionary Bodies: Chinese Dance and the Socialist Legacy*. California: University of California Press, 2018. Https://www.luminosoa.org/site/books/10.1525/luminos.58/

Wong, Aida Yuen 阮圓. "Gao Jianfu shuhua de canpomei yu beixue de guanxi" 高劍父書畫的殘破美與碑學的關係 [Relationship between Gao Jianfu's aesthetic of dilapidation in painting and calligraphy and the Stele School]. In *Guohua fuhuo yundong yu Guangdong zhongguohua*, ed. Chen Ruilin and Wei Chenghong, vol. 2, 356–68. Guangzhou: Lingnan meishu chubanshe, 2017.

Wong, Aida Yuen. *Parting the Mists: Discovering Japan and the Rise of National-Style Painting in Modern China*. Honolulu: University of Hawai'i Press, 2006.

Wong, Alvin Ka Hin. "Transgenderism as a Heuristic Device: On the Cross-Historical and Transnational Adaptations of the *Legend of the White Snake*." In *Transgender China*, ed. Howard Chiang, 263–86. New York: Palgrave Macmillan, 2012.

Woodbridge, Samuel I. *Fifty Years in China*. Richmond: Presbyterian Committee Publication, [1918] 1919.

Woodbridge, Samuel I, trans. *The Golden-Horned Dragon King, or The Emperor's Visit to the Spirit World*. Shanghai: printed at the office of the North-China Herald, 1895.

Woodbridge, Samuel I., trans. *China's Only Hope: An Appeal by Her Greatest Viceroy, Chang Chih-tung, with the Sanction of the Present Emperor, Kwang Sü*. New York: Revell, 1900.

Wu Guo 伍國. "Qian Zhongshu dui Chen Yinque 'yishi zhengshi' de piping" 錢鐘書對陳寅恪 '以詩証史' 的批評 [Qain Zhongshu's criticism of Chen Yinque's 'using poetry to support history']. *Shuwu* 6 (2017): 38–42.

Wu, Hung. *A Story of Ruins: Presence and Absence in Chinese Art and Visual Culture*. London: Reaktion Books, 2012.

Wu, Hung. *Zooming In: Histories of Photography in China*. London: Reaktion Books, 2016.

Wu, Pei-yi. "'The White Snake,' The Evolution of a Myth in China," PhD diss., Columbia University, 1969.

Wu, Shengqing. *Photo Poetics: Chinese Lyricism and Modern Media Culture*. New York: Columbia University Press, 2020.

Wu Shengqing 吳盛青, ed. *Lüxing de tuxiang yu wenben: Xiandai huayu yujing zhong de meijie hudong* 旅行的圖像與文本：現代華語語境中的媒介互動 [Traveling image and text in modern China]. Shanghai: Fudan daxue chubanshe, 2016.

Wu Xiaofang 吳曉芳. "'Buchong yongsheng Shangdi zhirong, fanbai suxiu shiren qinshou kunchong zhixiang': lun Wu Banqiao dui shenshu Xiyou gushi de yingyi (1895)" "不崇永生上帝之榮，反拜速朽世人禽獸昆蟲之像": 論吳板橋對神書西遊故事的英譯 (1895) [God vs. dragon: on Samuel I. Woodbridge's English translation 'Westward Journey Stories' (1895) contained in a script of Tongzi drama]. *Dangdai zhongguo yanjiu* 25, no. 2 (2018): 145–65.

Wu Xueshan 吳雪杉. "Leifeng xizhao: 'Yiji' de guankan yu zaixian" 雷峰夕照: "遺跡"的觀看與再現 [Evening illumination of Thunder Peak: viewing and reconstructing the 'ruins']. *Gugong bowuyuan yuankan* 1 (2019): 59–76.

Xiao, Hui Faye. *Youth Economy, Crisis, and Reinvention in Twenty-First-Century China: Morning Sun in the Tiny Times*. London: Routledge, 2020.

Xu Guowei 徐國衛, ed. *Chumo lishi: Zhongguo xiyanghua de kaituozhe* 觸摸歷史: 中國西洋畫的開拓者 [Touching history: pioneers of Western-style painting in China], vol. 2. Jinan: Shangdong renmin chubanshe, 2010.

Xu, Lanjun. "The Lure of Sadness: The Fever of *Yueju* and *The Butterfly Lovers* in the Early PRC." *Asian Theatre Journal* 33, no. 1 (Spring 2016): 104–29.

Yam, Shui-Yin Sharon. *Inconvenient Strangers: Transnational Subjects and the Politics of Citizenship*. Columbus: The Ohio State University Press, 2019.

Yamanashi, Makiko. *A History of the Takarazuka Revue Since 1914: Modernity, Girls' Culture, Japan Pop*. Leiden: Global Oriental & Brill, 2012.

Yang, Gene Luen, Viktor Bogdanovic, and Richard Friend, et al. *New Super-Man, Vol. 1: Made in China*. DC Universe Rebirth. Burbank: DC Comics, 2017.

Yang Hoiseok 양회석. "Zhongguo xiqu gaige yundong yanjiu: 'Liangzhu,' 'Baishe zhuan,' 'Shiwu guan' euljungsim-eulo" 中國戲曲改革運動硏究:「梁祝」,「白蛇傳」,「十五貫」을중심으로 [A study on the movement of xiqu reform in China: centered on *Butterfly Lovers, Legend of White Snake*, and *Fifteen Strings of Cash]. Chungguk hyŏndae munhak* 32 (March 2005): 377–404.

Yang Lianfen 楊聯芬. *Langman de Zhongguo: xingbie shijiao xia jijinzhuyi sichao yu wenxue (1890–1940)* 浪漫的中國: 性別視角下激進主義思潮與文學 (1890–1940) [Romantic China: radical thought and literature from a gender perspective, 1890–1940]. Beijing: Renmin wenxue chubanshe, 2015.

Yang, Xianyi. *White Tiger: An Autobiography of Yang Xianyi*. Hong Kong: The Chinese University Press, 2002.

Yang, Xiaobin. *The Chinese Postmodern: Trauma and Irony in Chinese Avant-Garde Fiction*. Ann Arbor: University of Michigan Press, 2002.

Yang, Zhiyi. "A Humanist in France: Wang Jingwei during the First World War." *Poetica* 49 (2017/2018): 163–92.

Yang, Zhiyi. "The Road to Lyric Martyrdom: Reading the Poetry of Wang Zhaoming (1883–1944)." *Chinese Literature: Essays, Articles, Reviews* 37 (2015): 135–64.

Yao Dadui 姚達兌. "Shuyi yu chuanjiao: Wu Banqiao yingyi *Baishe zhimi: Leifengta chuanqi* (1896) yanjiu" 述異與傳教: 吳板橋英譯《白蛇之謎:雷峰塔傳奇》(1896) 研究 [Narrating the bizarre and preaching Christianity in China: Samuel Woodbridge's English translation of *The Mystery of the White Snake: A Legend of Thunder Peak Tower* in 1896]. *Guoji bijiao wenxue* 3, no. 1 (2020): 136–48.

Yau, Shuk Ting Kinnia 邱淑婷. *Honkon, Nihon eiga kōryūshi: Ajia eiga nettowāku no rūtsu o saguru* 香港・日本映画交流史: アジア映画ネットワークのツールを探る [A history of Hong Kong and Japanese film cooperation: Understanding the origins of East Asian film networks]. Tokyo: Tōkyō daigaku shuppankai, 2007.

Yau, Shuk Ting Kinnia. *Japanese and Hong Kong Film Industries: Understanding the Origins of East Asian Film Networks*. London: Routledge, 2009.

Yecies, Brian, Aegyung Shim, and Jack Yang. "Chinese Transcreators, Webtoons and the Korean Digital Wave." In *Digital Transactions in Asia: Economic, Informational, and Social Exchanges*, ed. Adrian Athique and Emma Baulch, 224–41. New York: Routledge, 2019.

Yeh, Emily Yueh-Yu. "From Shaw Brothers to Grand Motion Picture: Localisation of *Huangmei Diao* Films." In *Li Han-hsiang, Storyteller*, ed. Wong Ai-ling. Hong Kong: Hong Kong Film Archive, 2007.

Yen, Yuan-shu, "Biography of the White Serpent: A Keatsian Interpretation." *Tamkang Review* 1, no. 2 (1970): 227–43.

Yü, Chün-fang. *Kuan-yin: the Chinese Transformation of Avalokitesìvara*. New York: Columbia University Press, 2000.

Yue, Isaac. "Barbarians and Monstrosity: A Thematic Study of the Representation of Foreignness in Early Chinese Vernacular Stories." *Études chinoises*, vol. xxix (2010): 221–41.

Zeitlin, Judith T. *The Phantom Heroine: Ghosts and Gender in Seventeenth-Century Chinese Literature*. Honolulu: University of Hawai'i Press, 2007.

Zhang, Charlie Yi. *Dreadful Desires: The Uses of Love in Neoliberal China*. Durham, NC: Duke University Press, forthcoming.

Zhang, Charlie Yi. "Queering the National Body of Contemporary China." *Frontiers: A Journal of Women's Studies* 37, no. 2 (2016): 1–26.

Zhang, Charlie Yi. "When Feminist Falls in Love with Queer: Dan Mei Culture as a Transnational Apparatus of Love." *Feminist Formations* 29, no. 2 (2017): 121–46.

Zhang Geng 張庚, Guo Hancheng 郭漢城, and He Wei 何為, eds. *Zhongguo xiqu tonglun* 中國戲曲通論 [A general history of Chinese *xiqu*]. Shanghai: Shanghai wenyi chubanshe, 1989.

Zhang Lianhong 張煉紅. *Lilian jinghun: Xin zhongguo xiqu gaizao kaolun* 歷練精魂: 新中國戲曲改造考論 [Tempering the spirit: on *xiqu* reform in the new China]. Shanghai: Shanghai renmin chubanshe, 2013.

Zhang, Longxi. *The Tao and the Logos: Literary Hermeneutics, East and West*. Durham, NC: Duke University Press, 1992.

Zhao Shuli 趙樹理. *Xiao Erhei jiehun* 小二黑結婚 [The marriage of young blacky]. Beijing: Renmin wenxue chubanshe, 1953.

Zhao, Zifeng. "Metamorphoses of Snake Women: Melusine and Madam White." In *Melusine's Footprint: Tracing the Legacy of a Medieval Myth*, ed. Misty Urban, Deva F. Kemmis, and Melissa Ridley Elmes, 282–300. Leiden: Brill, 2017.

Zhong, Xueping, Wang Zheng, and Bai Di, eds. *Some of Us: Chinese Women Growing Up in the Mao Era*. New Brunswick: Rutgers University Press, 2001.

Zhu, Ping. "Chinese Literature at Large: Wong Chin Foo's Border-Crossing writing," paper manuscript shared by the author, 2021.

Index